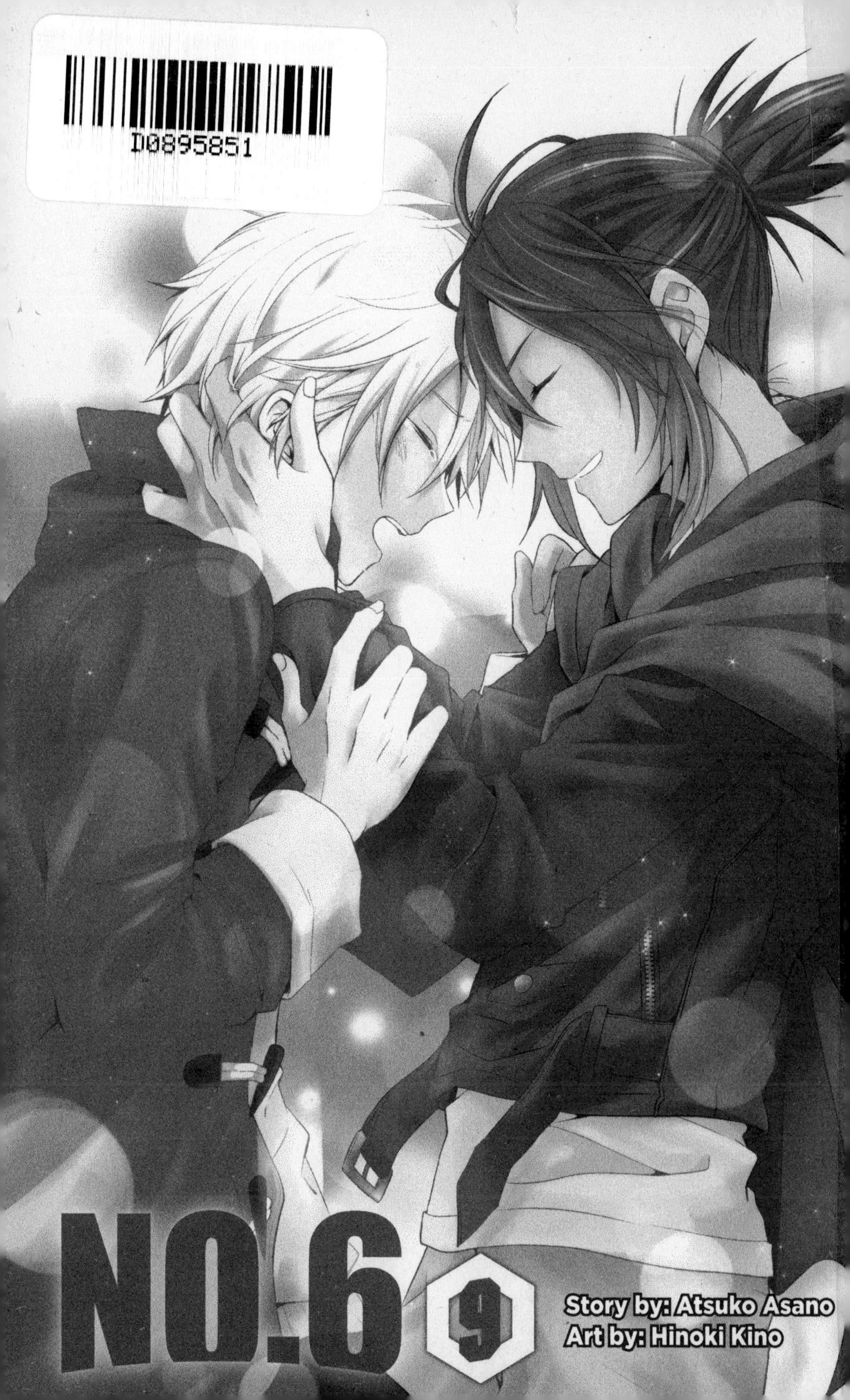
NO.6
9
Story by: Atsuko Asano
Art by: Hinoki Kino

NO.6

#9

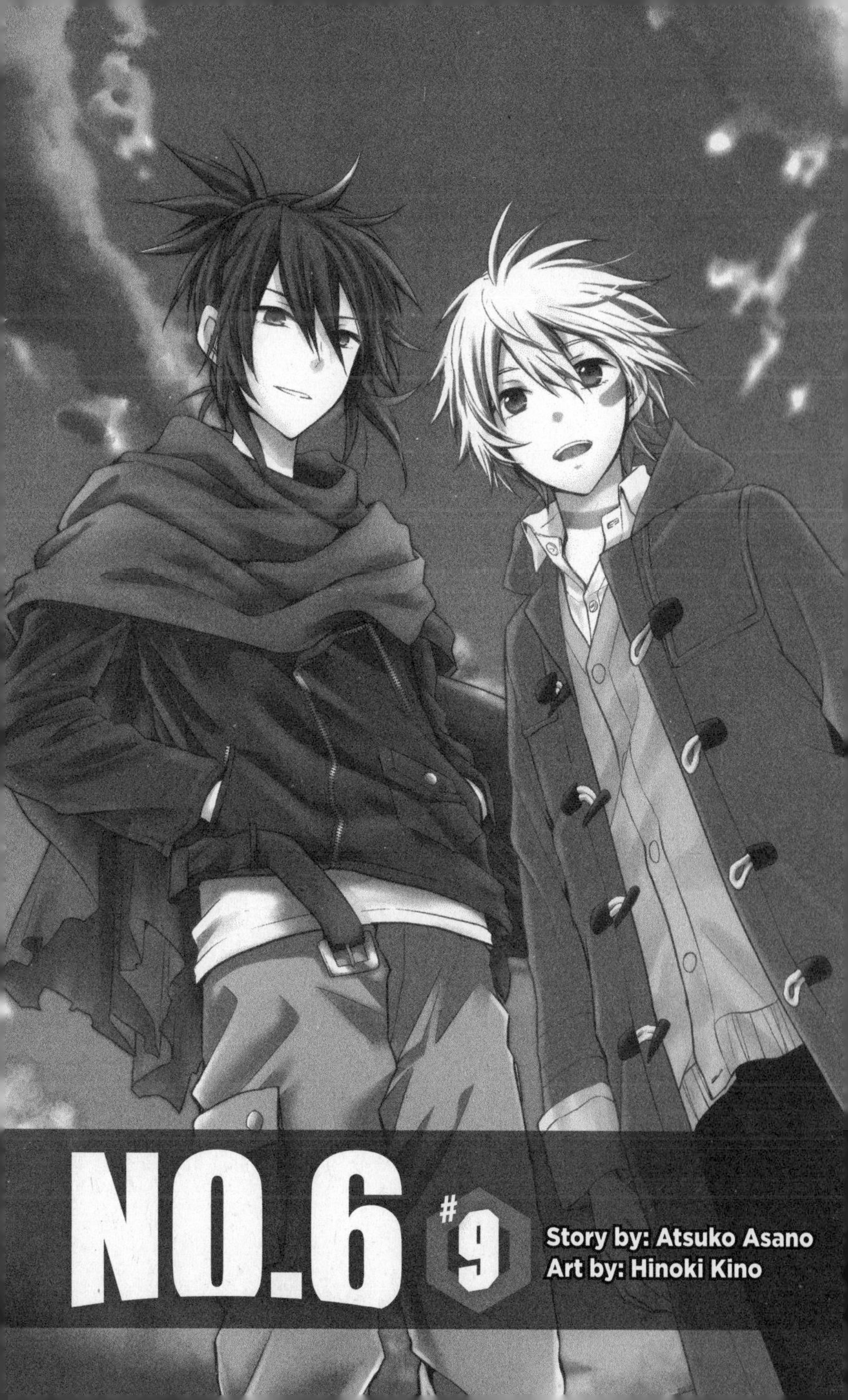
NO.6
#9
Story by: Atsuko Asano
Art by: Hinoki Kino

STORY and CHARACTERS

on was raised as a privileged elite in the holy
ty of NO. 6. As the Public Security Bureau
was arresting him on charges of murder, a
boy named Rat, whom Shion helped during
a storm four years earlier, stepped in to
save him. Together they escaped NO.
6 and fled to West Block, a place
of violence and chaos. Shion was
infected by a mysterious parasitic
bee, but survived, living together with Rat.
After hearing that his childhood friend Safu had been detained and taken
to the Correctional Facility, Shion decided to go free her, with assistance
from Dogkeeper and Rikiga. There the two saw with their own eyes
the hideous torture and murder perpetrated by NO. 6. Despite
being beaten to a pulp, they finally made it to the top floor. But
when they finally found Safu, they realized that all that was
left of her was her brain, which had been implanted into the
Mother computer. Following Safu's wishes, they destroyed
the computer. Then, just as Shion and Rat were making
their escape, Rat was shot through the chest...

Chronos

The top-class residential
area, open only to special
elite citizens.

YOMIN
He's doubted
NO. 6 since his
wife and child
died.

SHION
A former elite candidate, he was
a kind, gentle youth, but as his life
has grown harsher, he has begun
to change.

RIKIGA
A former journalist who
now publishes a porno
magazine in West Block.
An old friend of Karan.

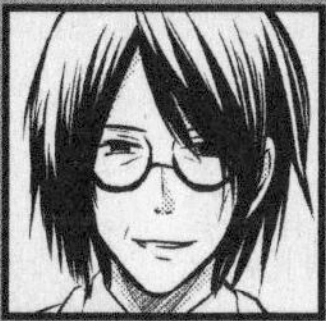

The Man in White
An ambitious research scientist.

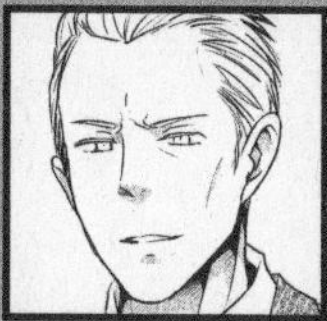

The Mayor
The most powerful man in No. 6.

Inside No. 6

Upper Class

The center of the city, with the Moondrop (City Hall) at its apex.

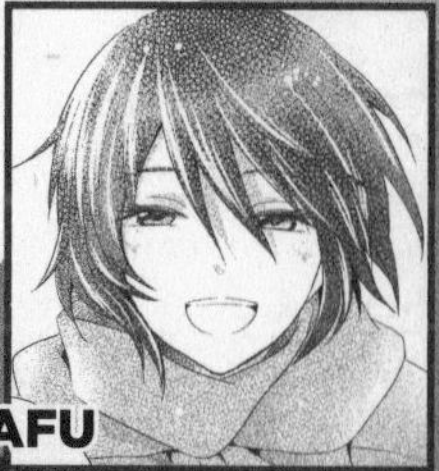

SAFU
A childhood friend who loved Shion. An elite researcher who specialized in neuroscience.

Arrested

The Correctional Facility

The prison for criminals from No. 6. Located in West Block.

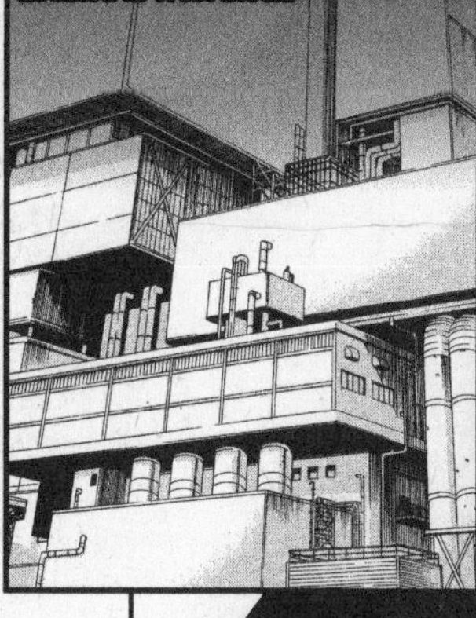

Lost Town

The lower-class residential area for the city's disenfranchised.

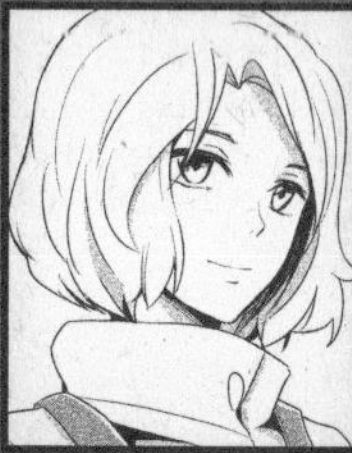

KARAN
Shion's mother. Operates a bakery in Lost Town.

The Outskirts

West Block

The dangerous special zone outside the walls of the city.

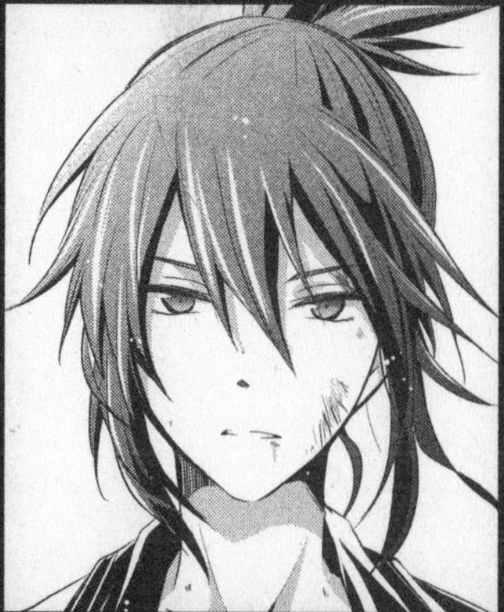

RAT
A youth who despises NO. 6. The sole survivor of the massacred "Forest People."

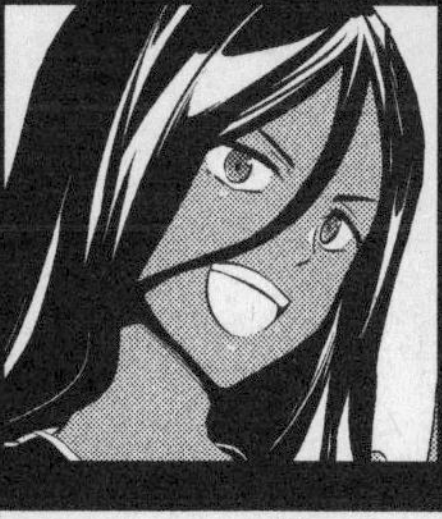

DOGKEEPER
Lives with dogs and operates a dilapidated hotel. Also gathers information for a price.

NO.6

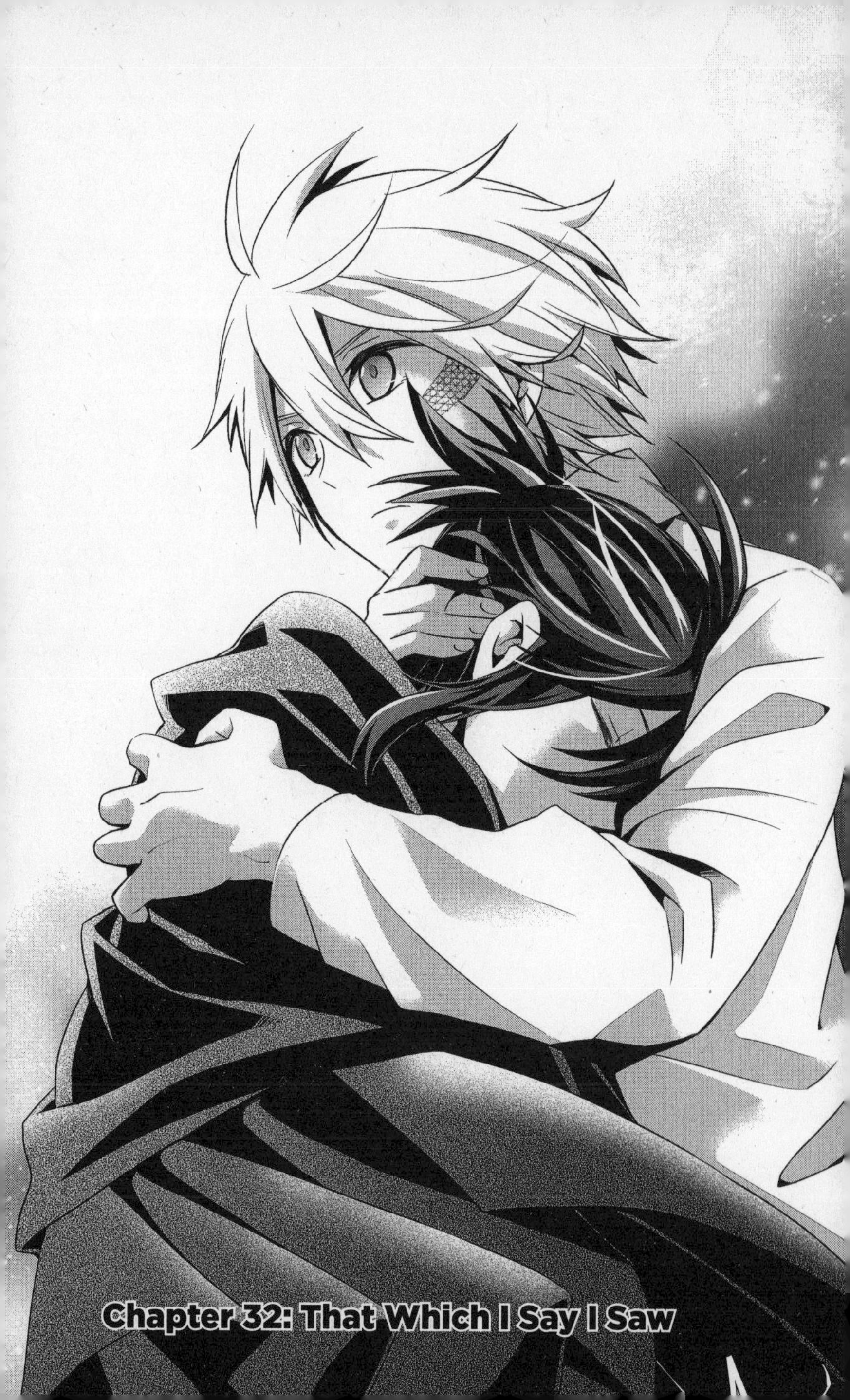

Chapter 32: That Which I Say I Saw

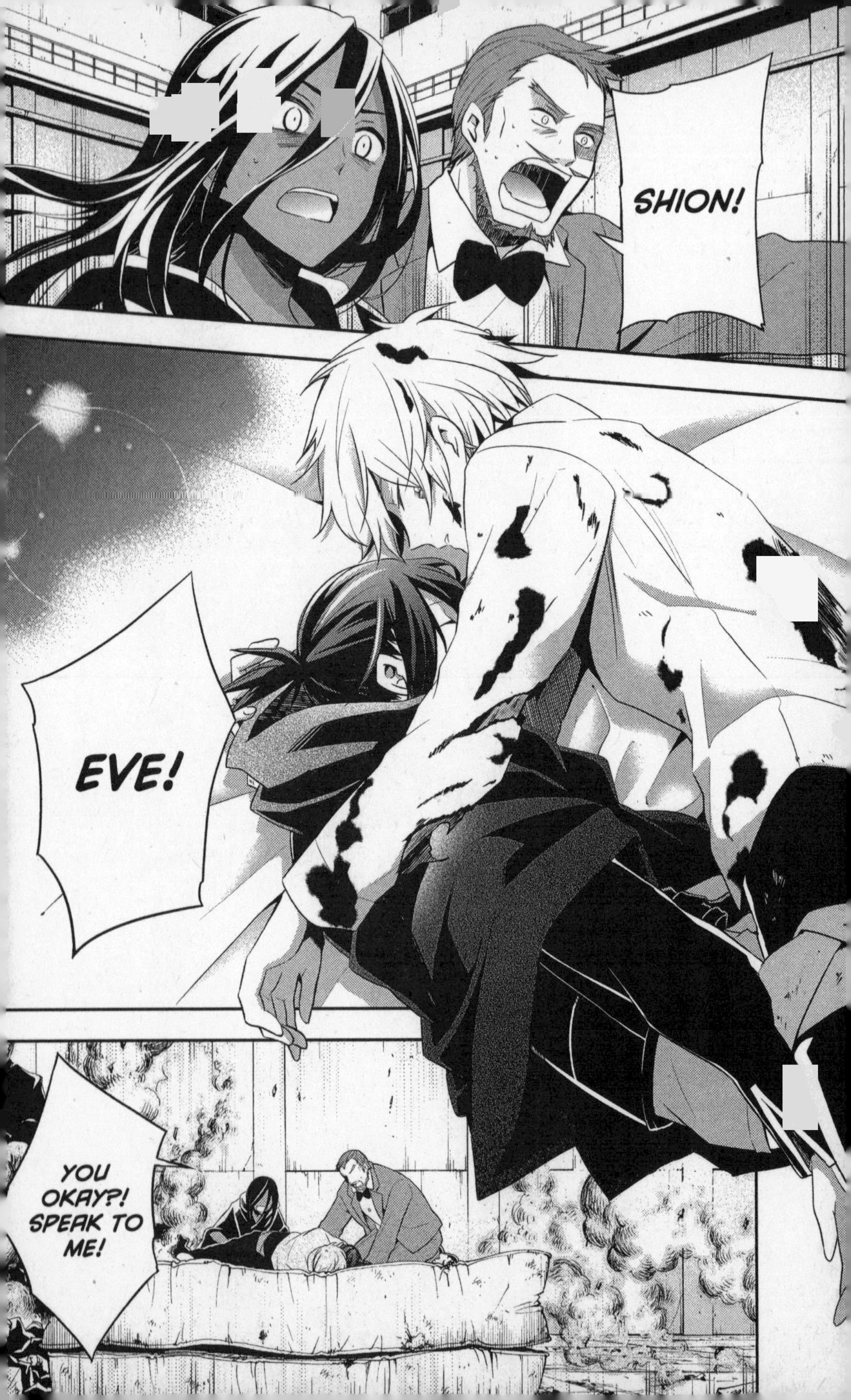
SHION!
EVE!
YOU OKAY?! SPEAK TO ME!

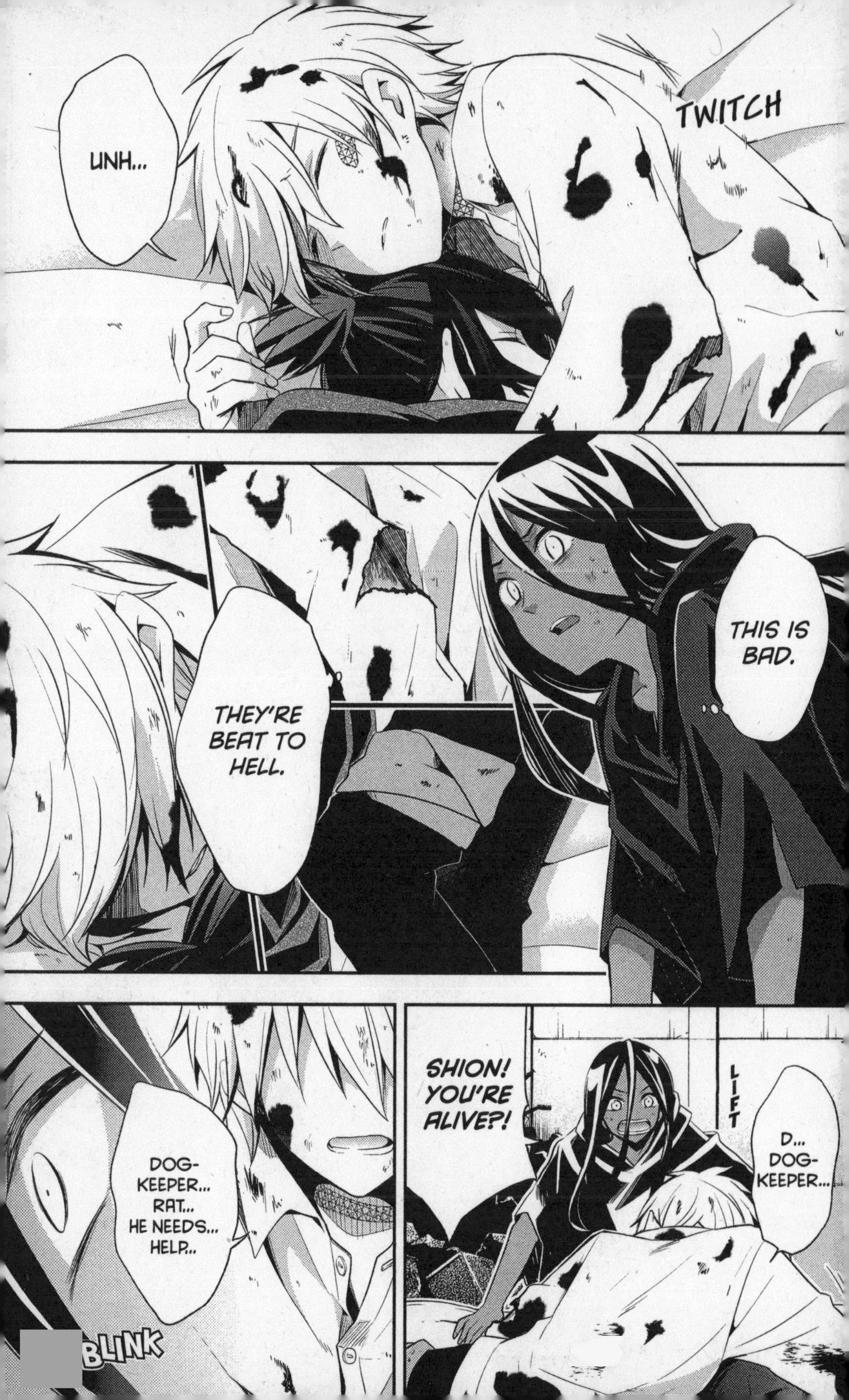
TWITCH
UNH...
THIS IS BAD.
THEY'RE BEAT TO HELL.
D... DOG-KEEPER...
LIFT
SHION! YOU'RE ALIVE?!
DOG-KEEPER... RAT... HE NEEDS... HELP...
BLINK

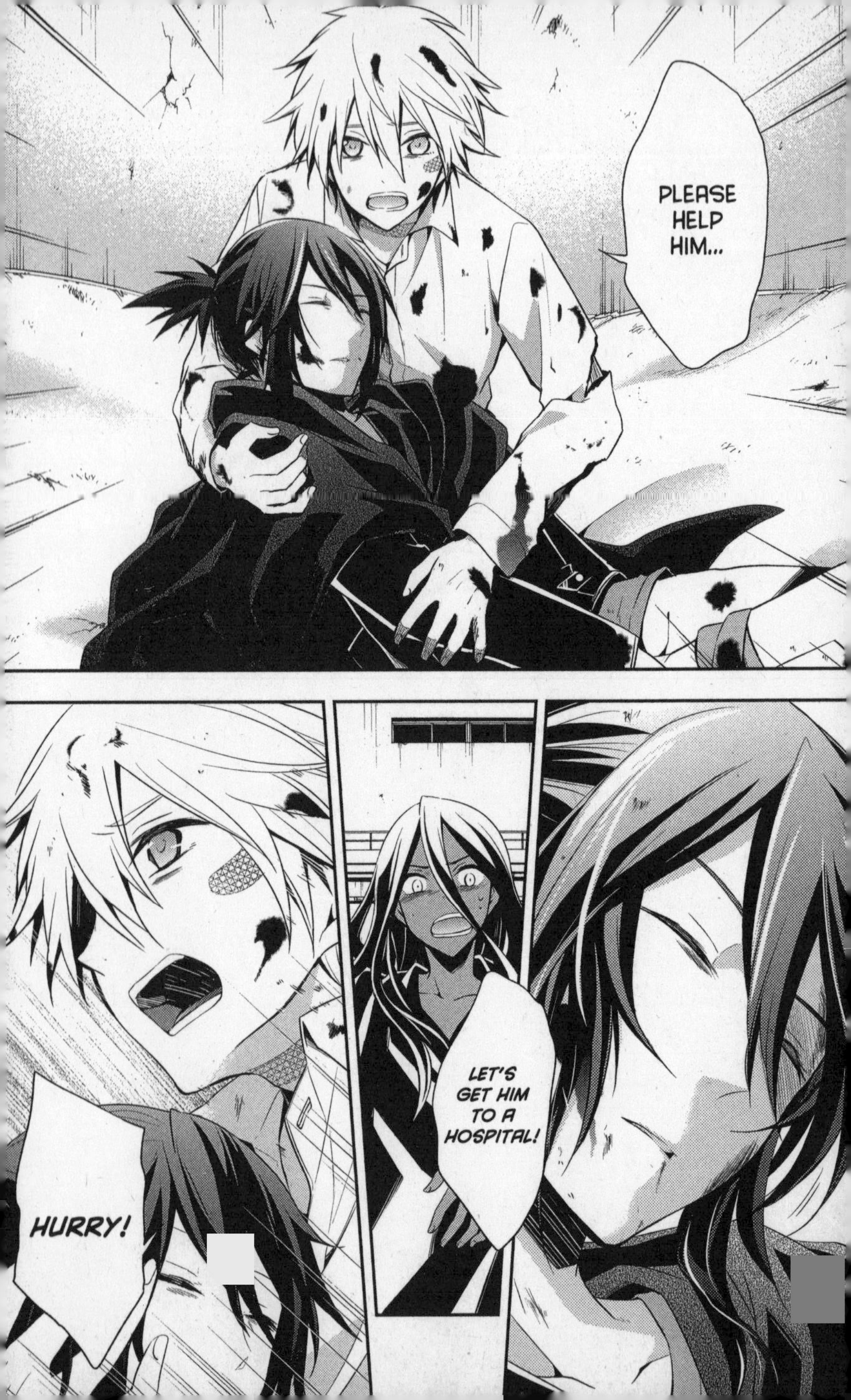
PLEASE HELP HIM...
LET'S GET HIM TO A HOSPITAL!
HURRY!

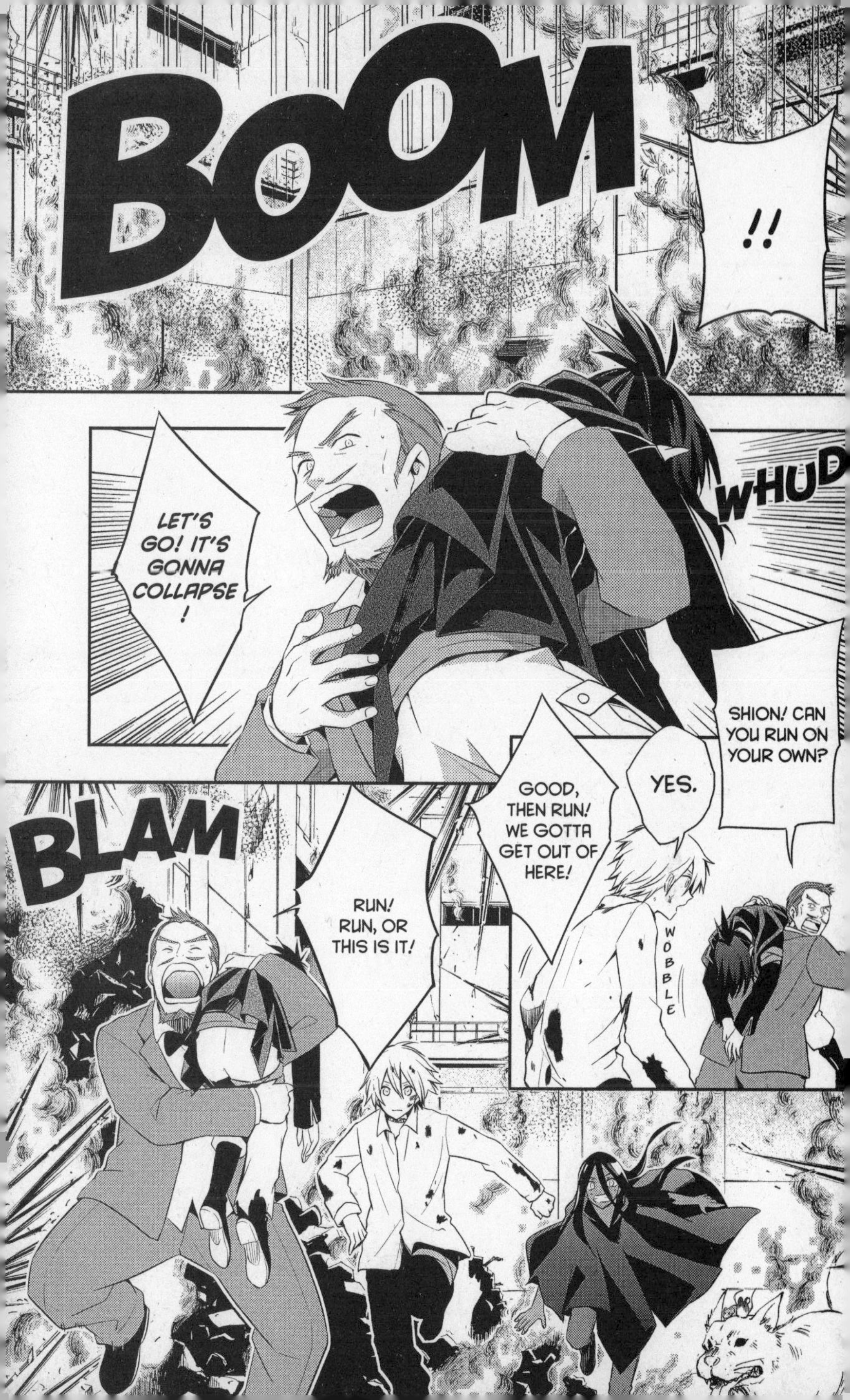
BOOM
!!
WHUD
LET'S GO! IT'S GONNA COLLAPSE!
SHION! CAN YOU RUN ON YOUR OWN?
YES.
GOOD, THEN RUN! WE GOTTA GET OUT OF HERE!
WOBBLE
BLAM
RUN! RUN, OR THIS IS IT!

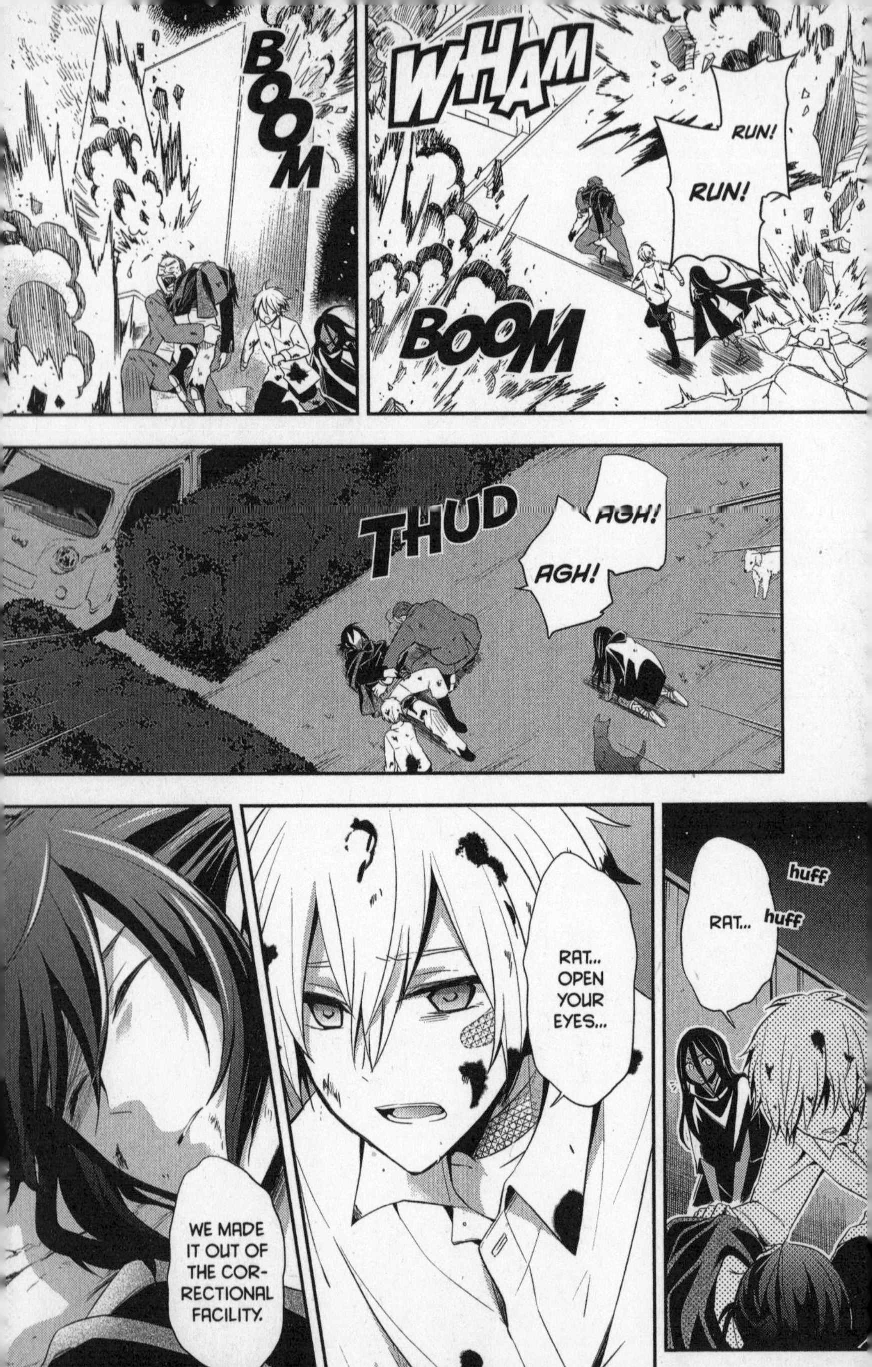
WHAM
RUN!
RUN!
BOOM
BOOM
AGH!
AGH!
THUD
RAT...
huff
huff
RAT... OPEN YOUR EYES...
WE MADE IT OUT OF THE COR-RECTIONAL FACILITY.

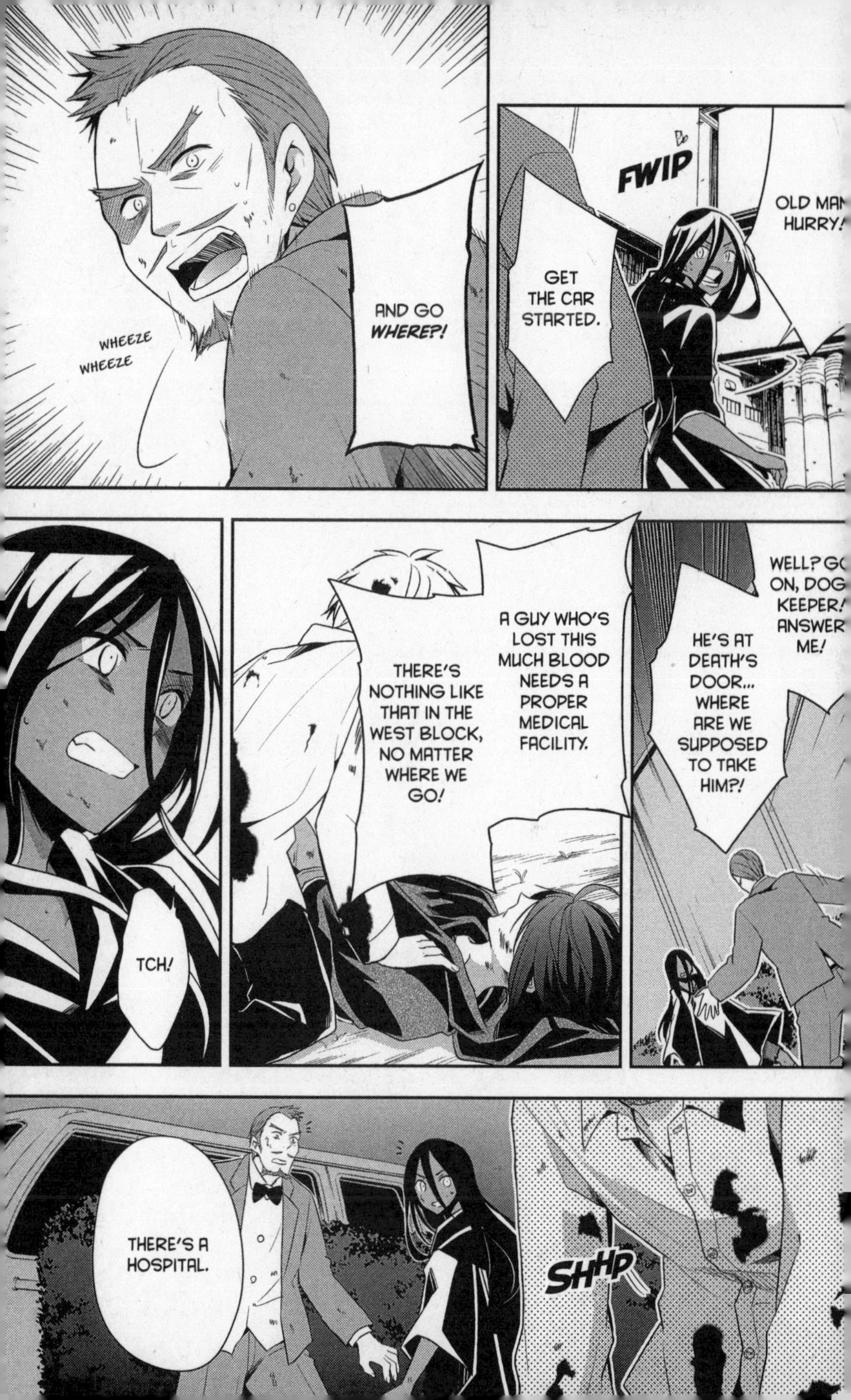
FWIP
OLD MAN HURRY!
GET THE CAR STARTED.
AND GO *WHERE?!*
WHEEZE WHEEZE
WELL? GO ON, DOG KEEPER! ANSWER ME!
HE'S AT DEATH'S DOOR... WHERE ARE WE SUPPOSED TO TAKE HIM?!
A GUY WHO'S LOST THIS MUCH BLOOD NEEDS A PROPER MEDICAL FACILITY.
THERE'S NOTHING LIKE THAT IN THE WEST BLOCK, NO MATTER WHERE WE GO!
TCH!
SHHP
THERE'S A HOSPITAL.

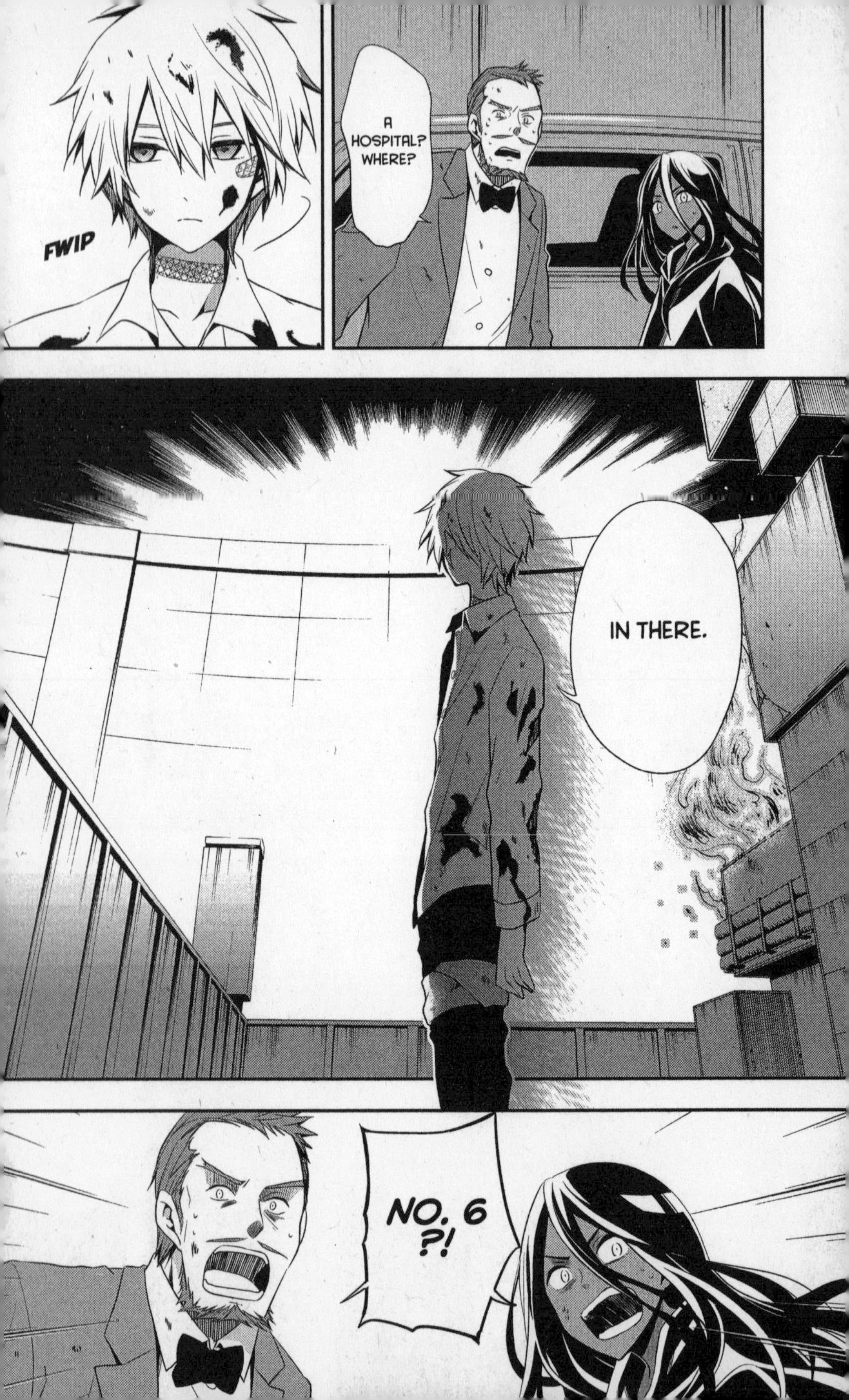
A HOSPITAL? WHERE?
FWIP
IN THERE.
NO. 6 ?!

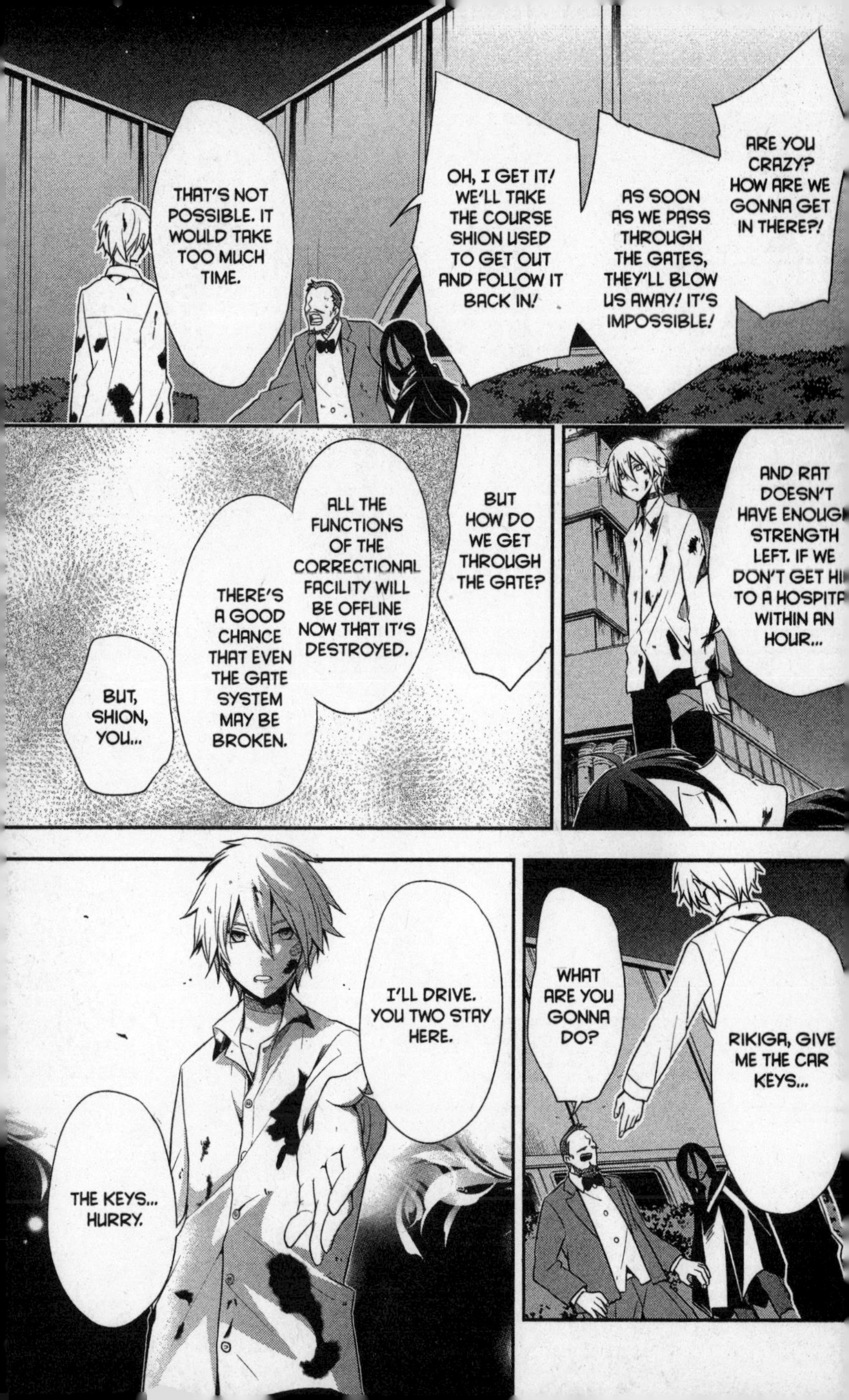
ARE YOU CRAZY? HOW ARE WE GONNA GET IN THERE?!
AS SOON AS WE PASS THROUGH THE GATES, THEY'LL BLOW US AWAY! IT'S IMPOSSIBLE!
OH, I GET IT! WE'LL TAKE THE COURSE SHION USED TO GET OUT AND FOLLOW IT BACK IN!
THAT'S NOT POSSIBLE. IT WOULD TAKE TOO MUCH TIME.
AND RAT DOESN'T HAVE ENOUG STRENGTH LEFT. IF WE DON'T GET HI TO A HOSPITA WITHIN AN HOUR...
BUT HOW DO WE GET THROUGH THE GATE?
ALL THE FUNCTIONS OF THE CORRECTIONAL FACILITY WILL BE OFFLINE NOW THAT IT'S DESTROYED.
THERE'S A GOOD CHANCE THAT EVEN THE GATE SYSTEM MAY BE BROKEN.
BUT, SHION, YOU...
RIKIGA, GIVE ME THE CAR KEYS...
WHAT ARE YOU GONNA DO?
I'LL DRIVE. YOU TWO STAY HERE.
THE KEYS... HURRY.

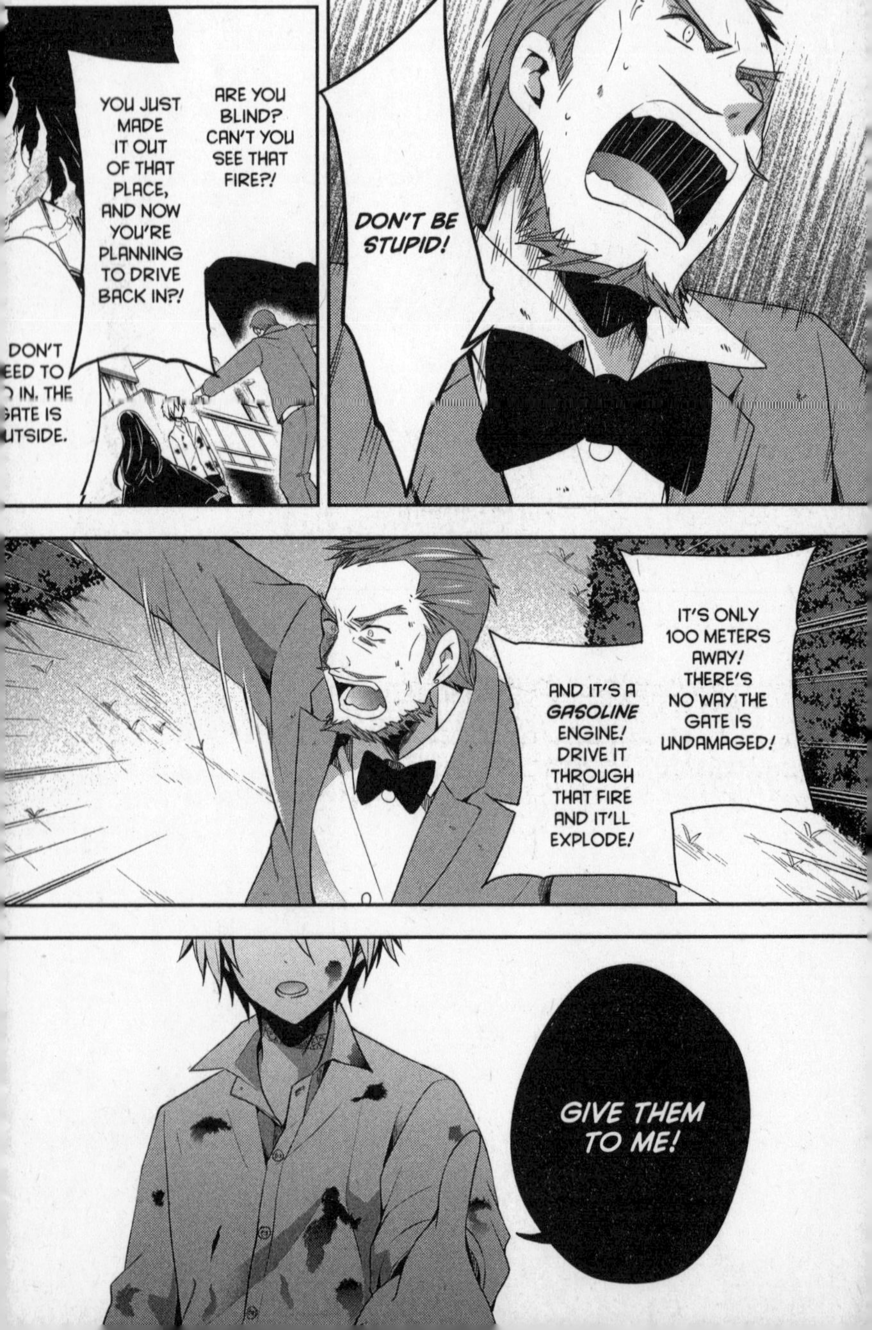
DON'T BE STUPID!
ARE YOU BLIND? CAN'T YOU SEE THAT FIRE?!
YOU JUST MADE IT OUT OF THAT PLACE, AND NOW YOU'RE PLANNING TO DRIVE BACK IN?!
DON'T EED TO IN. THE ATE IS UTSIDE.
IT'S ONLY 100 METERS AWAY! THERE'S NO WAY THE GATE IS UNDAMAGED!
AND IT'S A *GASOLINE* ENGINE! DRIVE IT THROUGH THAT FIRE AND IT'LL EXPLODE!
GIVE THEM TO ME!

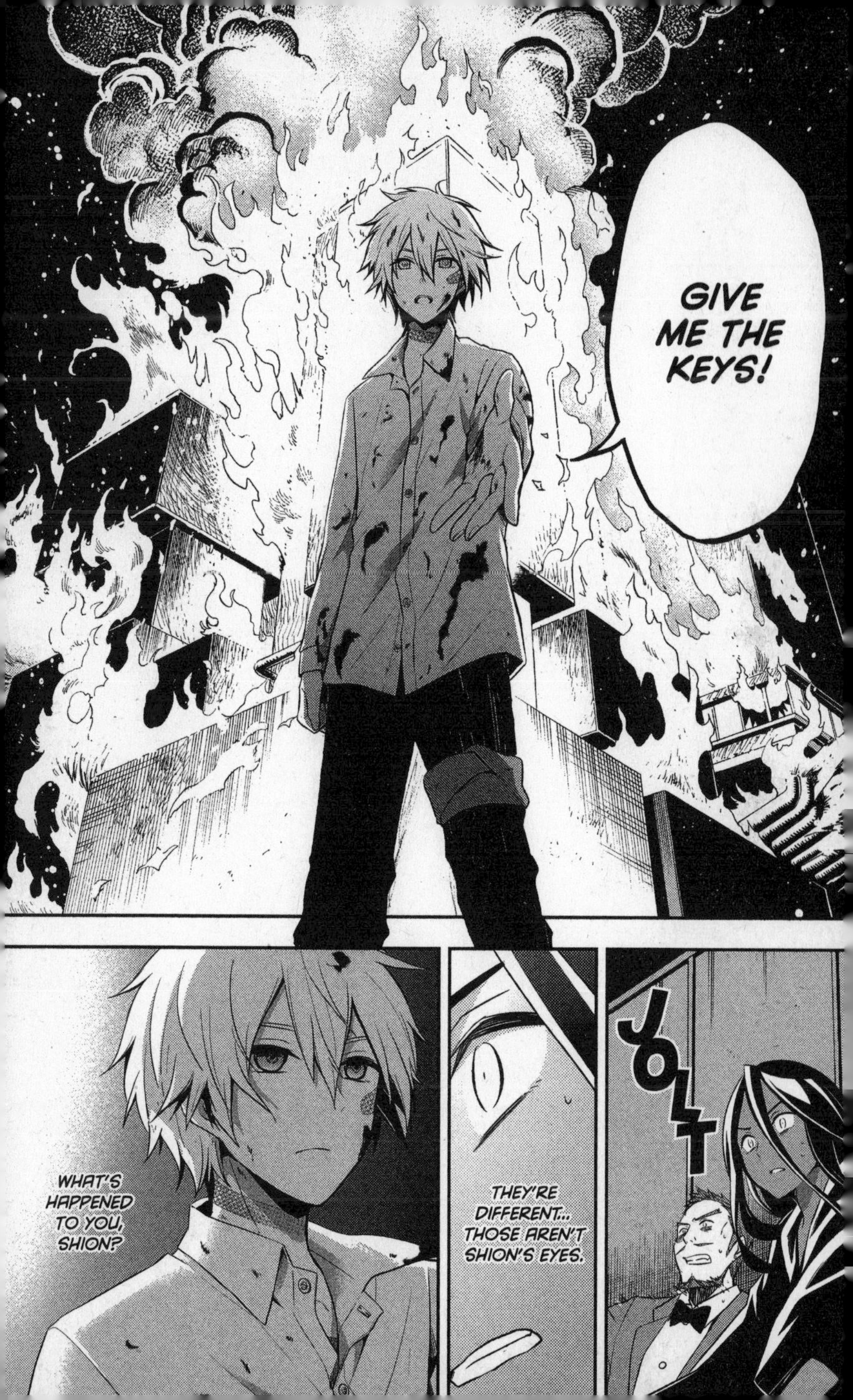
GIVE ME THE KEYS!
JOLT
THEY'RE DIFFERENT... THOSE AREN'T SHION'S EYES.
WHAT'S HAPPENED TO YOU, SHION?

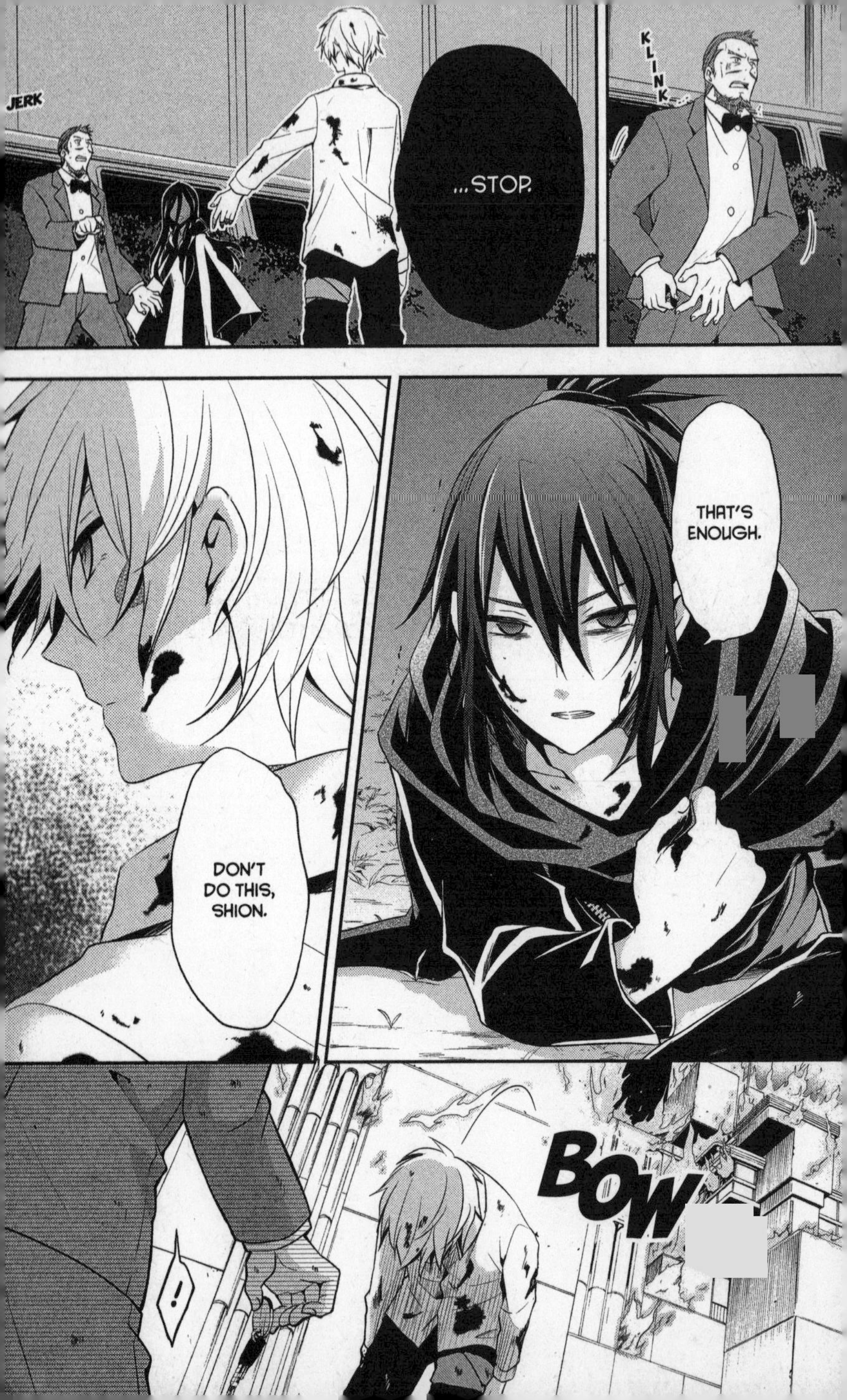
KLINK
...STOP.
JERK
THAT'S ENOUGH.
DON'T DO THIS, SHION.
BOW
!

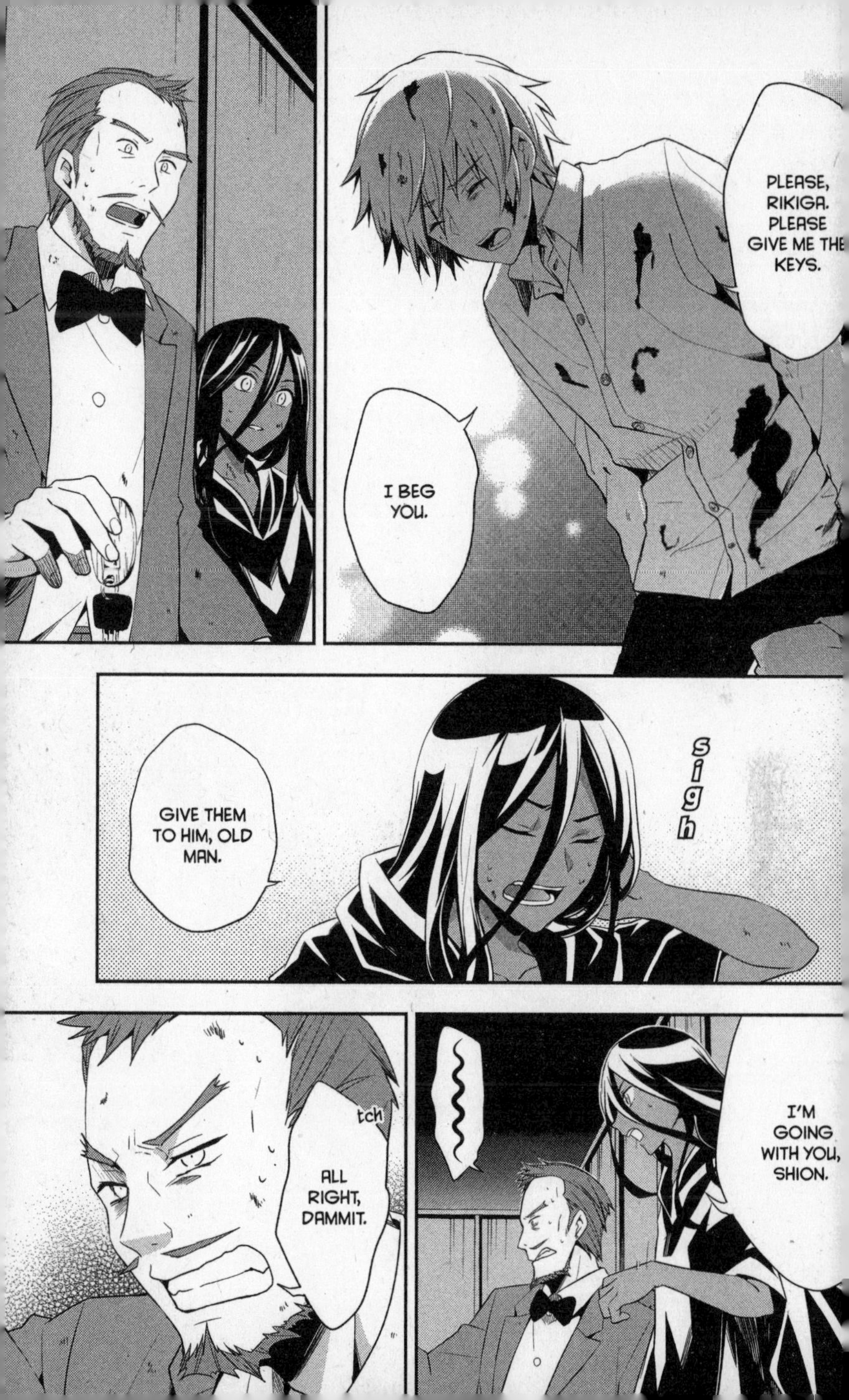
PLEASE, RIKIGA. PLEASE GIVE ME THE KEYS.
I BEG YOU.
sigh
GIVE THEM TO HIM, OLD MAN.
I'M GOING WITH YOU, SHION.
tch
ALL RIGHT, DAMMIT.

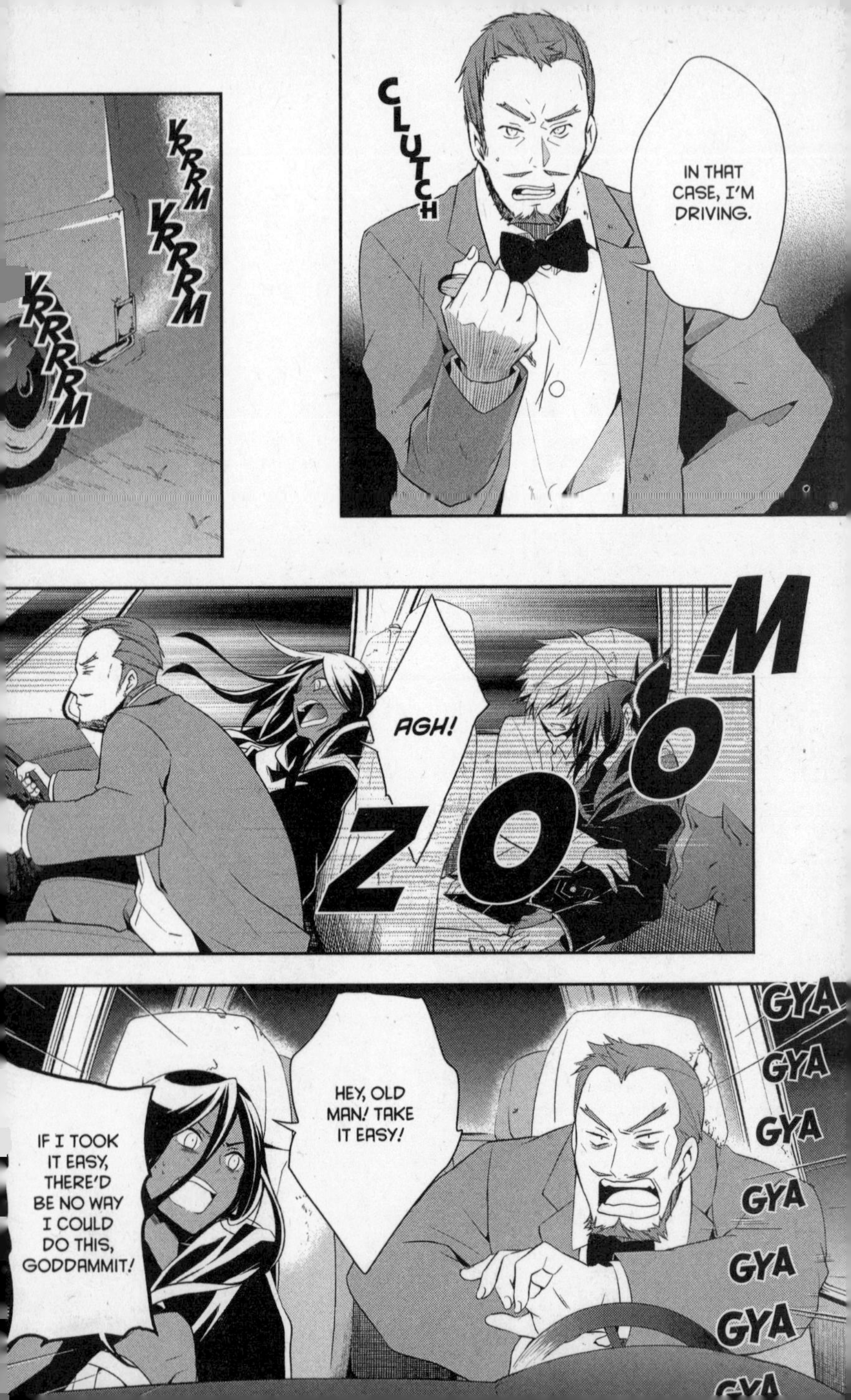
IN THAT CASE, I'M DRIVING.
CLUTCH
VRRRM
VRRRRM
VRRRRRM
ZOOOM
AGH!
GYA
GYA
GYA
GYA
GYA
GYA
HEY, OLD MAN! TAKE IT EASY!
IF I TOOK IT EASY, THERE'D BE NO WAY I COULD DO THIS, GODDAMMIT!

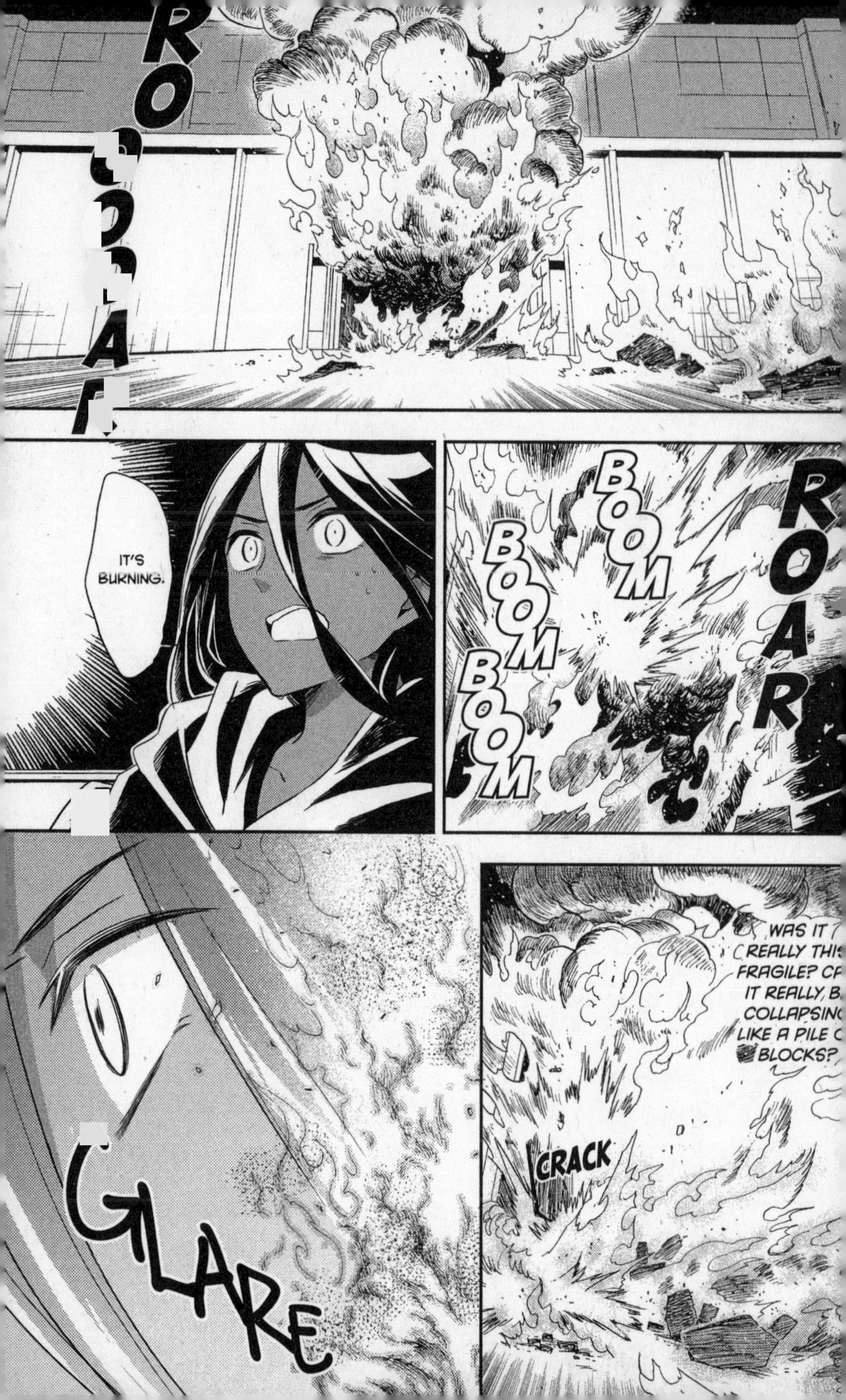
ROOOOAR
ROAR
BOOM
BOOM
BOOM
IT'S BURNING.
WAS IT REALLY THIS FRAGILE?
IT REALLY,
COLLAPSING LIKE A PILE
BLOCKS?
CRACK
GLARE

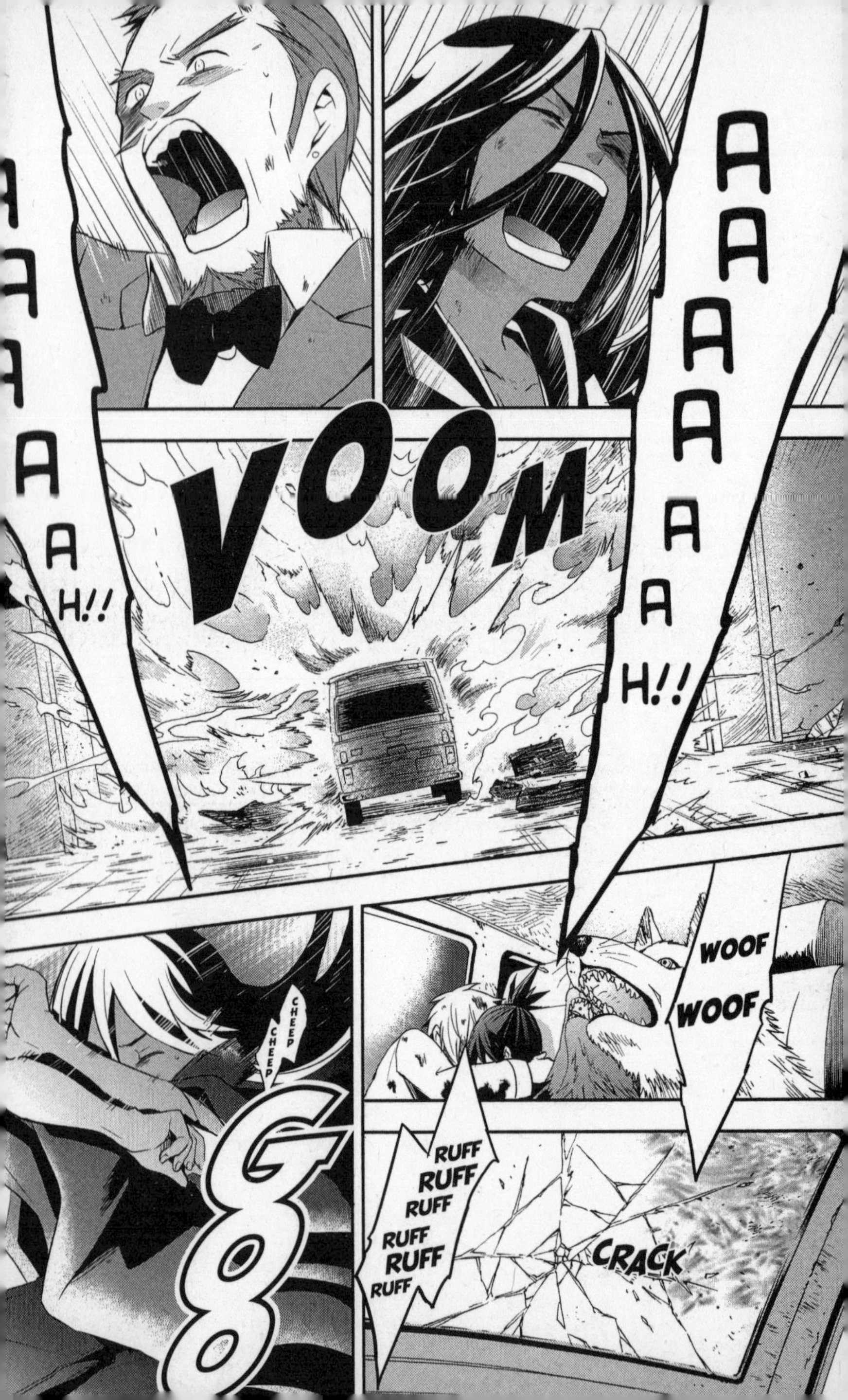

AAAAAAAAH!!
AAAAAAH!!
VOOM
WOOF WOOF
CHEEP CHEEP
GO
RUFF RUFF RUFF RUFF RUFF RUFF
CRACK

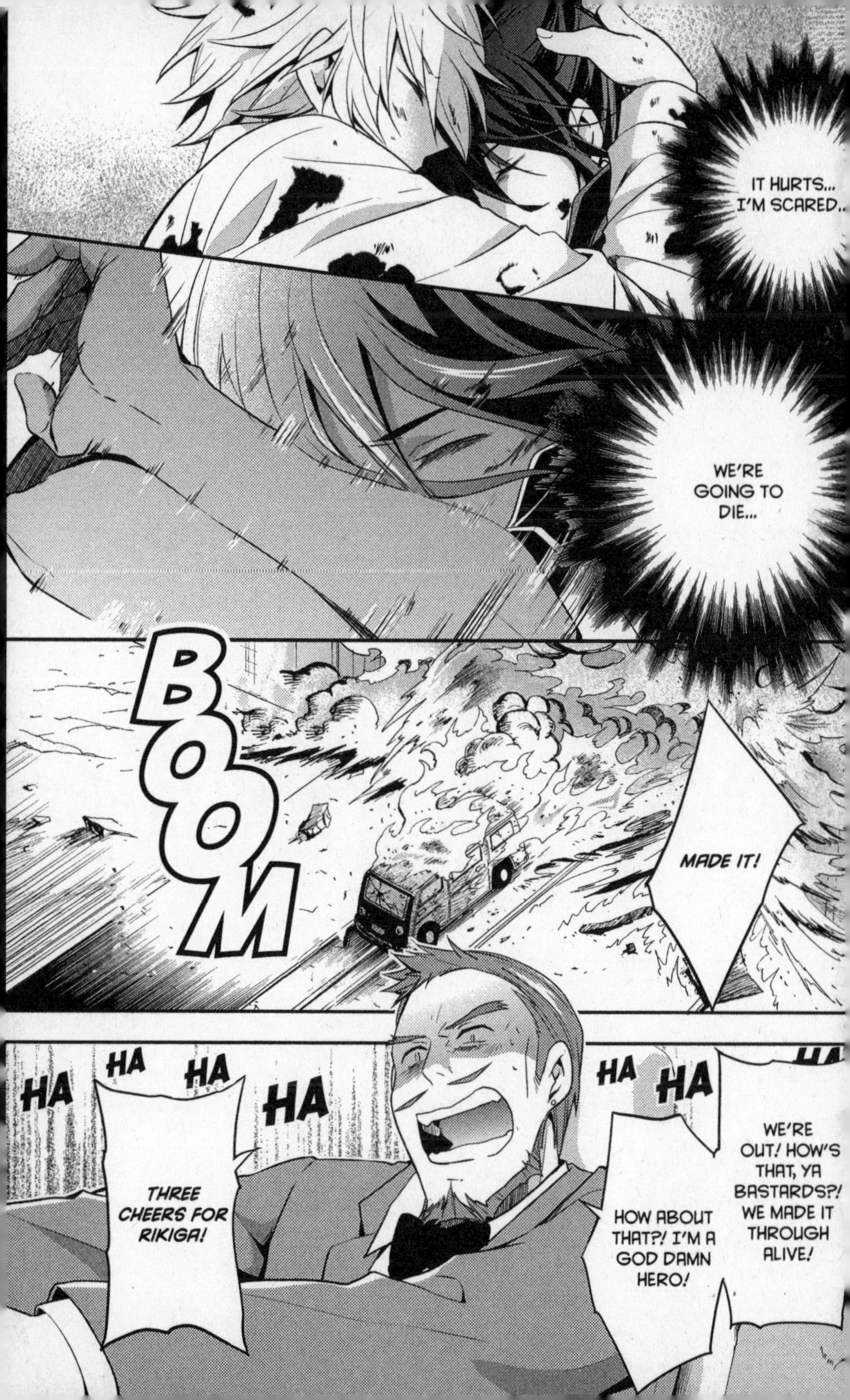
IT HURTS... I'M SCARED...
WE'RE GOING TO DIE...
MADE IT!
BOOM
WE'RE OUT! HOW'S THAT, YA BASTARDS?! WE MADE IT THROUGH ALIVE!
HOW ABOUT THAT?! I'M A GOD DAMN HERO!
HA HA HA HA HA HA
THREE CHEERS FOR RIKIGA!

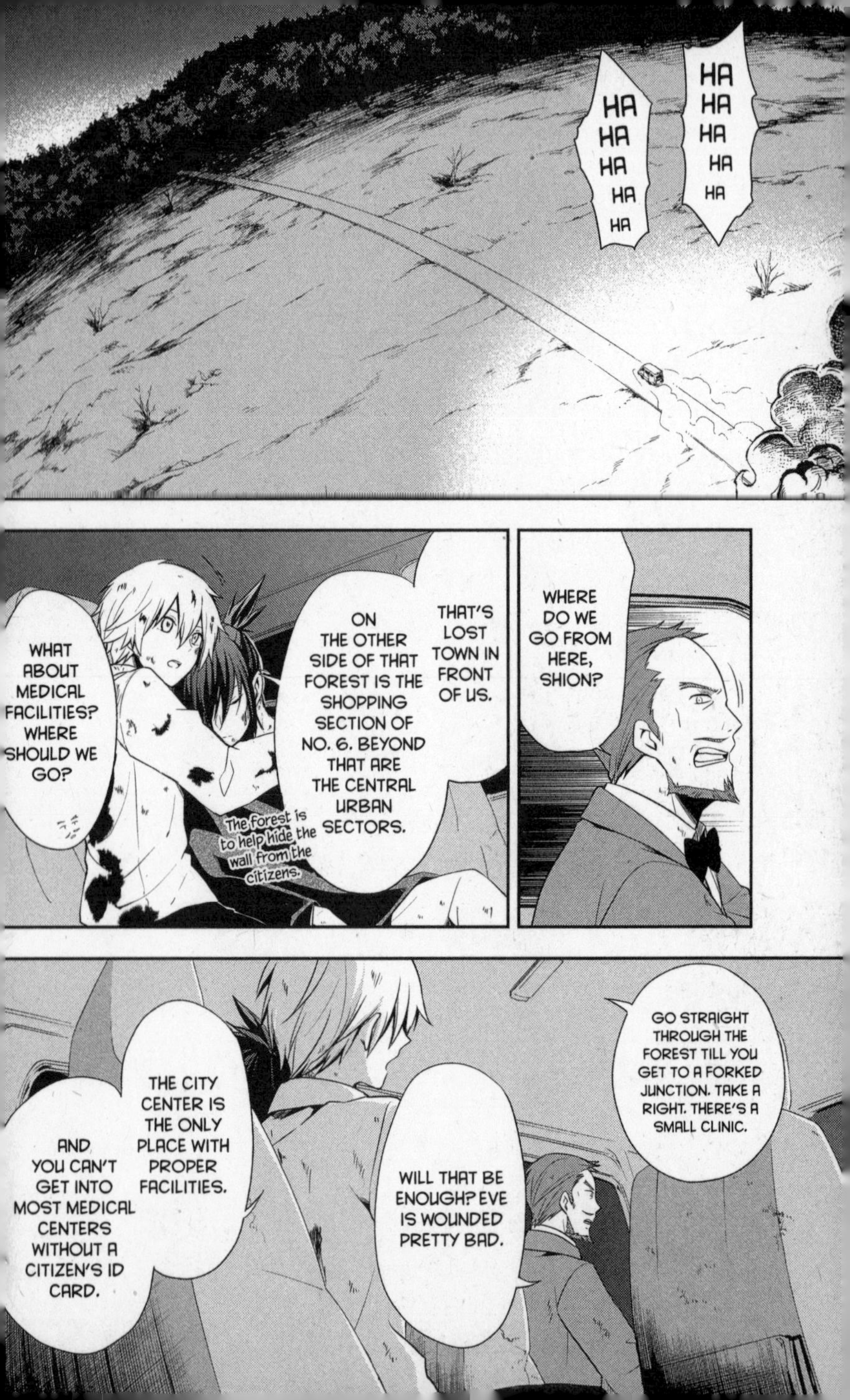
HA HA HA HA HA
HA HA HA HA HA
WHERE DO WE GO FROM HERE, SHION?
THAT'S LOST TOWN IN FRONT OF US.
ON THE OTHER SIDE OF THAT FOREST IS THE SHOPPING SECTION OF NO. 6. BEYOND THAT ARE THE CENTRAL URBAN SECTORS.
The forest is to help hide the wall from the citizens.
WHAT ABOUT MEDICAL FACILITIES? WHERE SHOULD WE GO?
GO STRAIGHT THROUGH THE FOREST TILL YOU GET TO A FORKED JUNCTION. TAKE A RIGHT. THERE'S A SMALL CLINIC.
WILL THAT BE ENOUGH? EVE IS WOUNDED PRETTY BAD.
THE CITY CENTER IS THE ONLY PLACE WITH PROPER FACILITIES.
AND YOU CAN'T GET INTO MOST MEDICAL CENTERS WITHOUT A CITIZEN'S ID CARD.

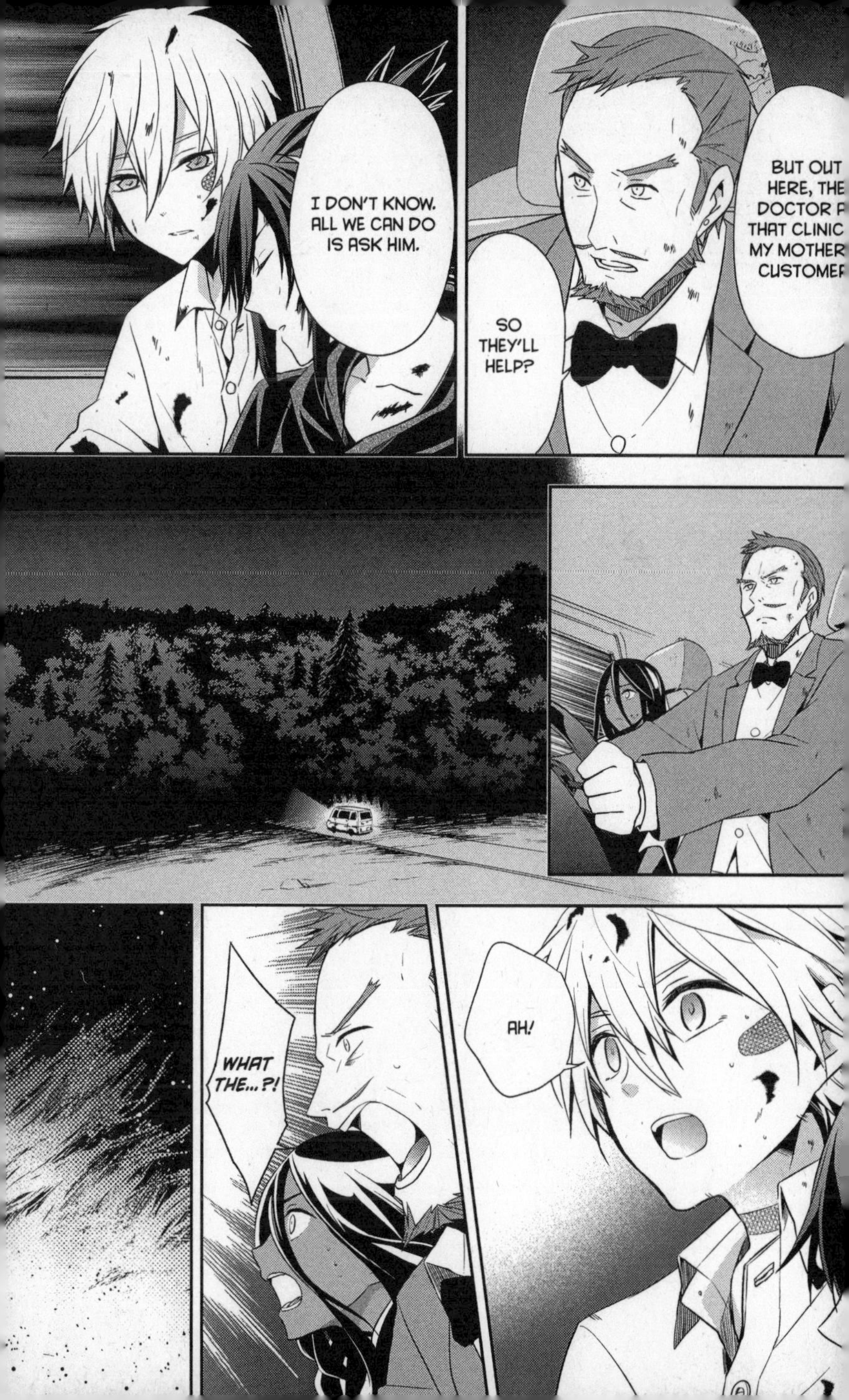
BUT OUT HERE, THE DOCTOR THAT CLINIC MY MOTHER CUSTOMER
SO THEY'LL HELP?
I DON'T KNOW. ALL WE CAN DO IS ASK HIM.
AH!
WHAT THE...?!

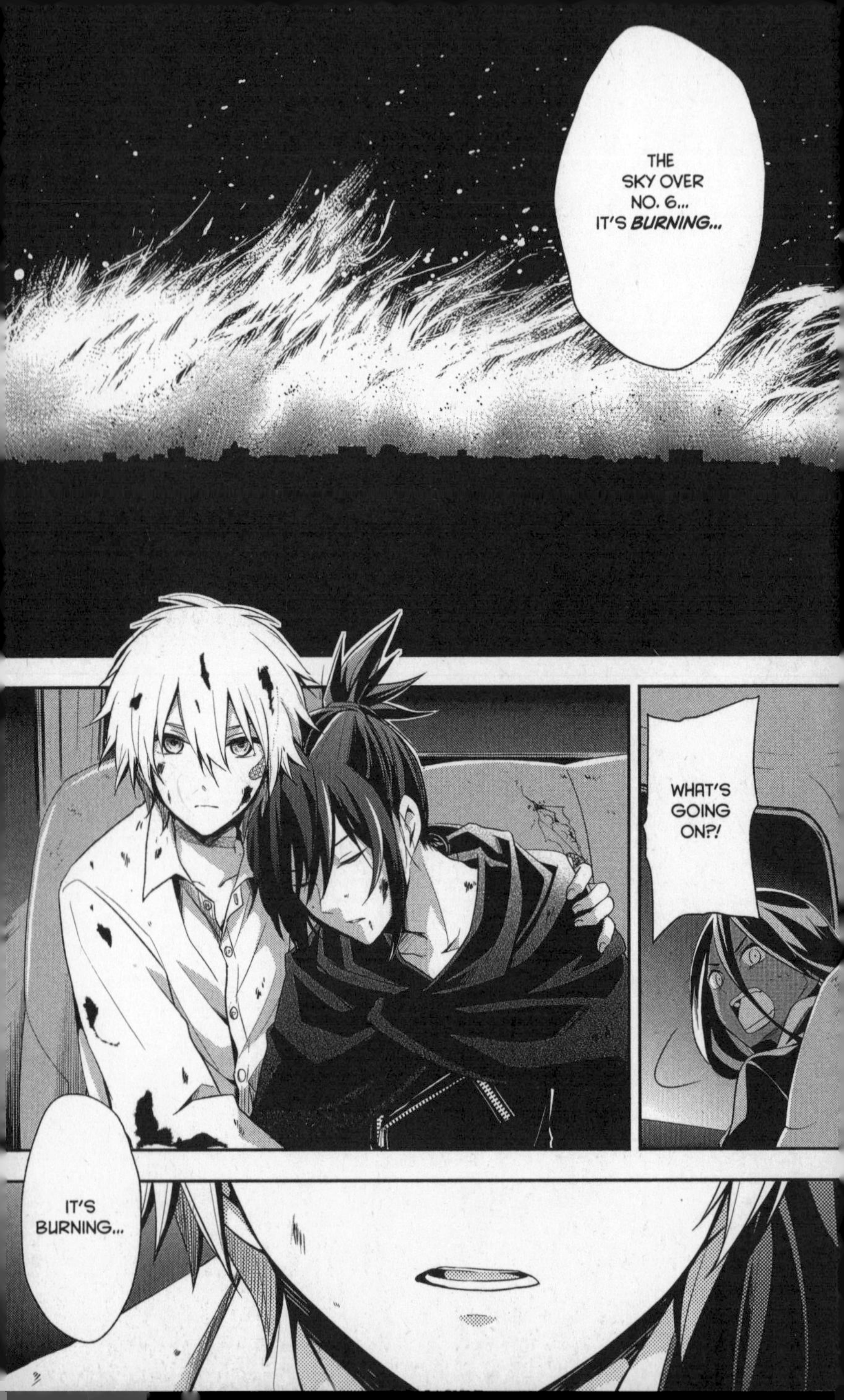
THE SKY OVER NO. 6... IT'S *BURNING*...
WHAT'S GOING ON?!
IT'S BURNING...

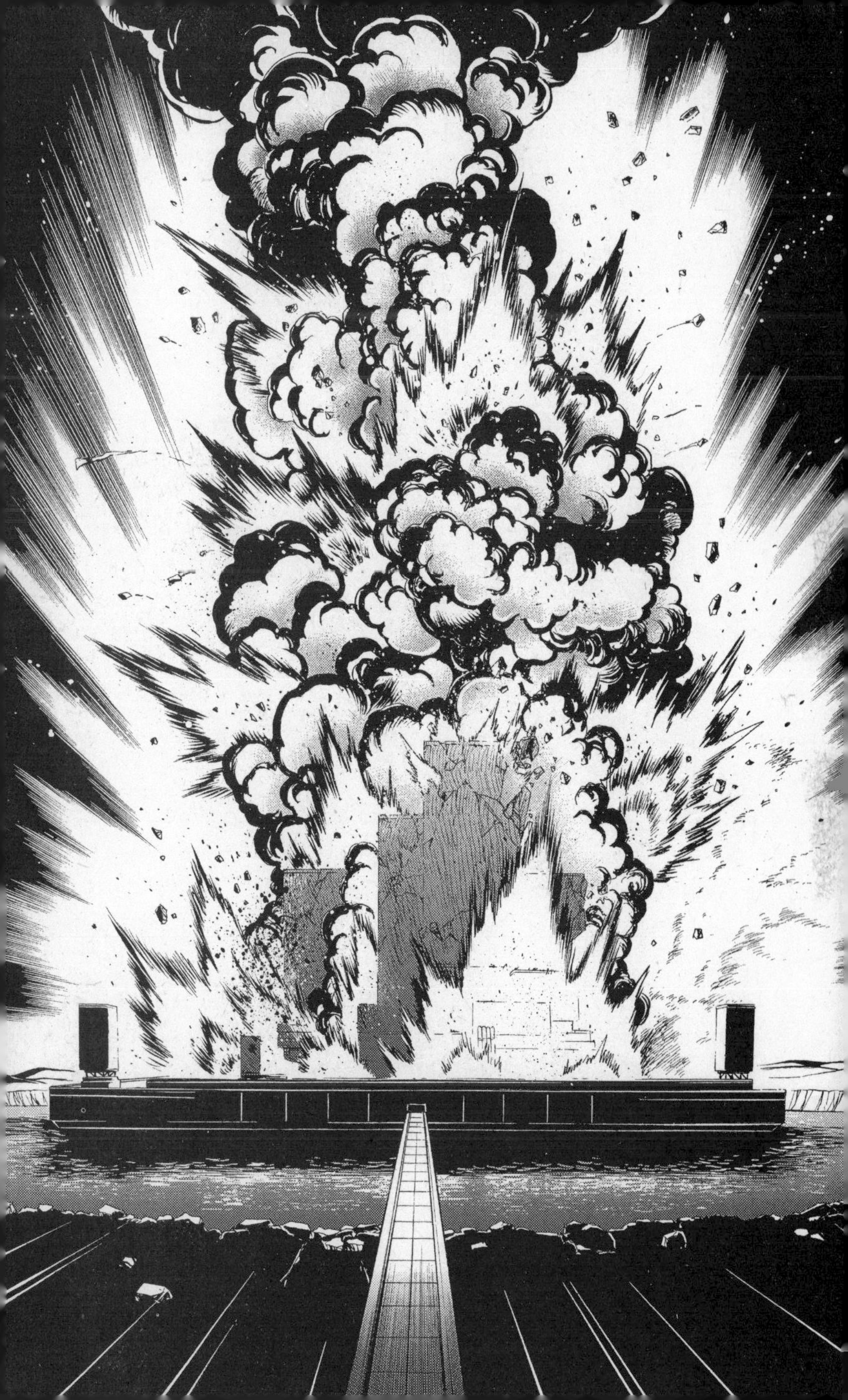

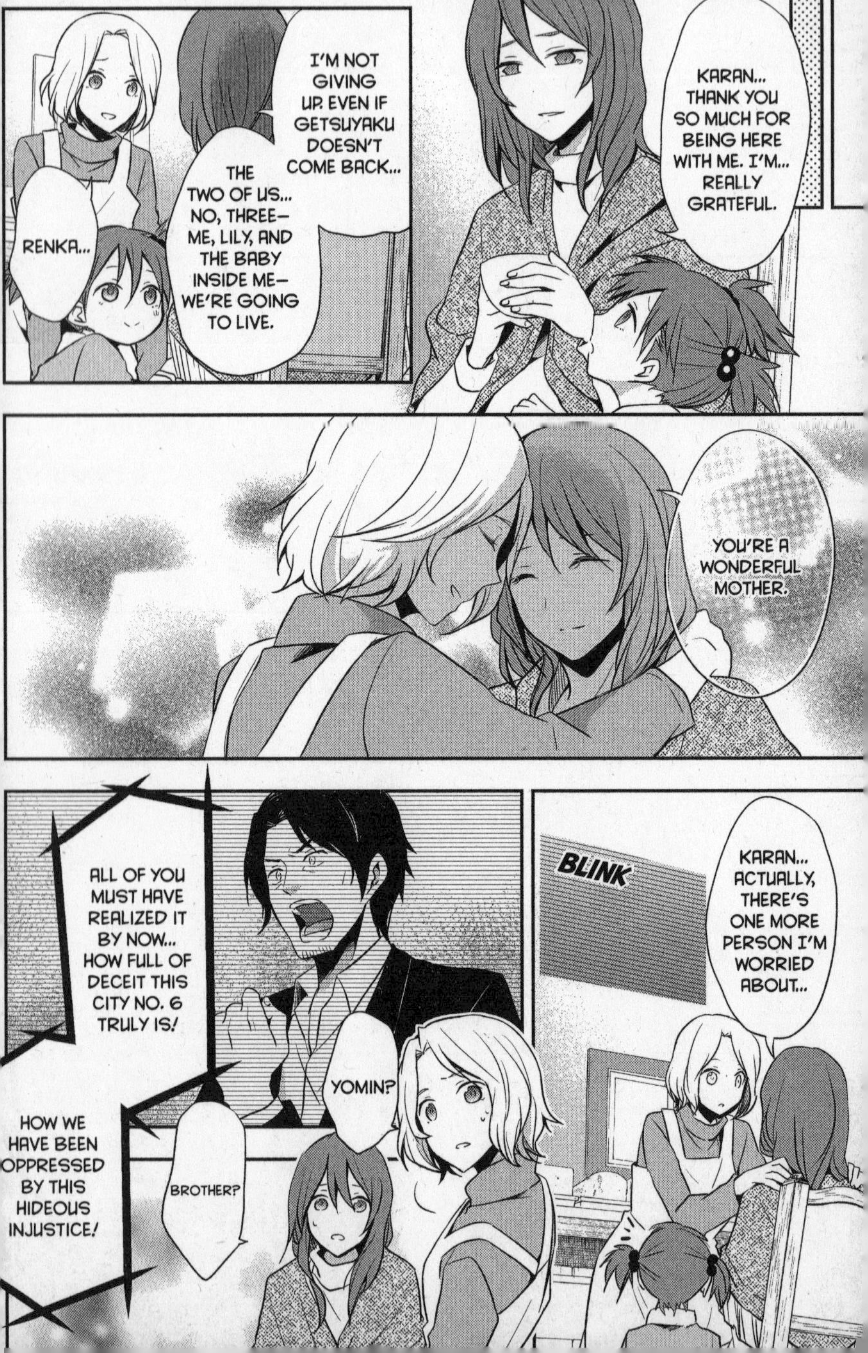
KARAN... THANK YOU SO MUCH FOR BEING HERE WITH ME. I'M... REALLY GRATEFUL.
I'M NOT GIVING UP. EVEN IF GETSUYAKU DOESN'T COME BACK...
THE TWO OF US... NO, THREE— ME, LILY, AND THE BABY INSIDE ME— WE'RE GOING TO LIVE.
RENKA...
YOU'RE A WONDERFUL MOTHER.
BLINK
KARAN... ACTUALLY, THERE'S ONE MORE PERSON I'M WORRIED ABOUT...
ALL OF YOU MUST HAVE REALIZED IT BY NOW... HOW FULL OF DECEIT THIS CITY NO. 6 TRULY IS!
YOMIN?
HOW WE HAVE BEEN OPPRESSED BY THIS HIDEOUS INJUSTICE!
BROTHER?

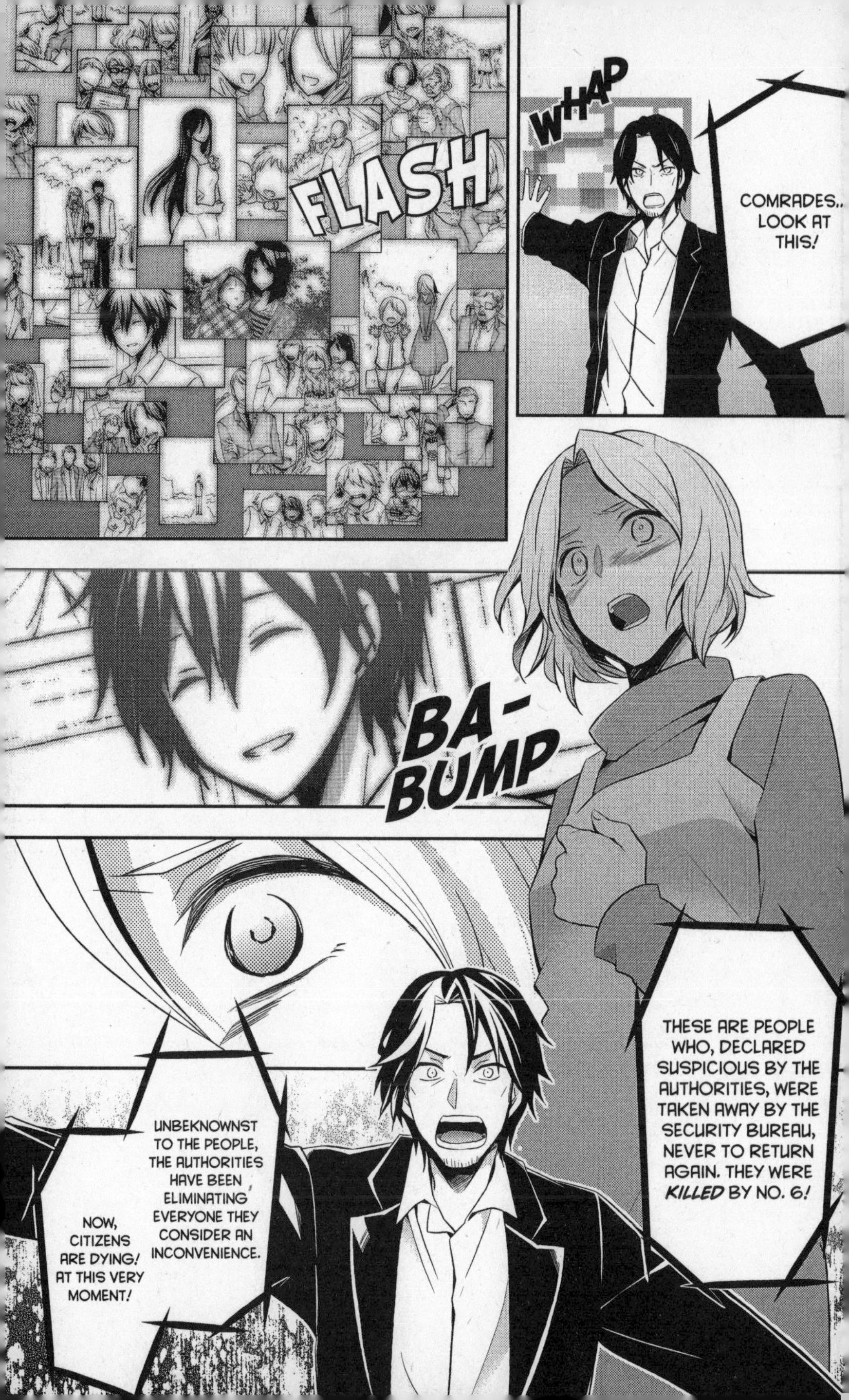
WHAP
COMRADES.. LOOK AT THIS!
FLASH
BA-BUMP
THESE ARE PEOPLE WHO, DECLARED SUSPICIOUS BY THE AUTHORITIES, WERE TAKEN AWAY BY THE SECURITY BUREAU, NEVER TO RETURN AGAIN. THEY WERE *KILLED* BY NO. 6!
UNBEKNOWNST TO THE PEOPLE, THE AUTHORITIES HAVE BEEN ELIMINATING EVERYONE THEY CONSIDER AN INCONVENIENCE.
NOW, CITIZENS ARE DYING! AT THIS VERY MOMENT!

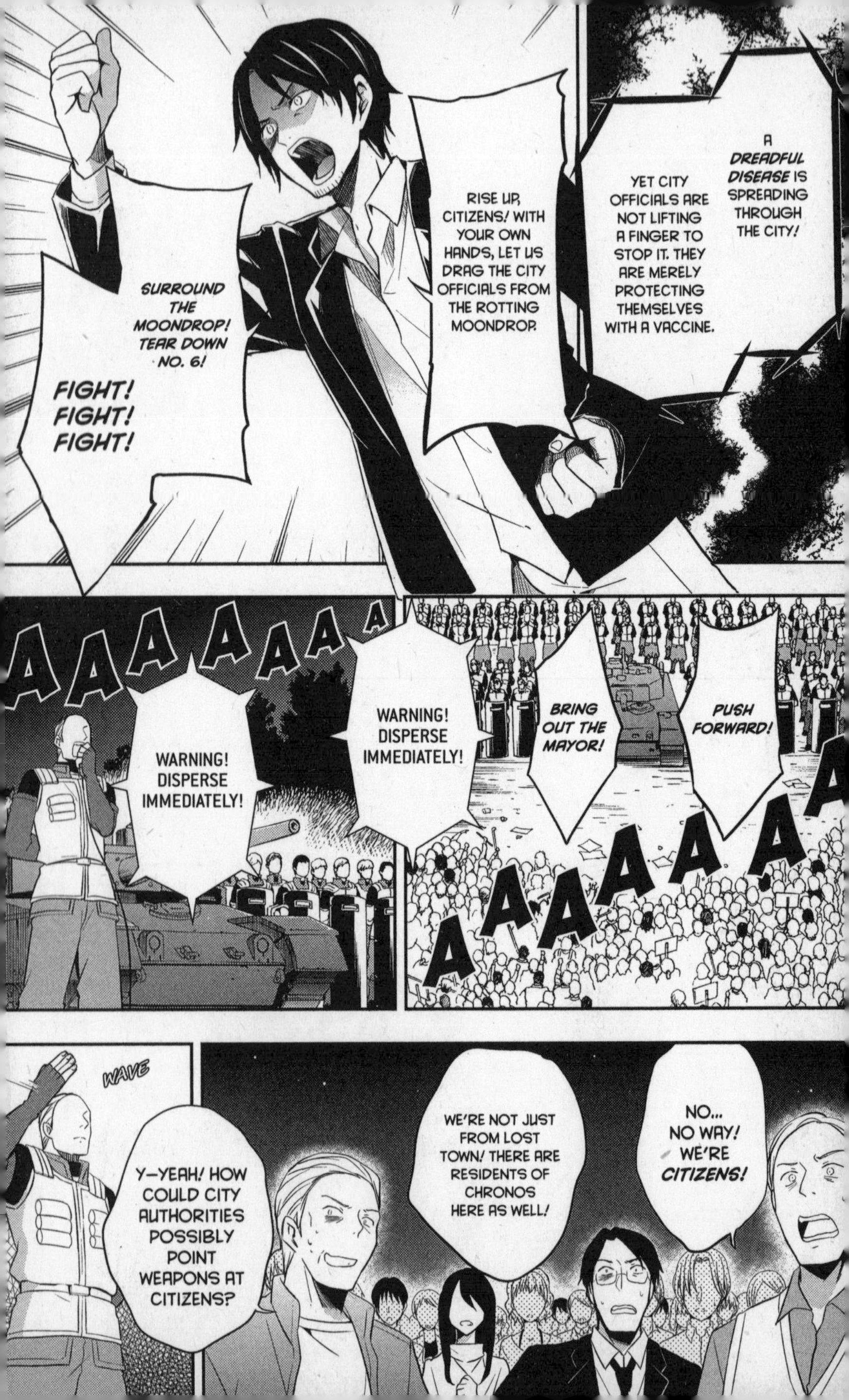
A DREADFUL DISEASE IS SPREADING THROUGH THE CITY!
YET CITY OFFICIALS ARE NOT LIFTING A FINGER TO STOP IT. THEY ARE MERELY PROTECTING THEMSELVES WITH A VACCINE.
RISE UP, CITIZENS! WITH YOUR OWN HANDS, LET US DRAG THE CITY OFFICIALS FROM THE ROTTING MOONDROP.
SURROUND THE MOONDROP! TEAR DOWN NO. 6!
FIGHT! FIGHT! FIGHT!
PUSH FORWARD!
BRING OUT THE MAYOR!
AAAAAAAA
WARNING! DISPERSE IMMEDIATELY!
WARNING! DISPERSE IMMEDIATELY!
AAAAAAA
NO... NO WAY! WE'RE CITIZENS!
WE'RE NOT JUST FROM LOST TOWN! THERE ARE RESIDENTS OF CHRONOS HERE AS WELL!
Y-YEAH! HOW COULD CITY AUTHORITIES POSSIBLY POINT WEAPONS AT CITIZENS?
WAVE

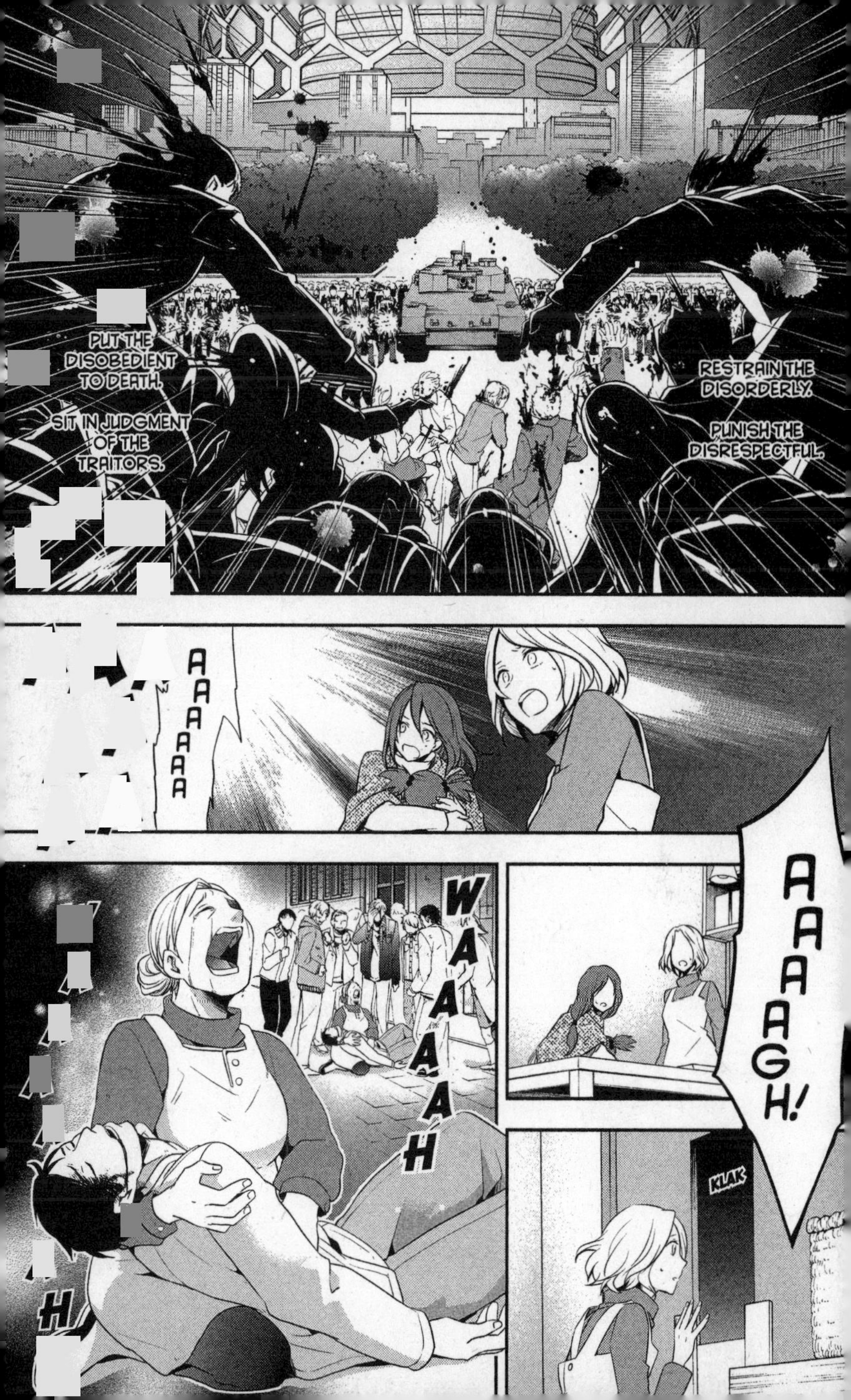
RESTRAIN THE DISORDERLY.
PUNISH THE DISRESPECTFUL.
PUT THE DISOBEDIENT TO DEATH.
SIT IN JUDGMENT OF THE TRAITORS.
AAAAAAA
AAAAGH!
KLAK
WAAAAH

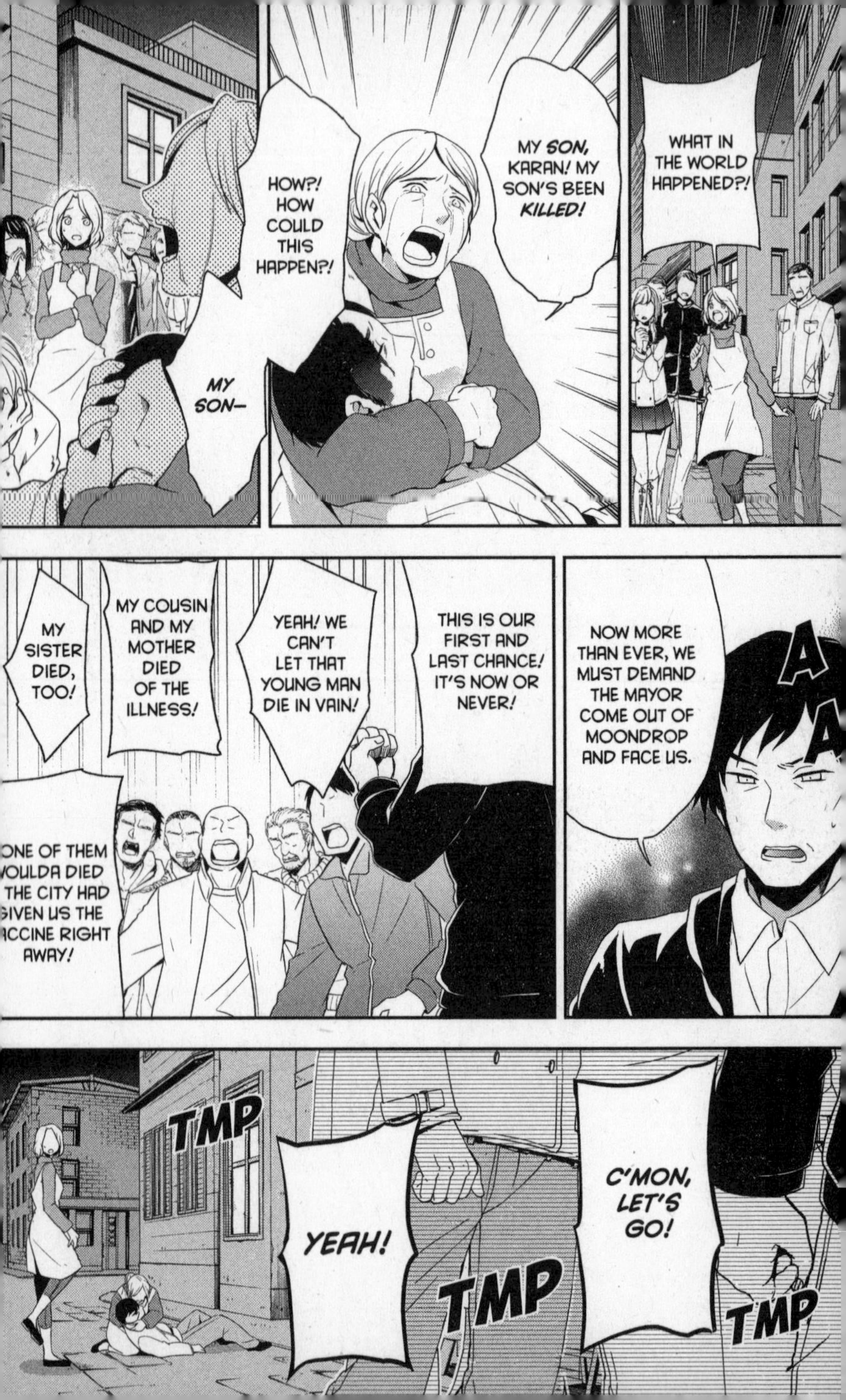
WHAT IN THE WORLD HAPPENED?!
MY SON, KARAN! MY SON'S BEEN KILLED!
HOW?! HOW COULD THIS HAPPEN?!
MY SON—
NOW MORE THAN EVER, WE MUST DEMAND THE MAYOR COME OUT OF MOONDROP AND FACE US.
THIS IS OUR FIRST AND LAST CHANCE! IT'S NOW OR NEVER!
YEAH! WE CAN'T LET THAT YOUNG MAN DIE IN VAIN!
MY COUSIN AND MY MOTHER DIED OF THE ILLNESS!
MY SISTER DIED, TOO!
ONE OF THEM OULDA DIED THE CITY HAD GIVEN US THE CCINE RIGHT AWAY!
C'MON, LET'S GO!
TMP
TMP
YEAH!
TMP

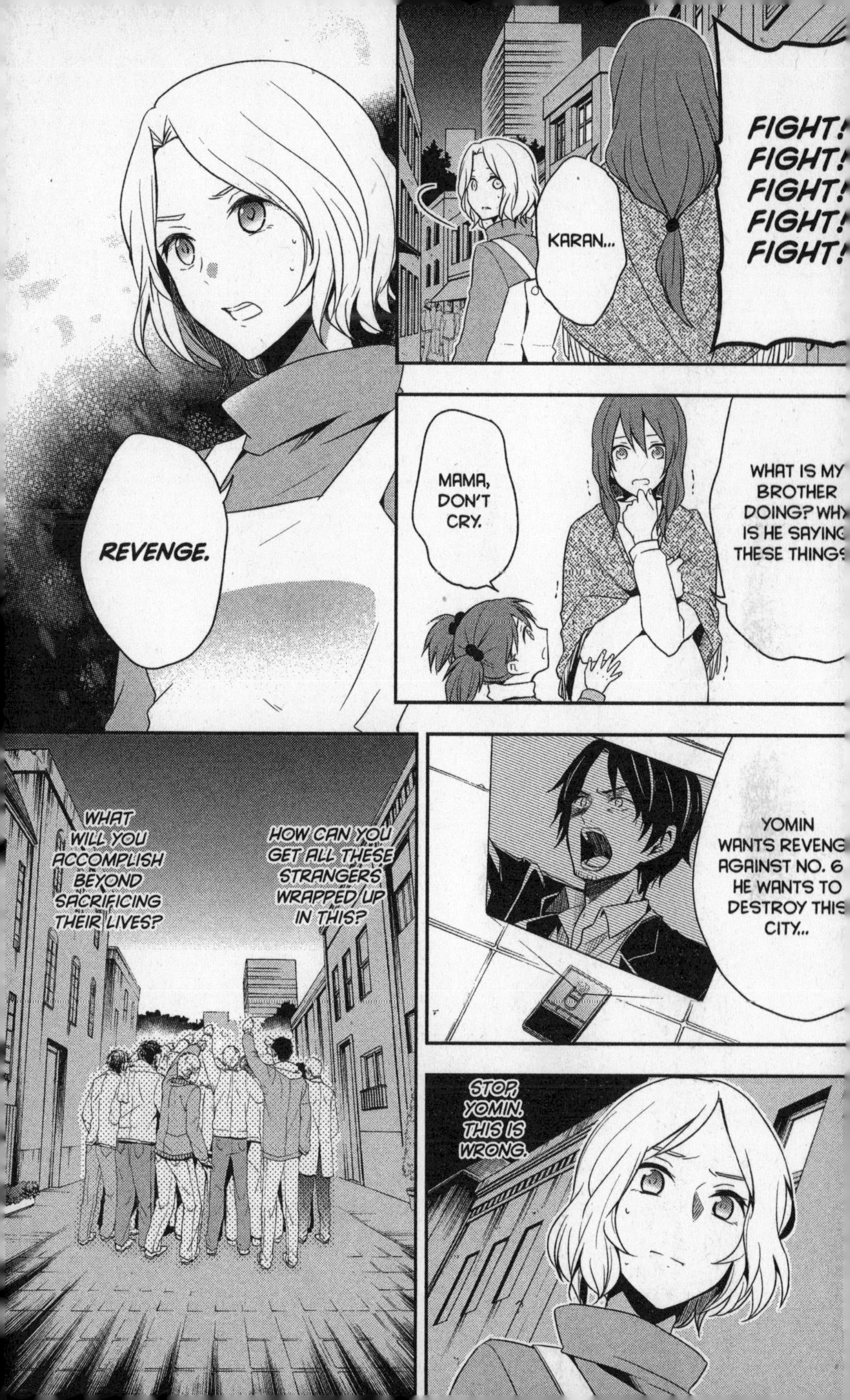
FIGHT! FIGHT! FIGHT! FIGHT! FIGHT!
KARAN...
WHAT IS MY BROTHER DOING? WH IS HE SAYING THESE THING
MAMA, DON'T CRY.
REVENGE.
YOMIN WANTS REVENG AGAINST NO. 6 HE WANTS TO DESTROY THIS CITY...
STOP, YOMIN. THIS IS WRONG.
HOW CAN YOU GET ALL THESE STRANGERS WRAPPED UP IN THIS?
WHAT WILL YOU ACCOMPLISH BEYOND SACRIFICING THEIR LIVES?

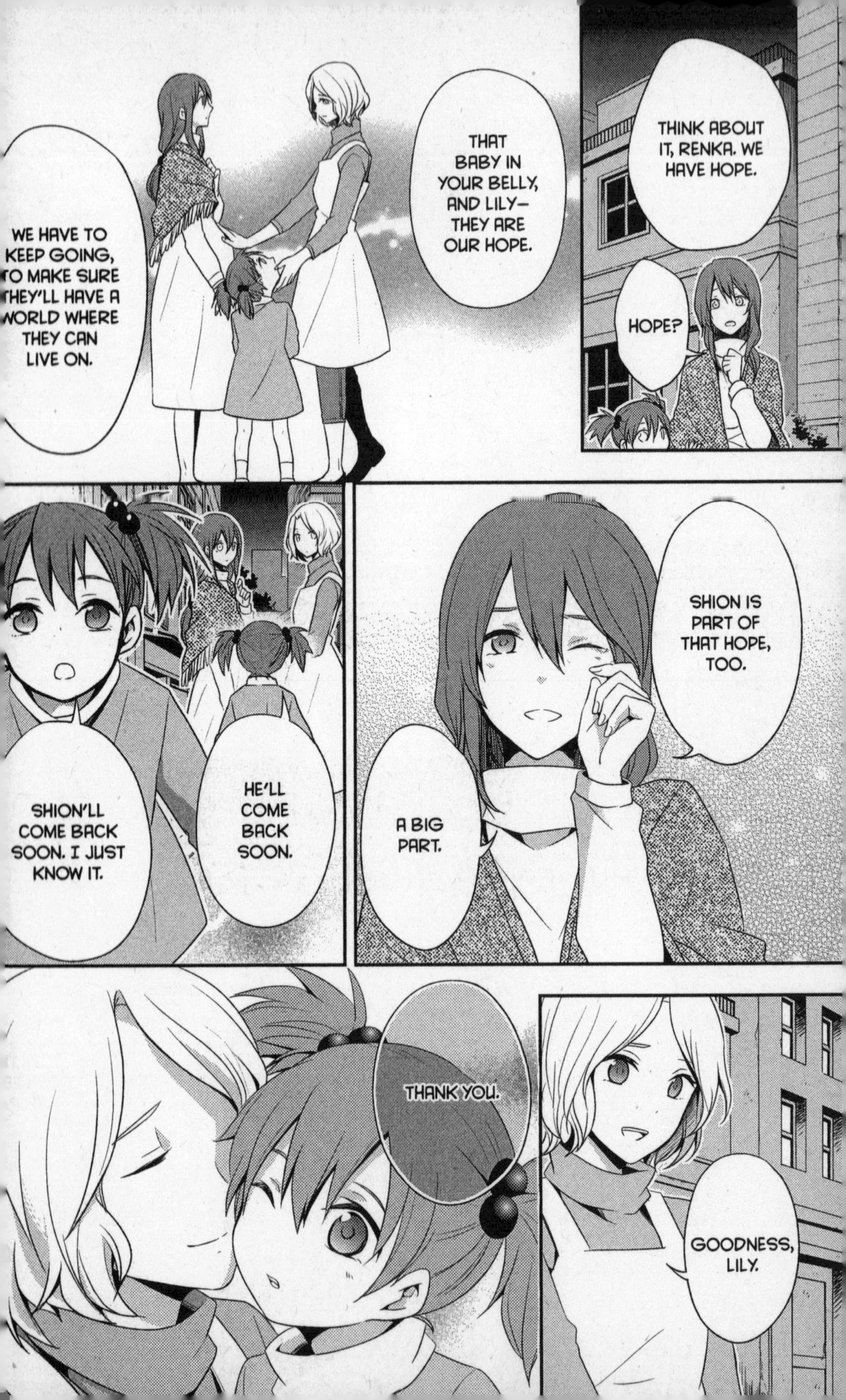
THINK ABOUT IT, RENKA. WE HAVE HOPE.
HOPE?
THAT BABY IN YOUR BELLY, AND LILY— THEY ARE OUR HOPE.
WE HAVE TO KEEP GOING, TO MAKE SURE THEY'LL HAVE A WORLD WHERE THEY CAN LIVE ON.
SHION IS PART OF THAT HOPE, TOO.
A BIG PART.
HE'LL COME BACK SOON.
SHION'LL COME BACK SOON. I JUST KNOW IT.
GOODNESS, LILY.
THANK YOU.

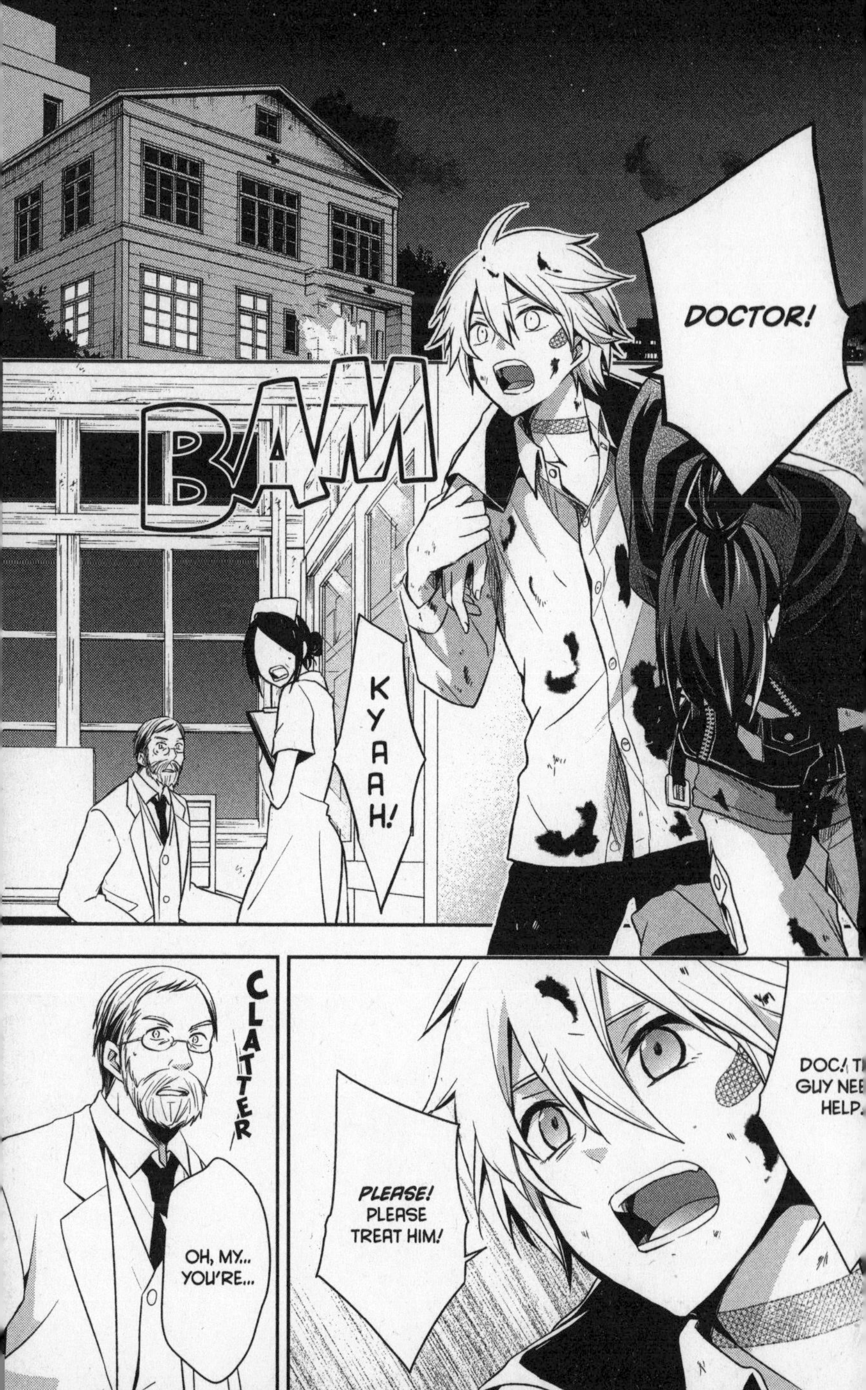
DOCTOR!
BAM
KYAAH!
DOC! T GUY NEE HELP.
PLEASE! PLEASE TREAT HIM!
CLATTER
OH, MY... YOU'RE...

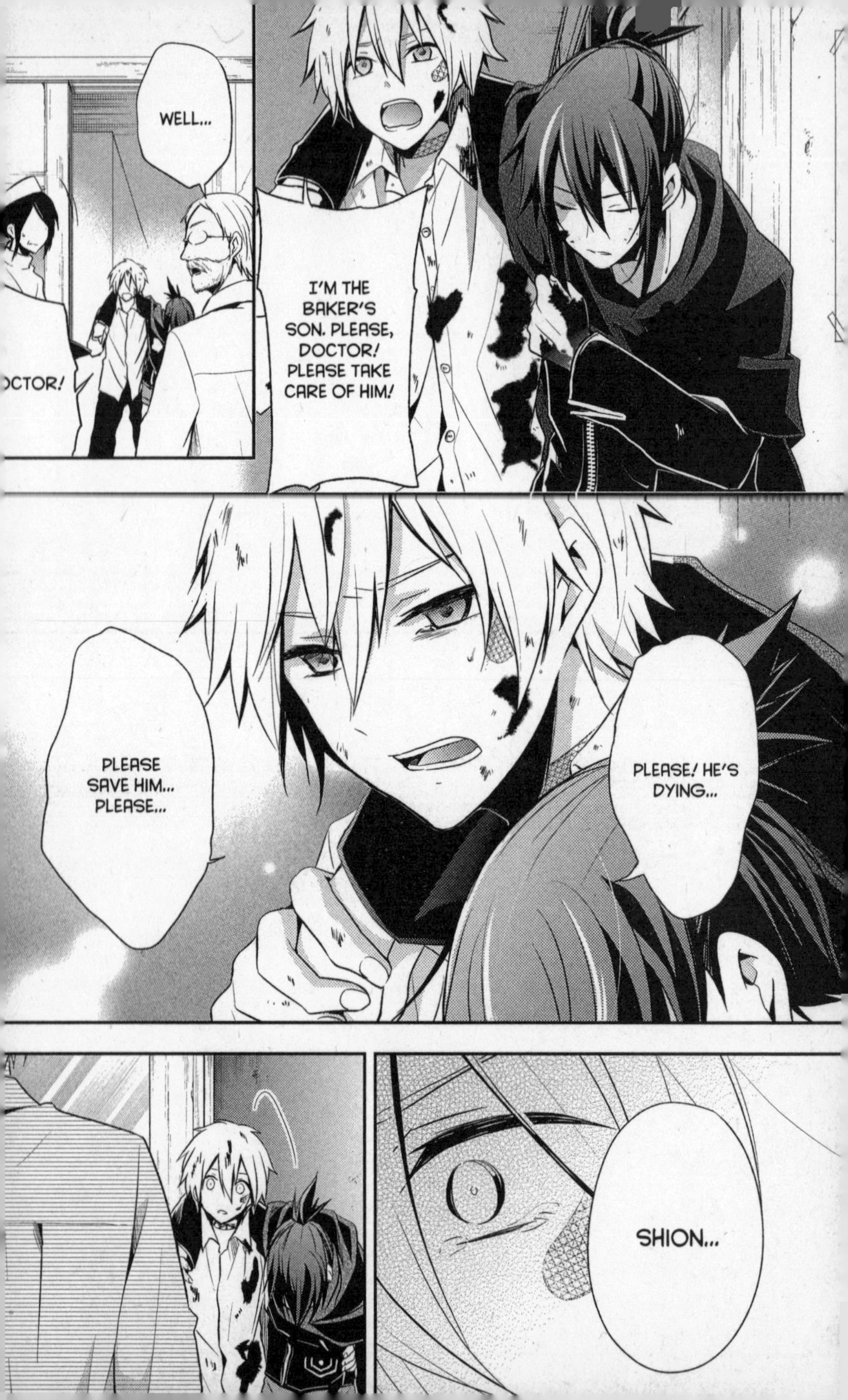
I'M THE BAKER'S SON. PLEASE, DOCTOR! PLEASE TAKE CARE OF HIM!
WELL...
OCTOR!
PLEASE! HE'S DYING...
PLEASE SAVE HIM... PLEASE...
SHION...

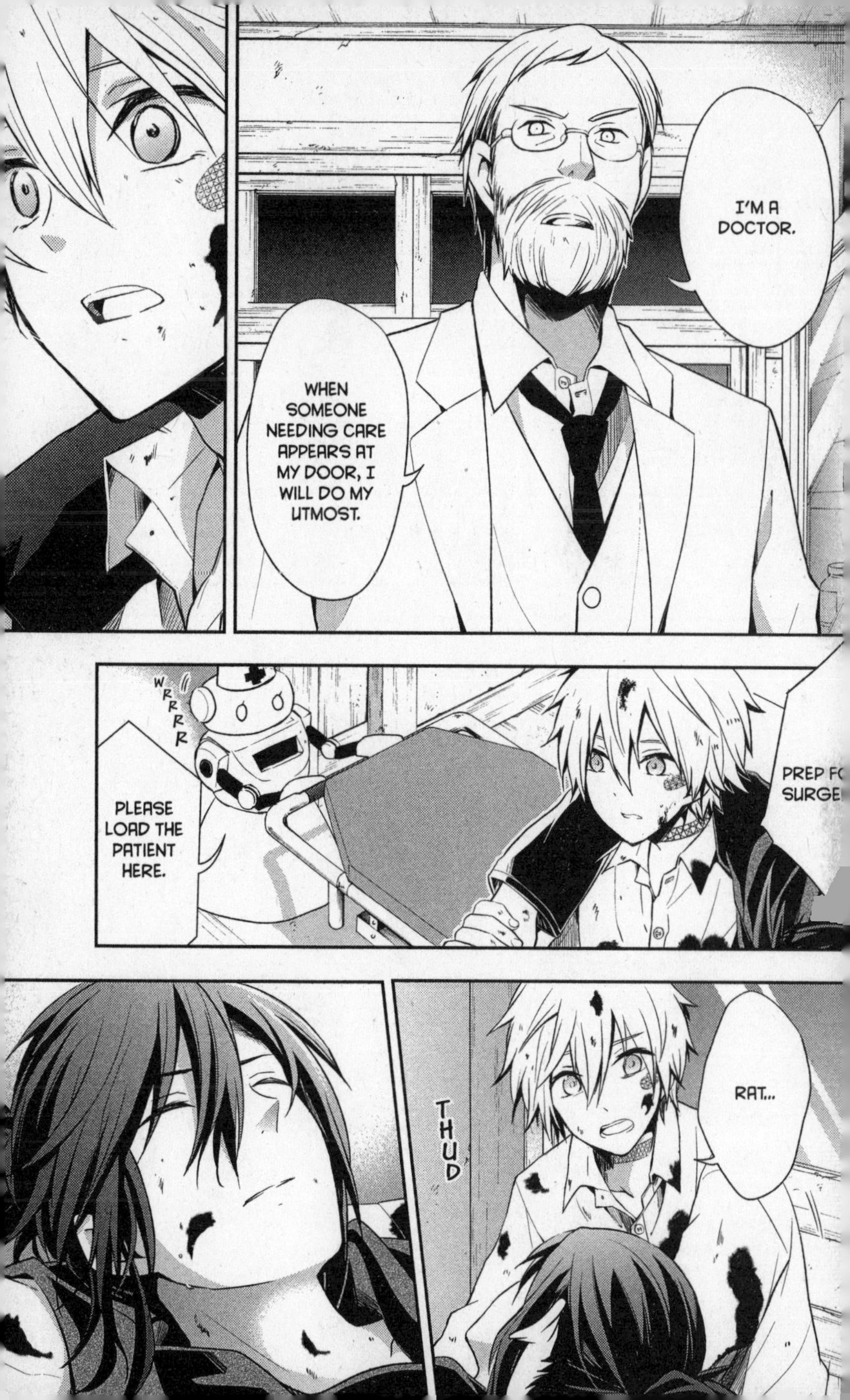
I'M A DOCTOR.
WHEN SOMEONE NEEDING CARE APPEARS AT MY DOOR, I WILL DO MY UTMOST.
WRRRR
PLEASE LOAD THE PATIENT HERE.
RAT...
THUD

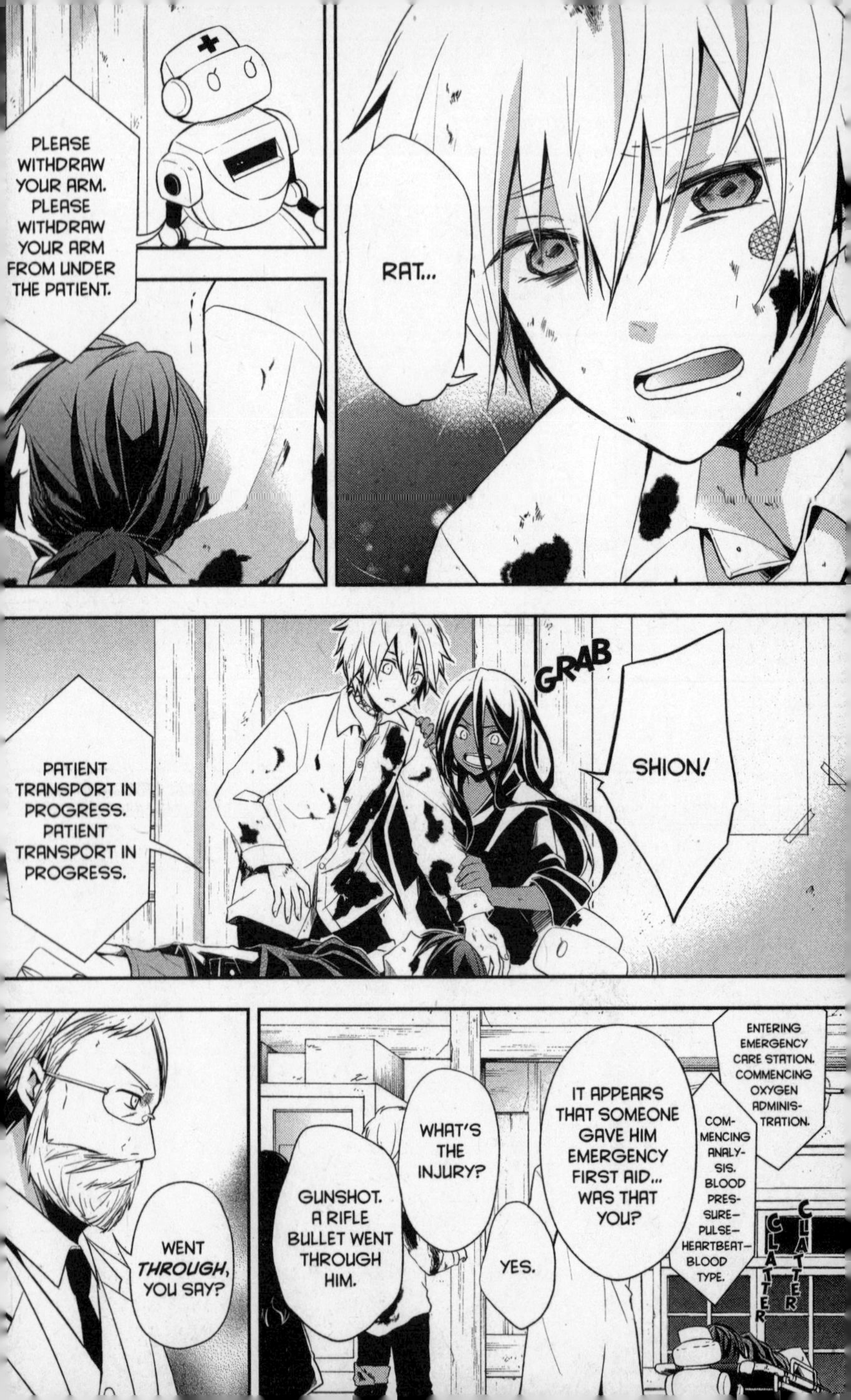
RAT...
PLEASE WITHDRAW YOUR ARM. PLEASE WITHDRAW YOUR ARM FROM UNDER THE PATIENT.
SHION!
GRAB
PATIENT TRANSPORT IN PROGRESS. PATIENT TRANSPORT IN PROGRESS.
ENTERING EMERGENCY CARE STATION. COMMENCING OXYGEN ADMINIS-TRATION.
COM-MENCING ANALY-SIS. BLOOD PRES-SURE—PULSE—HEARTBEAT—BLOOD TYPE.
CLATTER CLATTER
IT APPEARS THAT SOMEONE GAVE HIM EMERGENCY FIRST AID... WAS THAT YOU?
YES.
WHAT'S THE INJURY?
GUNSHOT. A RIFLE BULLET WENT THROUGH HIM.
WENT *THROUGH*, YOU SAY?

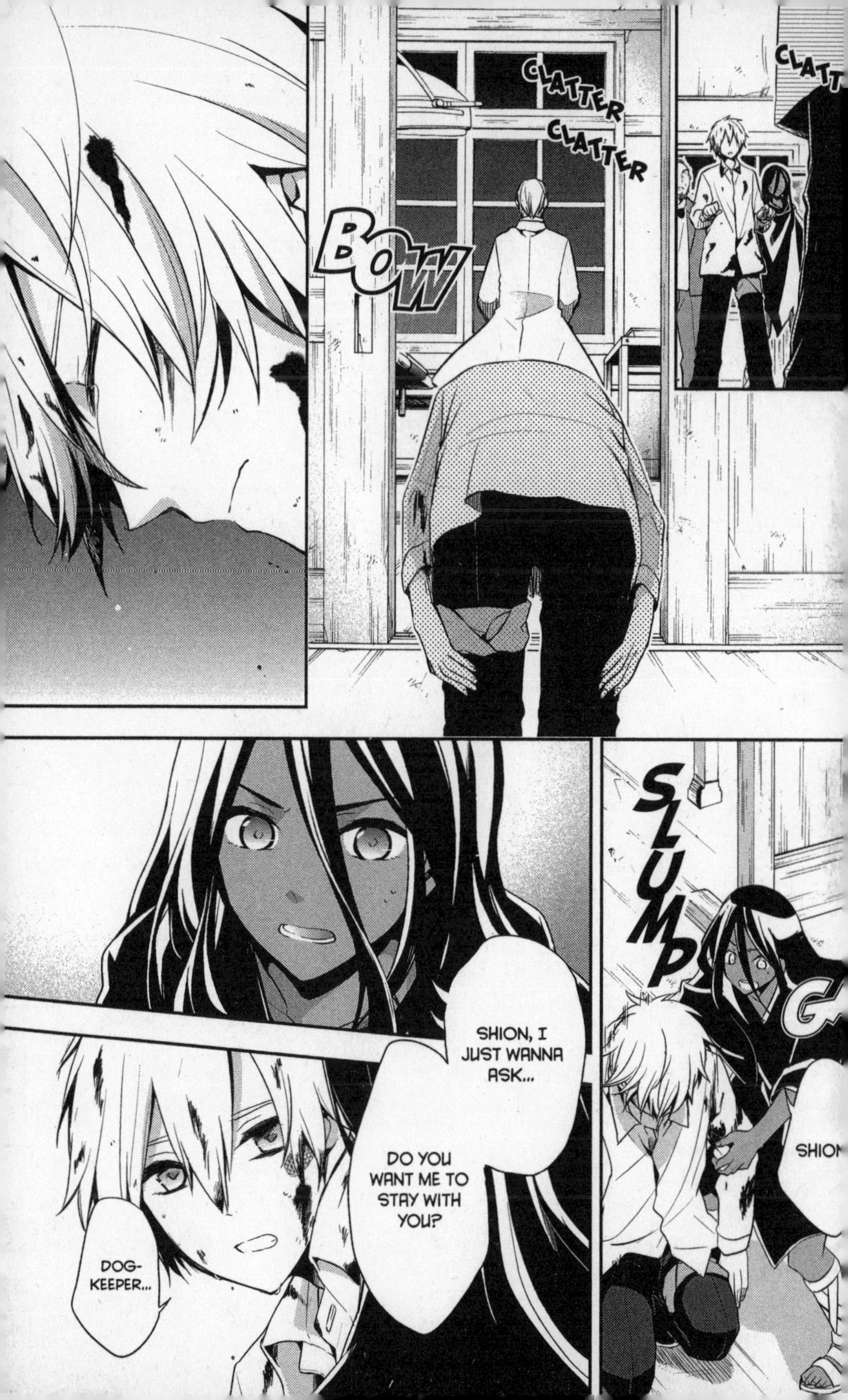
CLATT
CLATTER
CLATTER
BOW
SLUMP
SHION
SHION, I JUST WANNA ASK...
DO YOU WANT ME TO STAY WITH YOU?
DOG-KEEPER...

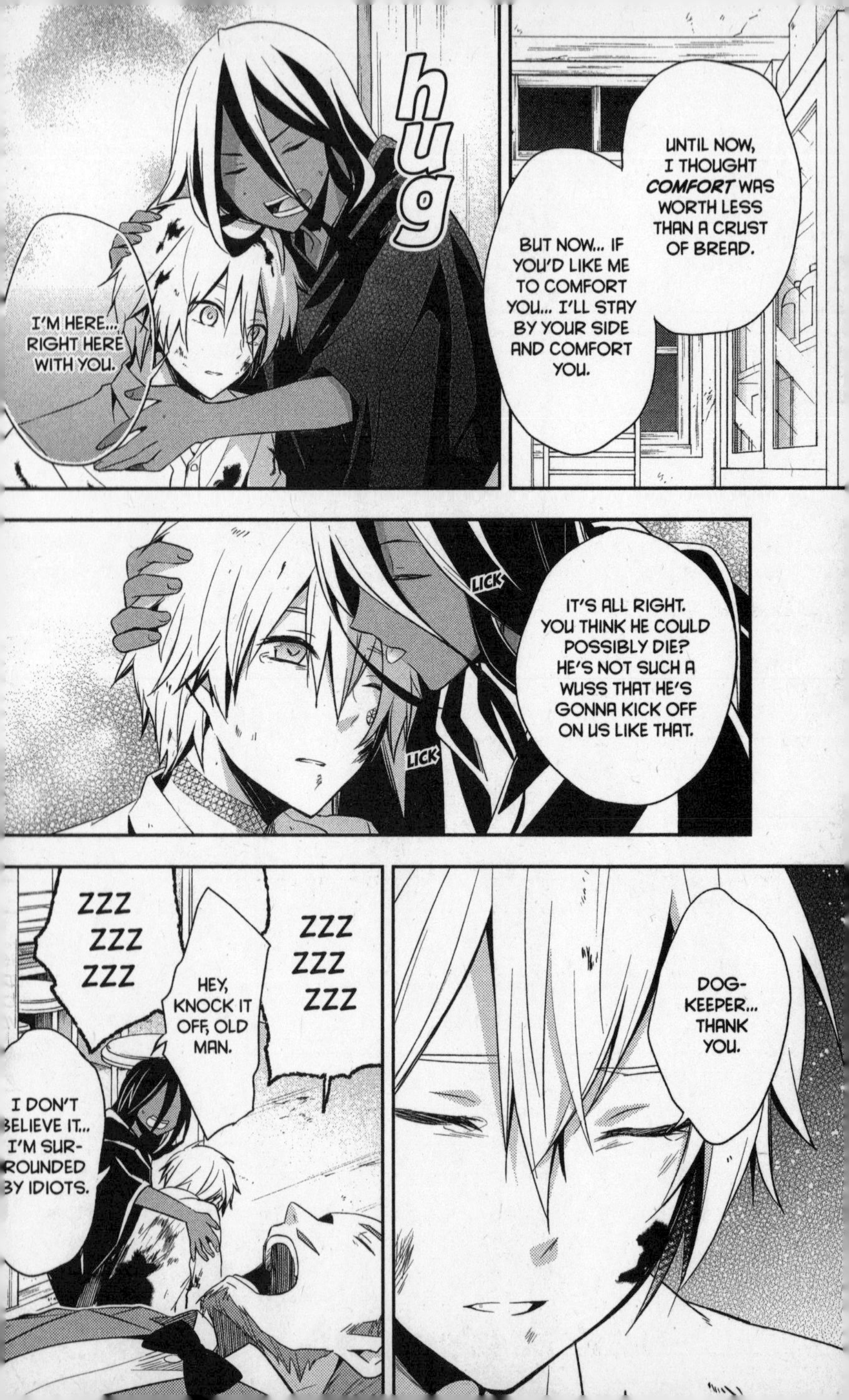
UNTIL NOW, I THOUGHT *COMFORT* WAS WORTH LESS THAN A CRUST OF BREAD.
BUT NOW... IF YOU'D LIKE ME TO COMFORT YOU... I'LL STAY BY YOUR SIDE AND COMFORT YOU.
hug
I'M HERE... RIGHT HERE WITH YOU.
LICK
IT'S ALL RIGHT. YOU THINK HE COULD POSSIBLY DIE? HE'S NOT SUCH A WUSS THAT HE'S GONNA KICK OFF ON US LIKE THAT.
LICK
DOG-KEEPER... THANK YOU.
ZZZ ZZZ ZZZ
HEY, KNOCK IT OFF, OLD MAN.
ZZZ ZZZ ZZZ
I DON'T BELIEVE IT... I'M SUR-ROUNDED BY IDIOTS.

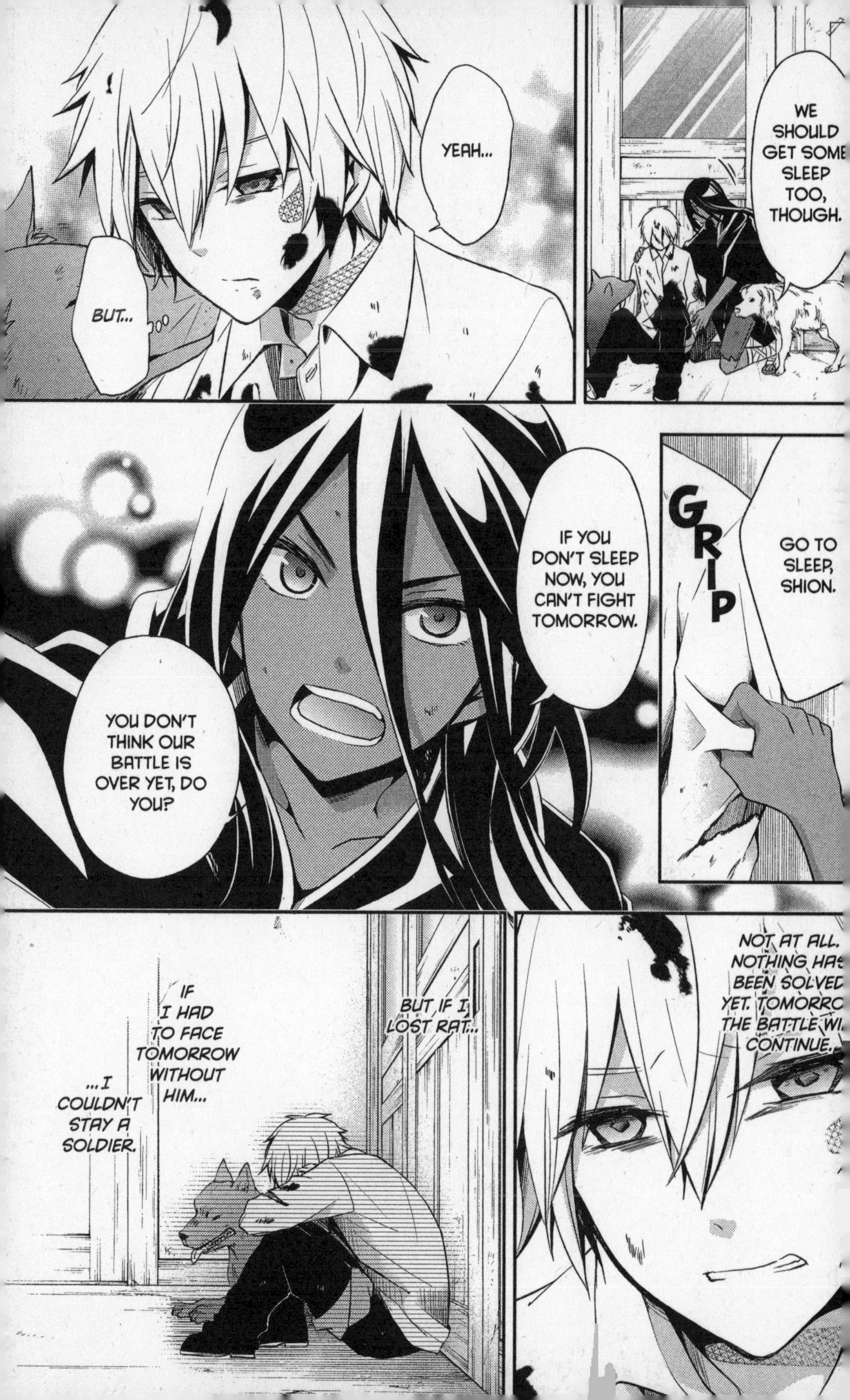
WE SHOULD GET SOME SLEEP TOO, THOUGH.
YEAH...
BUT...
GO TO SLEEP, SHION.
GRIP
IF YOU DON'T SLEEP NOW, YOU CAN'T FIGHT TOMORROW.
YOU DON'T THINK OUR BATTLE IS OVER YET, DO YOU?
NOT AT ALL. NOTHING HAS BEEN SOLVED YET. TOMORRO THE BATTLE WI CONTINUE.
BUT IF I LOST RAT...
IF I HAD TO FACE TOMORROW WITHOUT HIM...
...I COULDN'T STAY A SOLDIER.

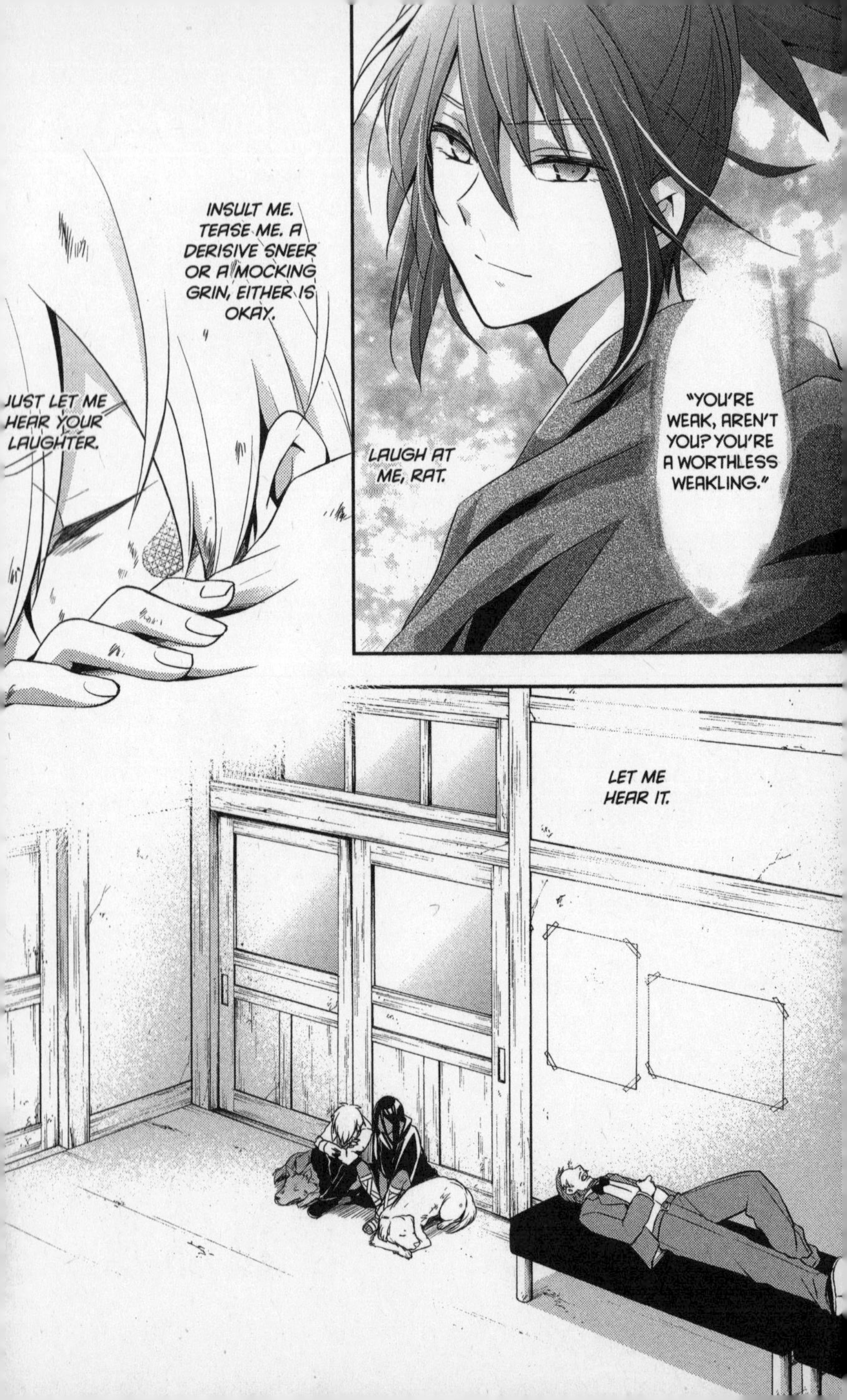
"YOU'RE WEAK, AREN'T YOU? YOU'RE A WORTHLESS WEAKLING."
LAUGH AT ME, RAT.
INSULT ME. TEASE ME. A DERISIVE SNEER OR A MOCKING GRIN, EITHER IS OKAY.
JUST LET ME HEAR YOUR LAUGHTER.
LET ME HEAR IT.

NO.6

Chapter 33: But Once

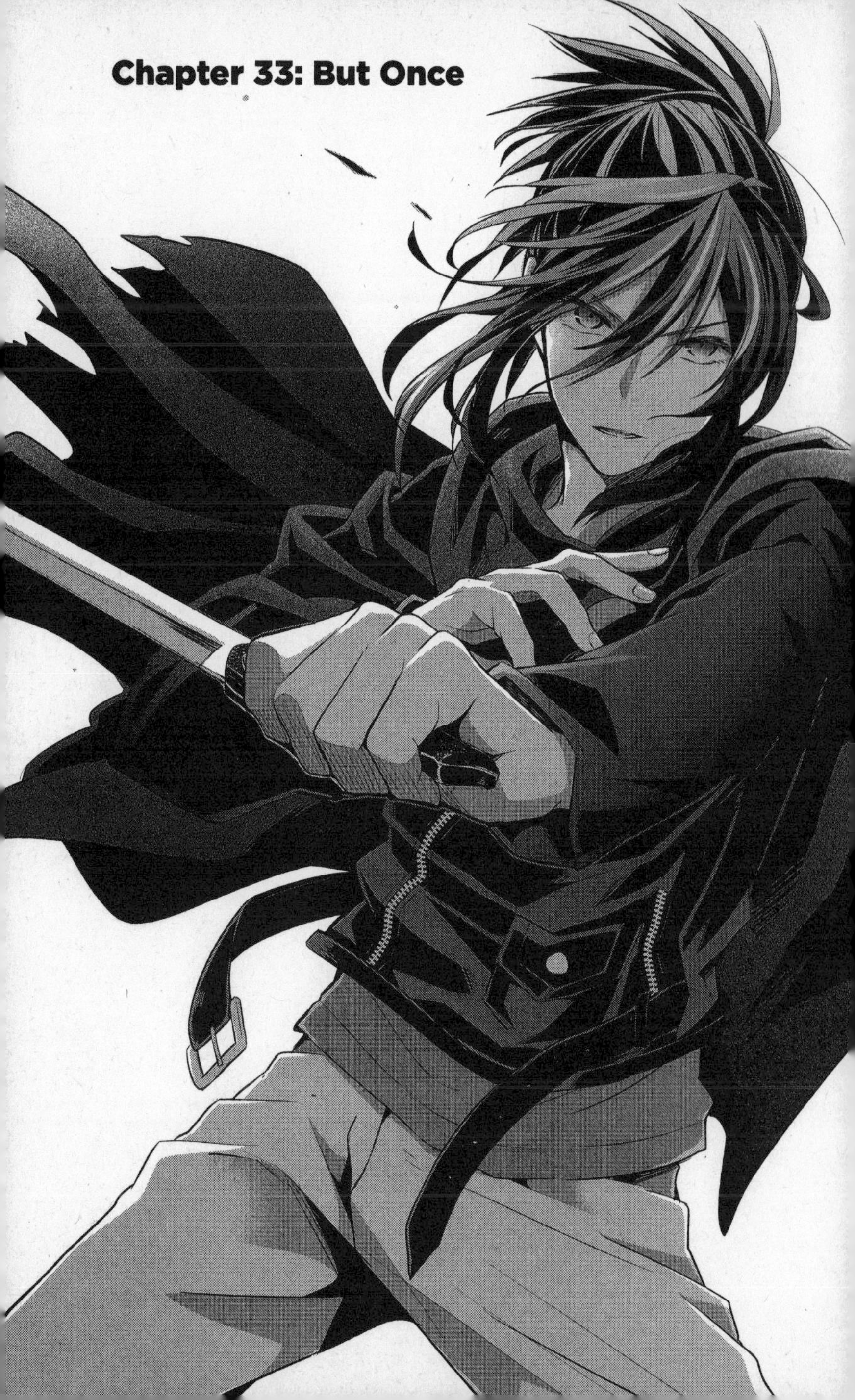

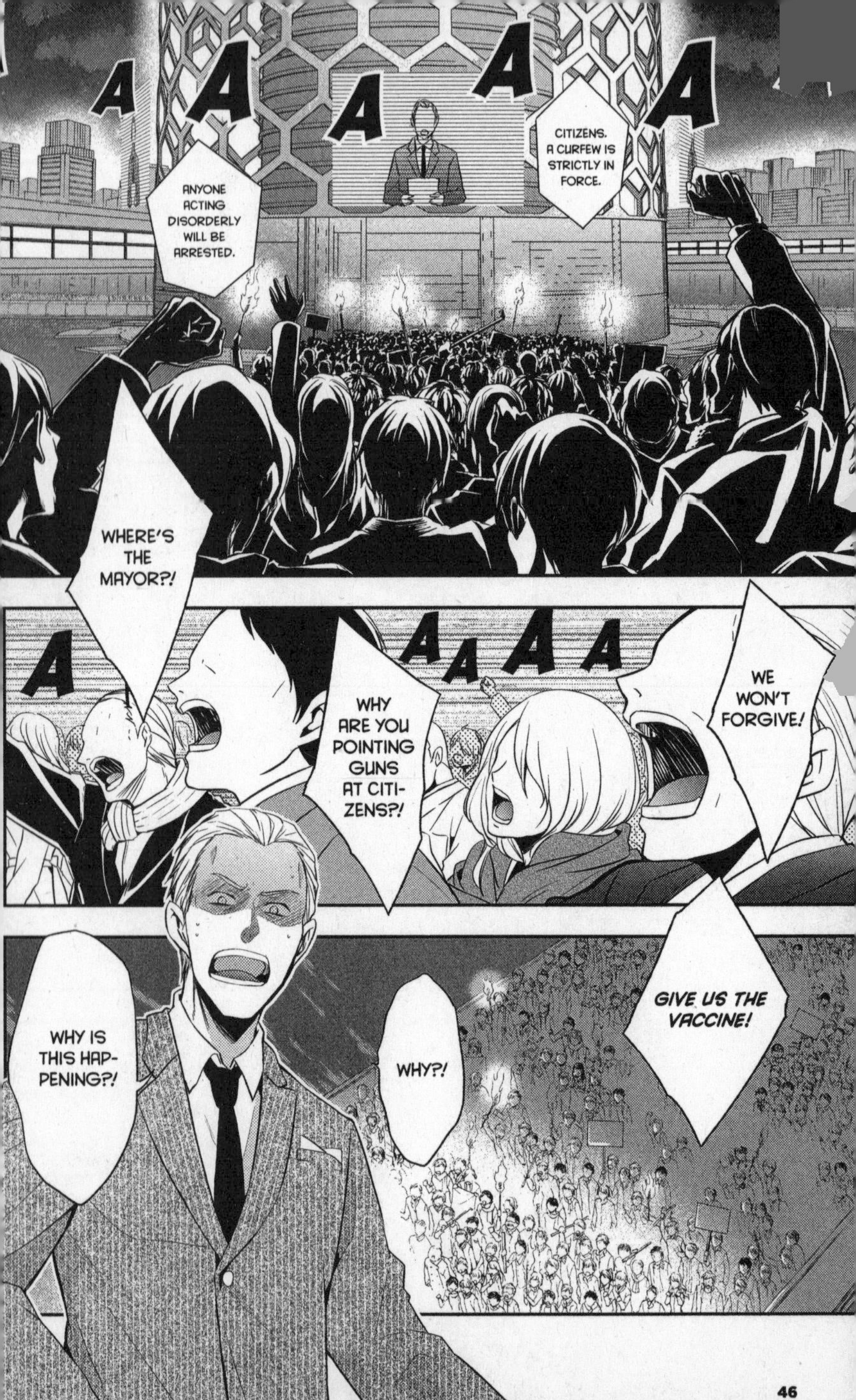
A A A A A
CITIZENS. A CURFEW IS STRICTLY IN FORCE.
ANYONE ACTING DISORDERLY WILL BE ARRESTED.
A A A A A
WE WON'T FORGIVE!
WHY ARE YOU POINTING GUNS AT CITI-ZENS?!
WHERE'S THE MAYOR?!
GIVE US THE VACCINE!
WHY?!
WHY IS THIS HAP-PENING?!

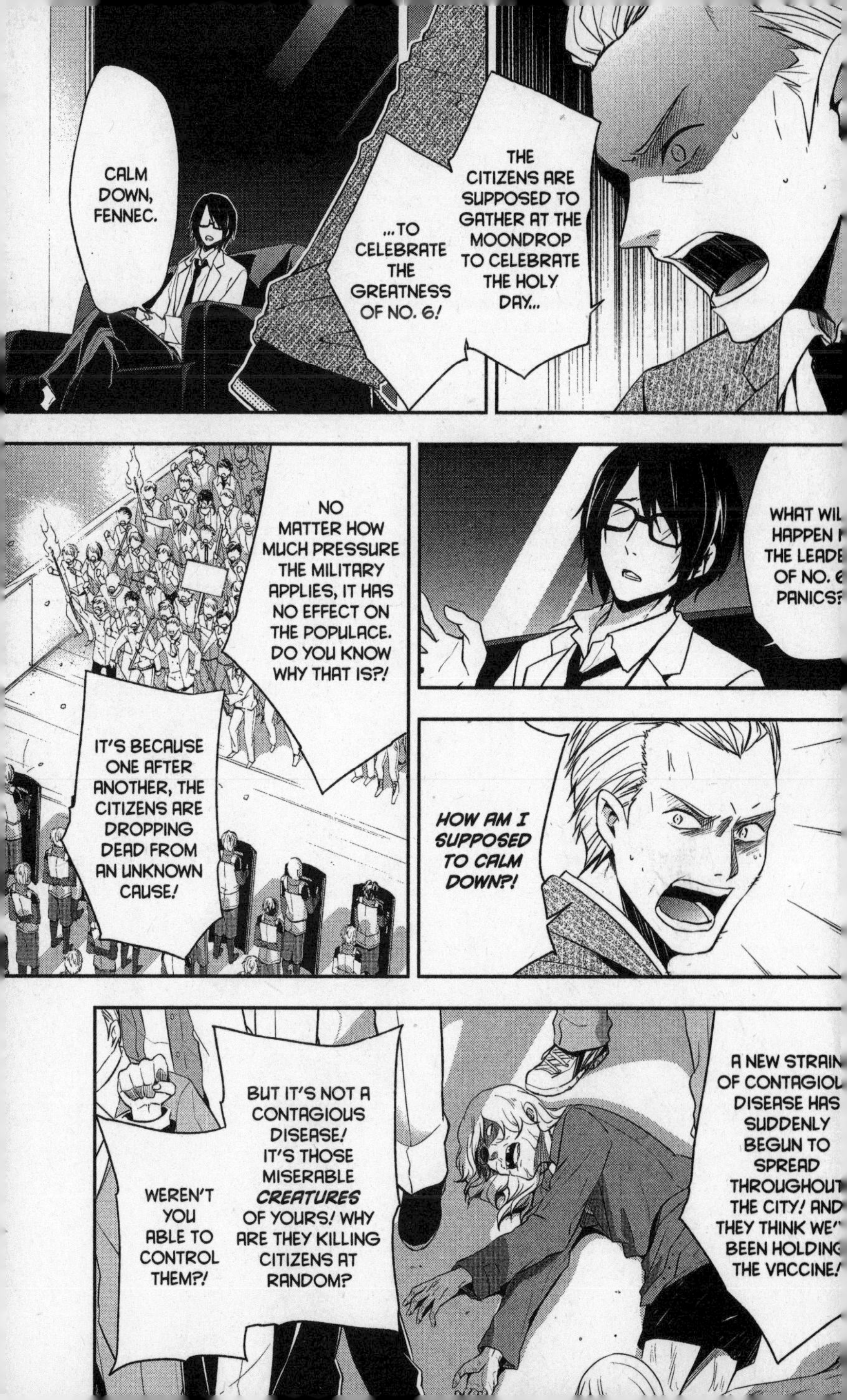
THE CITIZENS ARE SUPPOSED TO GATHER AT THE MOONDROP TO CELEBRATE THE HOLY DAY...
...TO CELEBRATE THE GREATNESS OF NO. 6!
CALM DOWN, FENNEC.
WHAT WIL HAPPEN I THE LEADE OF NO. 6 PANICS?
HOW AM I SUPPOSED TO CALM DOWN?!
NO MATTER HOW MUCH PRESSURE THE MILITARY APPLIES, IT HAS NO EFFECT ON THE POPULACE. DO YOU KNOW WHY THAT IS?!
IT'S BECAUSE ONE AFTER ANOTHER, THE CITIZENS ARE DROPPING DEAD FROM AN UNKNOWN CAUSE!
A NEW STRAIN OF CONTAGIOL DISEASE HAS SUDDENLY BEGUN TO SPREAD THROUGHOUT THE CITY! AND THEY THINK WE' BEEN HOLDING THE VACCINE!
BUT IT'S NOT A CONTAGIOUS DISEASE! IT'S THOSE MISERABLE *CREATURES* OF YOURS! WHY ARE THEY KILLING CITIZENS AT RANDOM?
WEREN'T YOU ABLE TO CONTROL THEM?!

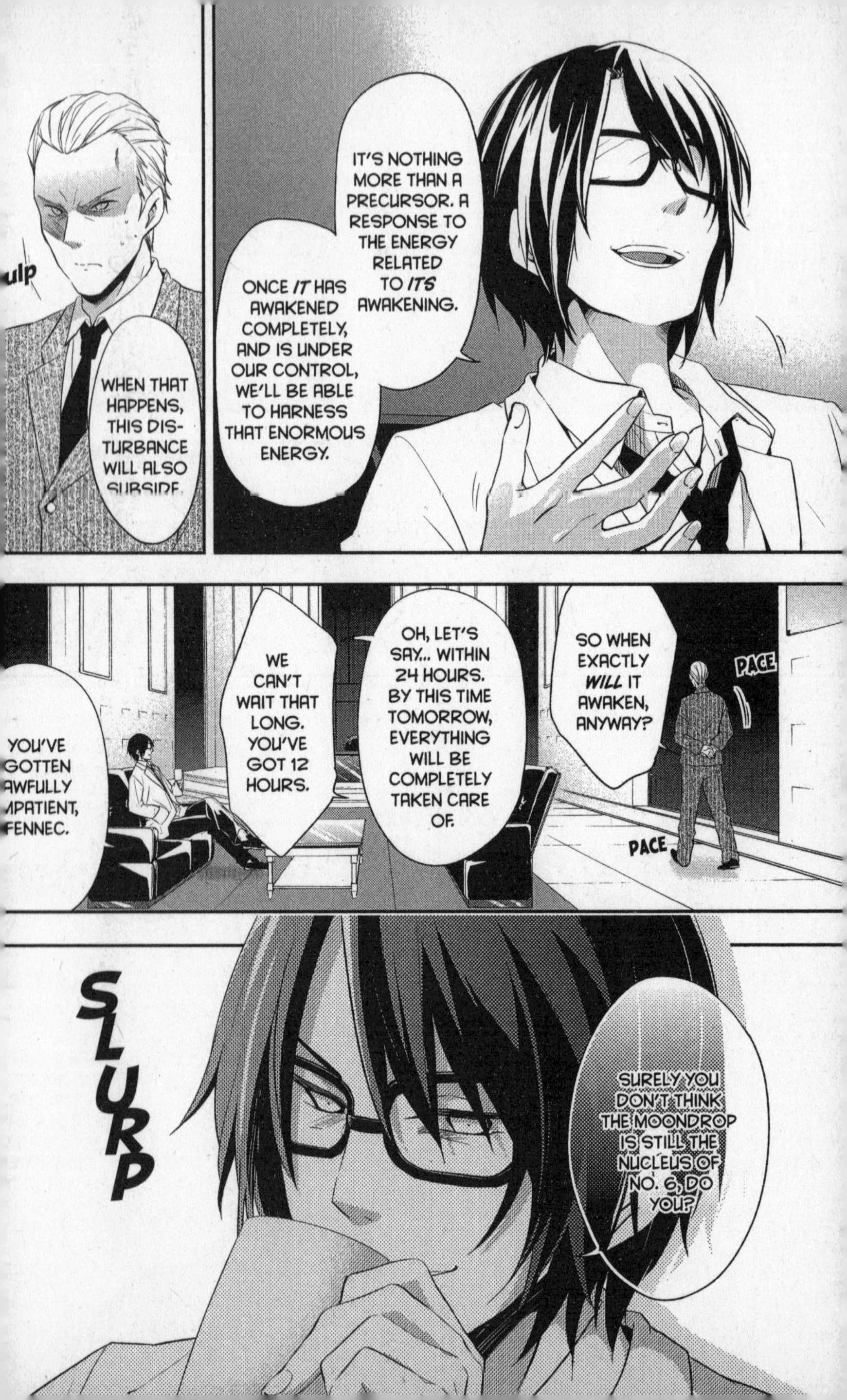
IT'S NOTHING MORE THAN A PRECURSOR. A RESPONSE TO THE ENERGY RELATED TO *ITS* AWAKENING.
ONCE *IT* HAS AWAKENED COMPLETELY, AND IS UNDER OUR CONTROL, WE'LL BE ABLE TO HARNESS THAT ENORMOUS ENERGY.
ulp
WHEN THAT HAPPENS, THIS DIS-TURBANCE WILL ALSO SUBSIDE.
SO WHEN EXACTLY *WILL* IT AWAKEN, ANYWAY?
PACE
PACE
OH, LET'S SAY... WITHIN 24 HOURS. BY THIS TIME TOMORROW, EVERYTHING WILL BE COMPLETELY TAKEN CARE OF.
WE CAN'T WAIT THAT LONG. YOU'VE GOT 12 HOURS.
YOU'VE GOTTEN AWFULLY MPATIENT, FENNEC.
SLURP
SURELY YOU DON'T THINK THE MOONDROP IS STILL THE NUCLEUS OF NO. 6, DO YOU?

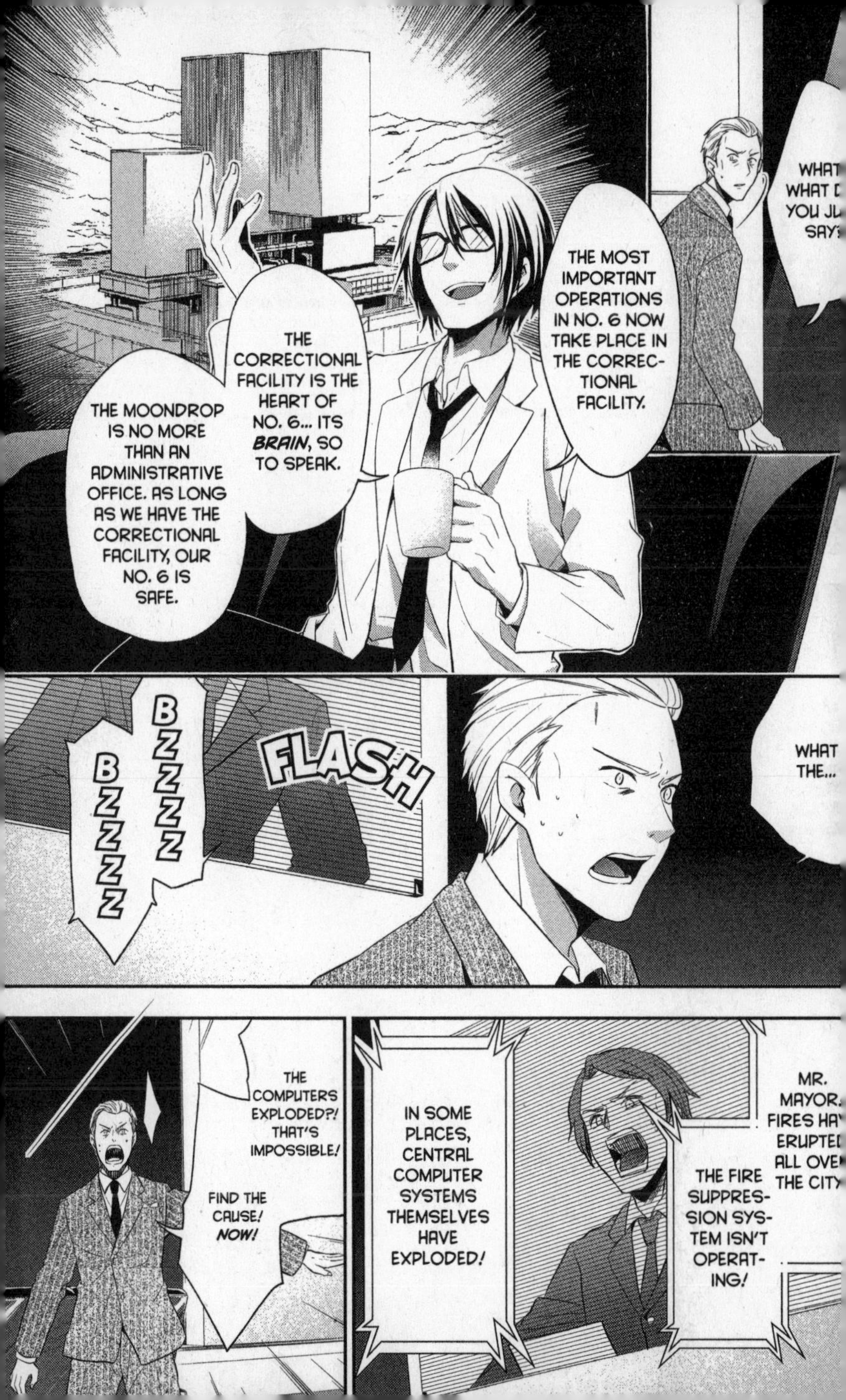
WHAT WHAT D YOU JU SAY
THE MOST IMPORTANT OPERATIONS IN NO. 6 NOW TAKE PLACE IN THE CORRECTIONAL FACILITY.
THE CORRECTIONAL FACILITY IS THE HEART OF NO. 6... ITS *BRAIN*, SO TO SPEAK.
THE MOONDROP IS NO MORE THAN AN ADMINISTRATIVE OFFICE. AS LONG AS WE HAVE THE CORRECTIONAL FACILITY, OUR NO. 6 IS SAFE.
WHAT THE...
FLASH
BZZZZ
BZZZZ
MR. MAYOR FIRES HAV ERUPTED ALL OVE THE CITY
THE FIRE SUPPRESSION SYSTEM ISN'T OPERATING!
IN SOME PLACES, CENTRAL COMPUTER SYSTEMS THEMSELVES HAVE EXPLODED!
THE COMPUTERS EXPLODED?! THAT'S IMPOSSIBLE!
FIND THE CAUSE! *NOW!*

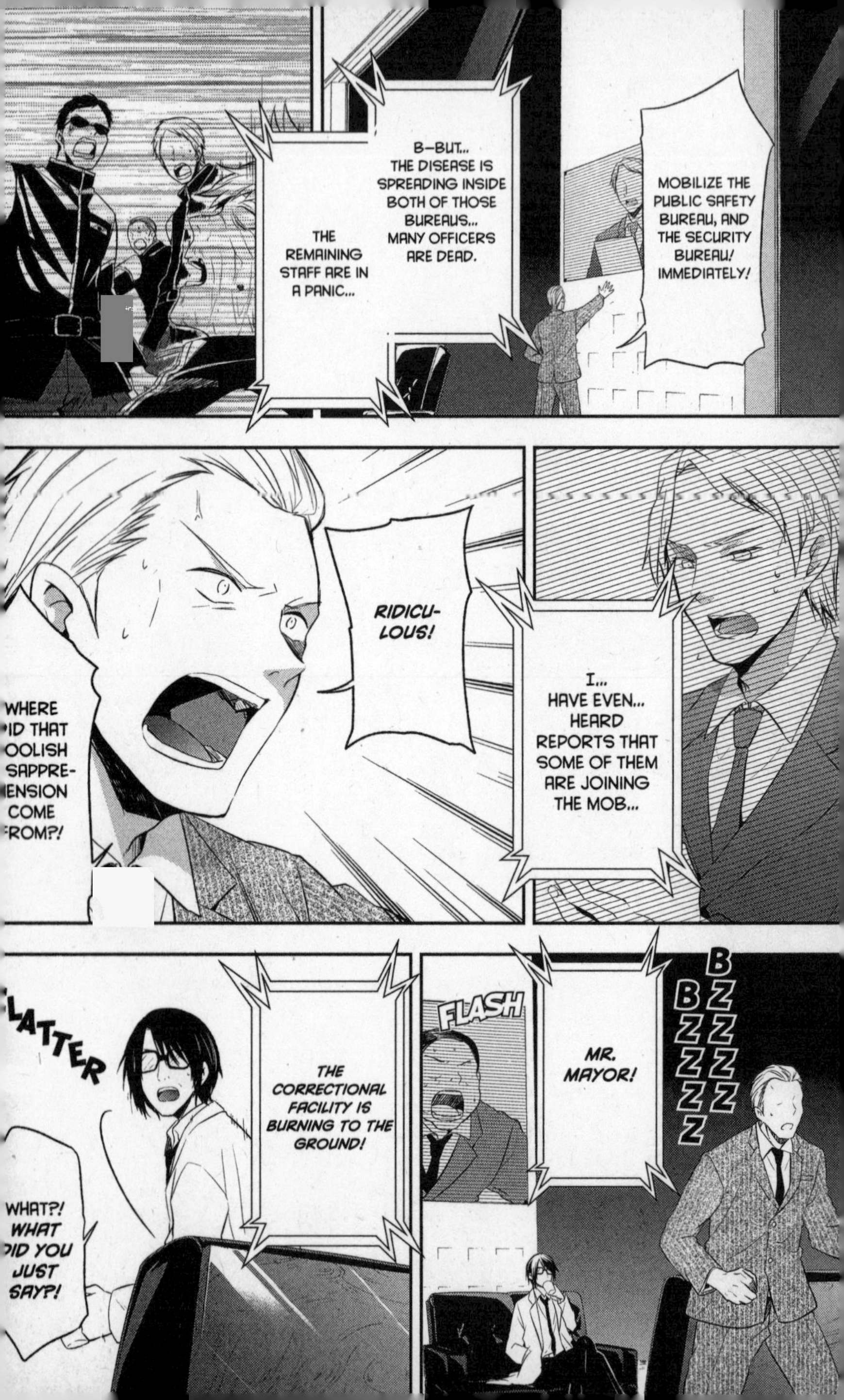
MOBILIZE THE PUBLIC SAFETY BUREAU, AND THE SECURITY BUREAU! IMMEDIATELY!
B—BUT... THE DISEASE IS SPREADING INSIDE BOTH OF THOSE BUREAUS... MANY OFFICERS ARE DEAD.
THE REMAINING STAFF ARE IN A PANIC...
I... HAVE EVEN... HEARD REPORTS THAT SOME OF THEM ARE JOINING THE MOB...
RIDICU-LOUS!
WHERE ID THAT OOLISH SAPPRE-ENSION COME ROM?!
BZZZZZ
BZZZZZ
FLASH
MR. MAYOR!
THE CORRECTIONAL FACILITY IS BURNING TO THE GROUND!
LATTER
WHAT?! WHAT ID YOU JUST SAY?!

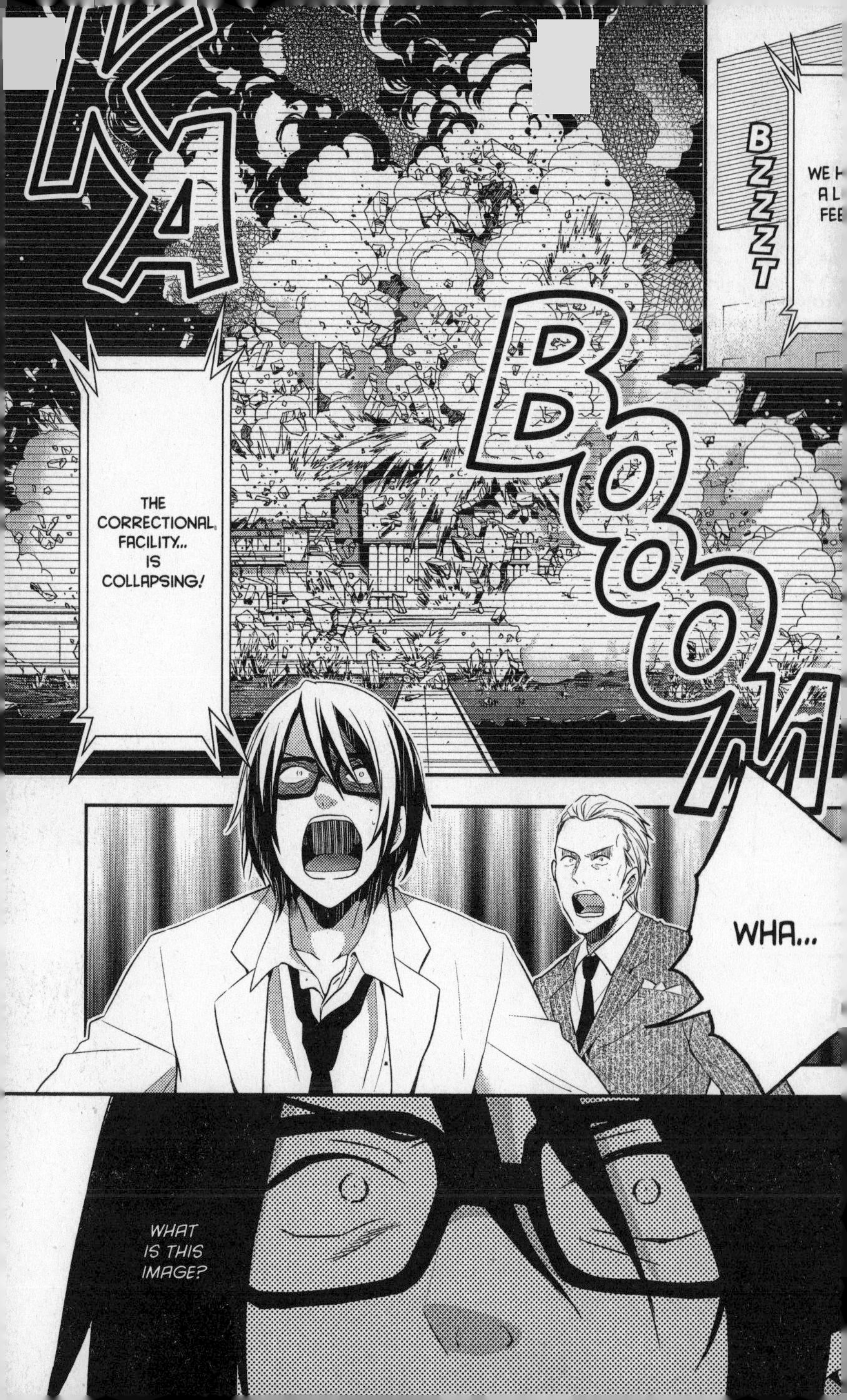
BZZZT
KA
BOOOOM
THE CORRECTIONAL FACILITY... IS COLLAPSING!
WHA...
WHAT IS THIS IMAGE?

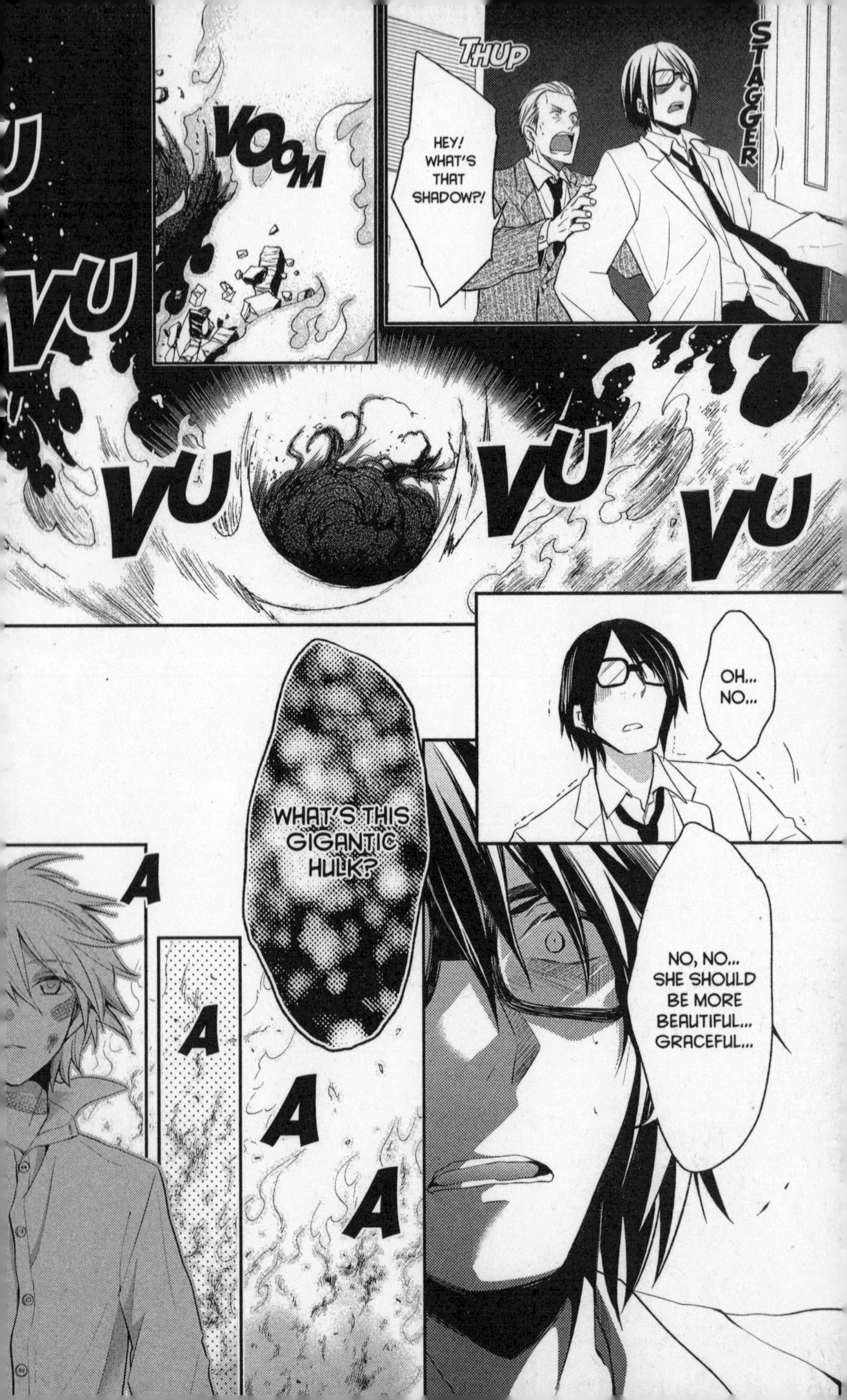
STAGGER
THUP
HEY! WHAT'S THAT SHADOW?!
VOOM
VU
VU
VU
VU
VU
OH... NO...
NO, NO... SHE SHOULD BE MORE BEAUTIFUL... GRACEFUL...
WHAT'S THIS GIGANTIC HULK?
A
A
A
A

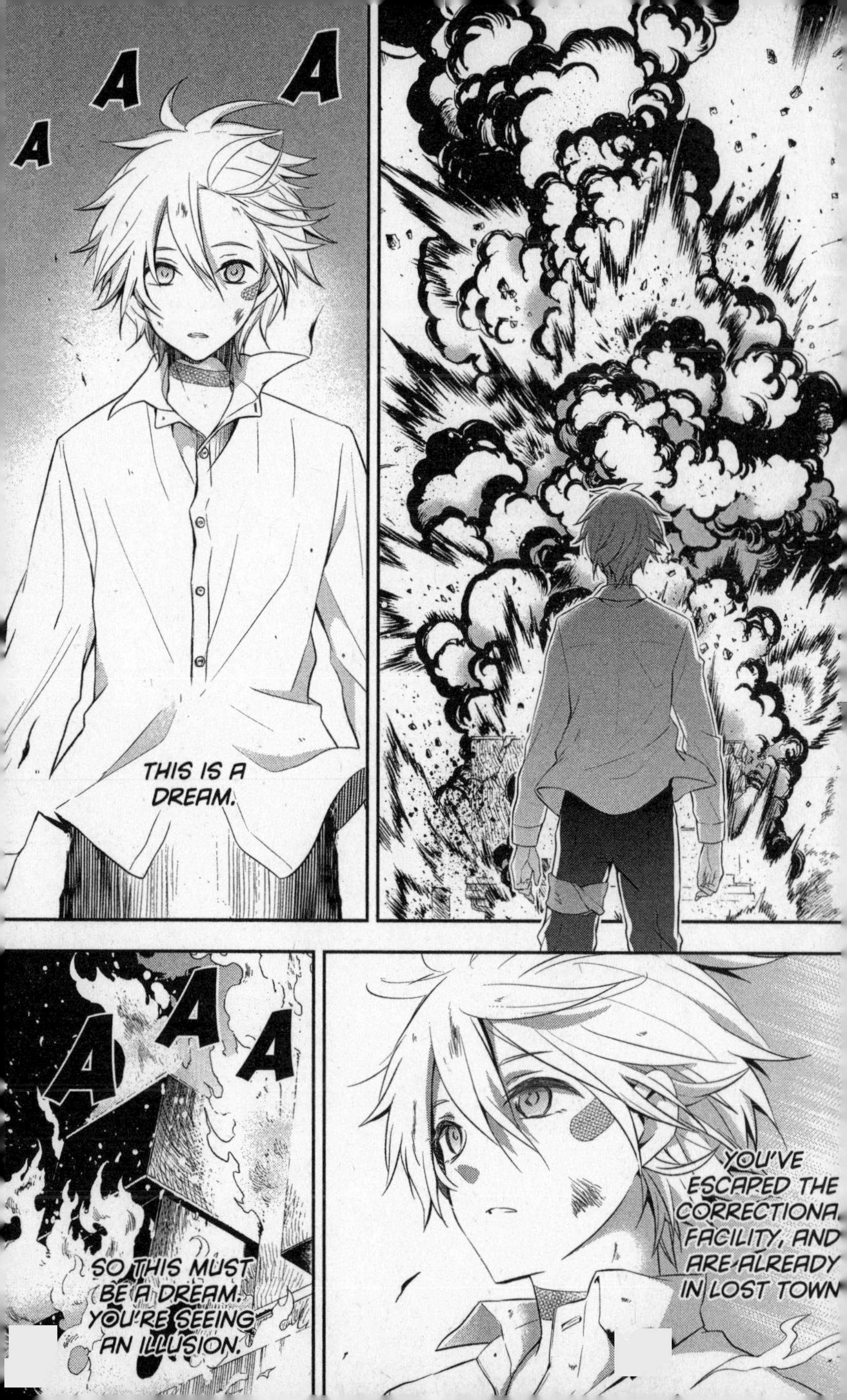
A A A A
THIS IS A DREAM.
YOU'VE ESCAPED THE CORRECTIONA FACILITY, AND ARE ALREADY IN LOST TOWN
A A A
SO THIS MUST BE A DREAM. YOU'RE SEEING AN ILLUSION.

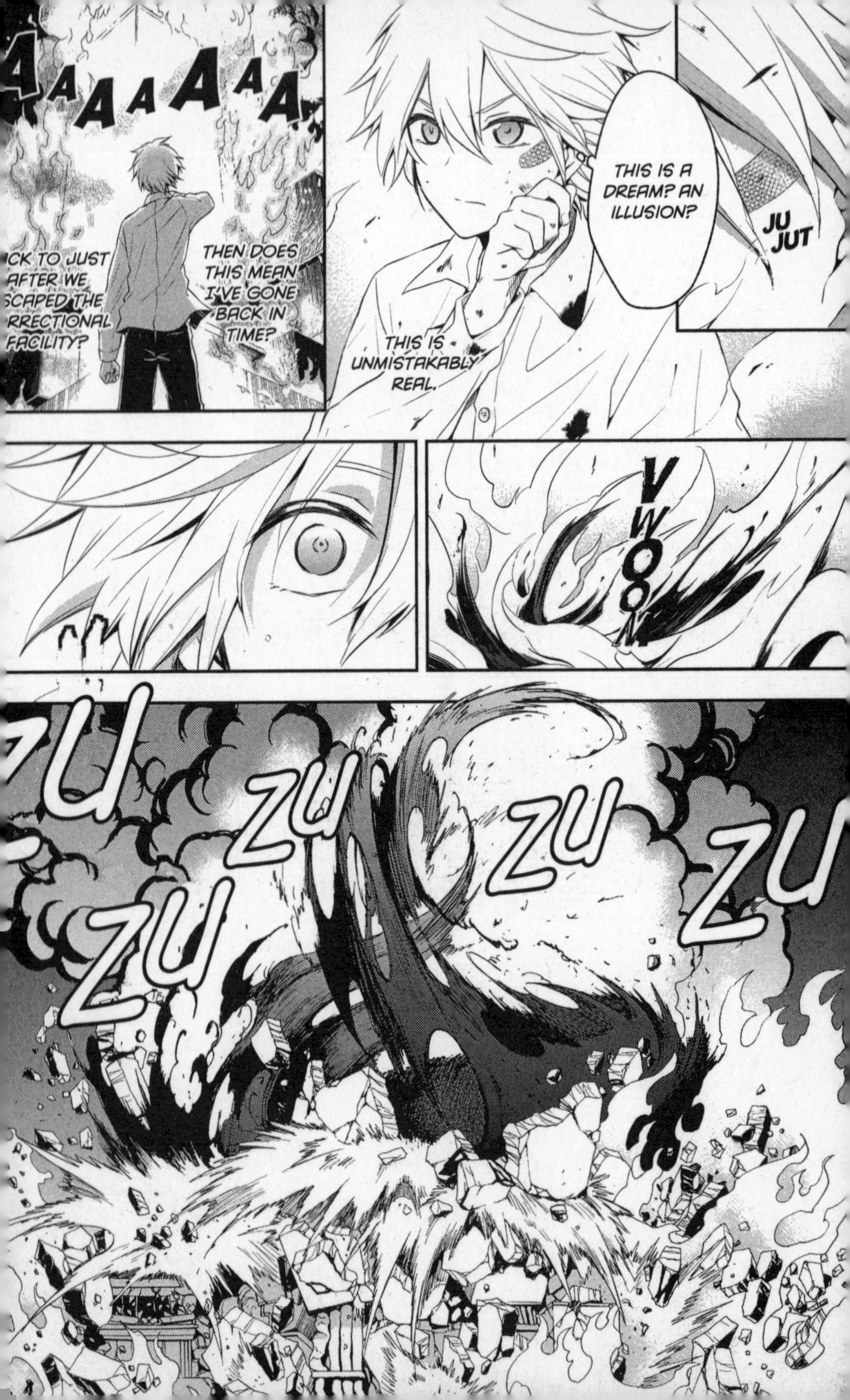
THIS IS A DREAM? AN ILLUSION?
JU JUT
THIS IS UNMISTAKABLY REAL.
AAAAAAAA
THEN DOES THIS MEAN I'VE GONE BACK IN TIME?
CK TO JUST AFTER WE SCAPED THE RRECTIONAL FACILITY?
VWOOOM
ZU ZU ZU ZU ZU

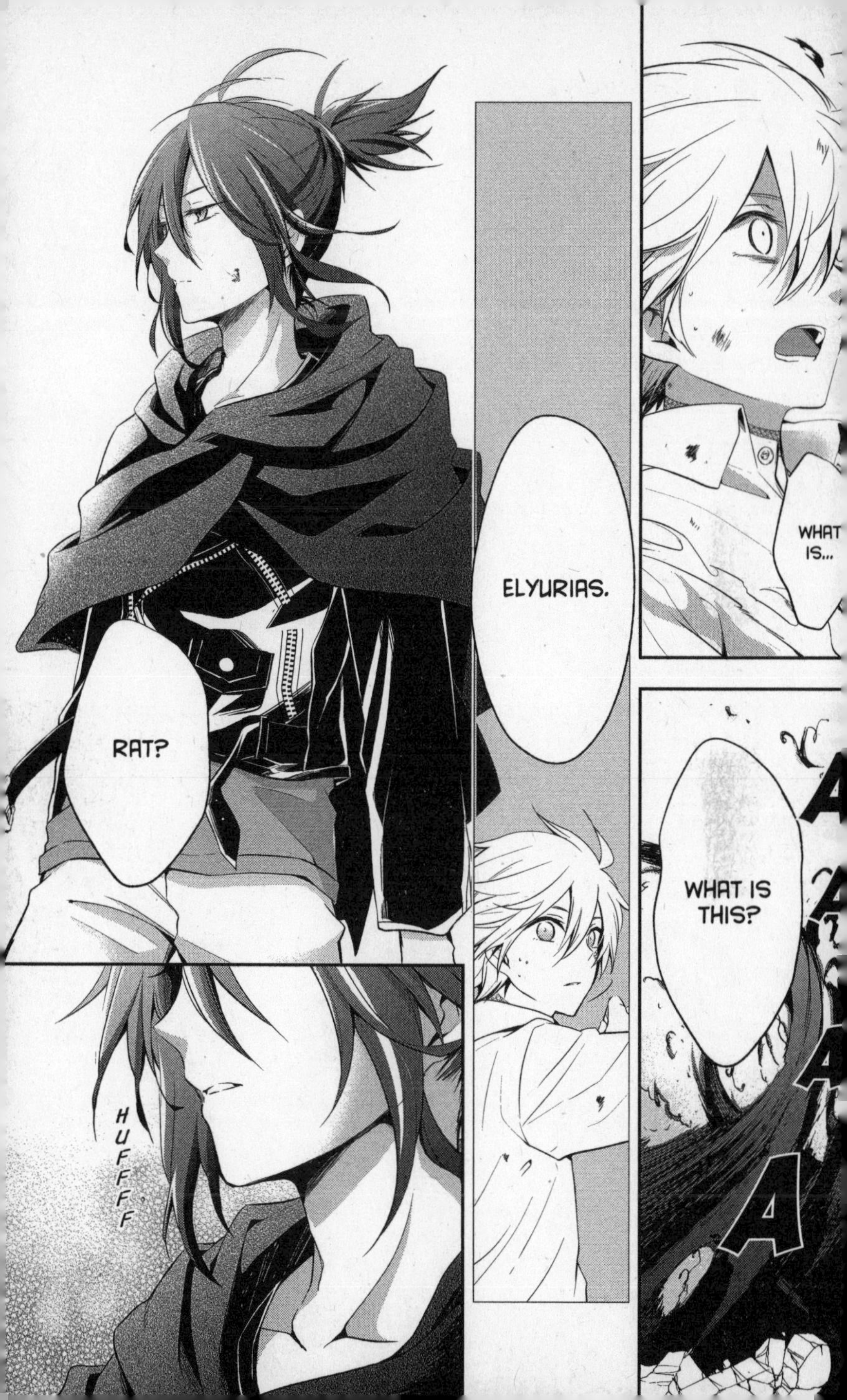
WHAT IS...
WHAT IS THIS?
AAAAA
ELYURIAS.
RAT?
HUFFFF

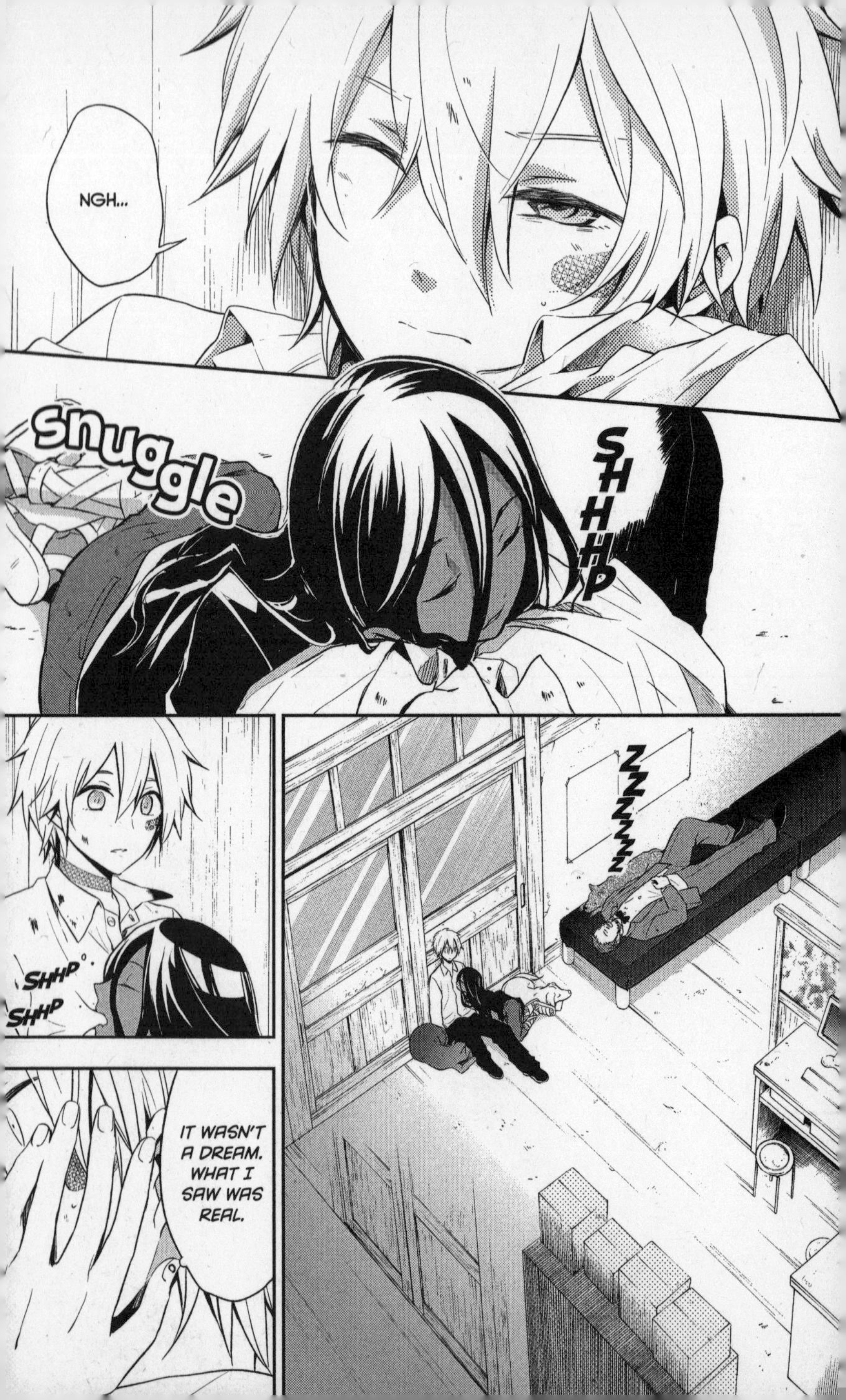
NGH...
SHHHP
Snuggle
ZZZZZZ
SHHP
SHHP
IT WASN'T A DREAM. WHAT I SAW WAS REAL.

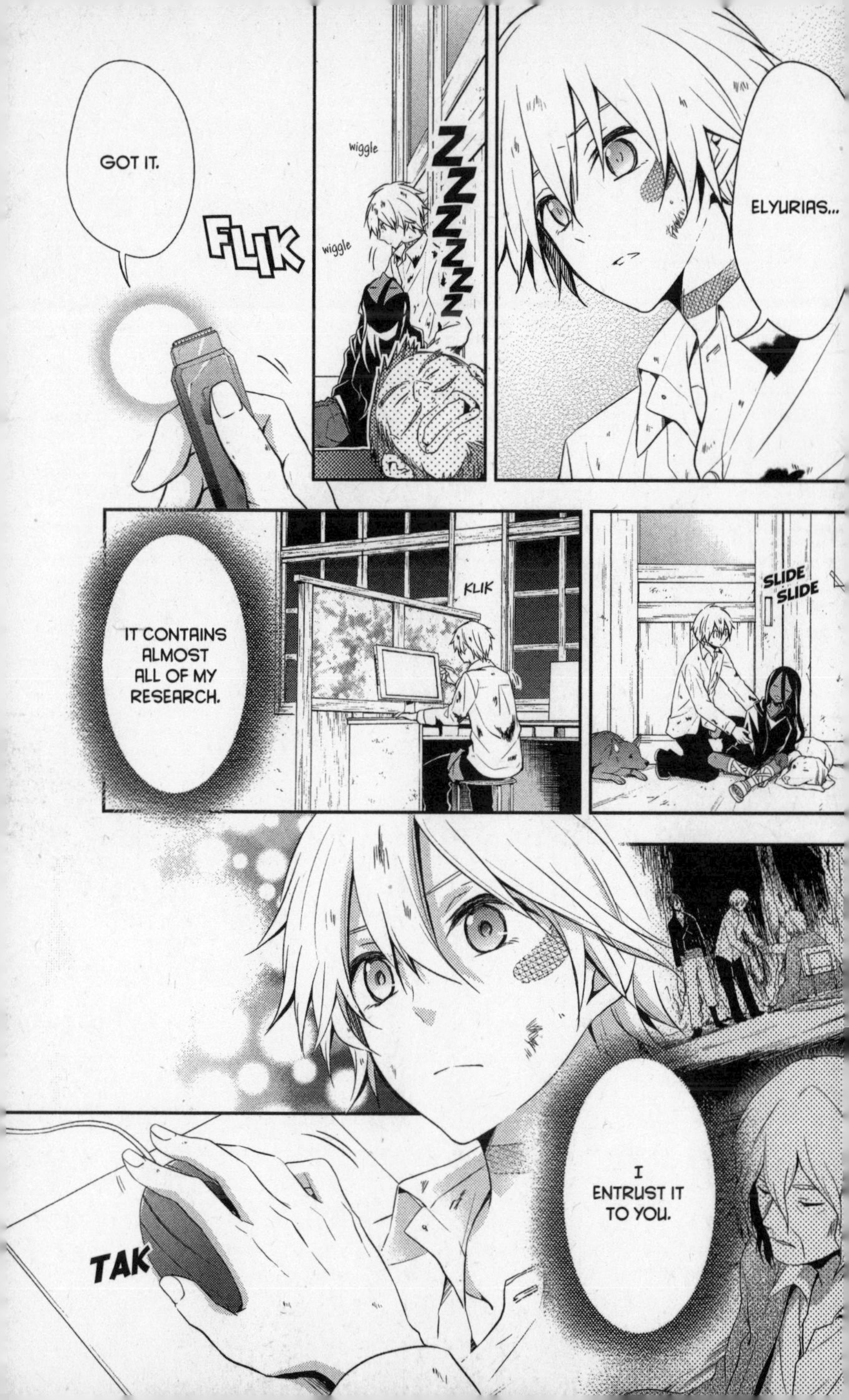
ELYURIAS...
wiggle
wiggle
ZZZZZZZ
GOT IT.
FLIK
SLIDE
SLIDE
KLIK
IT CONTAINS ALMOST ALL OF MY RESEARCH.
I ENTRUST IT TO YOU.
TAK

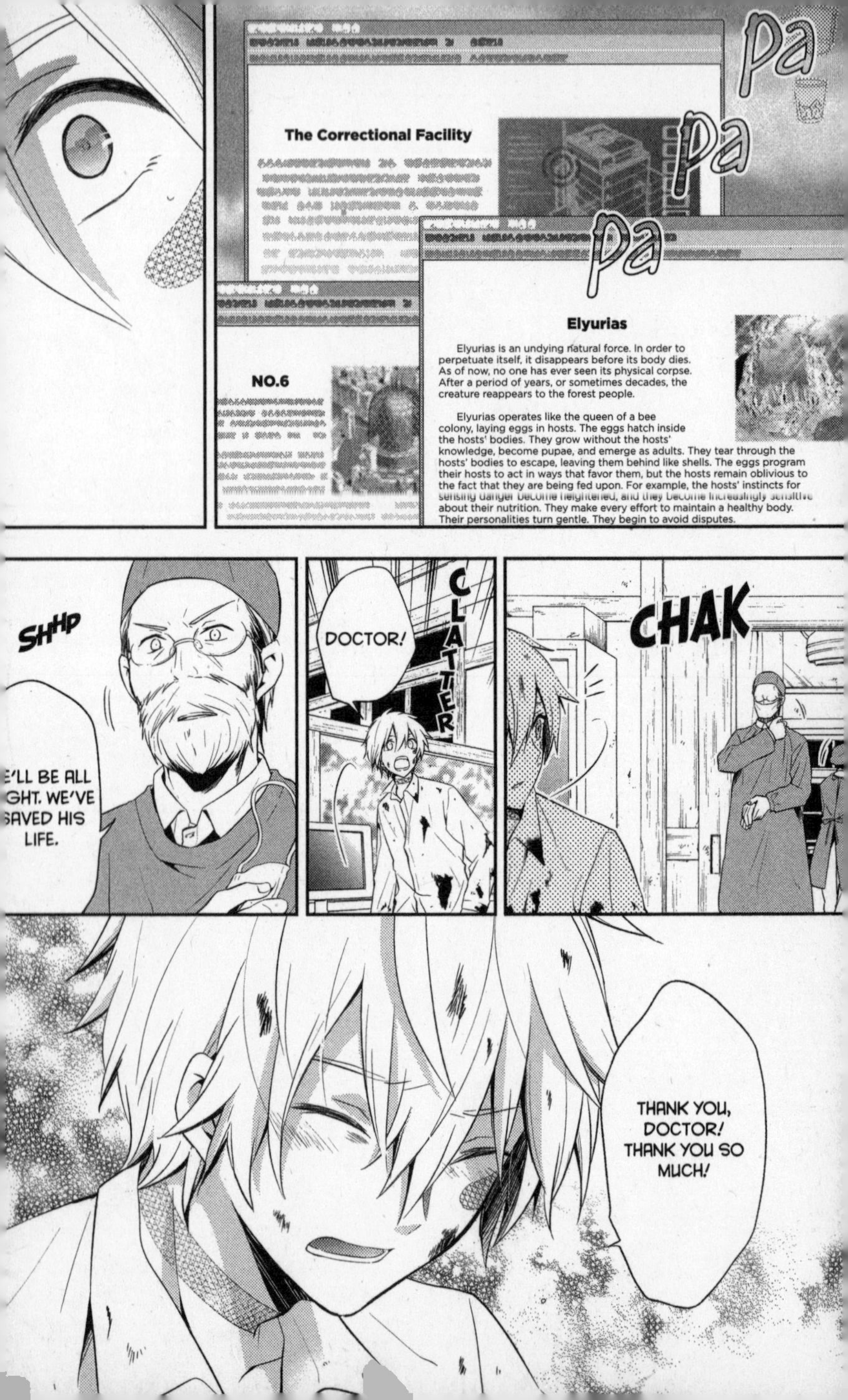
Pa
Pa
Pa
The Correctional Facility
Elyurias
Elyurias is an undying natural force. In order to perpetuate itself, it disappears before its body dies. As of now, no one has ever seen its physical corpse. After a period of years, or sometimes decades, the creature reappears to the forest people.
Elyurias operates like the queen of a bee colony, laying eggs in hosts. The eggs hatch inside the hosts' bodies. They grow without the hosts' knowledge, become pupae, and emerge as adults. They tear through the hosts' bodies to escape, leaving them behind like shells. The eggs program their hosts to act in ways that favor them, but the hosts remain oblivious to the fact that they are being fed upon. For example, the hosts' instincts for sensing danger become heightened, and they become increasingly sensitive about their nutrition. They make every effort to maintain a healthy body. Their personalities turn gentle. They begin to avoid disputes.
NO.6
CHAK
CLATTER
DOCTOR!
SHHP
E'LL BE ALL GHT. WE'VE SAVED HIS LIFE.
THANK YOU, DOCTOR! THANK YOU SO MUCH!

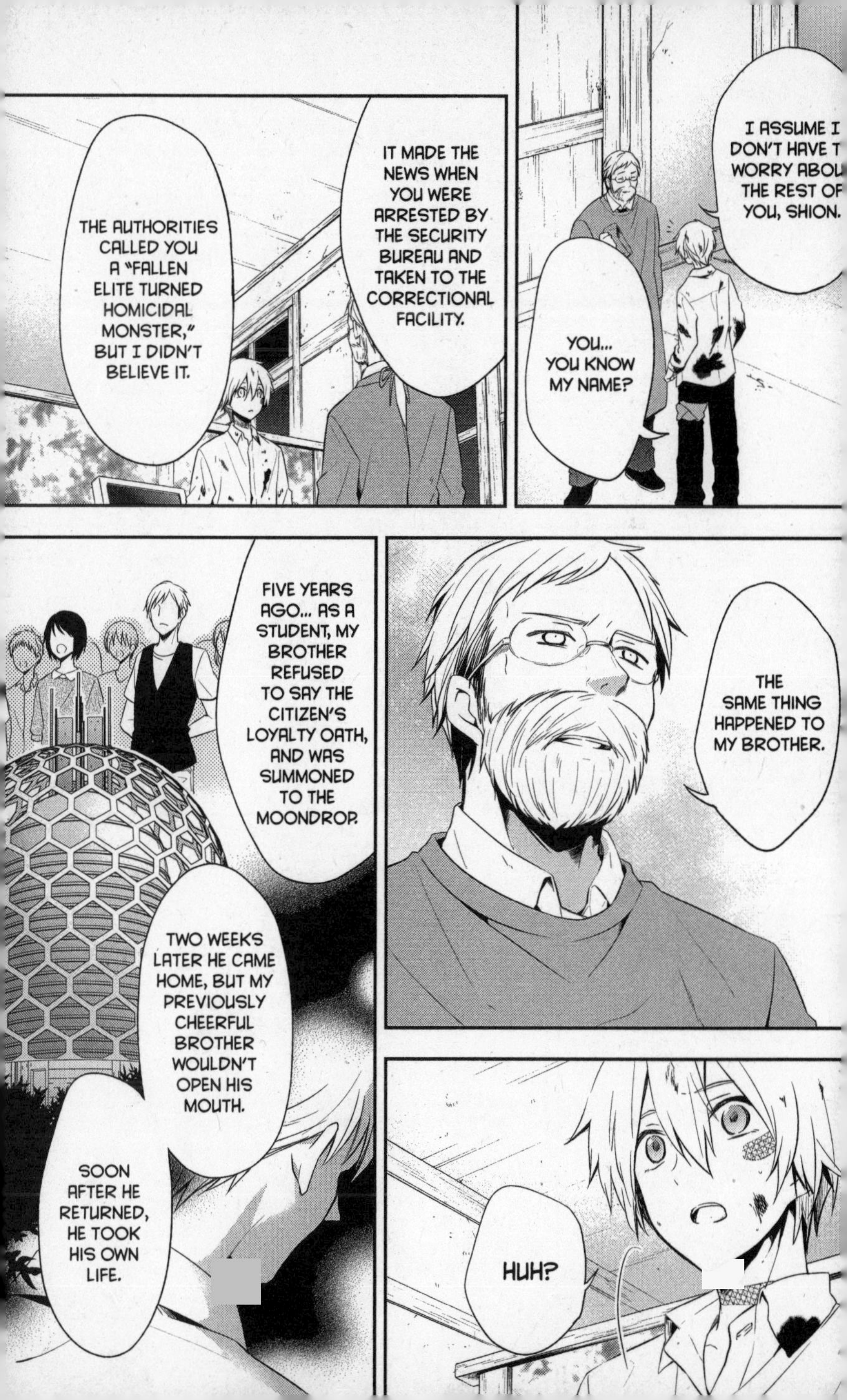
I ASSUME I DON'T HAVE T WORRY ABOU THE REST OF YOU, SHION.
YOU... YOU KNOW MY NAME?
IT MADE THE NEWS WHEN YOU WERE ARRESTED BY THE SECURITY BUREAU AND TAKEN TO THE CORRECTIONAL FACILITY.
THE AUTHORITIES CALLED YOU A "FALLEN ELITE TURNED HOMICIDAL MONSTER," BUT I DIDN'T BELIEVE IT.
THE SAME THING HAPPENED TO MY BROTHER.
HUH?
FIVE YEARS AGO... AS A STUDENT, MY BROTHER REFUSED TO SAY THE CITIZEN'S LOYALTY OATH, AND WAS SUMMONED TO THE MOONDROP.
TWO WEEKS LATER HE CAME HOME, BUT MY PREVIOUSLY CHEERFUL BROTHER WOULDN'T OPEN HIS MOUTH.
SOON AFTER HE RETURNED, HE TOOK HIS OWN LIFE.

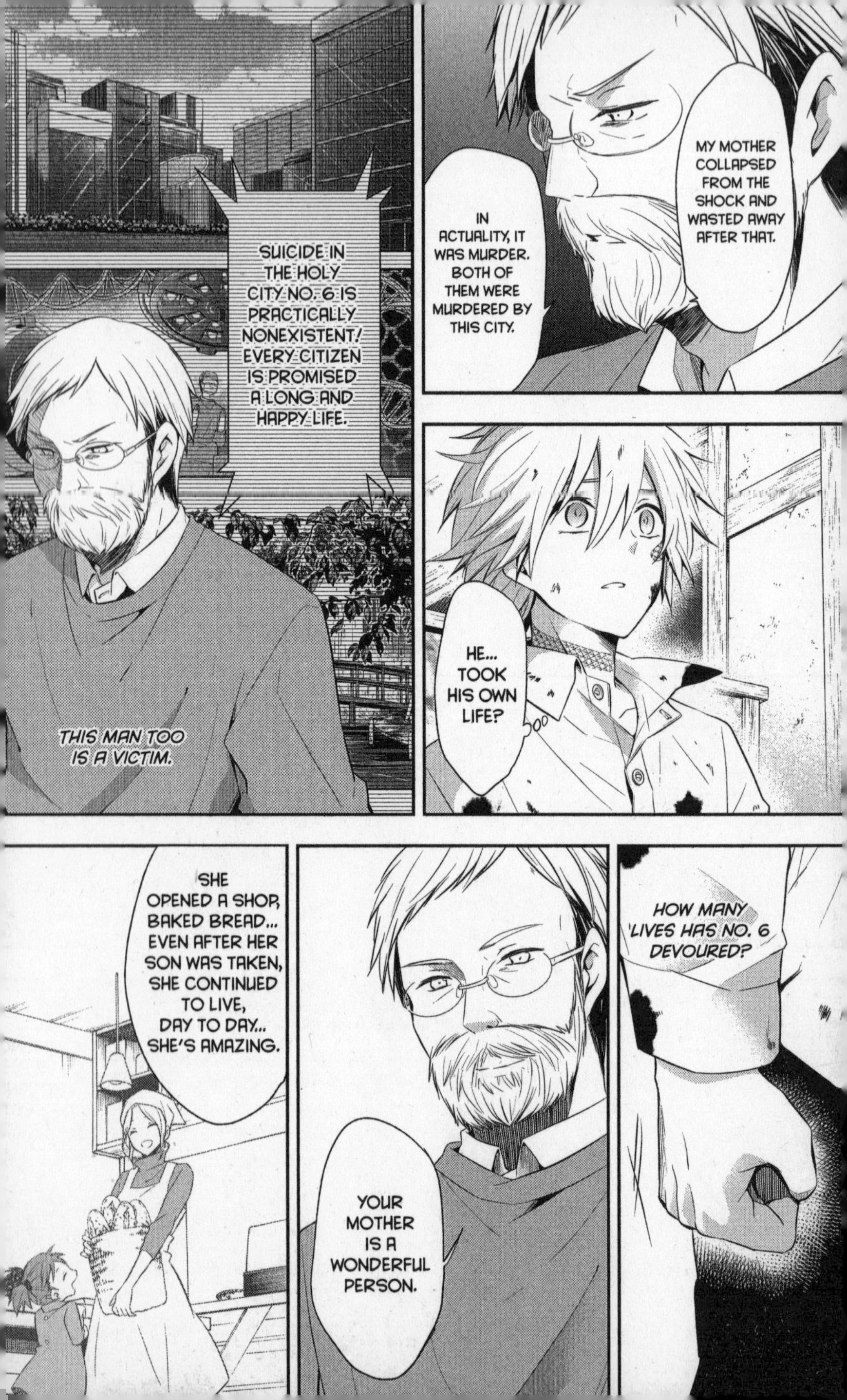
MY MOTHER COLLAPSED FROM THE SHOCK AND WASTED AWAY AFTER THAT.
IN ACTUALITY, IT WAS MURDER. BOTH OF THEM WERE MURDERED BY THIS CITY.
HE... TOOK HIS OWN LIFE?
SUICIDE IN THE HOLY CITY NO. 6 IS PRACTICALLY NONEXISTENT! EVERY CITIZEN IS PROMISED A LONG AND HAPPY LIFE.
THIS MAN TOO IS A VICTIM.
HOW MANY LIVES HAS NO. 6 DEVOURED?
YOUR MOTHER IS A WONDERFUL PERSON.
SHE OPENED A SHOP, BAKED BREAD... EVEN AFTER HER SON WAS TAKEN, SHE CONTINUED TO LIVE, DAY TO DAY... SHE'S AMAZING.

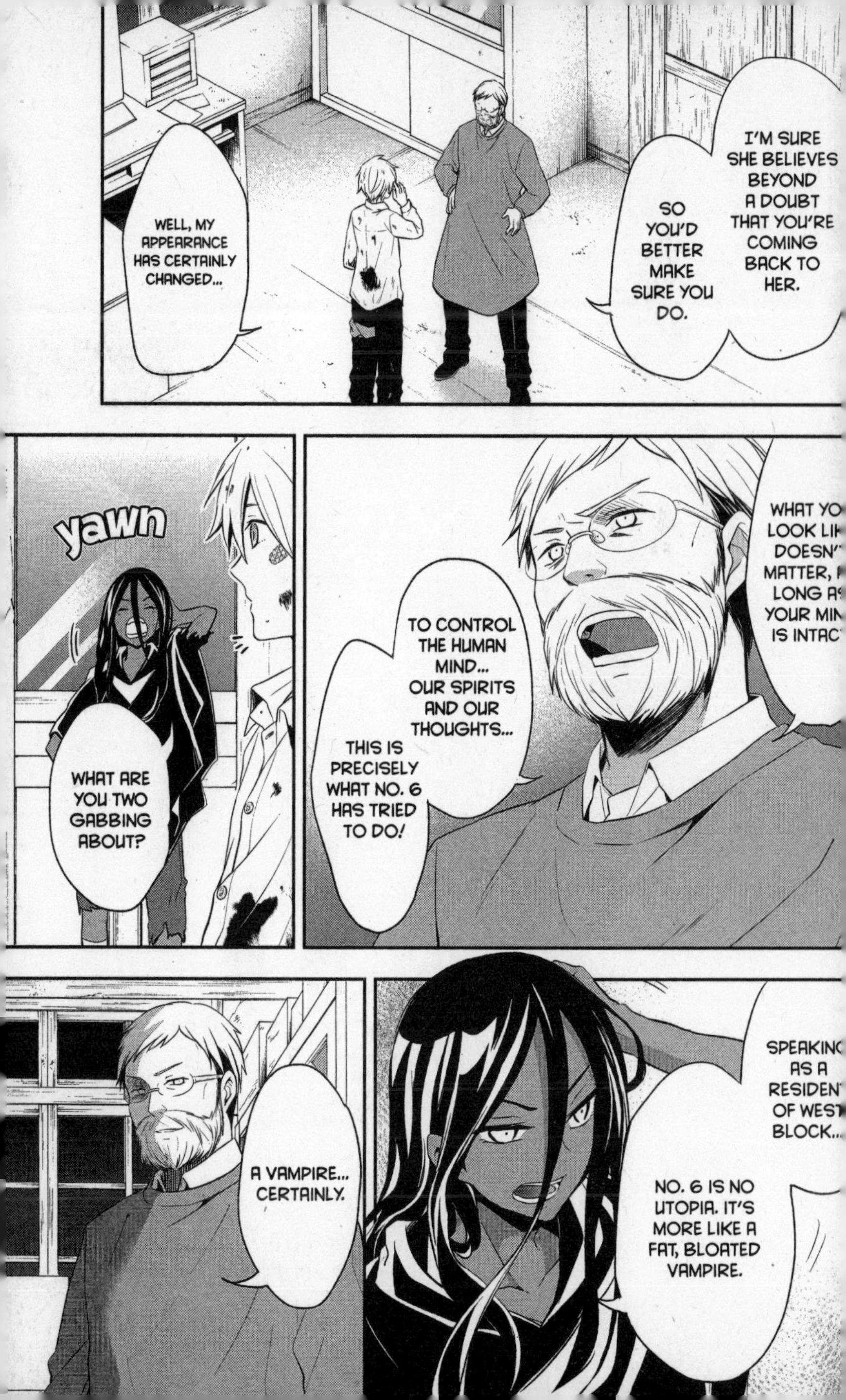
I'M SURE SHE BELIEVES BEYOND A DOUBT THAT YOU'RE COMING BACK TO HER.
SO YOU'D BETTER MAKE SURE YOU DO.
WELL, MY APPEARANCE HAS CERTAINLY CHANGED...
WHAT YO LOOK LIK DOESN' MATTER, LONG A YOUR MIN IS INTAC
TO CONTROL THE HUMAN MIND... OUR SPIRITS AND OUR THOUGHTS...
THIS IS PRECISELY WHAT NO. 6 HAS TRIED TO DO!
yawn
WHAT ARE YOU TWO GABBING ABOUT?
SPEAKIN AS A RESIDEN OF WES BLOCK...
NO. 6 IS NO UTOPIA. IT'S MORE LIKE A FAT, BLOATED VAMPIRE.
A VAMPIRE... CERTAINLY.

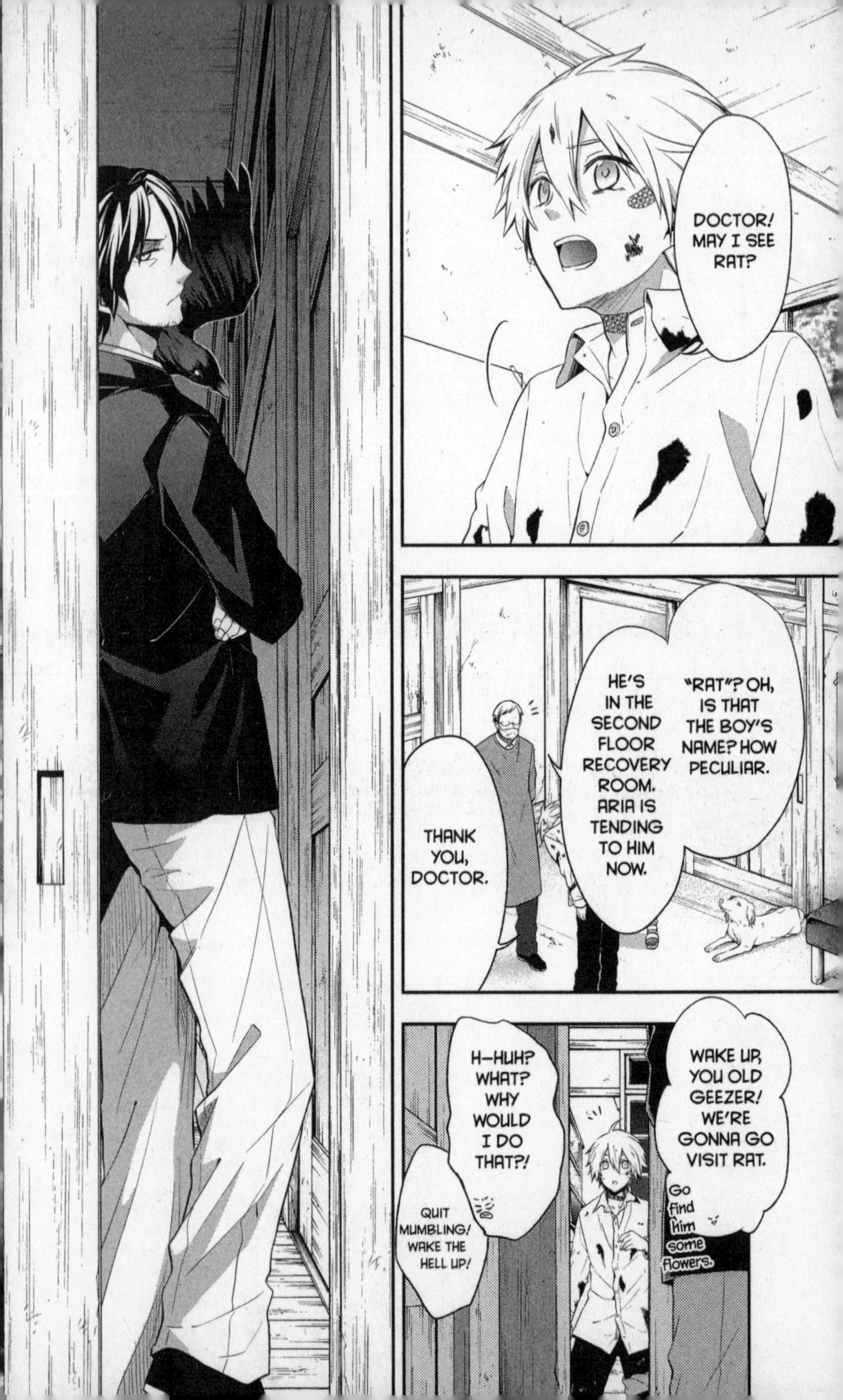
DOCTOR! MAY I SEE RAT?
"RAT"? OH, IS THAT THE BOY'S NAME? HOW PECULIAR.
HE'S IN THE SECOND FLOOR RECOVERY ROOM. ARIA IS TENDING TO HIM NOW.
THANK YOU, DOCTOR.
WAKE UP, YOU OLD GEEZER! WE'RE GONNA GO VISIT RAT.
Go find him some flowers.
H-HUH? WHAT? WHY WOULD I DO THAT?!
QUIT MUMBLING! WAKE THE HELL UP!

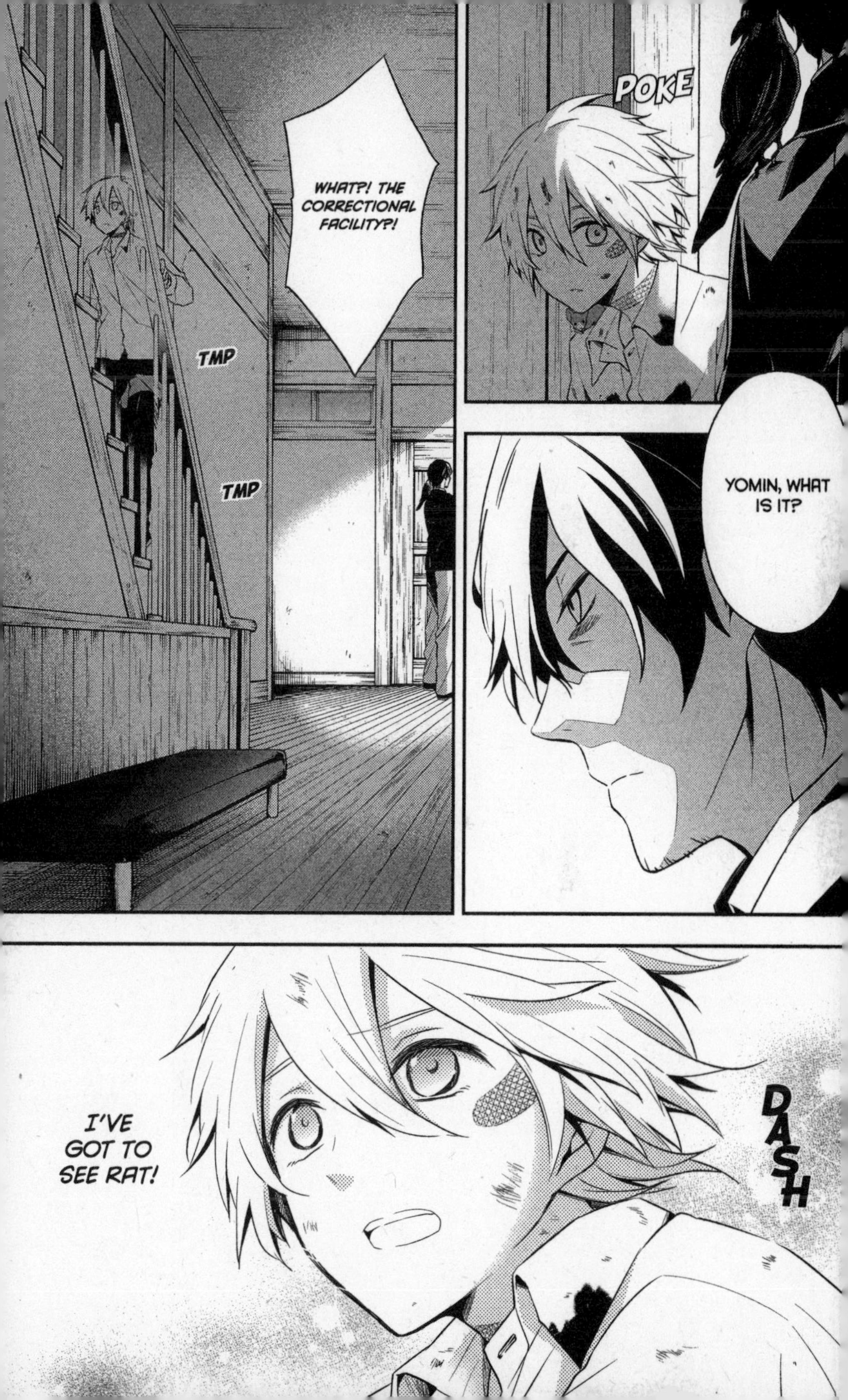
POKE
YOMIN, WHAT IS IT?
WHAT?! THE CORRECTIONAL FACILITY?!
TMP
TMP
DASH
I'VE GOT TO SEE RAT!

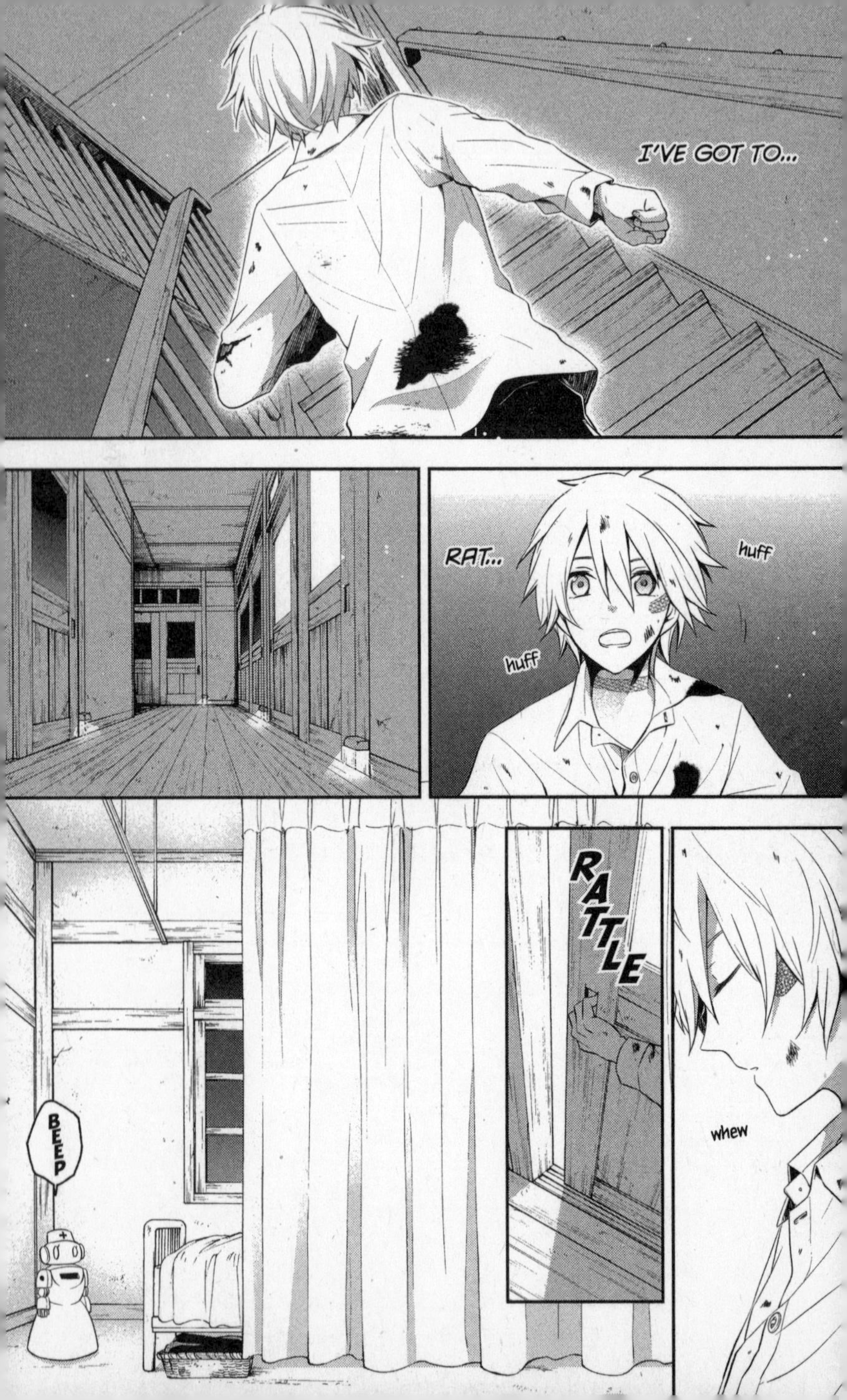
I'VE GOT TO...
RAT...
huff
huff
whew
RATTLE
BEEP

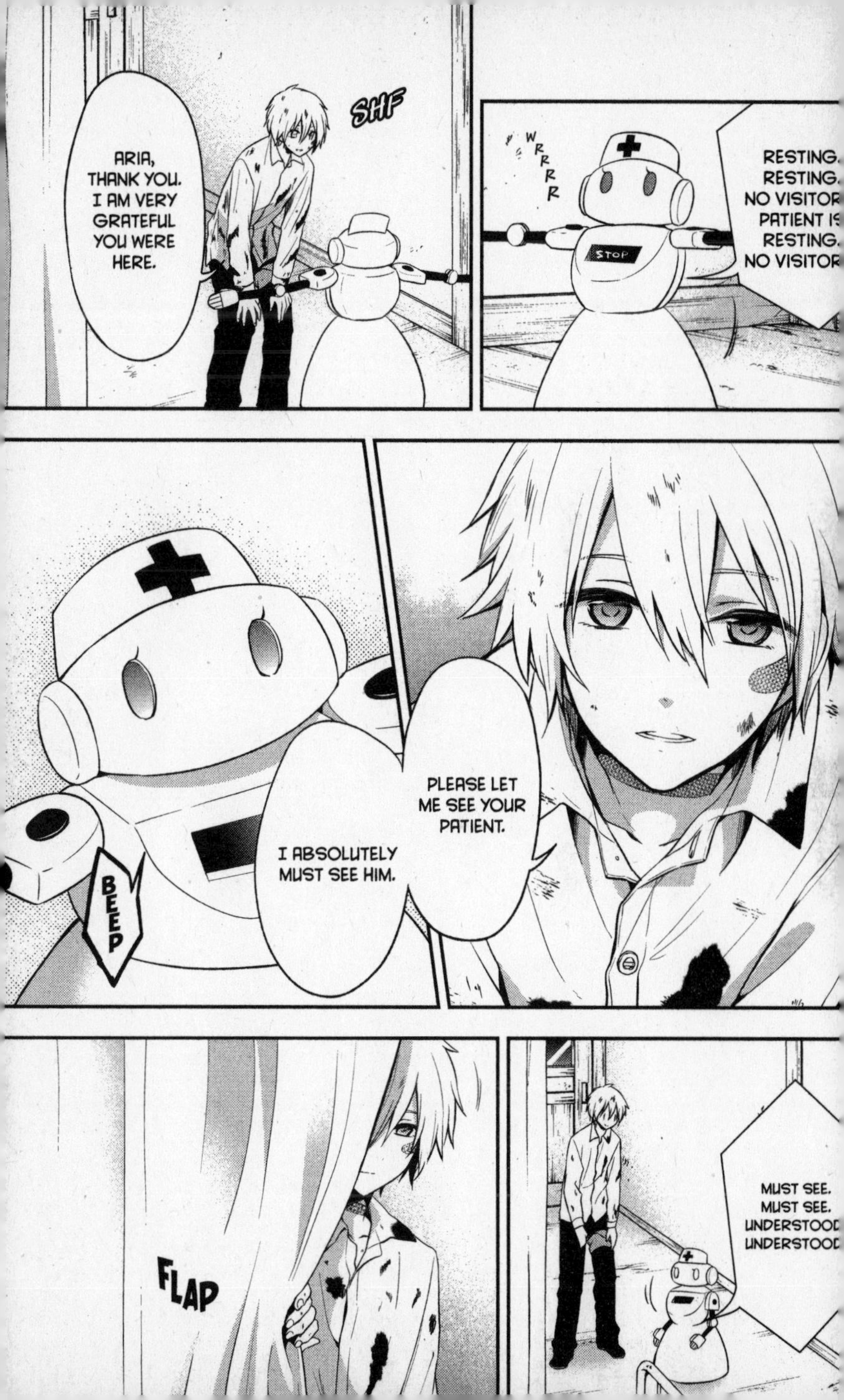

RESTING. RESTING. NO VISITOR PATIENT IS RESTING. NO VISITOR
WRRRR
ARIA, THANK YOU. I AM VERY GRATEFUL YOU WERE HERE.
SHF
PLEASE LET ME SEE YOUR PATIENT.
I ABSOLUTELY MUST SEE HIM.
BEEP
STOP
MUST SEE. MUST SEE. UNDERSTOOD UNDERSTOOD
FLAP

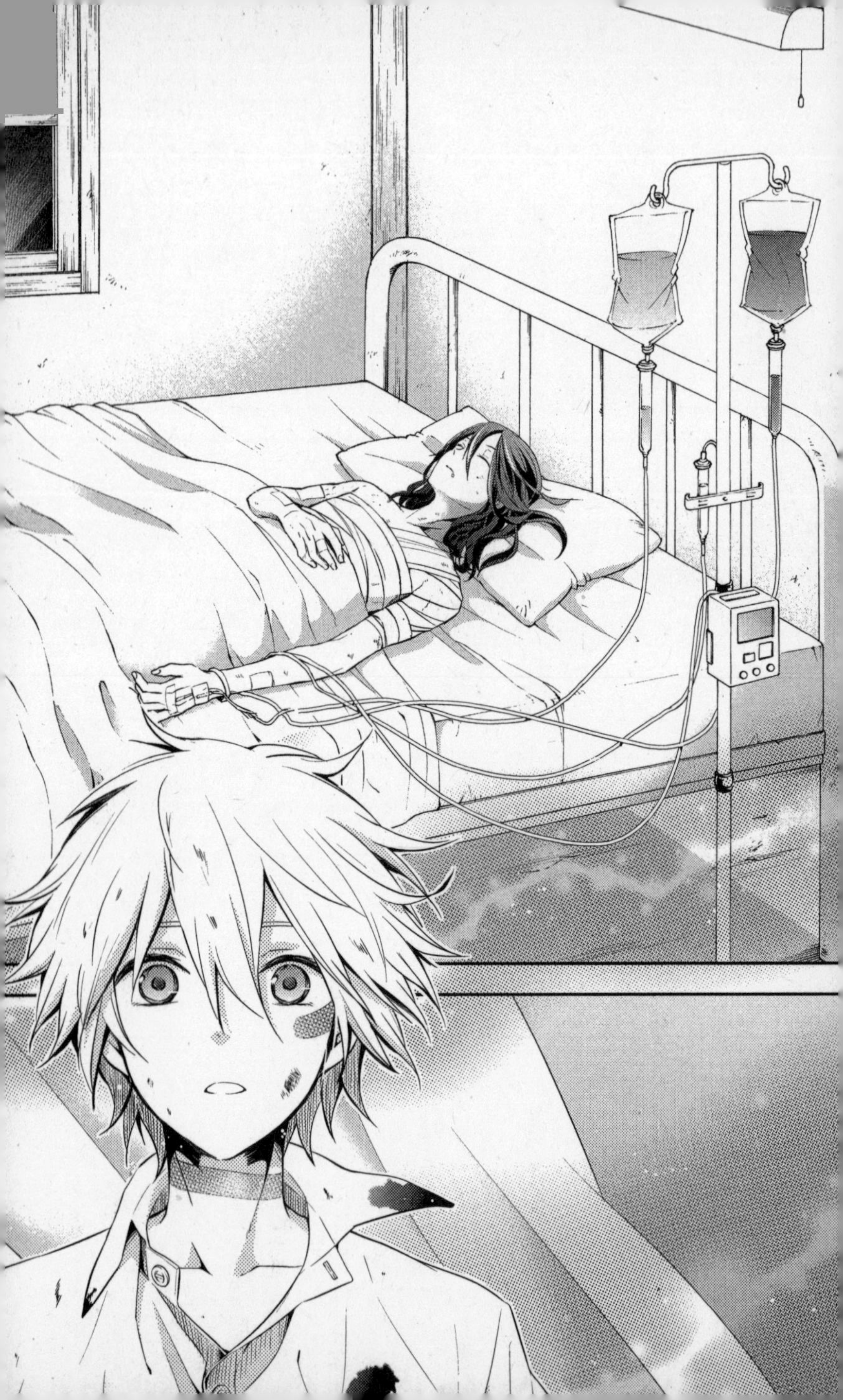

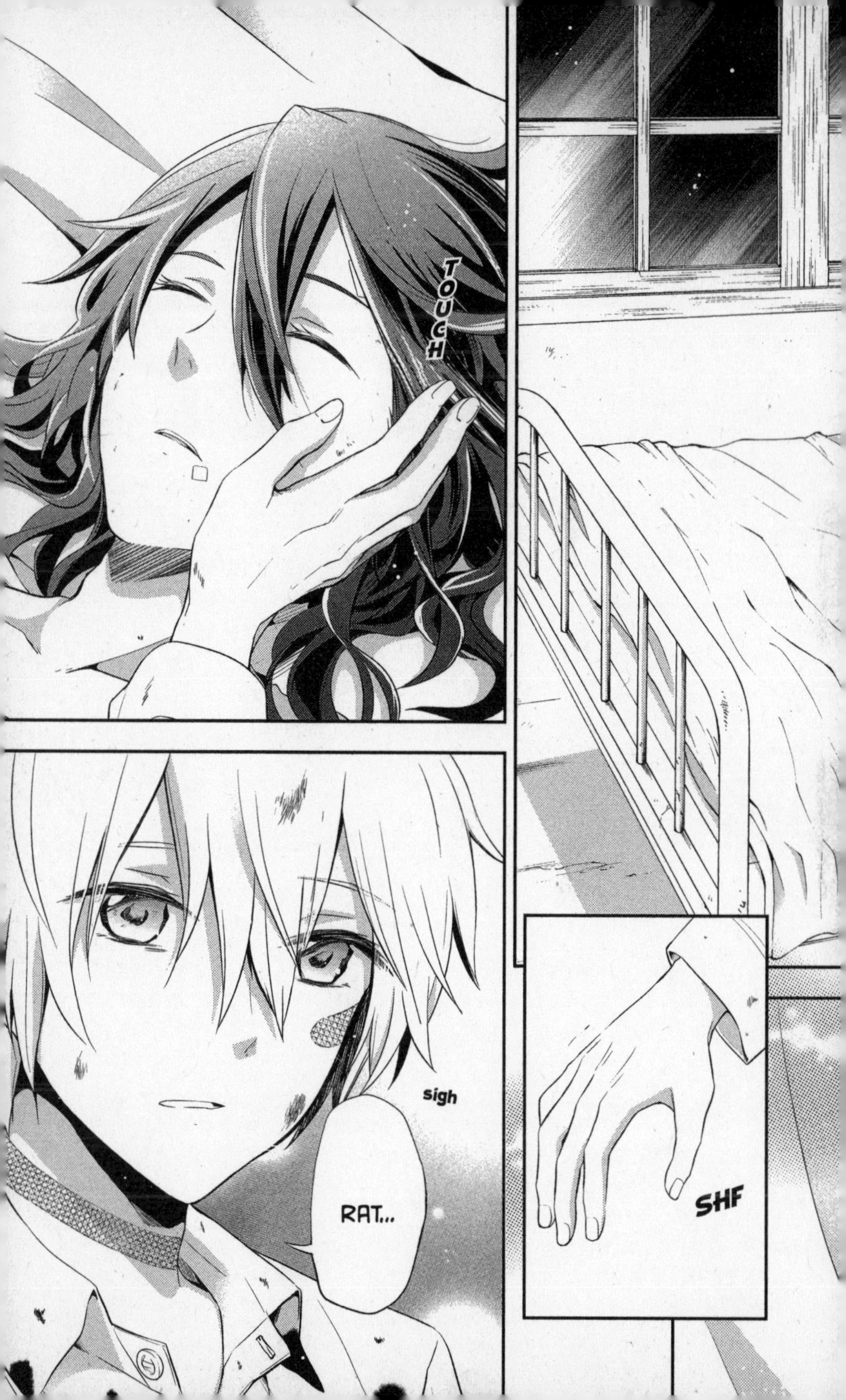
TOUCH
SHF
sigh
RAT...

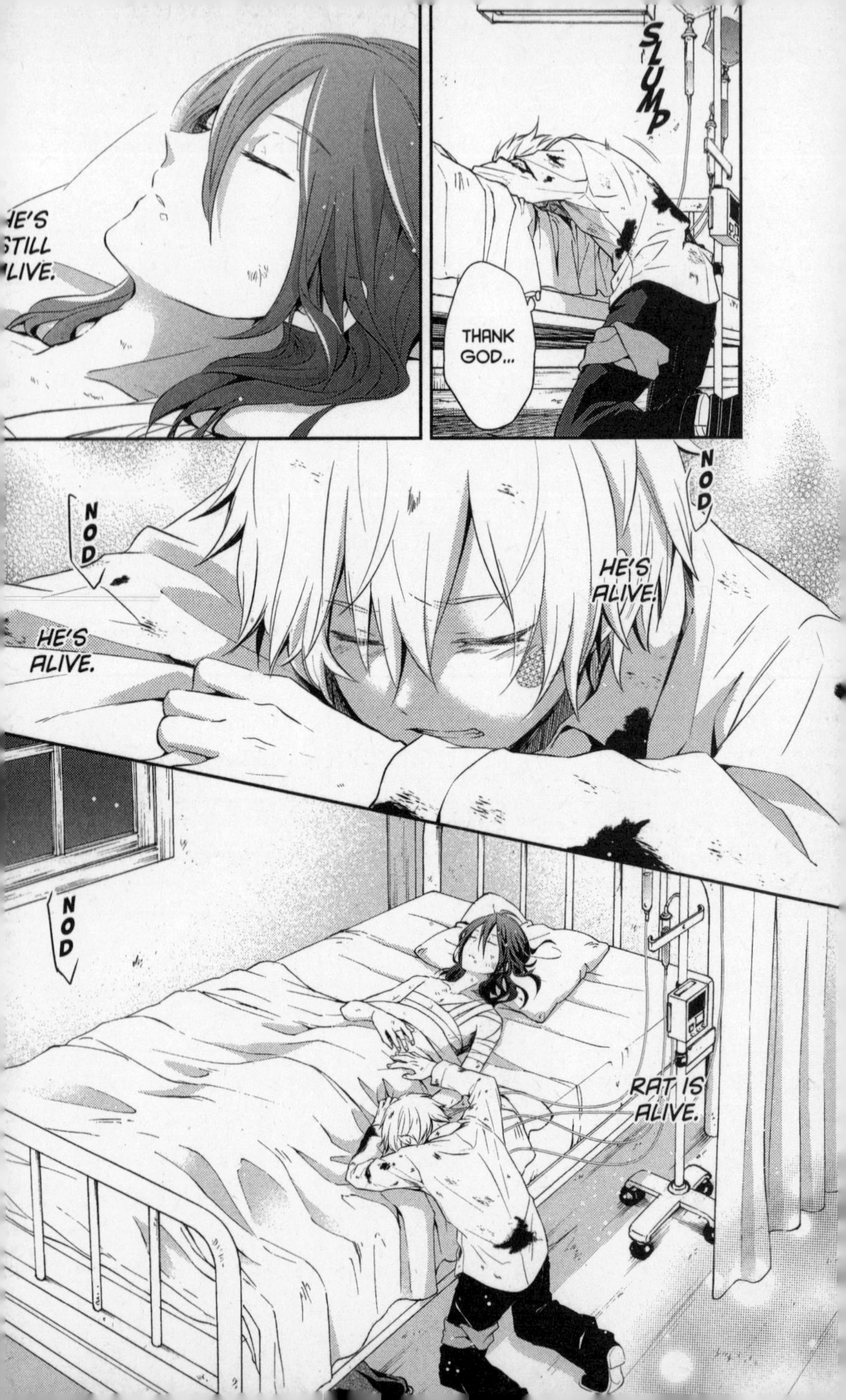
SLUMP
THANK GOD...
HE'S STILL ALIVE.
NOD
HE'S ALIVE.
NOD
HE'S ALIVE.
NOD
RAT IS ALIVE.

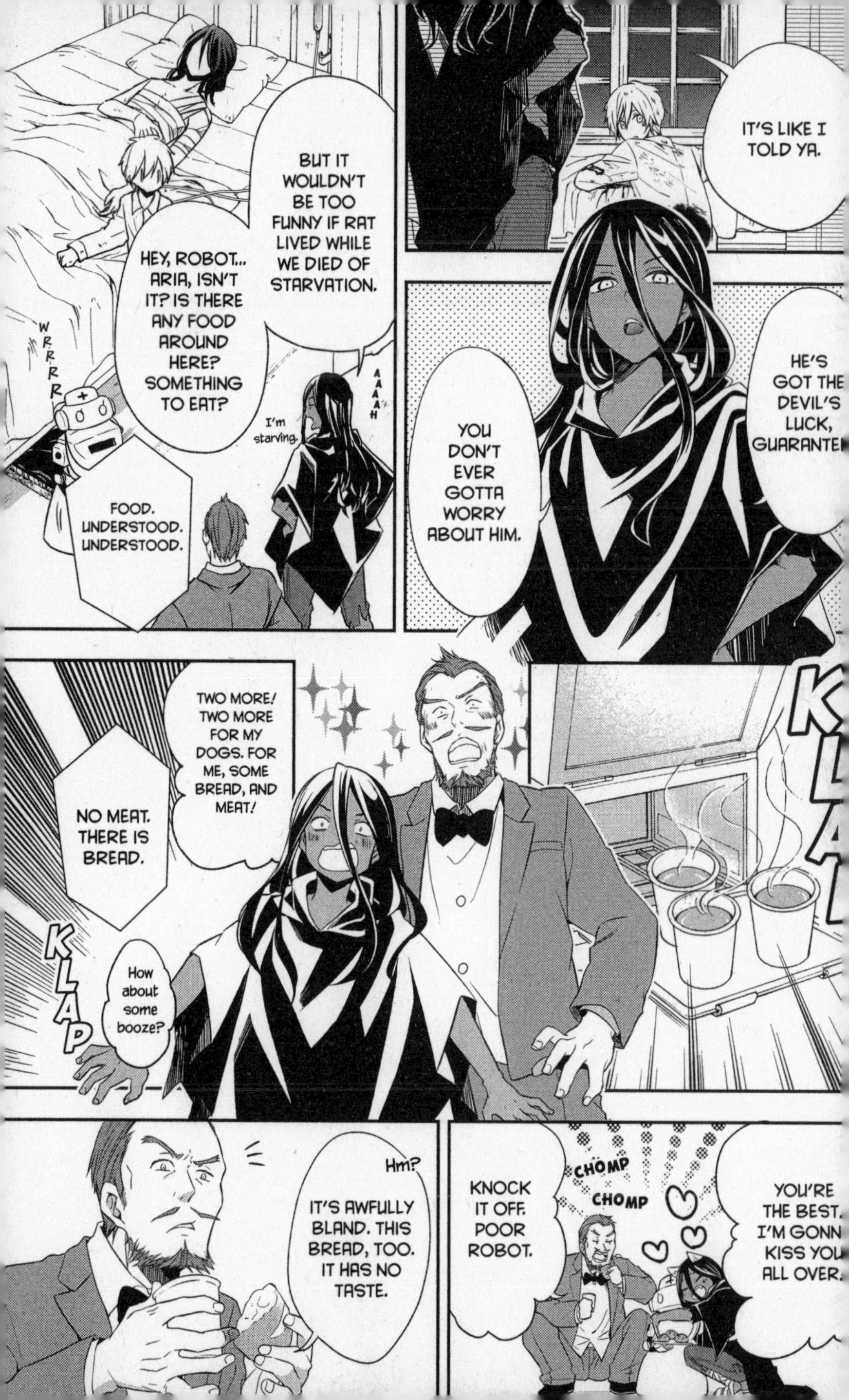
IT'S LIKE I TOLD YA.
HE'S GOT THE DEVIL'S LUCK, GUARANTE
YOU DON'T EVER GOTTA WORRY ABOUT HIM.
BUT IT WOULDN'T BE TOO FUNNY IF RAT LIVED WHILE WE DIED OF STARVATION.
HEY, ROBOT... ARIA, ISN'T IT? IS THERE ANY FOOD AROUND HERE? SOMETHING TO EAT?
AAAAH
I'm starving.
WRRRR
FOOD. UNDERSTOOD. UNDERSTOOD.
KLA
TWO MORE! TWO MORE FOR MY DOGS. FOR ME, SOME BREAD, AND MEAT!
NO MEAT. THERE IS BREAD.
How about some booze?
KLAP
YOU'RE THE BEST. I'M GONN KISS YOU ALL OVER.
CHOMP
CHOMP
KNOCK IT OFF. POOR ROBOT.
Hm?
IT'S AWFULLY BLAND. THIS BREAD, TOO. IT HAS NO TASTE.

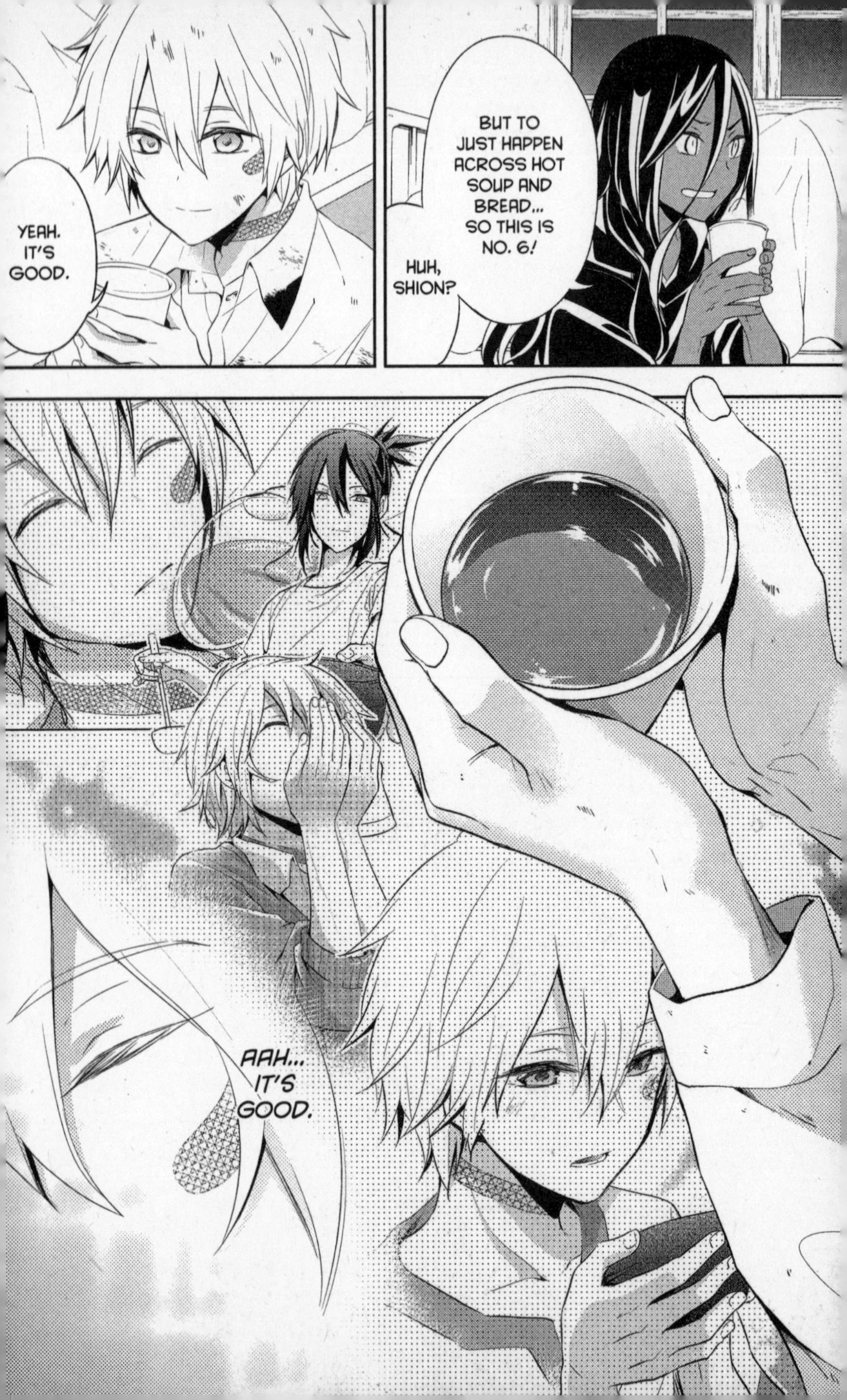
BUT TO JUST HAPPEN ACROSS HOT SOUP AND BREAD... SO THIS IS NO. 6!
HUH, SHION?
YEAH. IT'S GOOD.
AAH... IT'S GOOD.

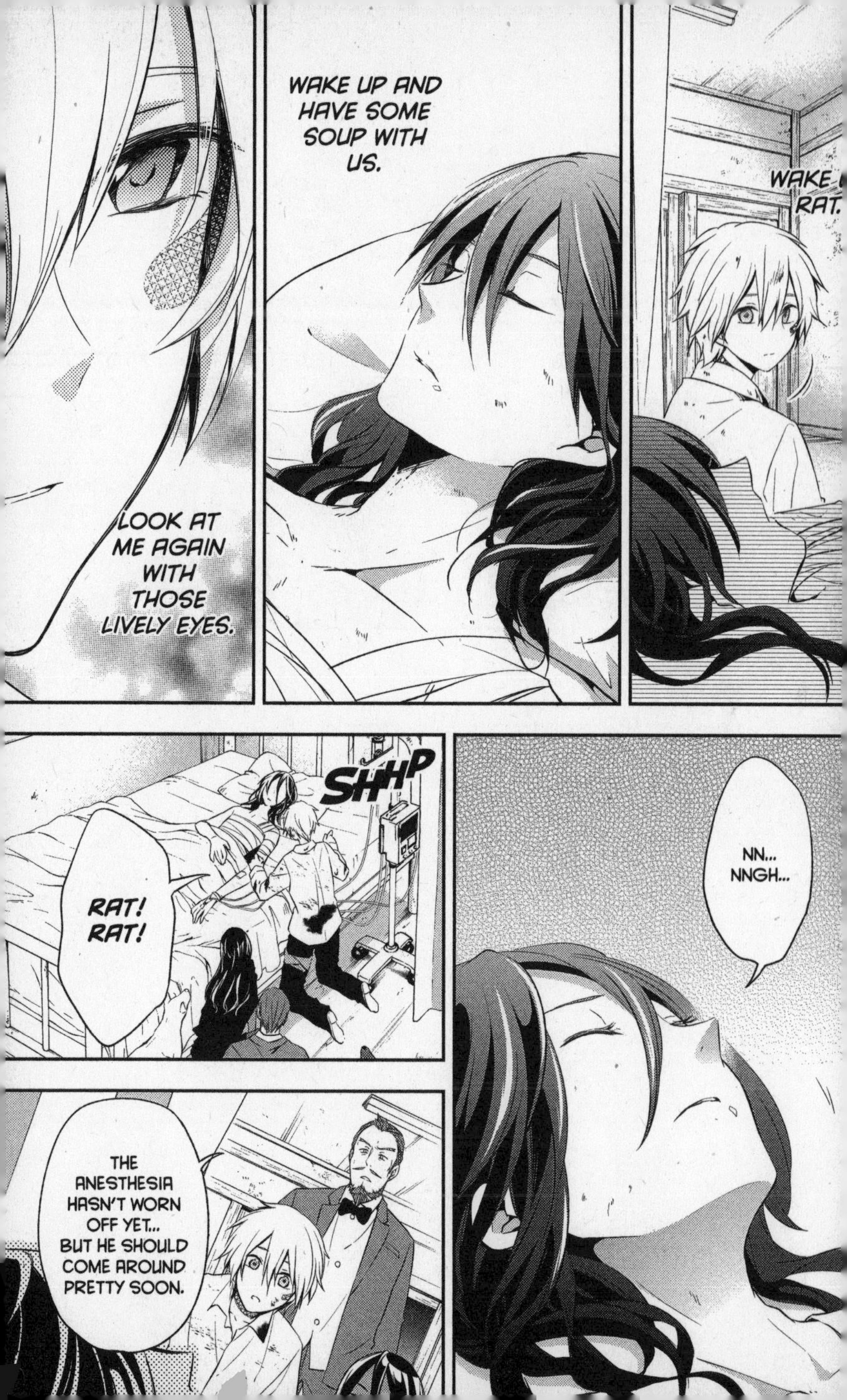
WAKE
RAT.
WAKE UP AND HAVE SOME SOUP WITH US.
LOOK AT ME AGAIN WITH THOSE LIVELY EYES.
NN... NNGH...
SHHP
RAT! RAT!
THE ANESTHESIA HASN'T WORN OFF YET... BUT HE SHOULD COME AROUND PRETTY SOON.

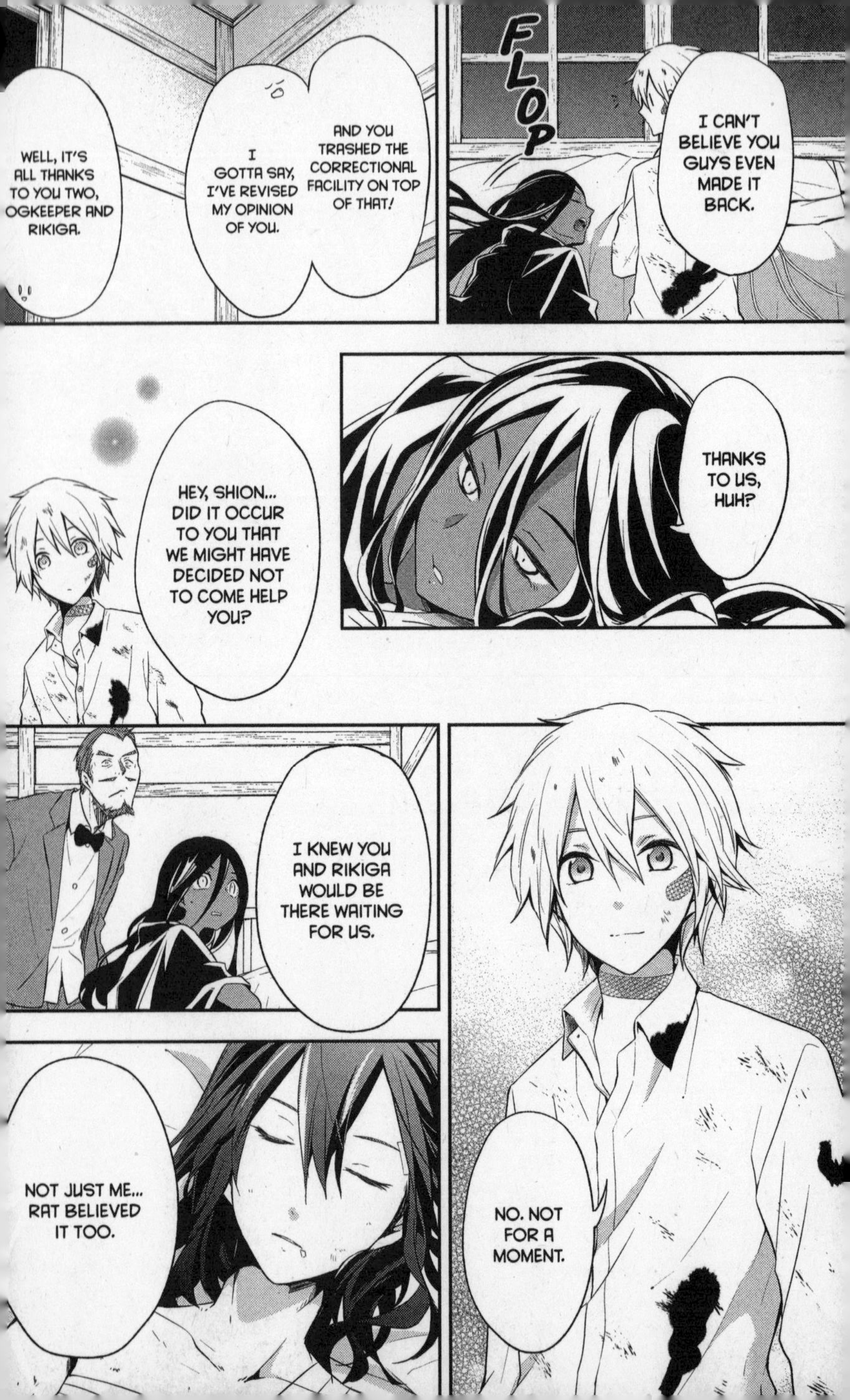
FLOP
I CAN'T BELIEVE YOU GUYS EVEN MADE IT BACK.
AND YOU TRASHED THE CORRECTIONAL FACILITY ON TOP OF THAT!
I GOTTA SAY, I'VE REVISED MY OPINION OF YOU.
WELL, IT'S ALL THANKS TO YOU TWO, OGKEEPER AND RIKIGA.
THANKS TO US, HUH?
HEY, SHION... DID IT OCCUR TO YOU THAT WE MIGHT HAVE DECIDED NOT TO COME HELP YOU?
NO. NOT FOR A MOMENT.
I KNEW YOU AND RIKIGA WOULD BE THERE WAITING FOR US.
NOT JUST ME... RAT BELIEVED IT TOO.

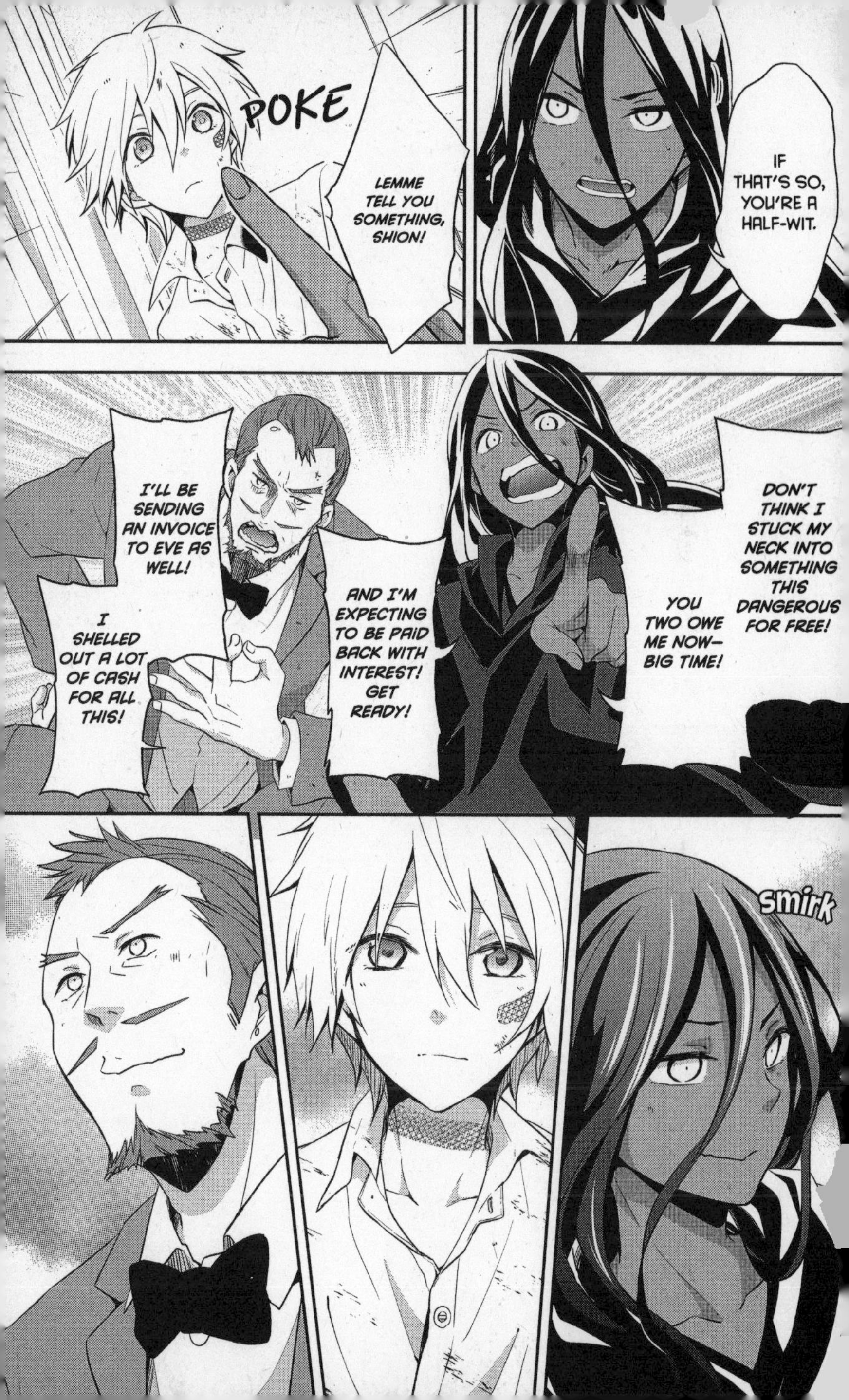
IF THAT'S SO, YOU'RE A HALF-WIT.
POKE
LEMME TELL YOU SOMETHING, SHION!
DON'T THINK I STUCK MY NECK INTO SOMETHING THIS DANGEROUS FOR FREE!
YOU TWO OWE ME NOW—BIG TIME!
I'LL BE SENDING AN INVOICE TO EVE AS WELL!
I SHELLED OUT A LOT OF CASH FOR ALL THIS!
AND I'M EXPECTING TO BE PAID BACK WITH INTEREST! GET READY!
smirk

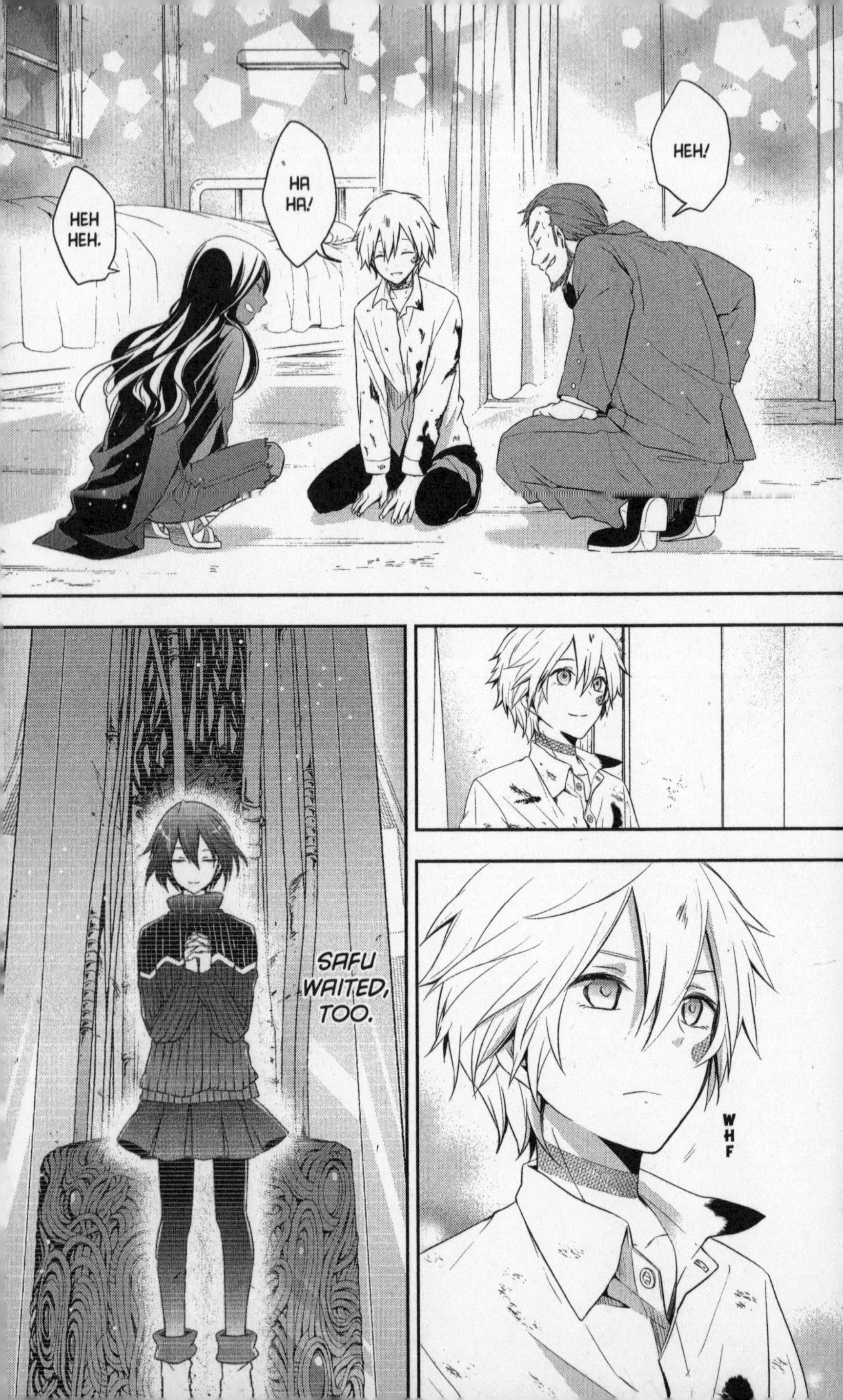
HEH!
HA HA!
HEH HEH.
WHF
SAFU WAITED, TOO.

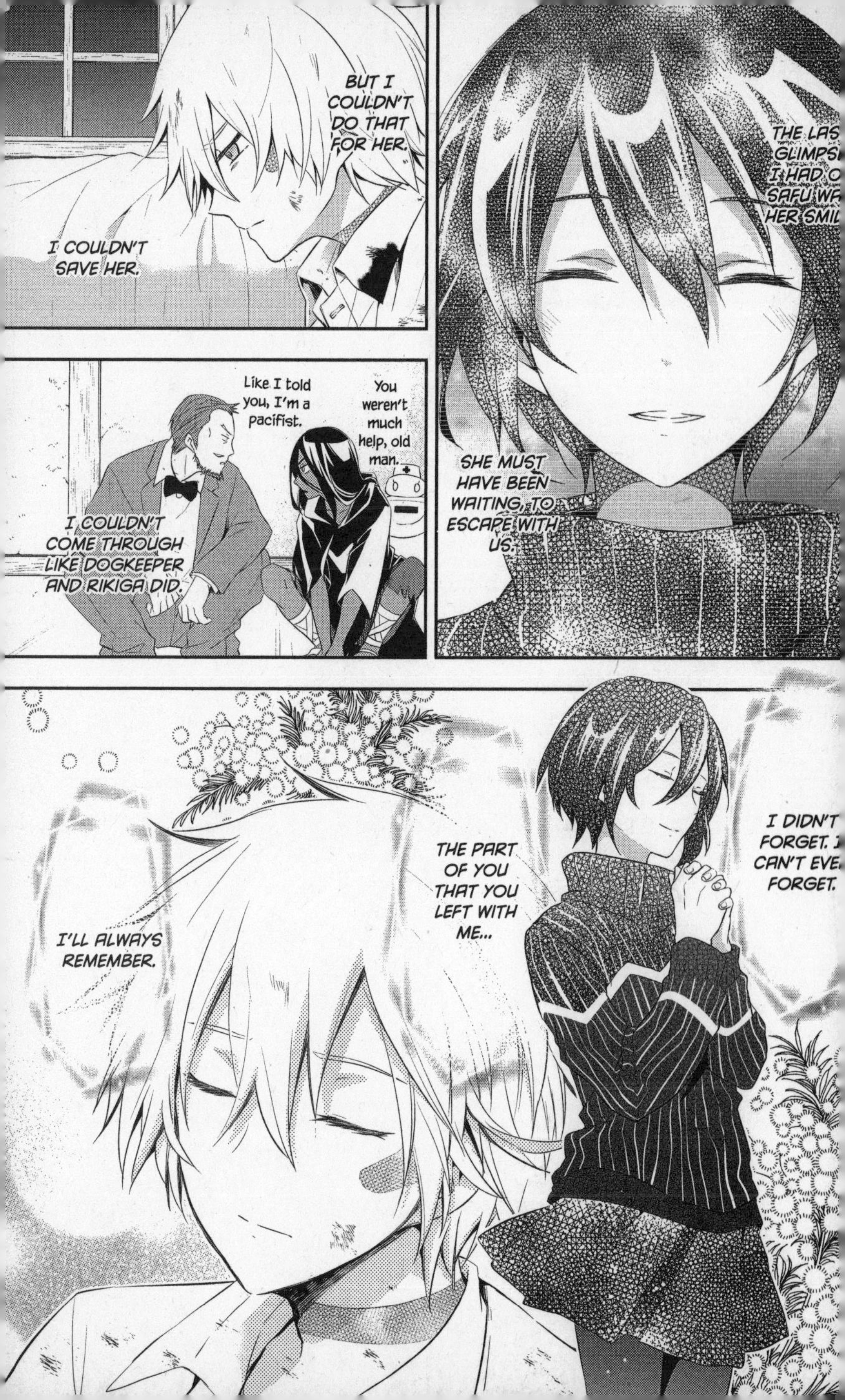
THE LAS GLIMPS I HAD O SAFU WA HER SMIL
SHE MUST HAVE BEEN WAITING, TO ESCAPE WITH US.
BUT I COULDN'T DO THAT FOR HER.
I COULDN'T SAVE HER.
You weren't much help, old man.
Like I told you, I'm a pacifist.
I COULDN'T COME THROUGH LIKE DOGKEEPER AND RIKIGA DID.
I DIDN'T FORGET. I CAN'T EVE FORGET.
THE PART OF YOU THAT YOU LEFT WITH ME...
I'LL ALWAYS REMEMBER.

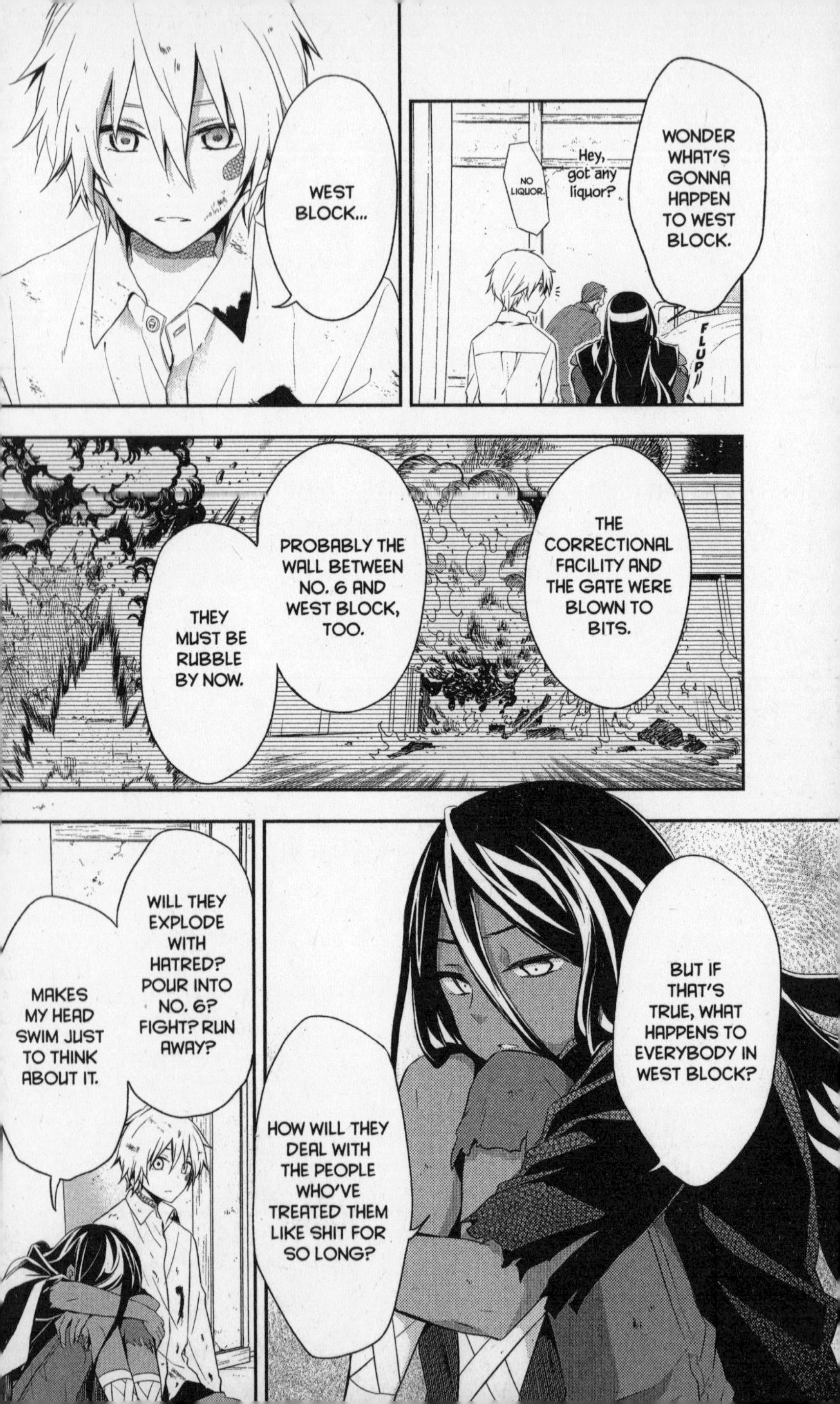
WONDER WHAT'S GONNA HAPPEN TO WEST BLOCK.
Hey, got any liquor?
NO LIQUOR.
FLUP!
WEST BLOCK...
THE CORRECTIONAL FACILITY AND THE GATE WERE BLOWN TO BITS.
PROBABLY THE WALL BETWEEN NO. 6 AND WEST BLOCK, TOO.
THEY MUST BE RUBBLE BY NOW.
BUT IF THAT'S TRUE, WHAT HAPPENS TO EVERYBODY IN WEST BLOCK?
HOW WILL THEY DEAL WITH THE PEOPLE WHO'VE TREATED THEM LIKE SHIT FOR SO LONG?
WILL THEY EXPLODE WITH HATRED? POUR INTO NO. 6? FIGHT? RUN AWAY?
MAKES MY HEAD SWIM JUST TO THINK ABOUT IT.

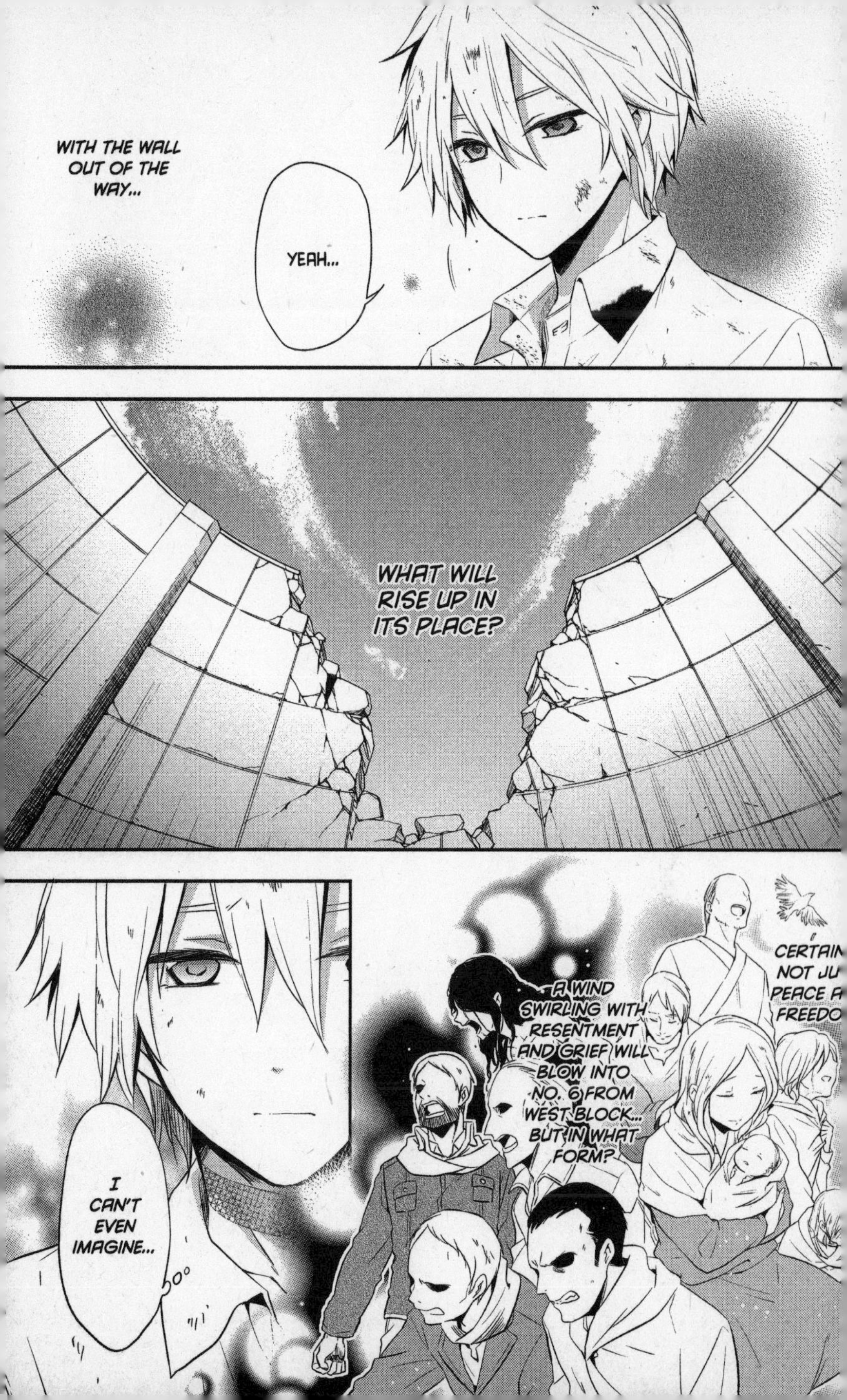
YEAH...
WITH THE WALL OUT OF THE WAY...
WHAT WILL RISE UP IN ITS PLACE?
CERTAIN NOT JU PEACE A FREEDO
A WIND SWIRLING WITH RESENTMENT AND GRIEF WILL BLOW INTO NO. 6 FROM WEST BLOCK... BUT IN WHAT FORM?
I CAN'T EVEN IMAGINE...

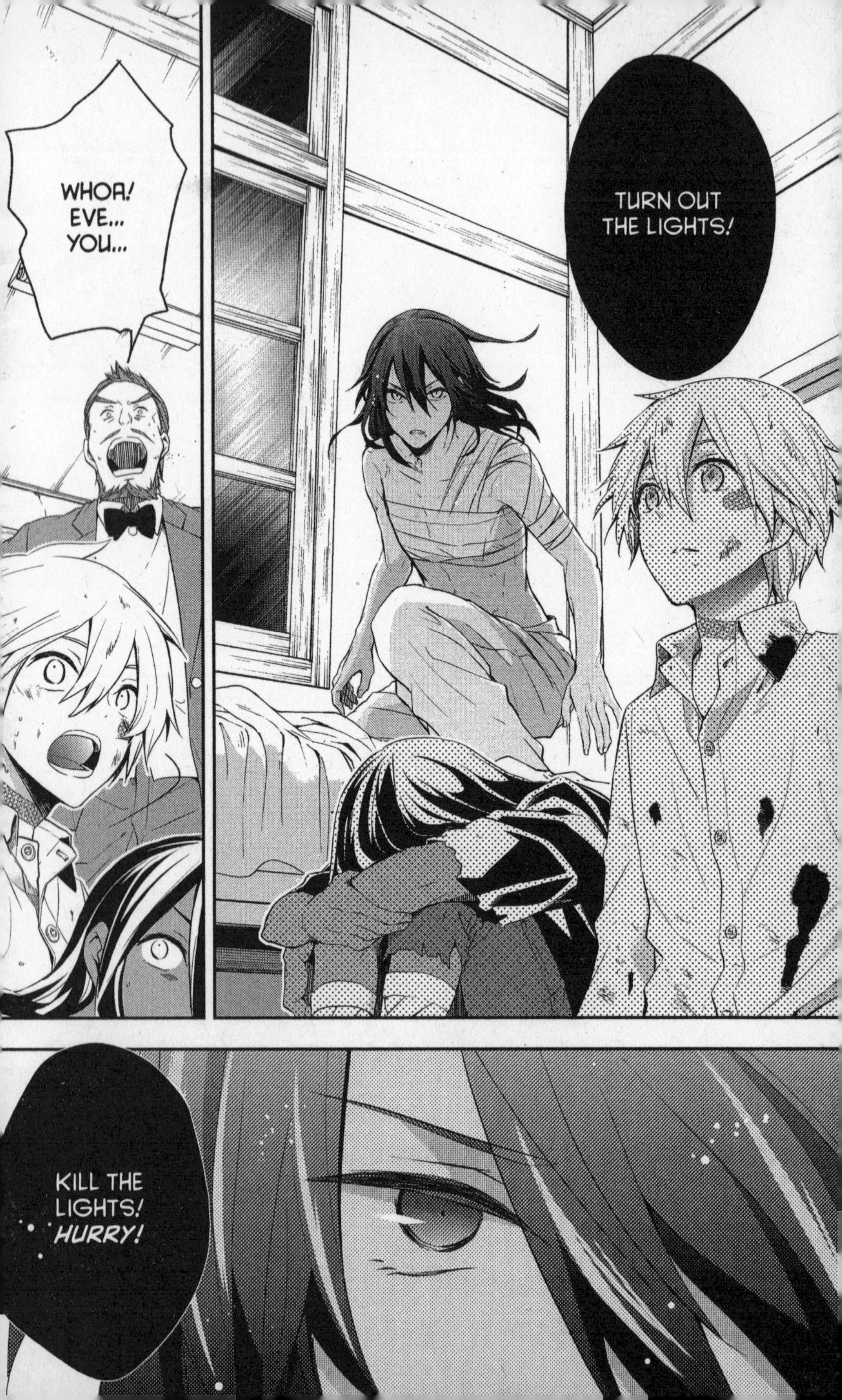
TURN OUT THE LIGHTS!
WHOA! EVE... YOU...
KILL THE LIGHTS! HURRY!

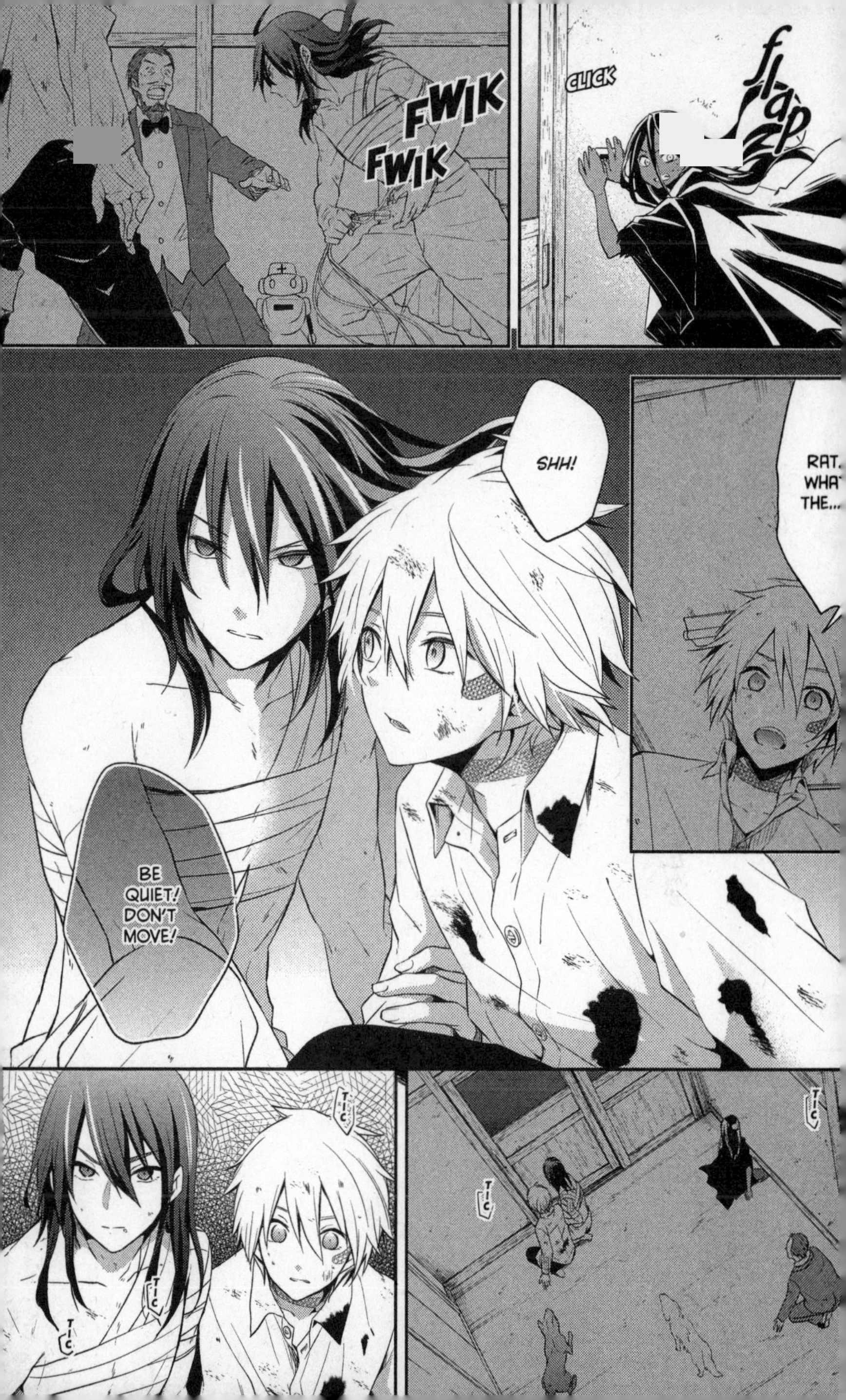
CLICK
flap
FWIK
FWIK
RAT. WHAT THE...
SHH!
BE QUIET! DON'T MOVE!
TIC
TIC
TIC
TIC
TIC

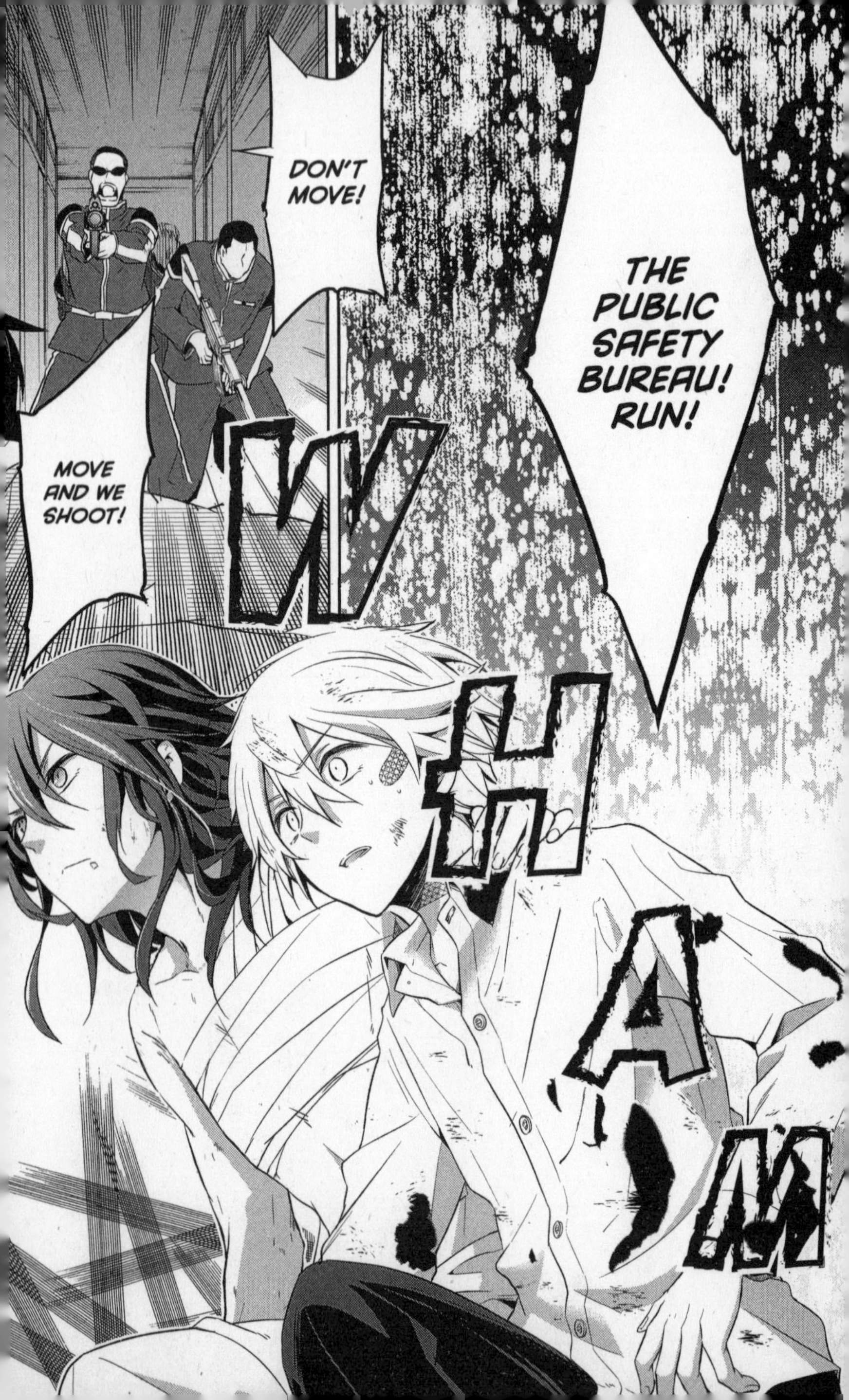
THE PUBLIC SAFETY BUREAU! RUN!
DON'T MOVE!
MOVE AND WE SHOOT!
WHAM

NO.6

Chapter 34: This Quintessence of Dust

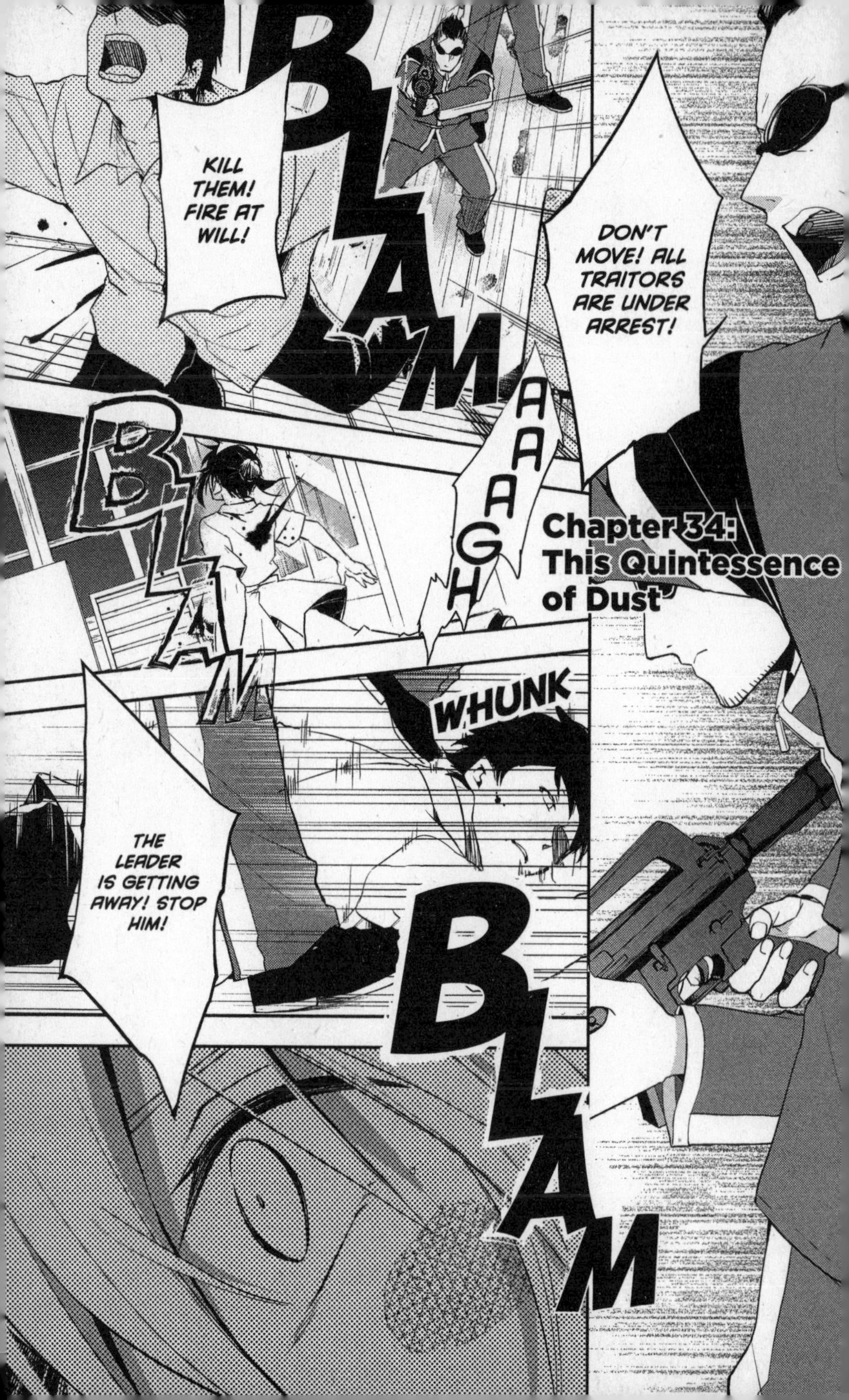
DON'T MOVE! ALL TRAITORS ARE UNDER ARREST!
KILL THEM! FIRE AT WILL!
BLAM
BLAM
AAAAGH
WHUNK
THE LEADER IS GETTING AWAY! STOP HIM!
BLAM

Chapter 34: This Quintessence of Dust

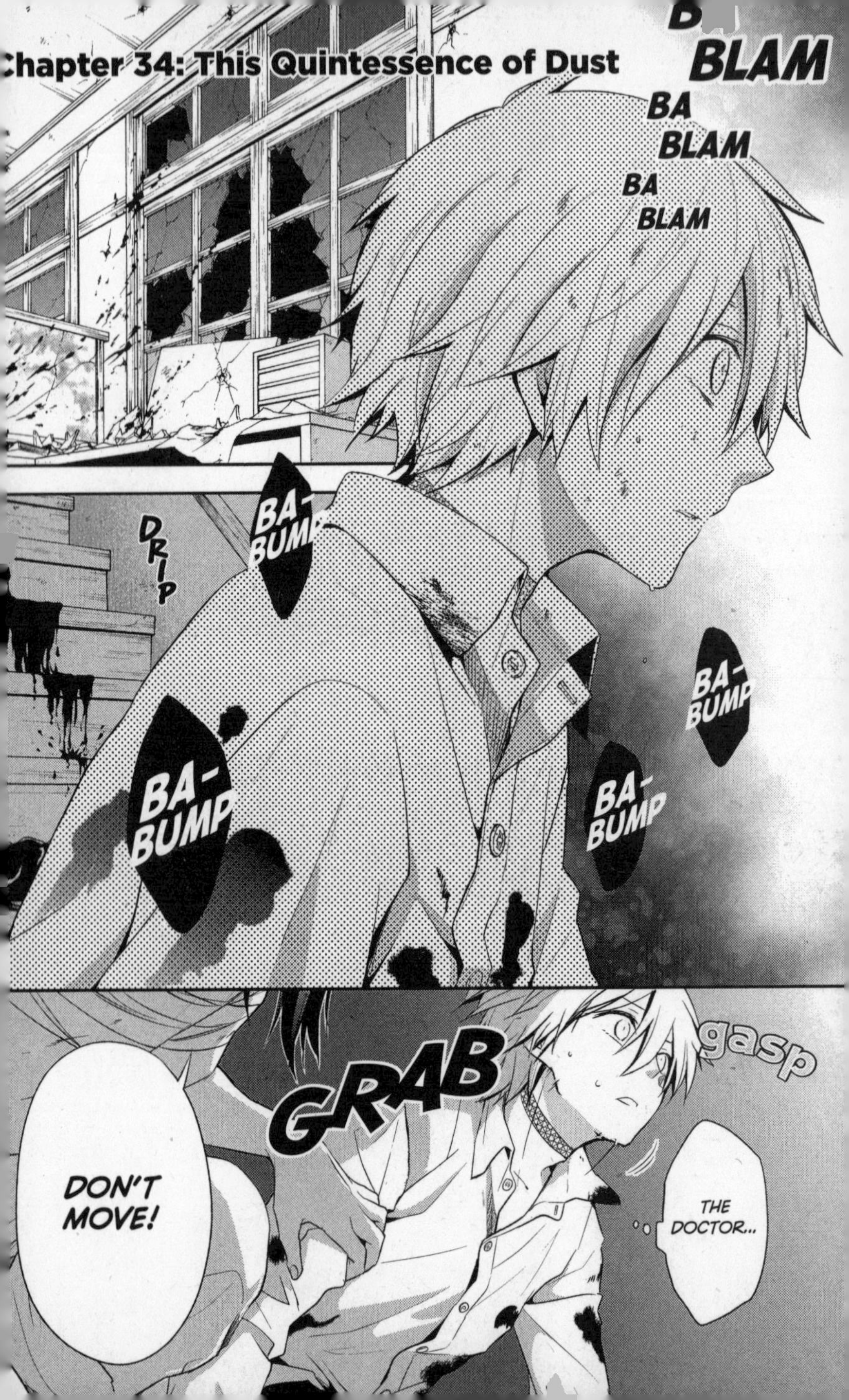
BLAM
BA BLAM
BA BLAM
BA-BUMP
DRIP
BA-BUMP
BA-BUMP
BA-BUMP
gasp
GRAB
THE DOCTOR...
DON'T MOVE!

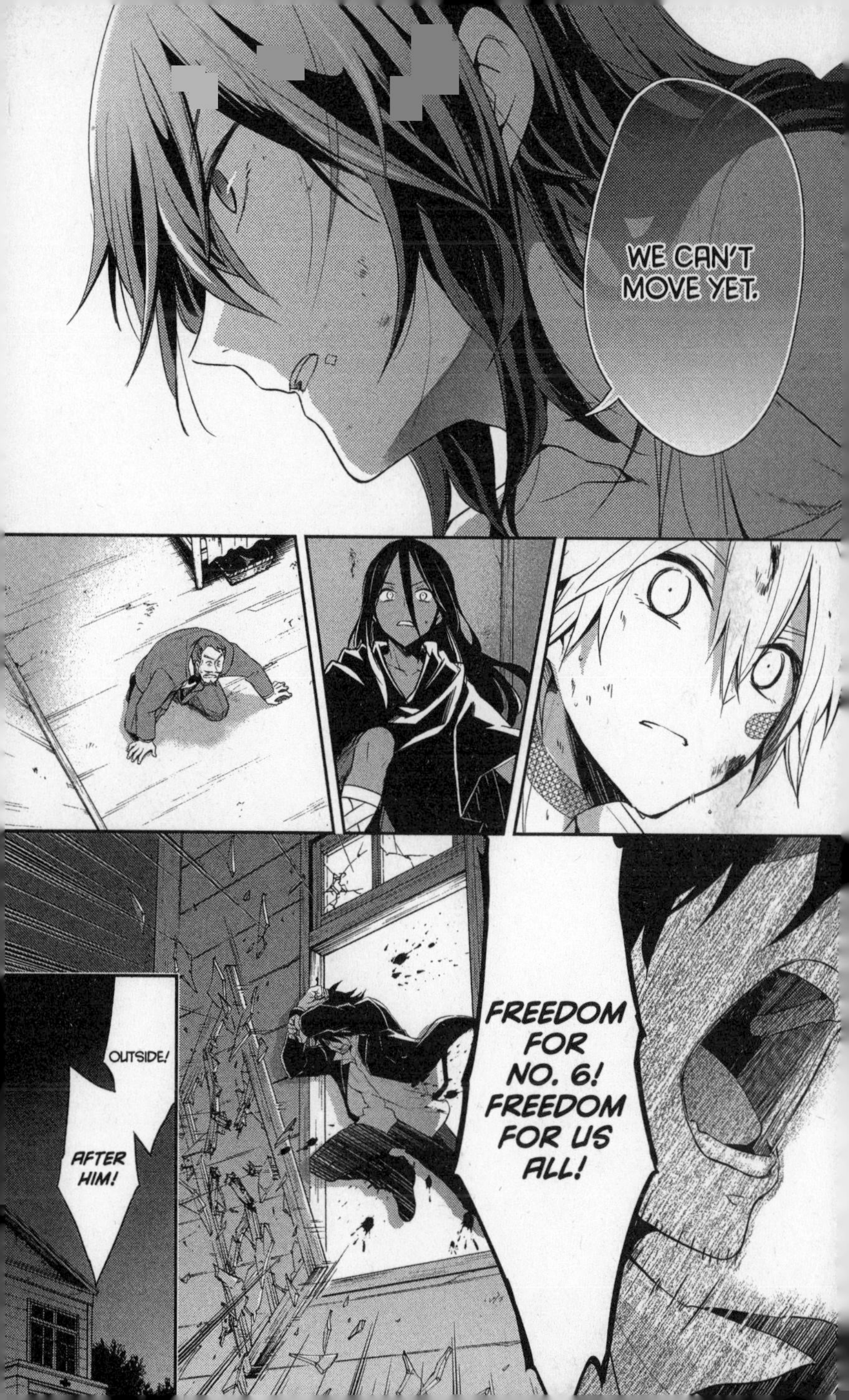
WE CAN'T MOVE YET.
FREEDOM FOR NO. 6! FREEDOM FOR US ALL!
OUTSIDE!
AFTER HIM!

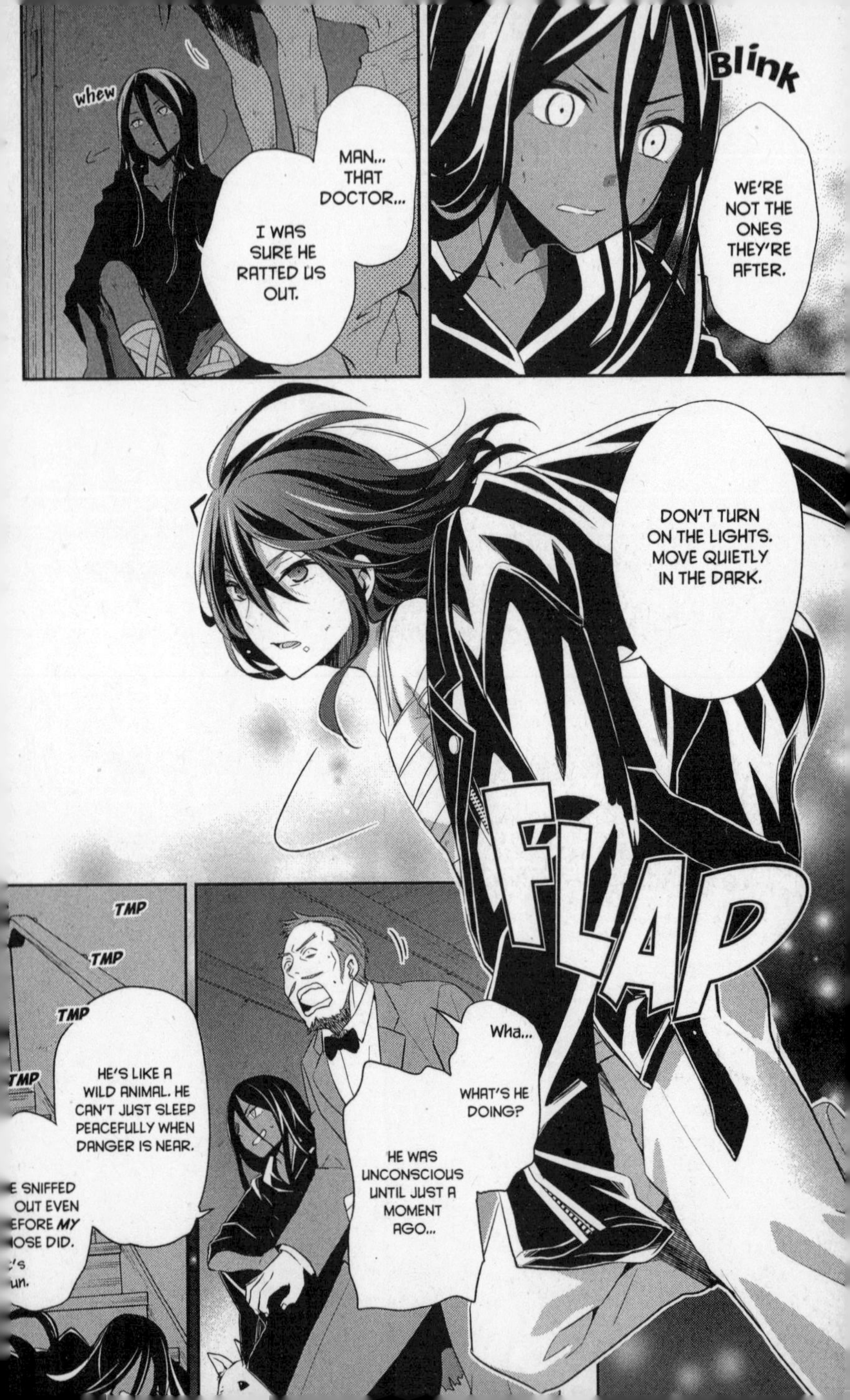
Blink
WE'RE NOT THE ONES THEY'RE AFTER.
whew
MAN... THAT DOCTOR...
I WAS SURE HE RATTED US OUT.
DON'T TURN ON THE LIGHTS. MOVE QUIETLY IN THE DARK.
FLAP
Wha...
WHAT'S HE DOING?
HE WAS UNCONSCIOUS UNTIL JUST A MOMENT AGO...
TMP
TMP
TMP
TMP
HE'S LIKE A WILD ANIMAL. HE CAN'T JUST SLEEP PEACEFULLY WHEN DANGER IS NEAR.
E SNIFFED OUT EVEN EFORE MY OSE DID.

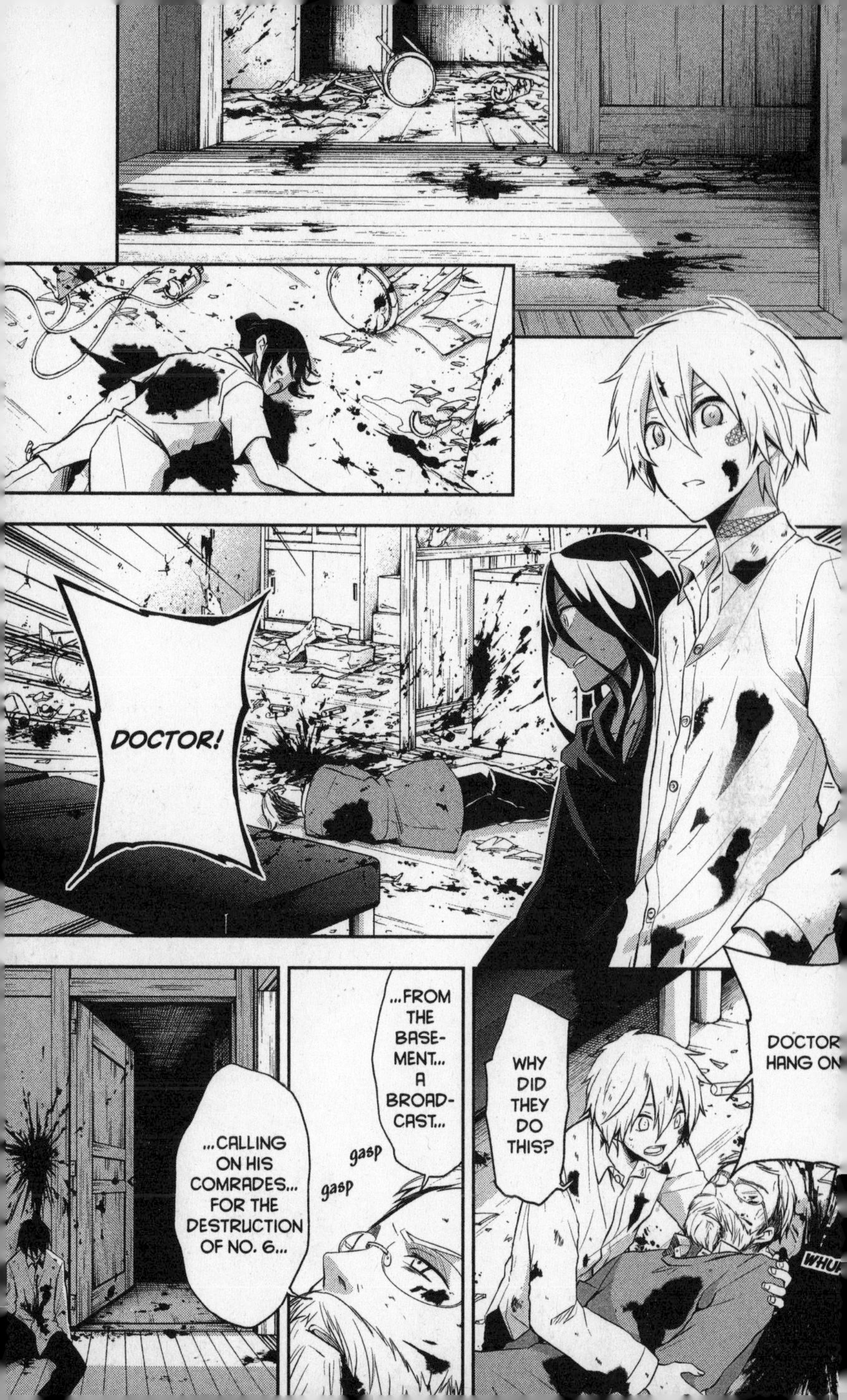
DOCTOR!
DOCTOR HANG ON
WHY DID THEY DO THIS?
WHU
...FROM THE BASEMENT... A BROADCAST...
gasp
gasp
...CALLING ON HIS COMRADES... FOR THE DESTRUCTION OF NO. 6...

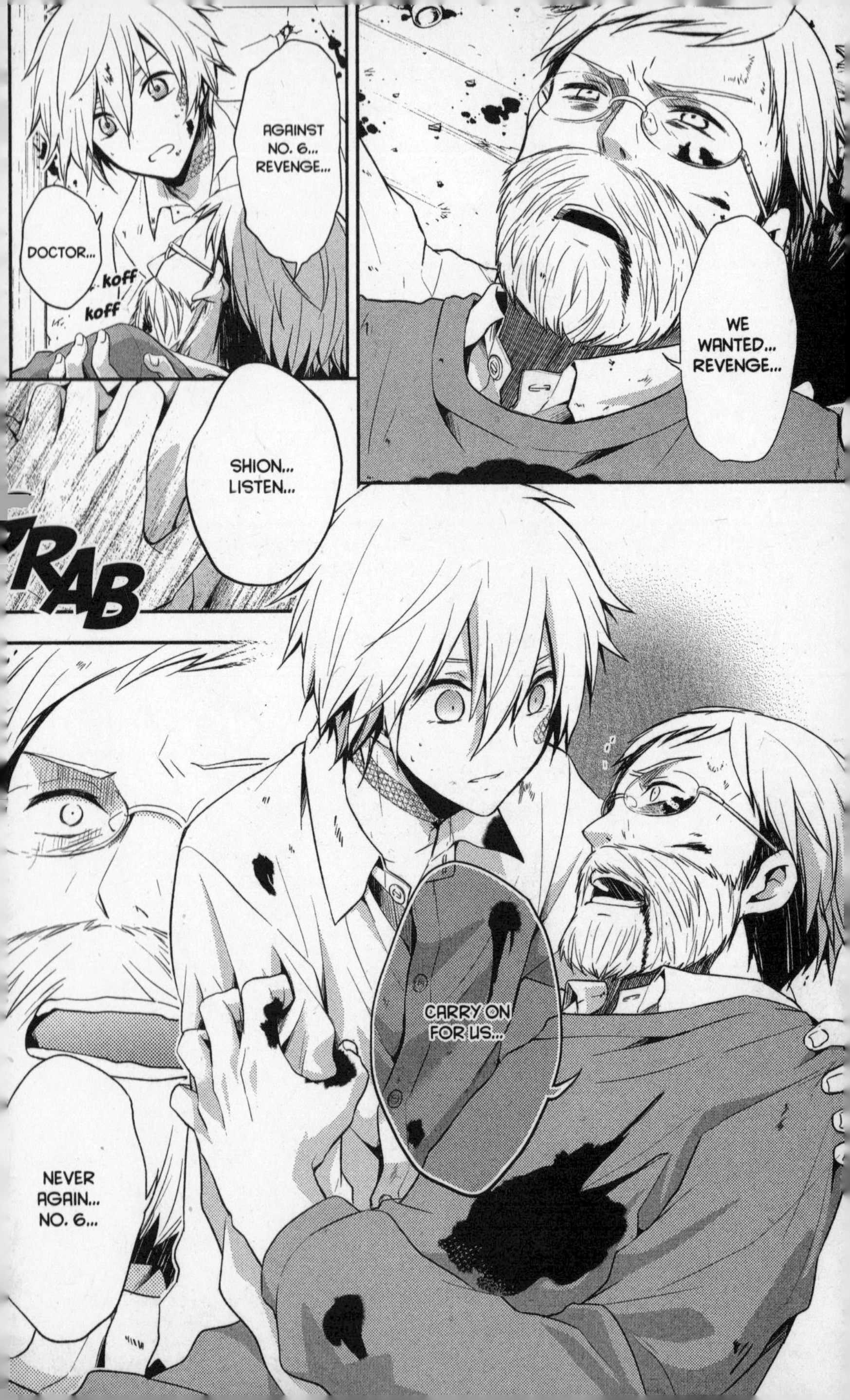
WE WANTED... REVENGE...
AGAINST NO. 6... REVENGE...
DOCTOR...
koff koff
RAB
SHION... LISTEN...
CARRY ON FOR US...
NEVER AGAIN... NO. 6...

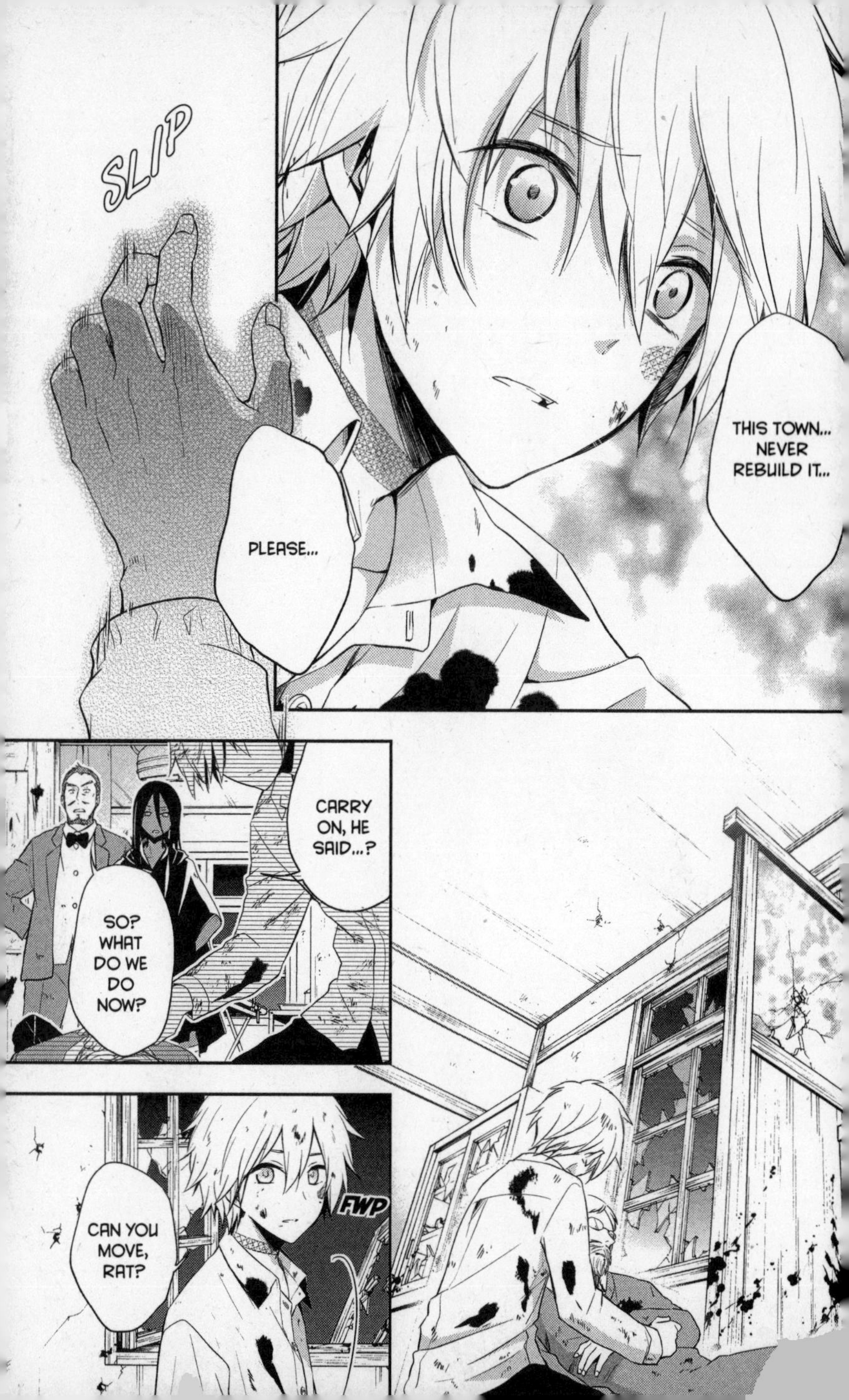
THIS TOWN... NEVER REBUILD IT...
PLEASE...
SLIP
CARRY ON, HE SAID...?
SO? WHAT DO WE DO NOW?
FWP
CAN YOU MOVE, RAT?

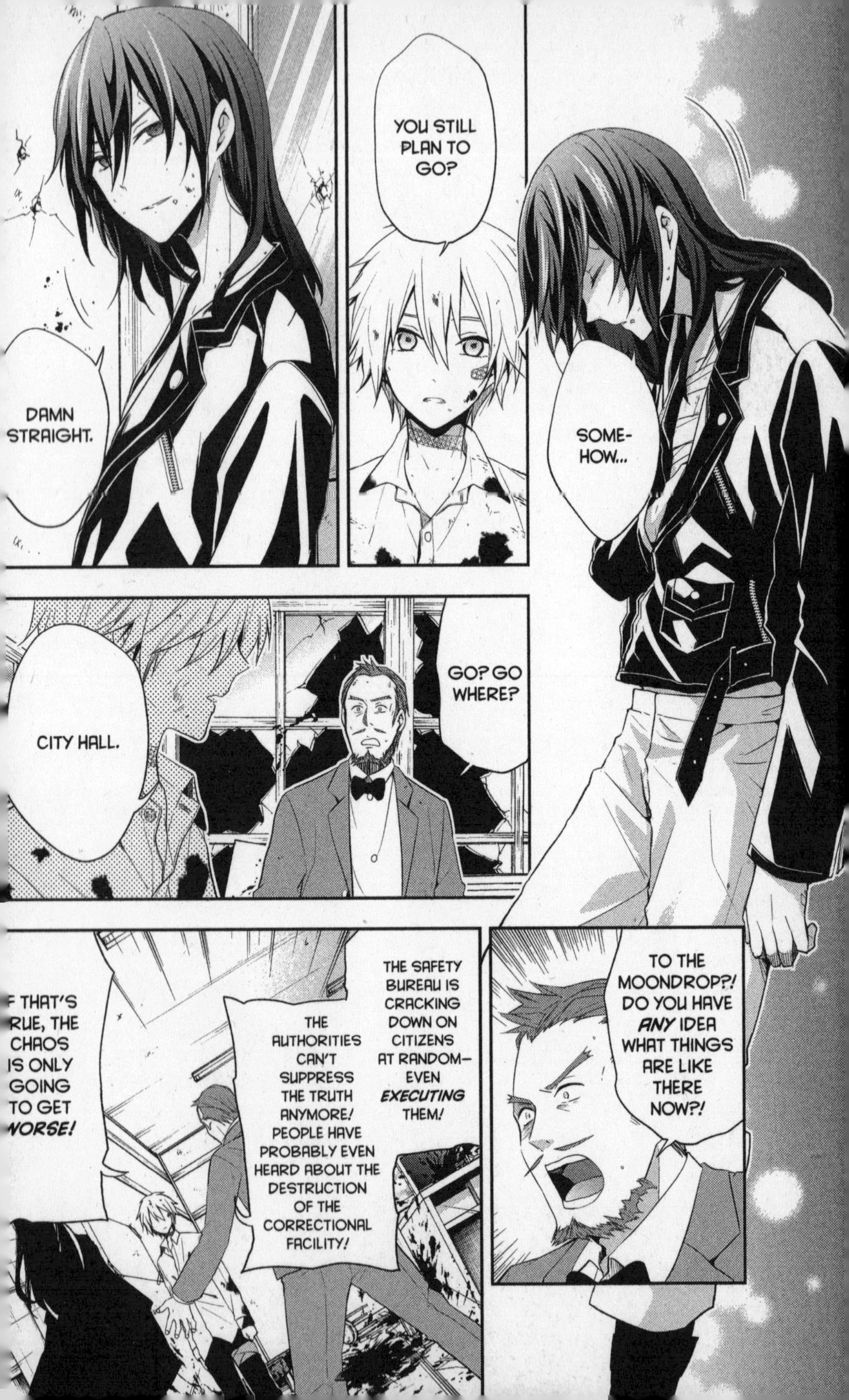
SOME-HOW...
YOU STILL PLAN TO GO?
DAMN STRAIGHT.
GO? GO WHERE?
CITY HALL.
TO THE MOONDROP?! DO YOU HAVE ANY IDEA WHAT THINGS ARE LIKE THERE NOW?!
THE SAFETY BUREAU IS CRACKING DOWN ON CITIZENS AT RANDOM— EVEN EXECUTING THEM!
THE AUTHORITIES CAN'T SUPPRESS THE TRUTH ANYMORE! PEOPLE HAVE PROBABLY EVEN HEARD ABOUT THE DESTRUCTION OF THE CORRECTIONAL FACILITY!
F THAT'S RUE, THE CHAOS IS ONLY GOING TO GET WORSE!

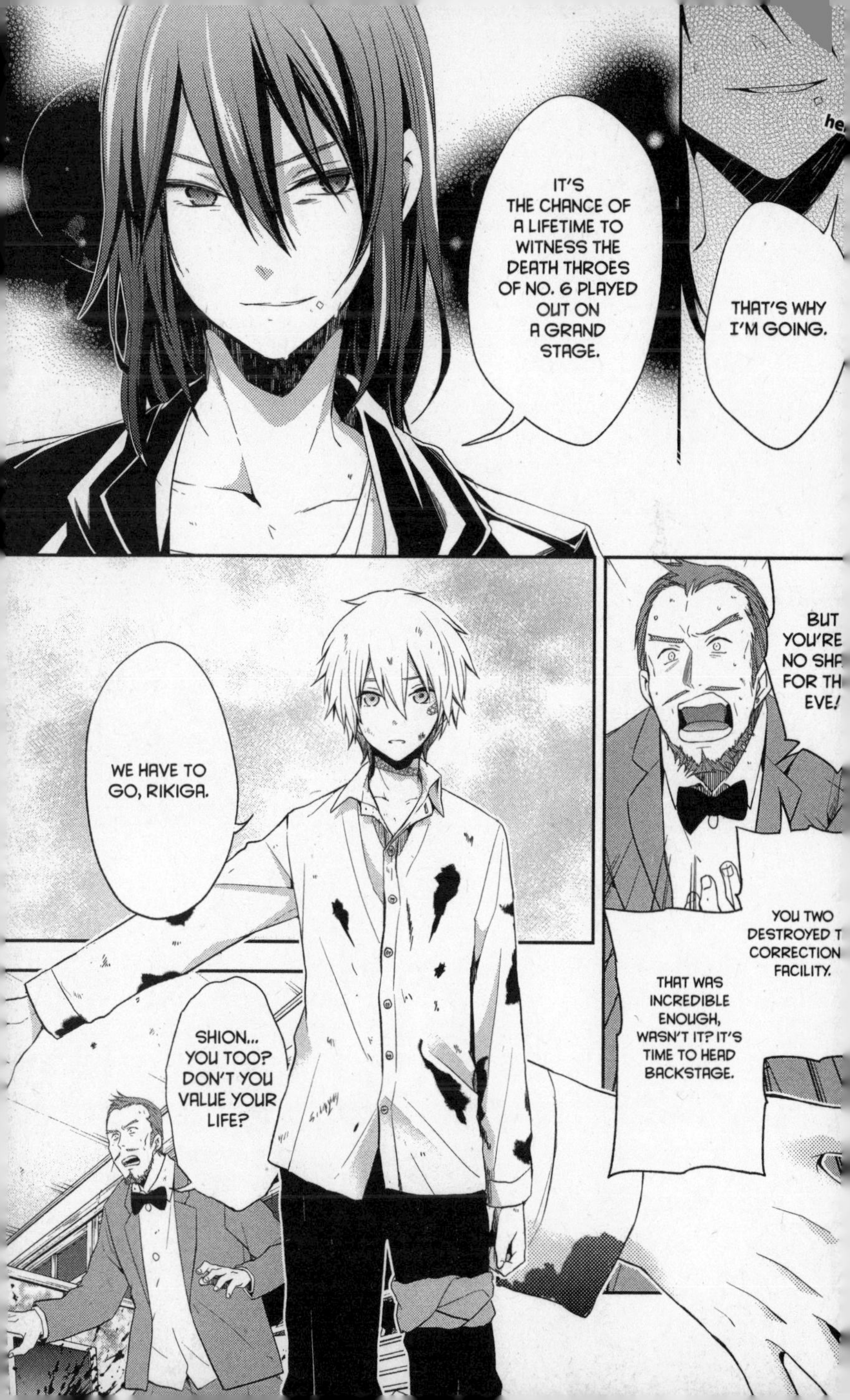
THAT'S WHY I'M GOING.
IT'S THE CHANCE OF A LIFETIME TO WITNESS THE DEATH THROES OF NO. 6 PLAYED OUT ON A GRAND STAGE.
BUT YOU'RE NO SHA FOR TH EVE!
YOU TWO DESTROYED T CORRECTION FACILITY.
THAT WAS INCREDIBLE ENOUGH, WASN'T IT? IT'S TIME TO HEAD BACKSTAGE.
WE HAVE TO GO, RIKIGA.
SHION... YOU TOO? DON'T YOU VALUE YOUR LIFE?

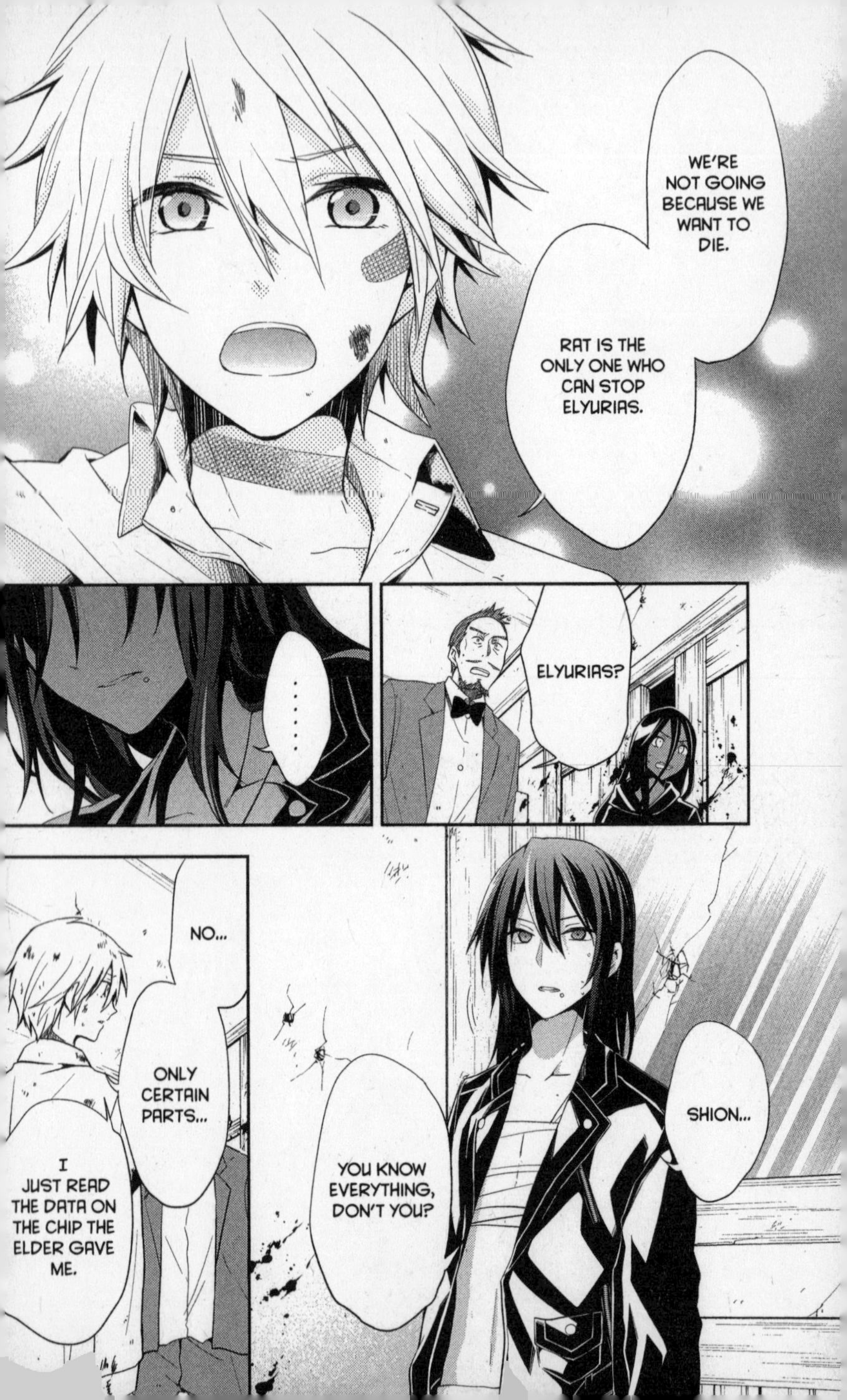
WE'RE NOT GOING BECAUSE WE WANT TO DIE.
RAT IS THE ONLY ONE WHO CAN STOP ELYURIAS.
ELYURIAS?
......
SHION...
YOU KNOW EVERYTHING, DON'T YOU?
NO...
ONLY CERTAIN PARTS...
I JUST READ THE DATA ON THE CHIP THE ELDER GAVE ME.

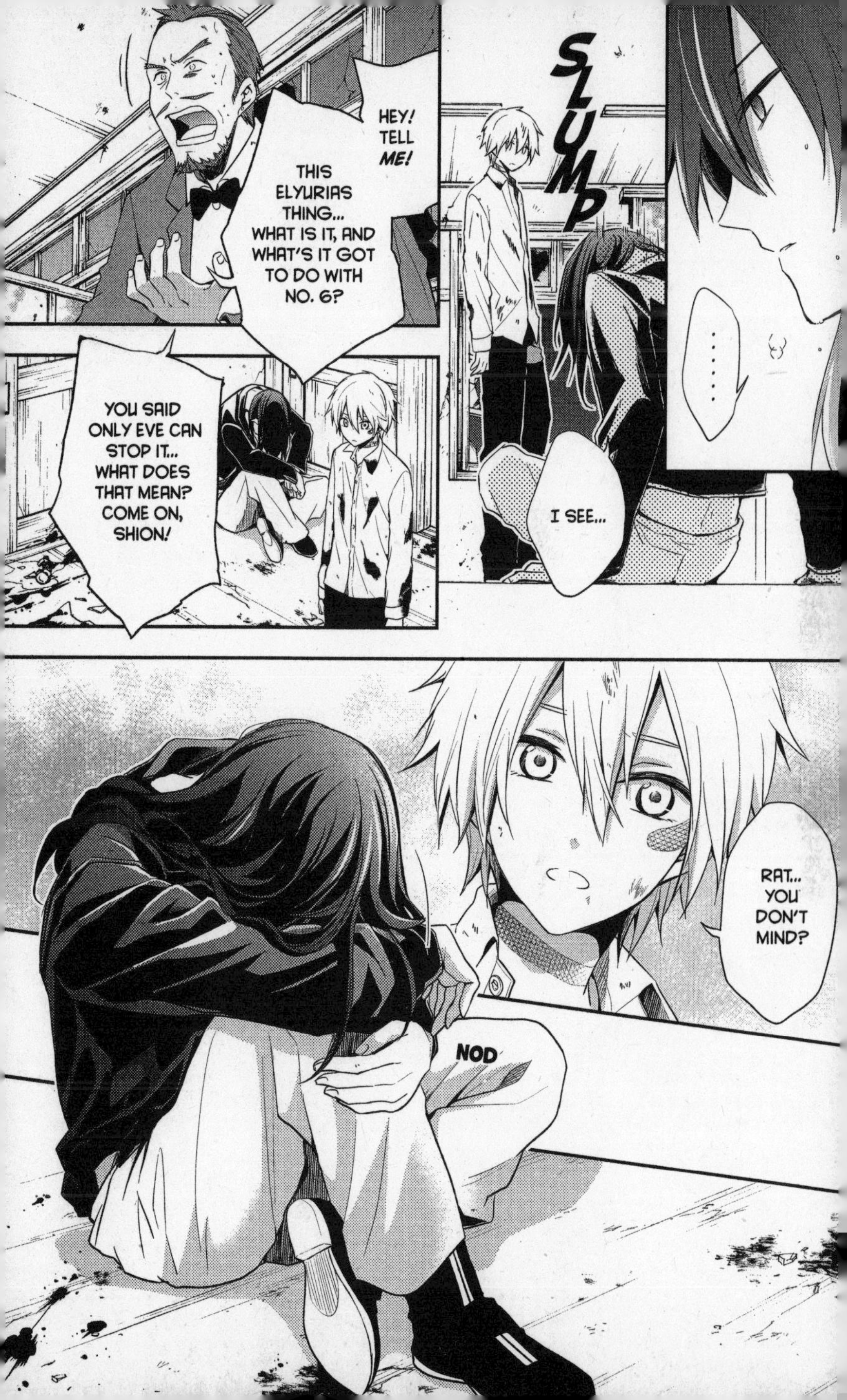
......
SLUMP
I SEE...
HEY! TELL *ME!*
THIS ELYURIAS THING... WHAT IS IT, AND WHAT'S IT GOT TO DO WITH NO. 6?
YOU SAID ONLY EVE CAN STOP IT... WHAT DOES THAT MEAN? COME ON, SHION!
RAT... YOU DON'T MIND?
NOD

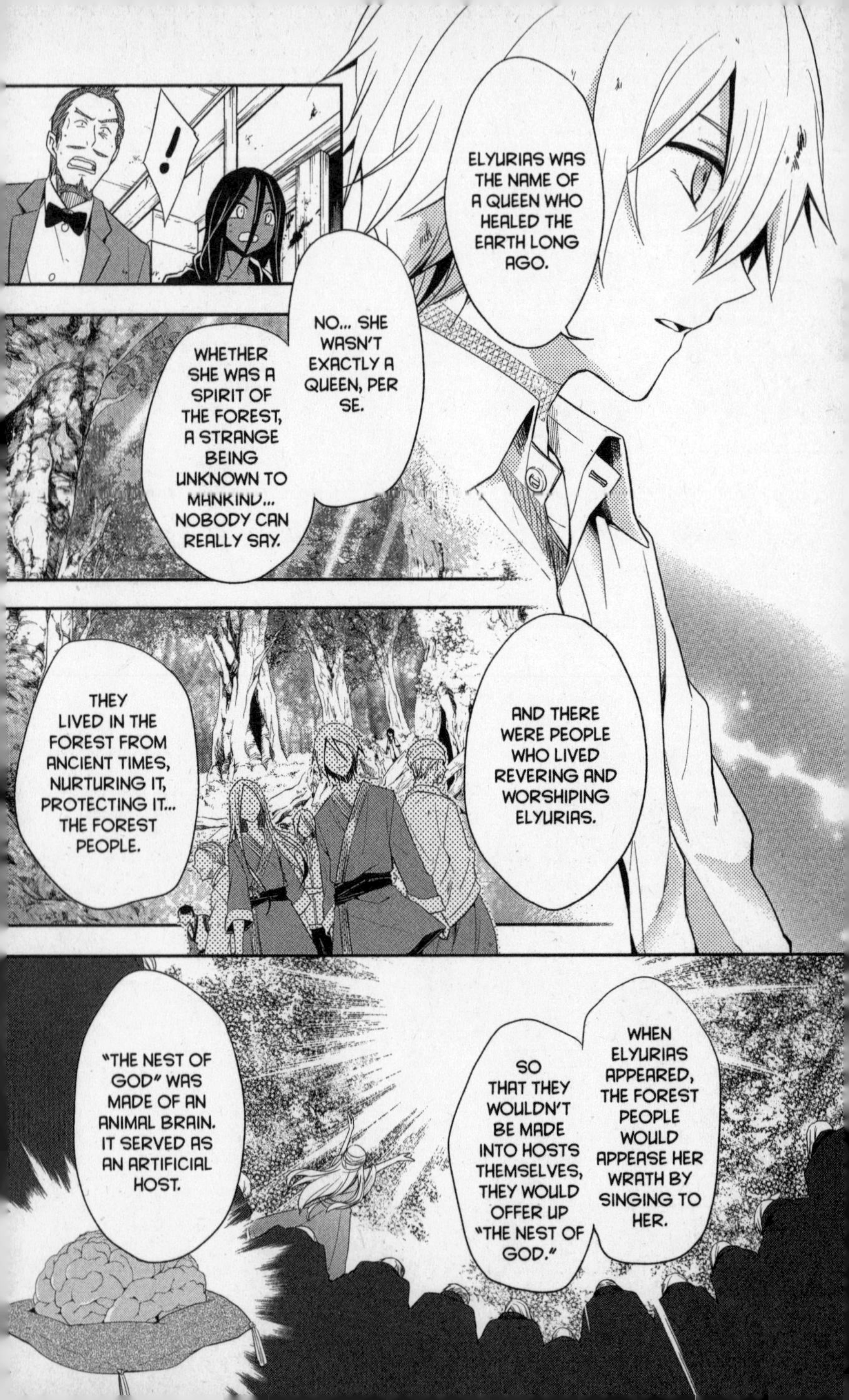
ELYURIAS WAS THE NAME OF A QUEEN WHO HEALED THE EARTH LONG AGO.
!
NO... SHE WASN'T EXACTLY A QUEEN, PER SE.
WHETHER SHE WAS A SPIRIT OF THE FOREST, A STRANGE BEING UNKNOWN TO MANKIND... NOBODY CAN REALLY SAY.
AND THERE WERE PEOPLE WHO LIVED REVERING AND WORSHIPING ELYURIAS.
THEY LIVED IN THE FOREST FROM ANCIENT TIMES, NURTURING IT, PROTECTING IT... THE FOREST PEOPLE.
WHEN ELYURIAS APPEARED, THE FOREST PEOPLE WOULD APPEASE HER WRATH BY SINGING TO HER.
SO THAT THEY WOULDN'T BE MADE INTO HOSTS THEMSELVES, THEY WOULD OFFER UP "THE NEST OF GOD."
"THE NEST OF GOD" WAS MADE OF AN ANIMAL BRAIN. IT SERVED AS AN ARTIFICIAL HOST.

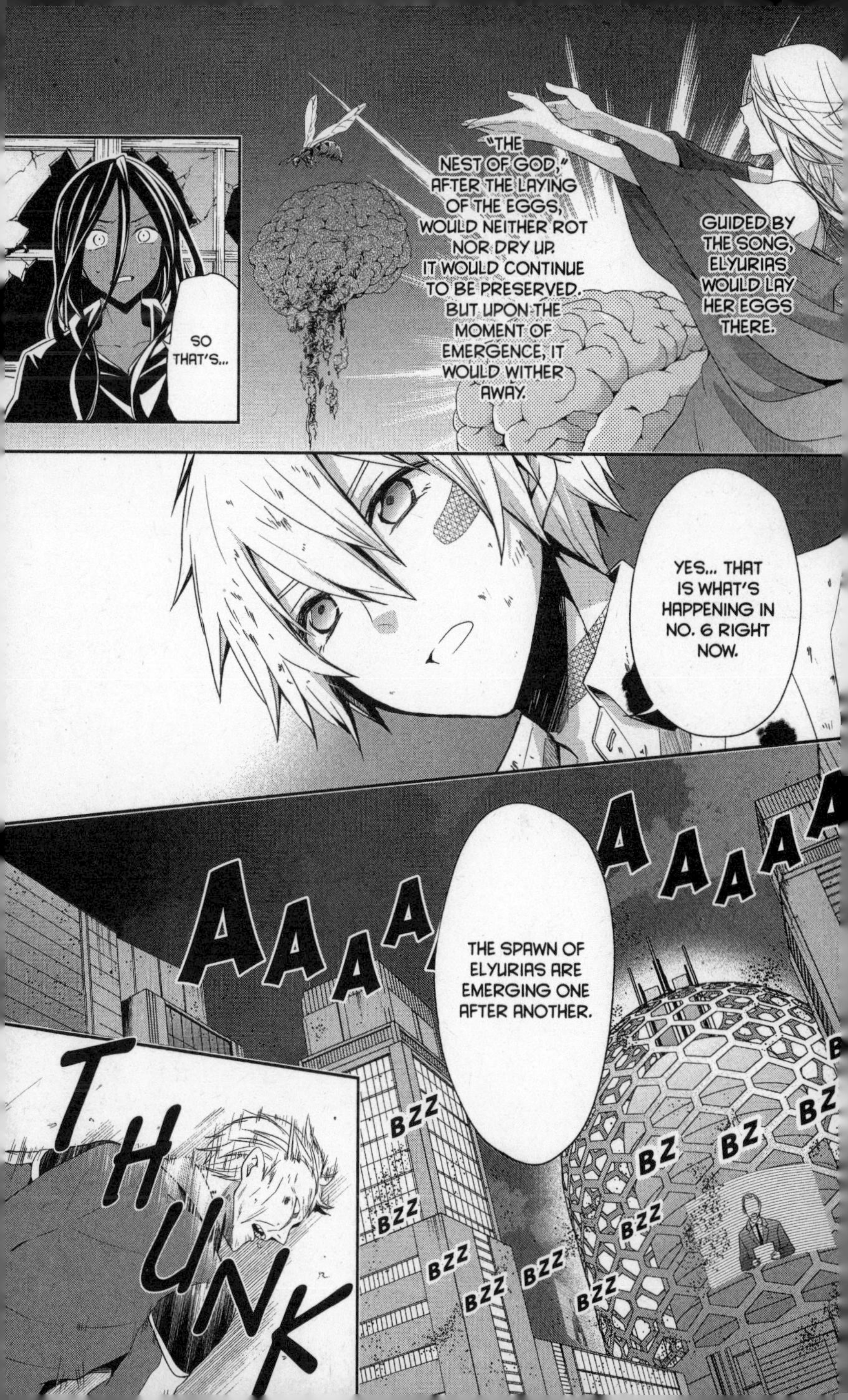
GUIDED BY THE SONG, ELYURIAS WOULD LAY HER EGGS THERE.
"THE NEST OF GOD," AFTER THE LAYING OF THE EGGS, WOULD NEITHER ROT NOR DRY UP. IT WOULD CONTINUE TO BE PRESERVED. BUT UPON THE MOMENT OF EMERGENCE, IT WOULD WITHER AWAY.
SO THAT'S...
YES... THAT IS WHAT'S HAPPENING IN NO. 6 RIGHT NOW.
AAAAAAAAA
THE SPAWN OF ELYURIAS ARE EMERGING ONE AFTER ANOTHER.
BZ BZ BZ BZ
BZZ BZZ BZZ BZZ BZZ BZZ BZZ
THUNK

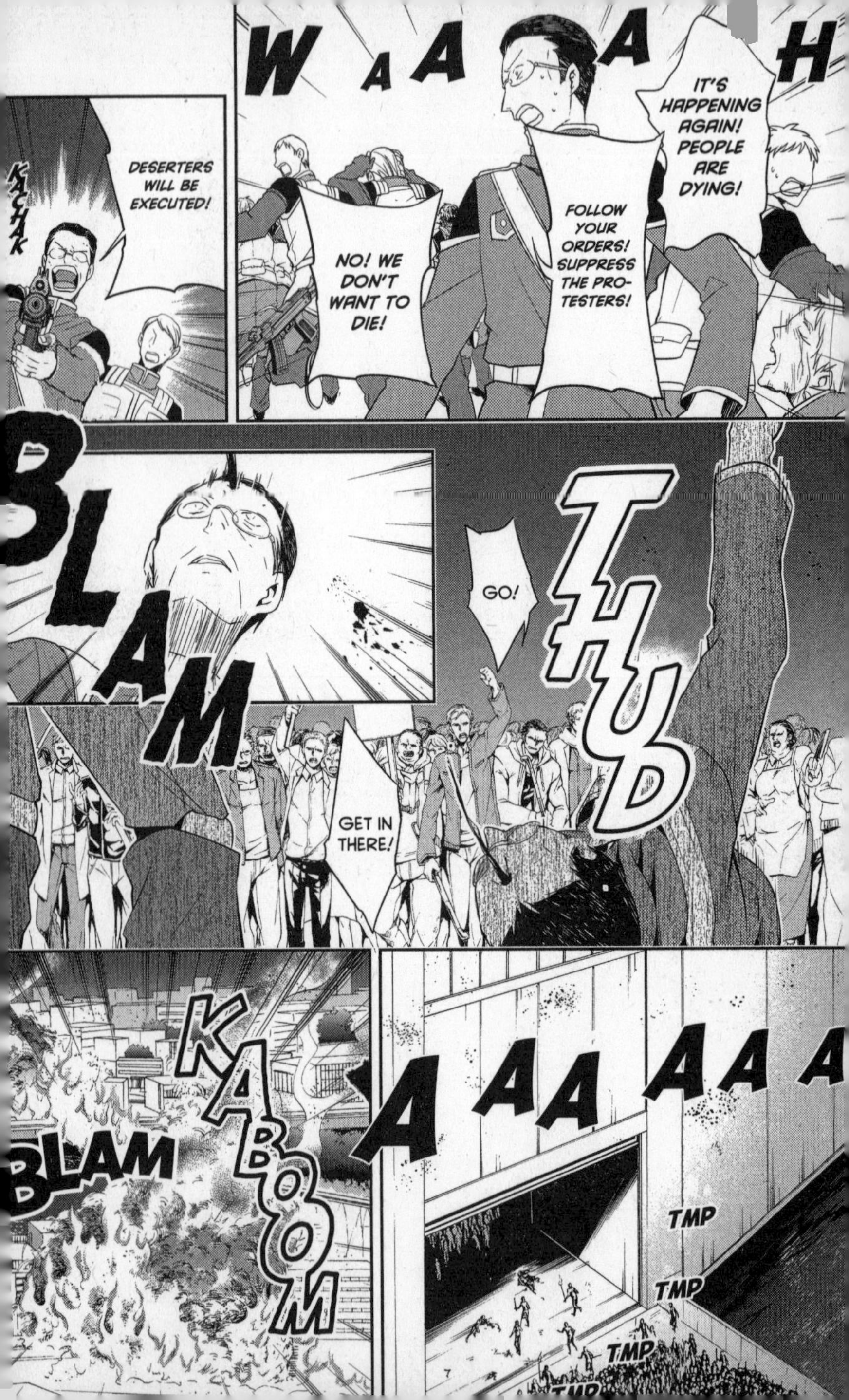
WAAAAH
IT'S HAPPENING AGAIN! PEOPLE ARE DYING!
FOLLOW YOUR ORDERS! SUPPRESS THE PROTESTERS!
NO! WE DON'T WANT TO DIE!
DESERTERS WILL BE EXECUTED!
KACHAK
BLAM
THUD
GO!
GET IN THERE!
AAAAAAAA
TMP
TMP
TMP
KABOOM
BLAM

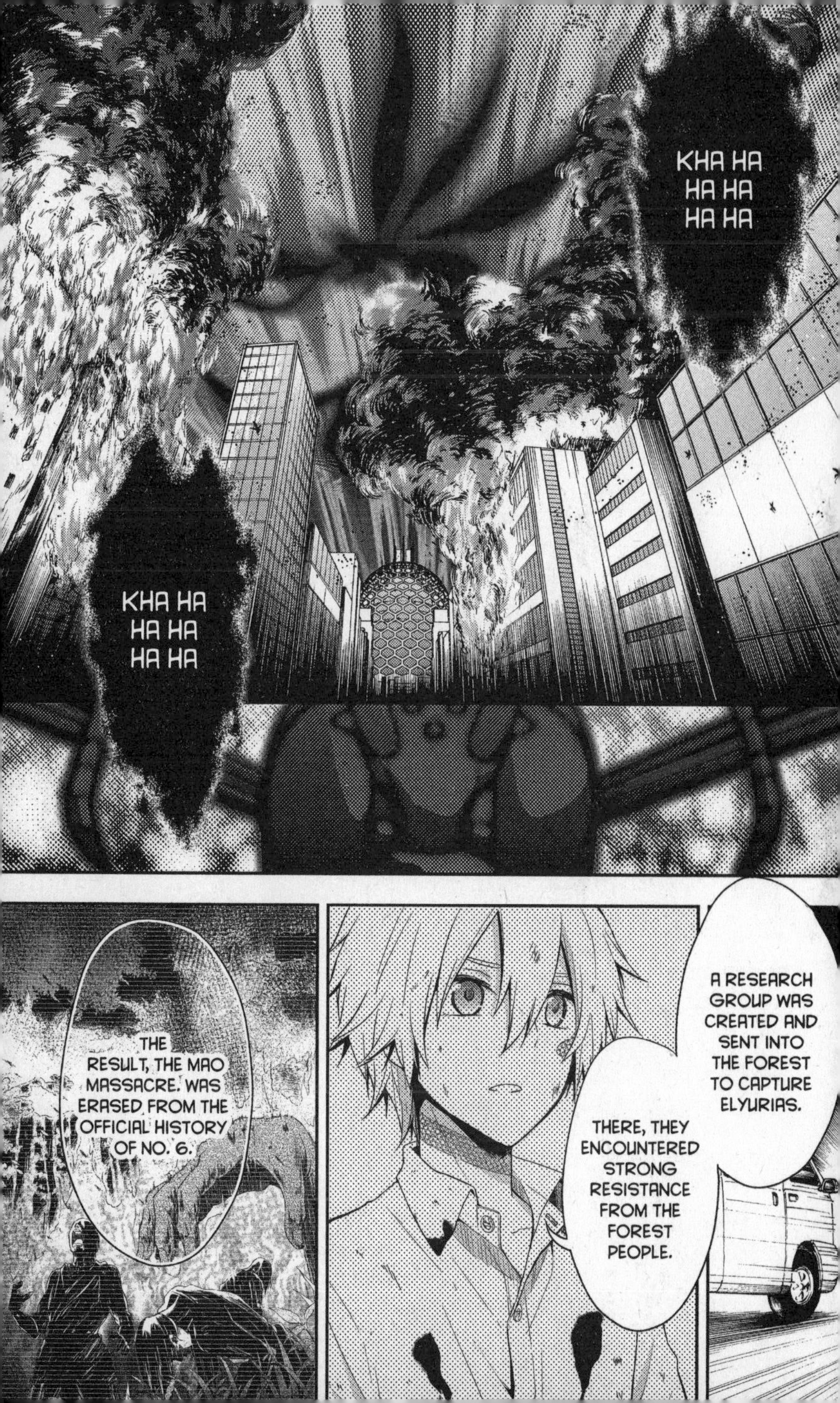
KHA HA HA HA HA HA
KHA HA HA HA HA HA
A RESEARCH GROUP WAS CREATED AND SENT INTO THE FOREST TO CAPTURE ELYURIAS.
THERE, THEY ENCOUNTERED STRONG RESISTANCE FROM THE FOREST PEOPLE.
THE RESULT, THE MAO MASSACRE, WAS ERASED FROM THE OFFICIAL HISTORY OF NO. 6.

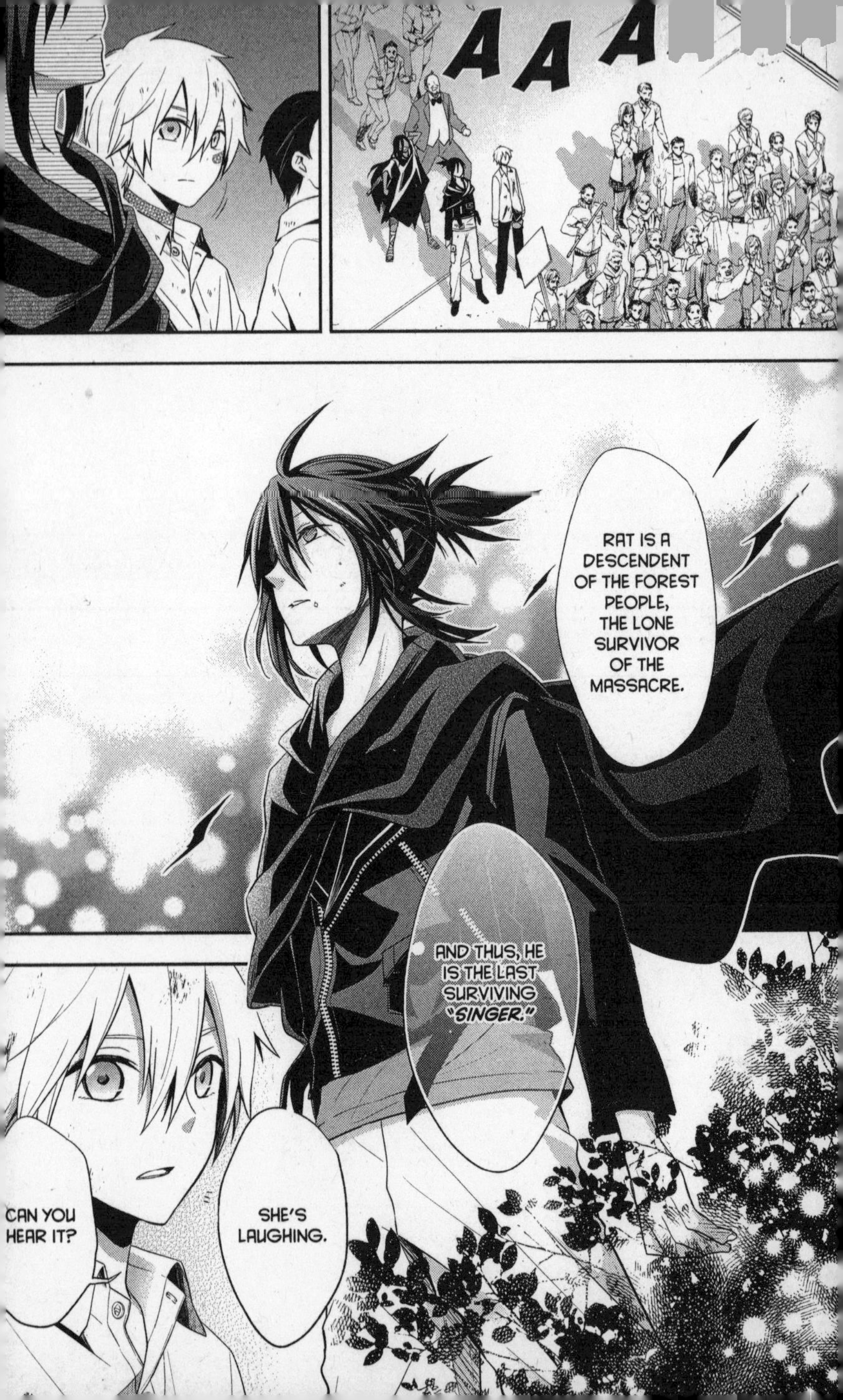
AAA
RAT IS A DESCENDENT OF THE FOREST PEOPLE, THE LONE SURVIVOR OF THE MASSACRE.
AND THUS, HE IS THE LAST SURVIVING "SINGER."
SHE'S LAUGHING.
CAN YOU HEAR IT?

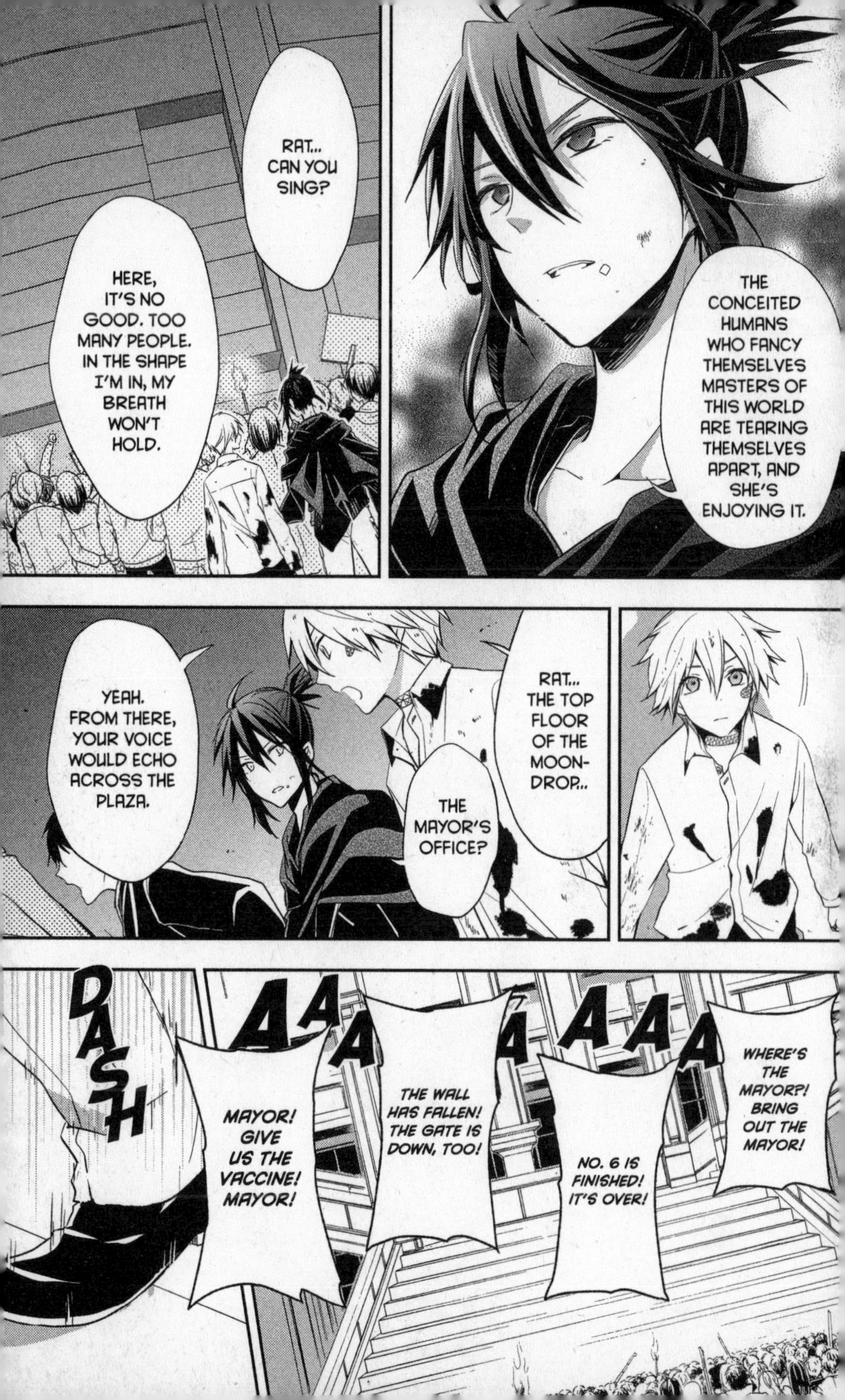
THE CONCEITED HUMANS WHO FANCY THEMSELVES MASTERS OF THIS WORLD ARE TEARING THEMSELVES APART, AND SHE'S ENJOYING IT.
RAT... CAN YOU SING?
HERE, IT'S NO GOOD. TOO MANY PEOPLE. IN THE SHAPE I'M IN, MY BREATH WON'T HOLD.
RAT... THE TOP FLOOR OF THE MOON-DROP...
THE MAYOR'S OFFICE?
YEAH. FROM THERE, YOUR VOICE WOULD ECHO ACROSS THE PLAZA.
AAAAAAAA
WHERE'S THE MAYOR?! BRING OUT THE MAYOR!
NO. 6 IS FINISHED! IT'S OVER!
THE WALL HAS FALLEN! THE GATE IS DOWN, TOO!
MAYOR! GIVE US THE VACCINE! MAYOR!
DASH

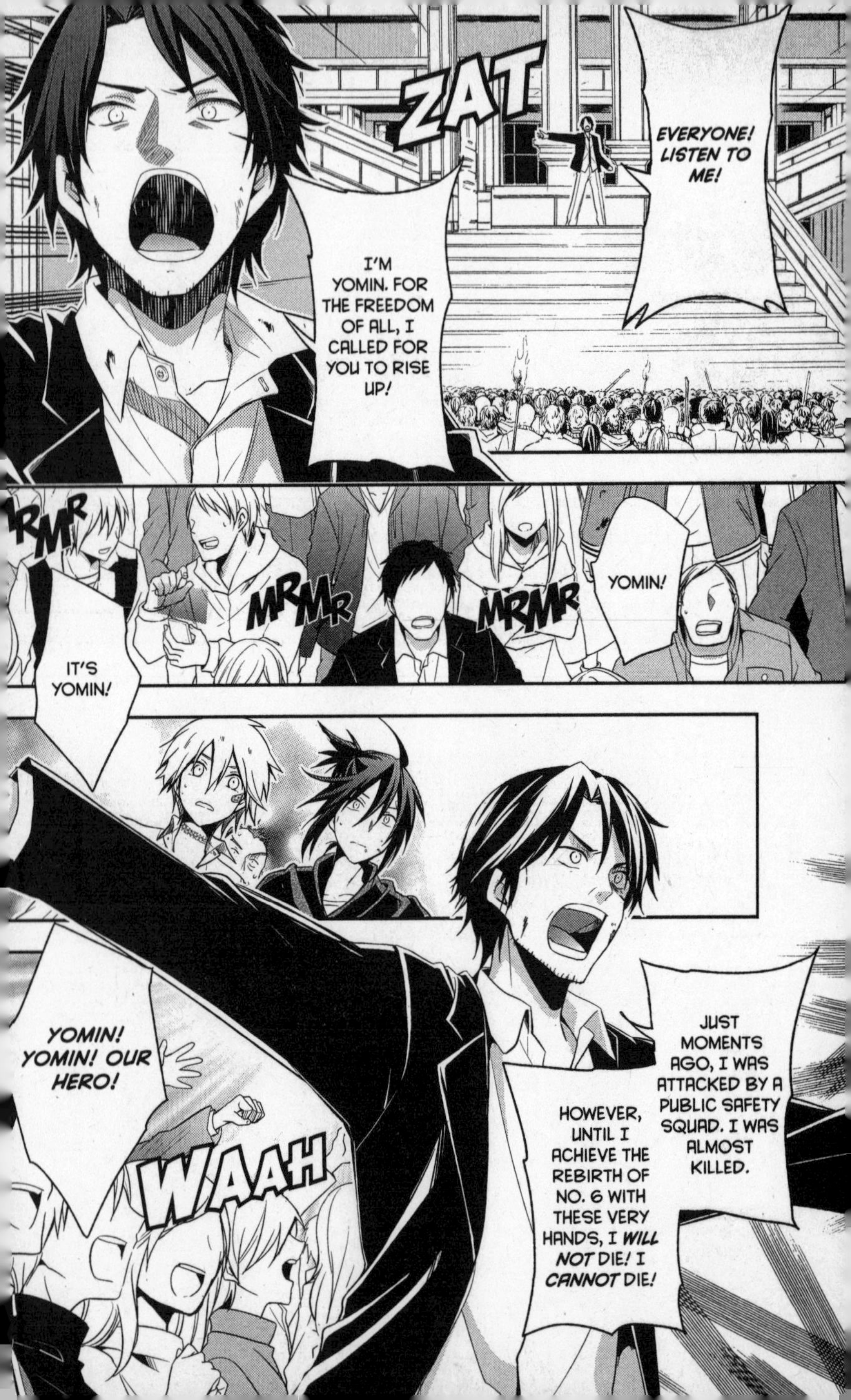
EVERYONE! LISTEN TO ME!
ZAT
I'M YOMIN. FOR THE FREEDOM OF ALL, I CALLED FOR YOU TO RISE UP!
YOMIN!
MRMR
MRMR
MRMR
IT'S YOMIN!
JUST MOMENTS AGO, I WAS ATTACKED BY A PUBLIC SAFETY SQUAD. I WAS ALMOST KILLED.
HOWEVER, UNTIL I ACHIEVE THE REBIRTH OF NO. 6 WITH THESE VERY HANDS, I *WILL NOT* DIE! I *CANNOT* DIE!
YOMIN! YOMIN! OUR HERO!
WAAH

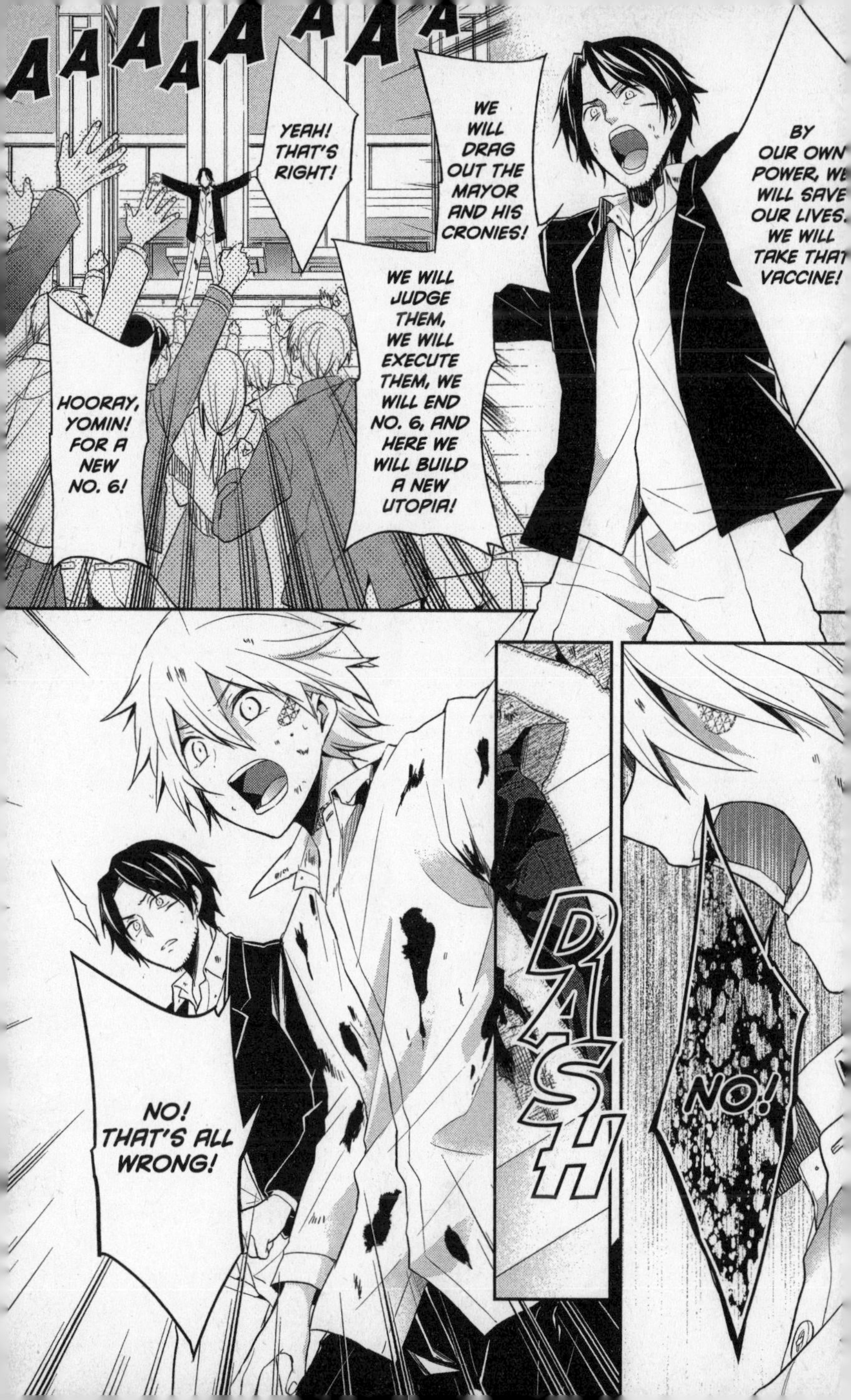
BY OUR OWN POWER, WE WILL SAVE OUR LIVES. WE WILL TAKE THAT VACCINE!
WE WILL DRAG OUT THE MAYOR AND HIS CRONIES!
YEAH! THAT'S RIGHT!
AAAAAAAA
WE WILL JUDGE THEM, WE WILL EXECUTE THEM, WE WILL END NO. 6, AND HERE WE WILL BUILD A NEW UTOPIA!
HOORAY, YOMIN! FOR A NEW NO. 6!
NO!
DASH
NO! THAT'S ALL WRONG!

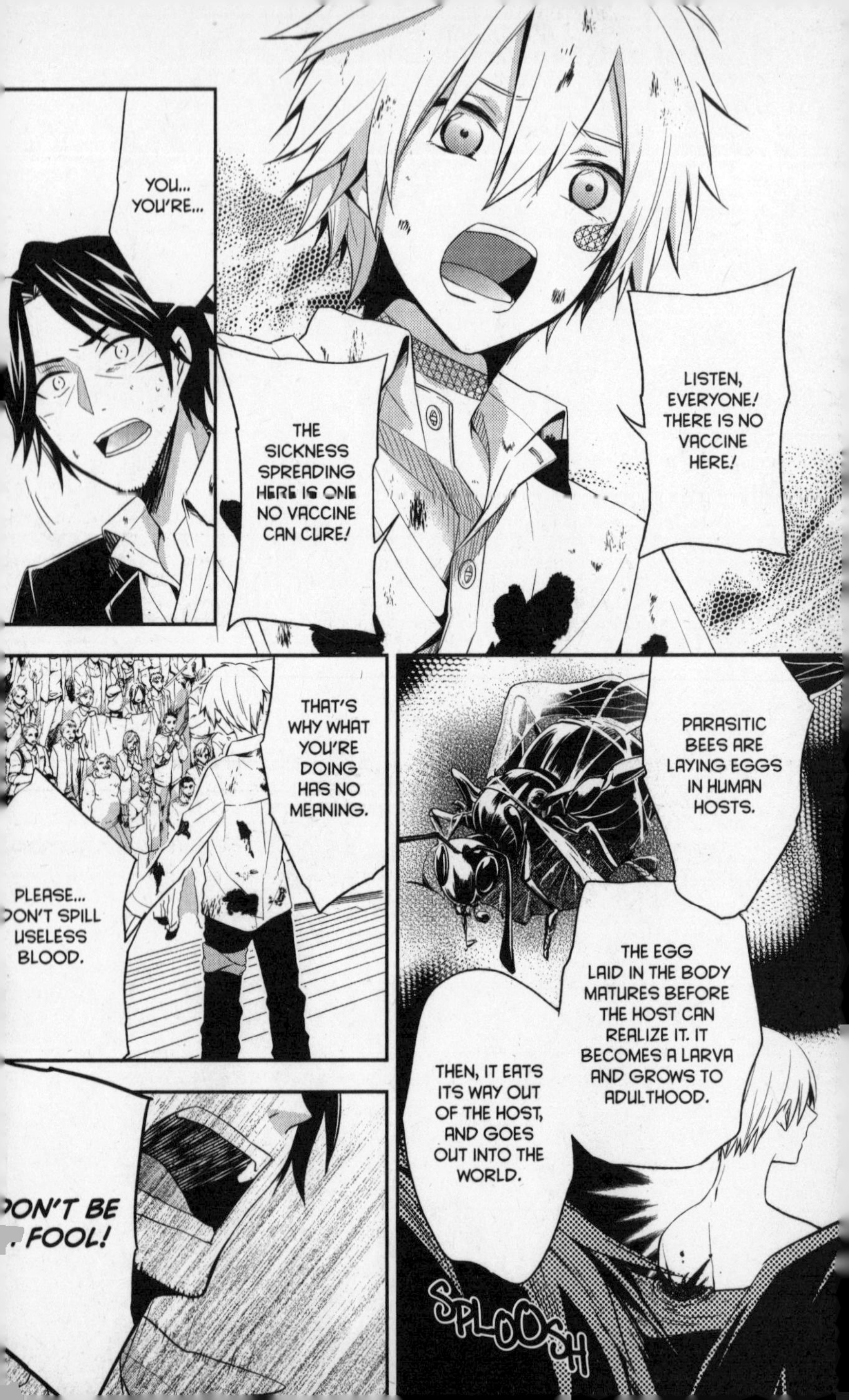
LISTEN, EVERYONE! THERE IS NO VACCINE HERE!
THE SICKNESS SPREADING HERE IS ONE NO VACCINE CAN CURE!
YOU... YOU'RE...
PARASITIC BEES ARE LAYING EGGS IN HUMAN HOSTS.
THE EGG LAID IN THE BODY MATURES BEFORE THE HOST CAN REALIZE IT. IT BECOMES A LARVA AND GROWS TO ADULTHOOD.
THEN, IT EATS ITS WAY OUT OF THE HOST, AND GOES OUT INTO THE WORLD.
SPLOOSH
THAT'S WHY WHAT YOU'RE DOING HAS NO MEANING.
PLEASE... DON'T SPILL USELESS BLOOD.
DON'T BE
FOOL!

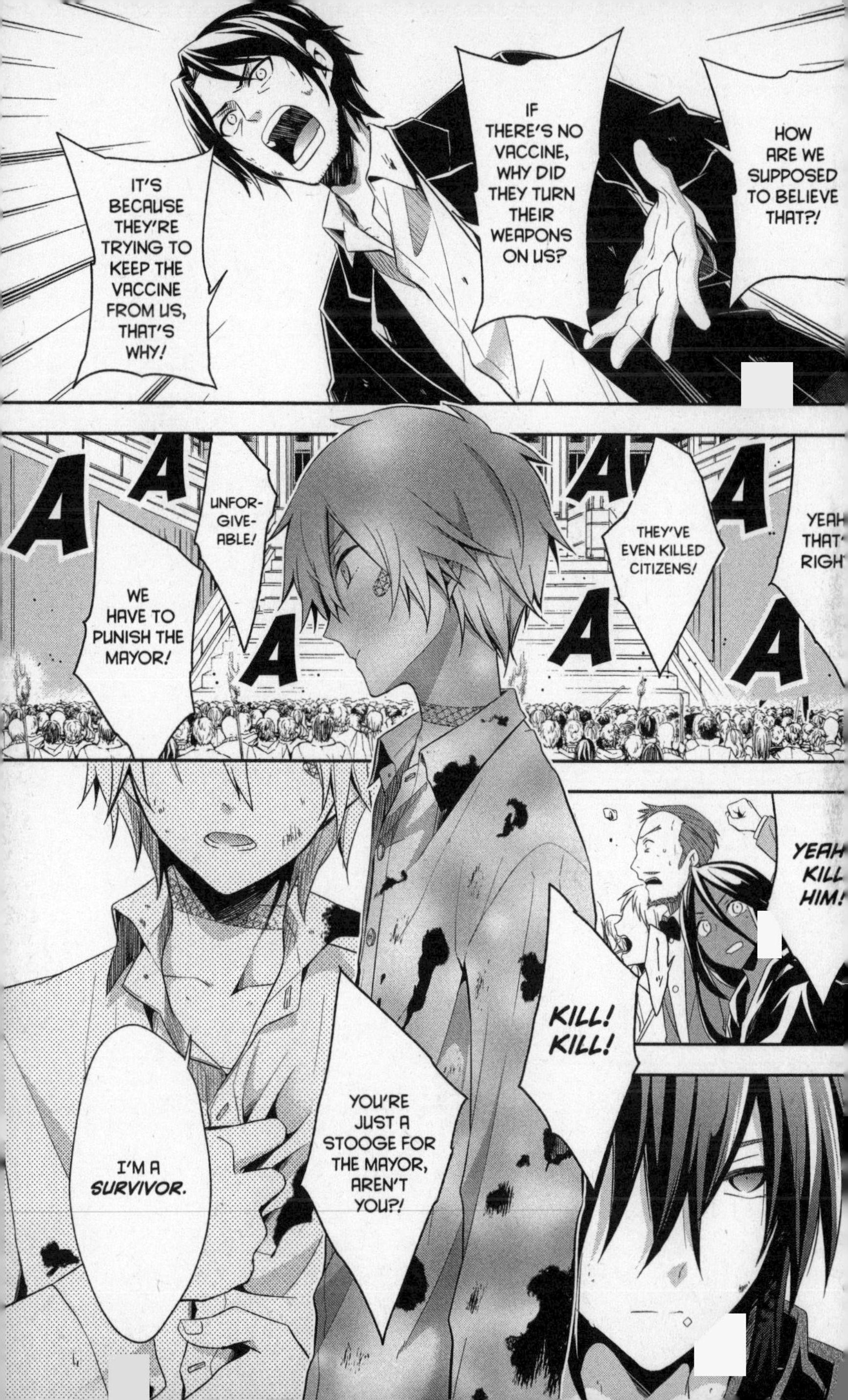
HOW ARE WE SUPPOSED TO BELIEVE THAT?!
IF THERE'S NO VACCINE, WHY DID THEY TURN THEIR WEAPONS ON US?
IT'S BECAUSE THEY'RE TRYING TO KEEP THE VACCINE FROM US, THAT'S WHY!
YEAH THAT' RIGH
A A A
THEY'VE EVEN KILLED CITIZENS!
UNFORGIVEABLE!
A A A
WE HAVE TO PUNISH THE MAYOR!
YEAH KILL HIM!
KILL! KILL!
YOU'RE JUST A STOOGE FOR THE MAYOR, AREN'T YOU?!
I'M A *SURVIVOR.*

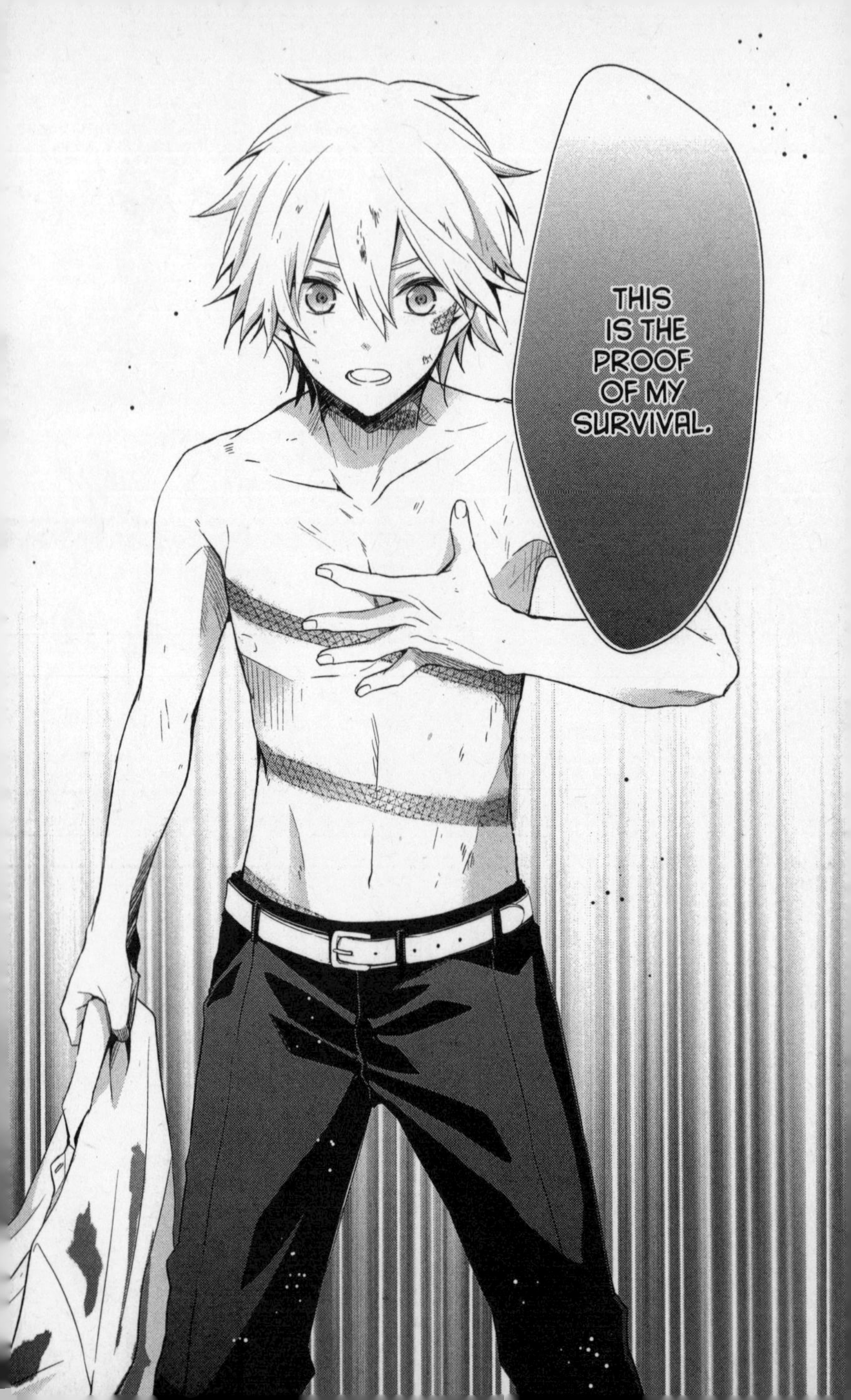
THIS IS THE PROOF OF MY SURVIVAL.

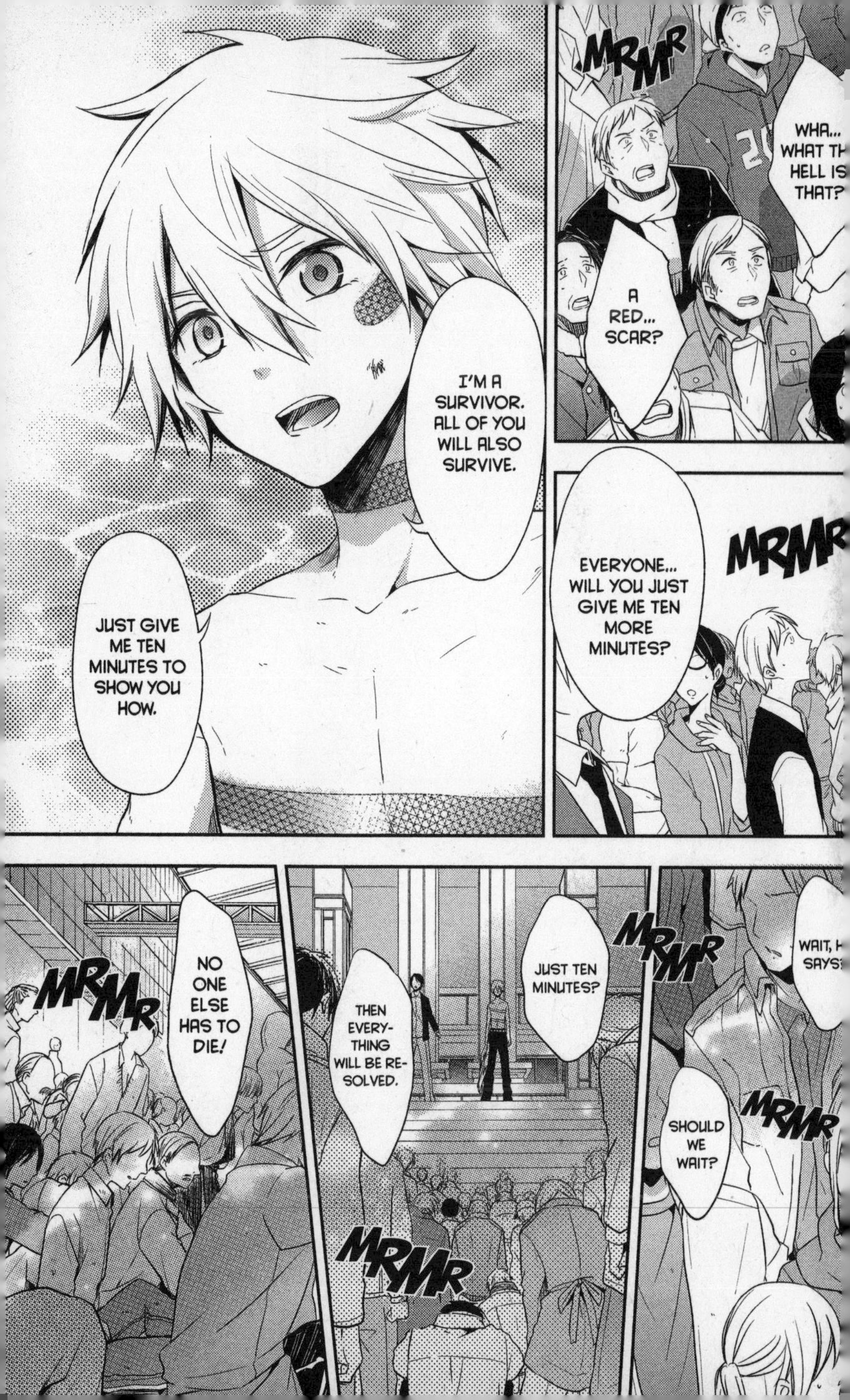
MRMR
WHA... WHAT TH HELL IS THAT?
A RED... SCAR?
MRMR
EVERYONE... WILL YOU JUST GIVE ME TEN MORE MINUTES?
I'M A SURVIVOR. ALL OF YOU WILL ALSO SURVIVE.
JUST GIVE ME TEN MINUTES TO SHOW YOU HOW.
WAIT, H SAYS?
MRMR
SHOULD WE WAIT?
MRMR
JUST TEN MINUTES?
THEN EVERY-THING WILL BE RE-SOLVED.
MRMR
NO ONE ELSE HAS TO DIE!
MRMR

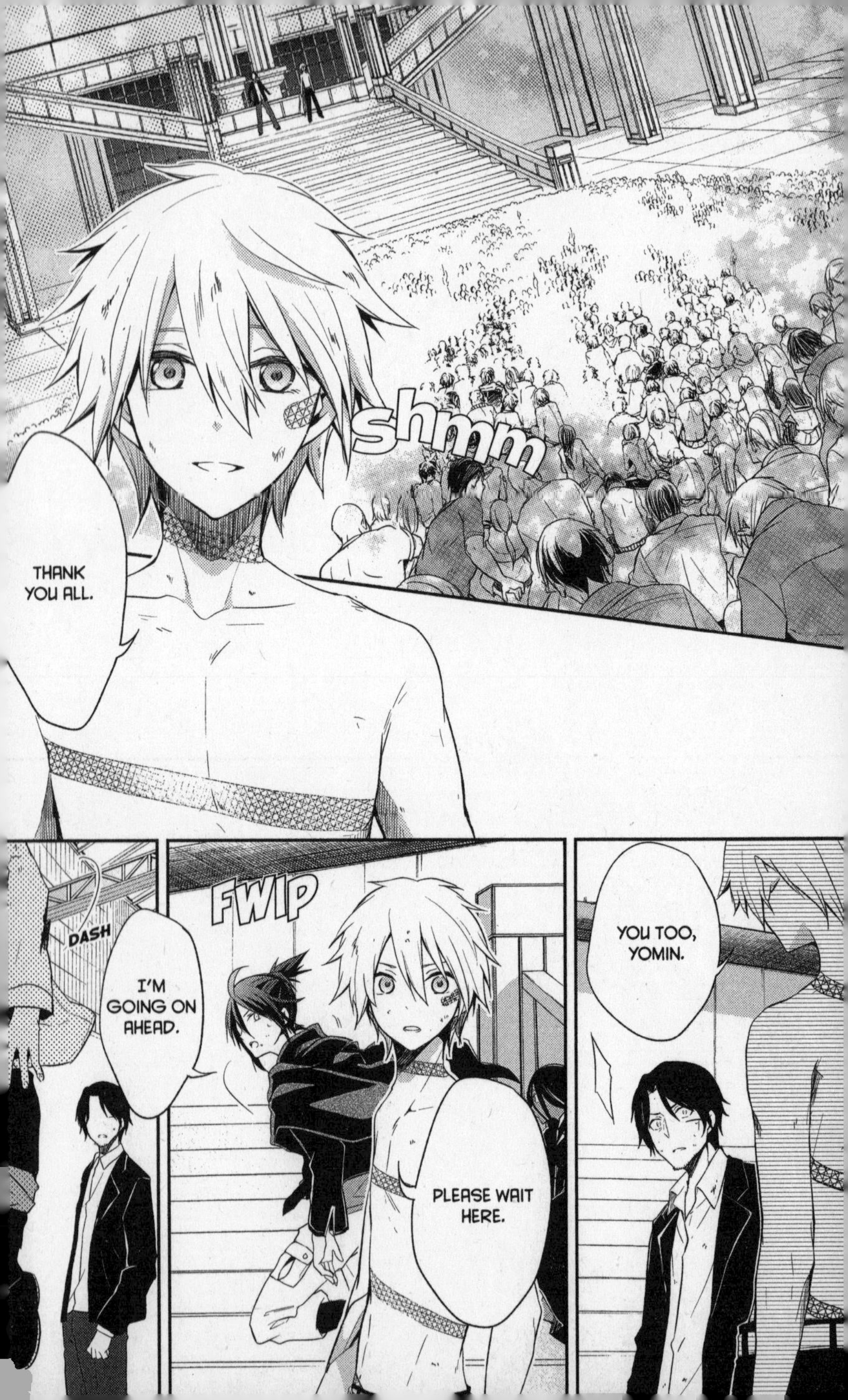
THANK YOU ALL.
shmm
DASH
FWIP
I'M GOING ON AHEAD.
PLEASE WAIT HERE.
YOU TOO, YOMIN.

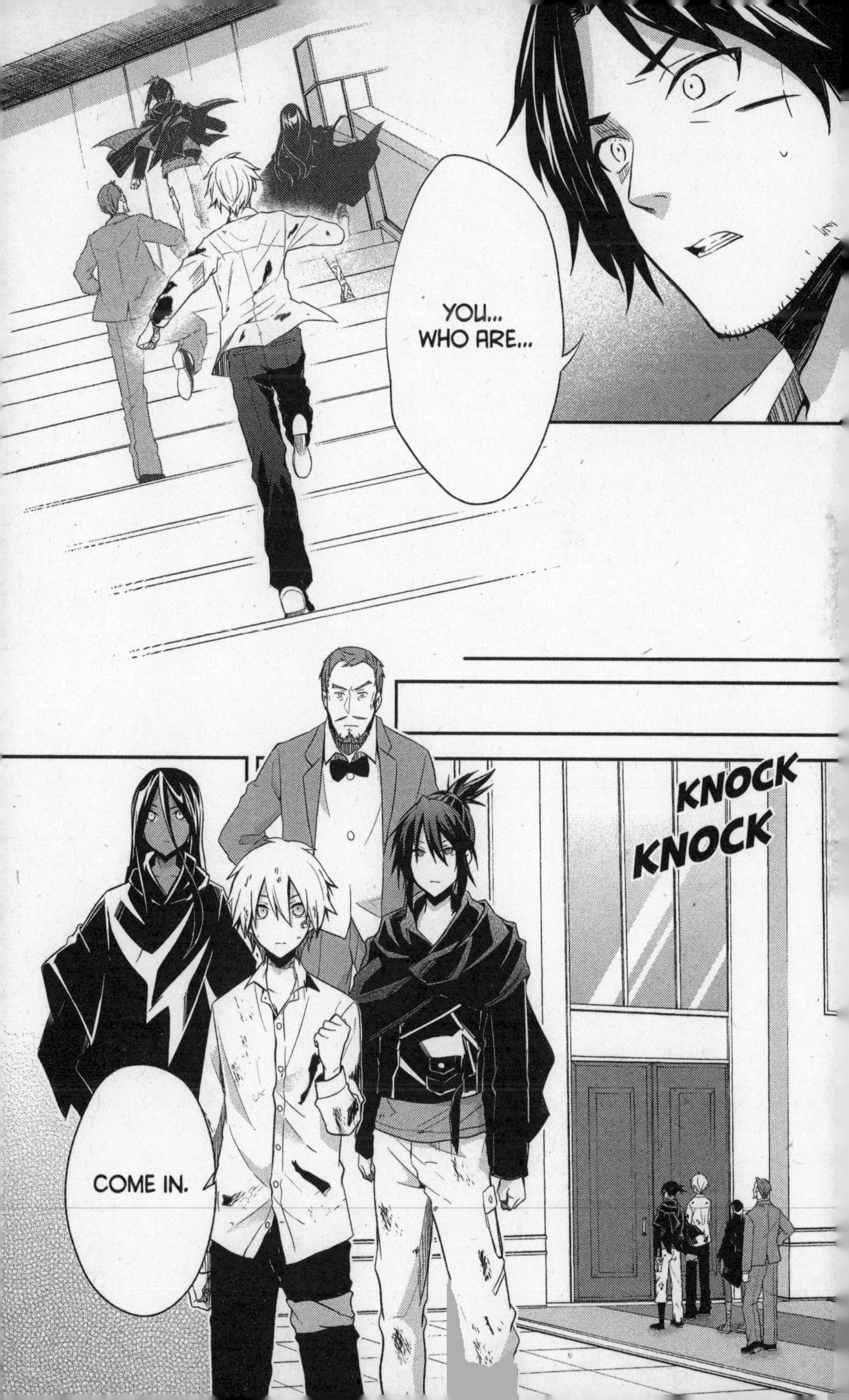
YOU... WHO ARE...
KNOCK KNOCK
COME IN.

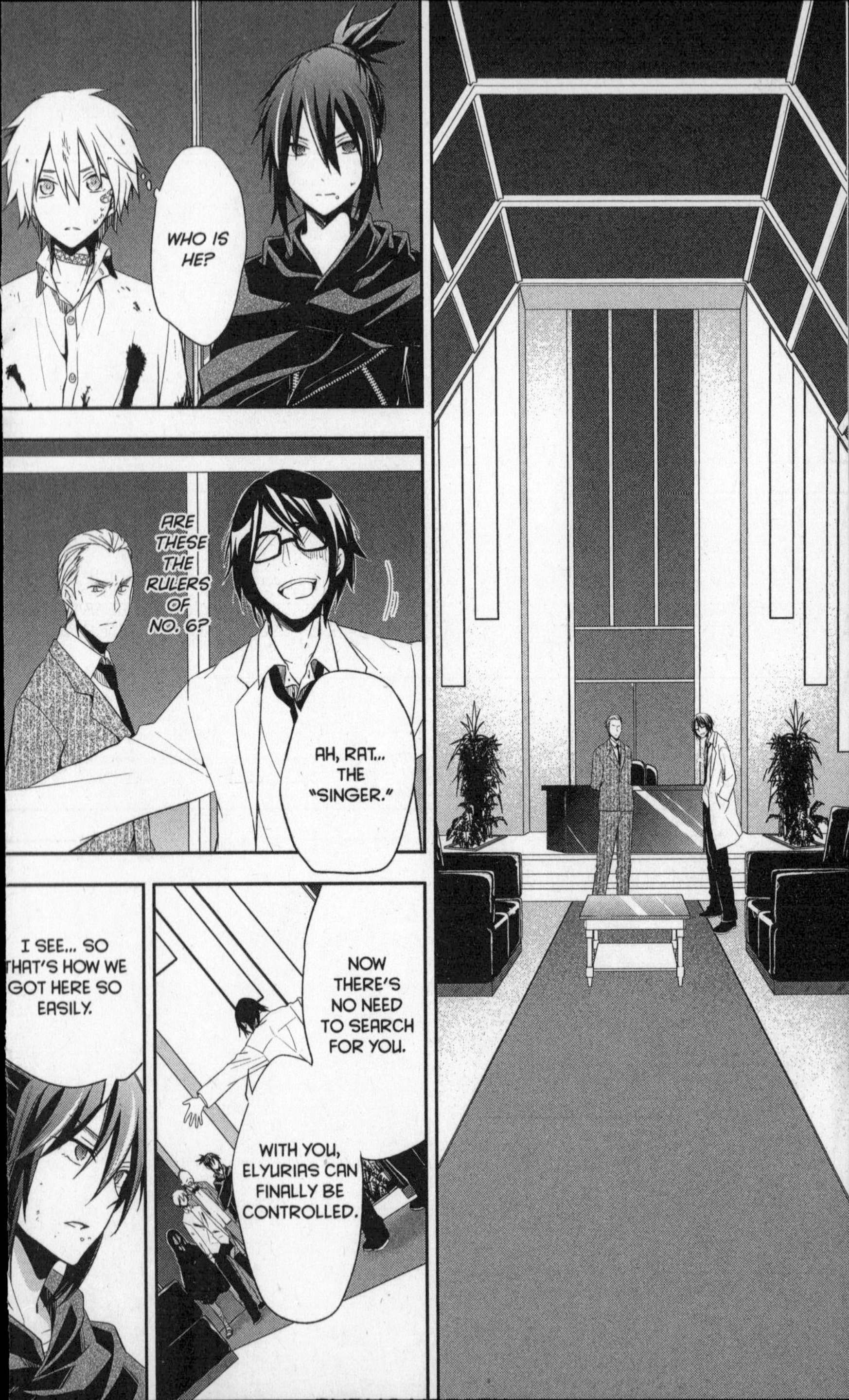
WHO IS HE?
ARE THESE THE RULERS OF NO. 6?
AH, RAT... THE "SINGER."
NOW THERE'S NO NEED TO SEARCH FOR YOU.
WITH YOU, ELYURIAS CAN FINALLY BE CONTROLLED.
I SEE... SO THAT'S HOW WE GOT HERE SO EASILY.

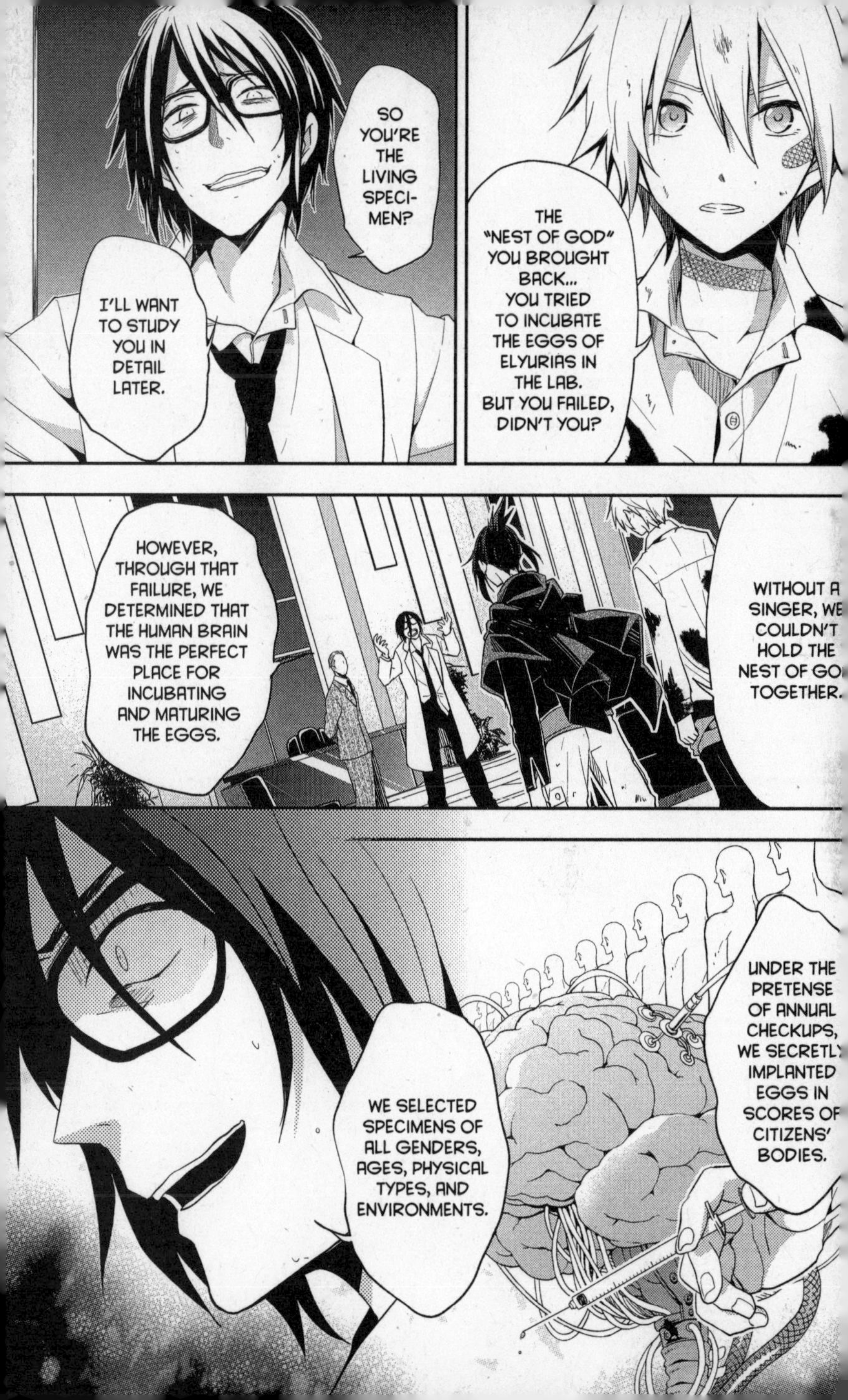
THE "NEST OF GOD" YOU BROUGHT BACK... YOU TRIED TO INCUBATE THE EGGS OF ELYURIAS IN THE LAB. BUT YOU FAILED, DIDN'T YOU?
SO YOU'RE THE LIVING SPECI-MEN?
I'LL WANT TO STUDY YOU IN DETAIL LATER.
WITHOUT A SINGER, WE COULDN'T HOLD THE NEST OF GO TOGETHER.
HOWEVER, THROUGH THAT FAILURE, WE DETERMINED THAT THE HUMAN BRAIN WAS THE PERFECT PLACE FOR INCUBATING AND MATURING THE EGGS.
UNDER THE PRETENSE OF ANNUAL CHECKUPS, WE SECRETL IMPLANTED EGGS IN SCORES OF CITIZENS' BODIES.
WE SELECTED SPECIMENS OF ALL GENDERS, AGES, PHYSICAL TYPES, AND ENVIRONMENTS.

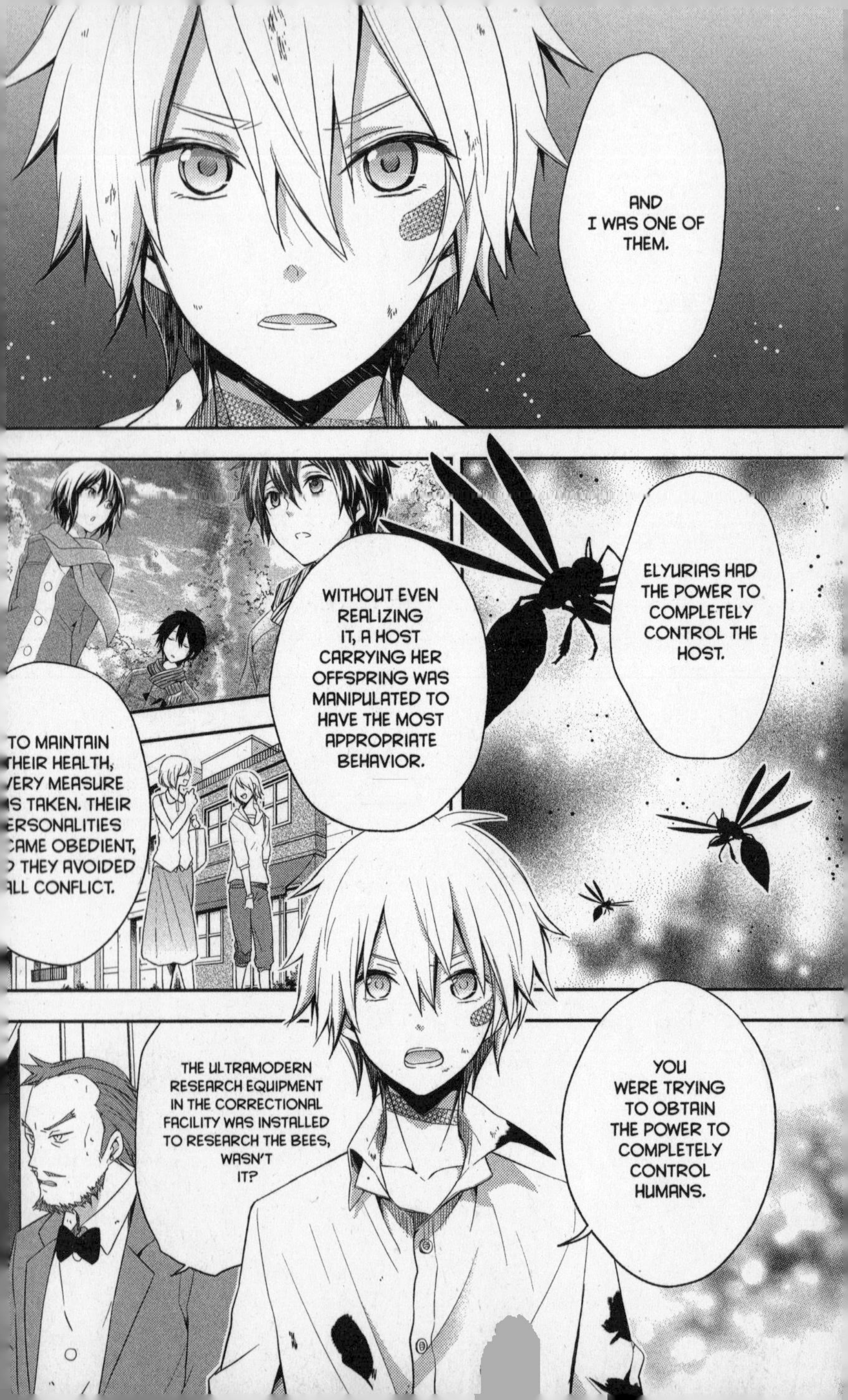
AND I WAS ONE OF THEM.
ELYURIAS HAD THE POWER TO COMPLETELY CONTROL THE HOST.
WITHOUT EVEN REALIZING IT, A HOST CARRYING HER OFFSPRING WAS MANIPULATED TO HAVE THE MOST APPROPRIATE BEHAVIOR.
TO MAINTAIN THEIR HEALTH, VERY MEASURE S TAKEN. THEIR ERSONALITIES CAME OBEDIENT, O THEY AVOIDED ALL CONFLICT.
YOU WERE TRYING TO OBTAIN THE POWER TO COMPLETELY CONTROL HUMANS.
THE ULTRAMODERN RESEARCH EQUIPMENT IN THE CORRECTIONAL FACILITY WAS INSTALLED TO RESEARCH THE BEES, WASN'T IT?

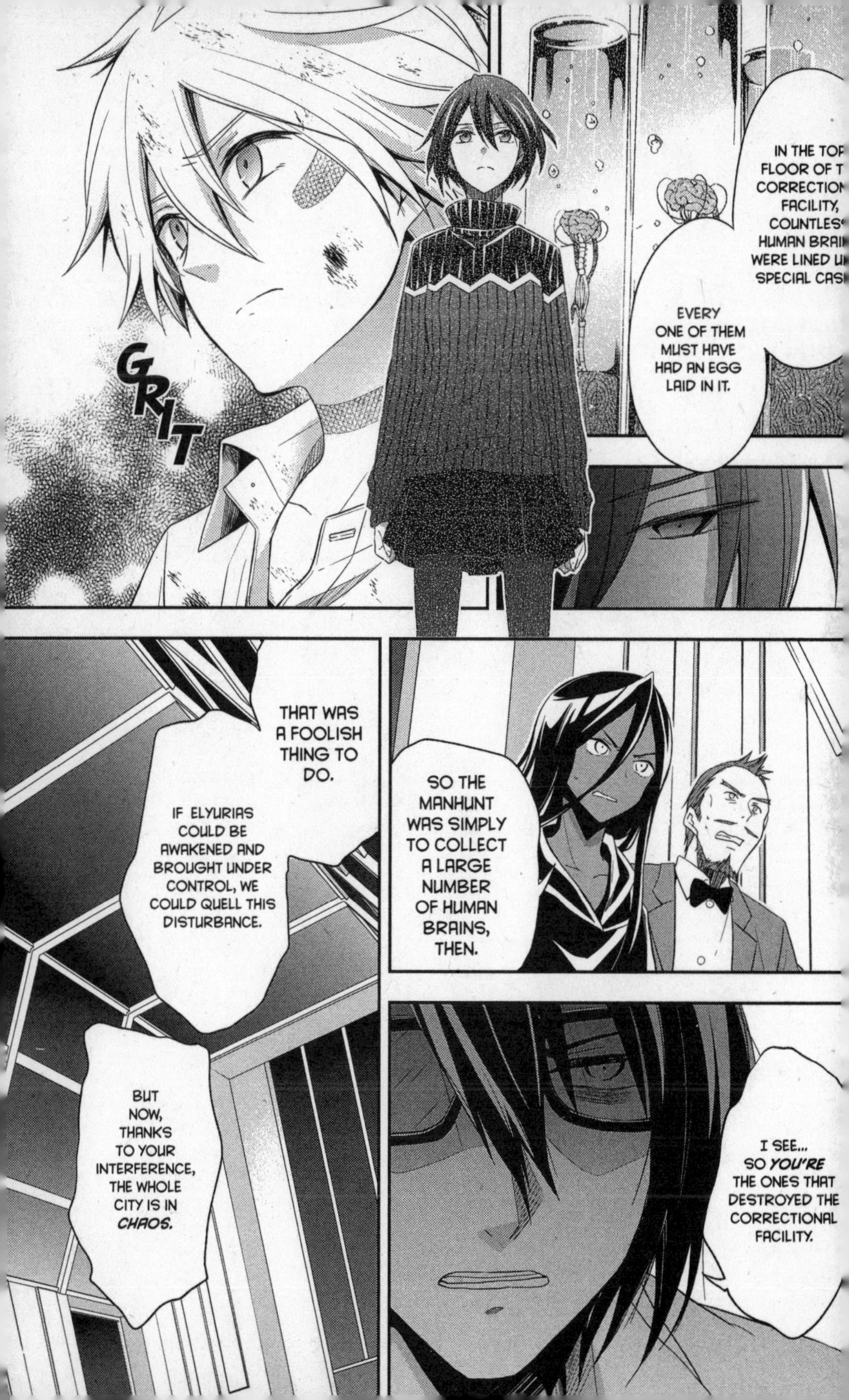
IN THE TOP FLOOR OF T CORRECTION FACILITY, COUNTLESS HUMAN BRAI WERE LINED U SPECIAL CAS
EVERY ONE OF THEM MUST HAVE HAD AN EGG LAID IN IT.
GRIT
SO THE MANHUNT WAS SIMPLY TO COLLECT A LARGE NUMBER OF HUMAN BRAINS, THEN.
I SEE... SO *YOU'RE* THE ONES THAT DESTROYED THE CORRECTIONAL FACILITY.
THAT WAS A FOOLISH THING TO DO.
IF ELYURIAS COULD BE AWAKENED AND BROUGHT UNDER CONTROL, WE COULD QUELL THIS DISTURBANCE.
BUT NOW, THANKS TO YOUR INTERFERENCE, THE WHOLE CITY IS IN *CHAOS.*

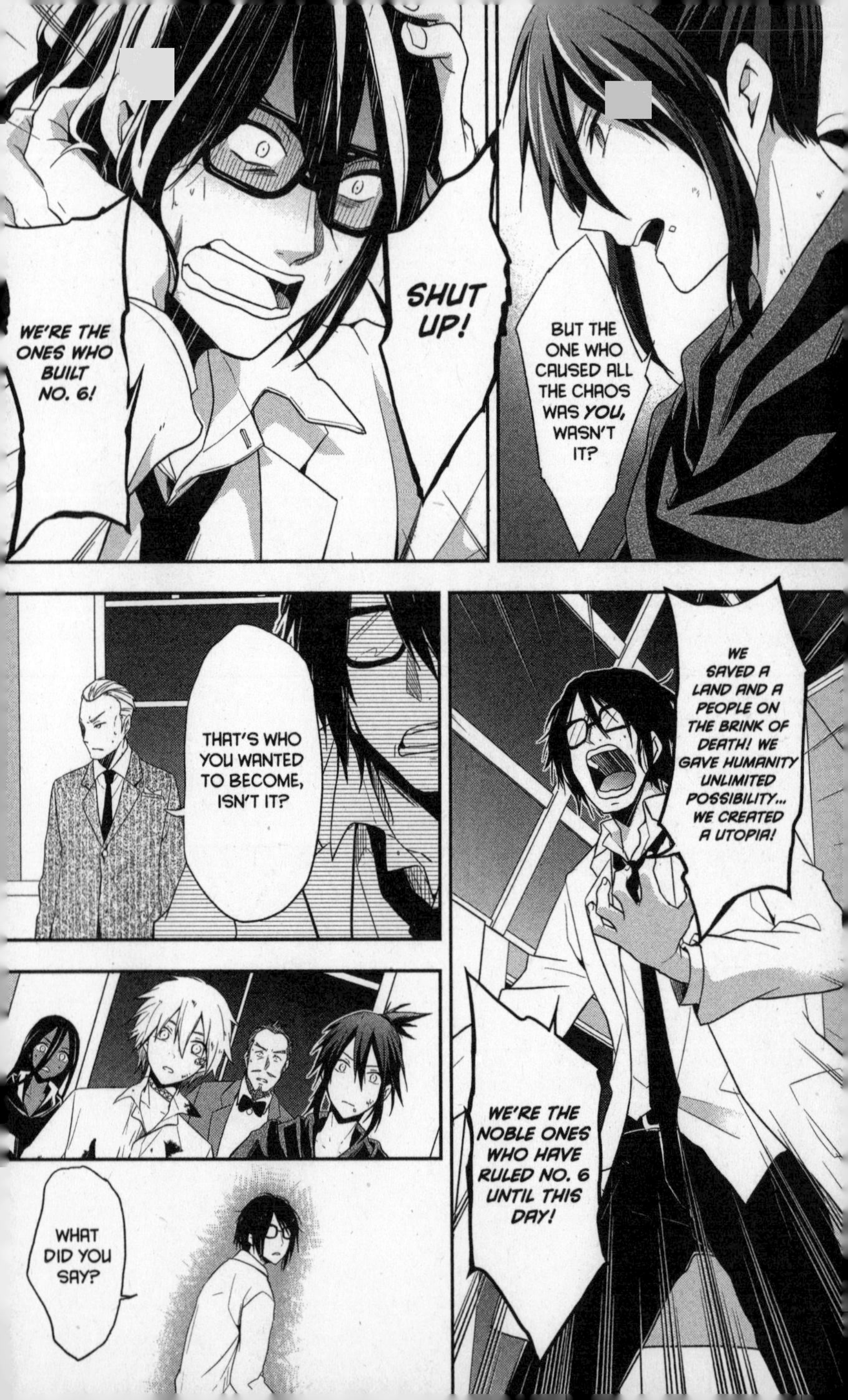
BUT THE ONE WHO CAUSED ALL THE CHAOS WAS *YOU*, WASN'T IT?
SHUT UP!
WE'RE THE ONES WHO BUILT NO. 6!
WE SAVED A LAND AND A PEOPLE ON THE BRINK OF DEATH! WE GAVE HUMANITY UNLIMITED POSSIBILITY... WE CREATED A UTOPIA!
WE'RE THE NOBLE ONES WHO HAVE RULED NO. 6 UNTIL THIS DAY!
THAT'S WHO YOU WANTED TO BECOME, ISN'T IT?
WHAT DID YOU SAY?

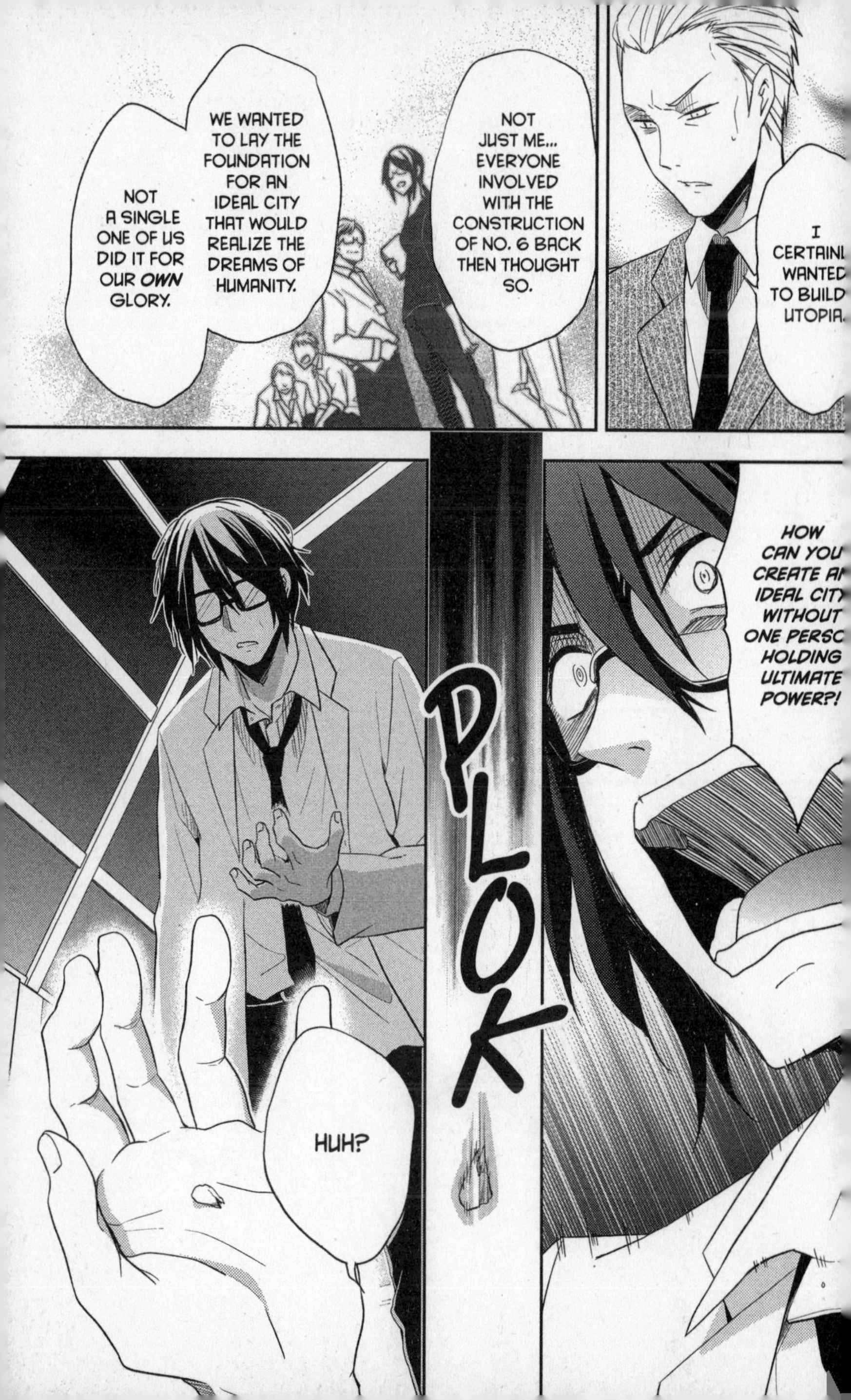
I CERTAINL WANTED TO BUILD UTOPIA.
NOT JUST ME... EVERYONE INVOLVED WITH THE CONSTRUCTION OF NO. 6 BACK THEN THOUGHT SO.
WE WANTED TO LAY THE FOUNDATION FOR AN IDEAL CITY THAT WOULD REALIZE THE DREAMS OF HUMANITY.
NOT A SINGLE ONE OF US DID IT FOR OUR *OWN* GLORY.
HOW CAN YOU CREATE A IDEAL CITY WITHOUT ONE PERSC HOLDING ULTIMATE POWER?!
PLOK
HUH?

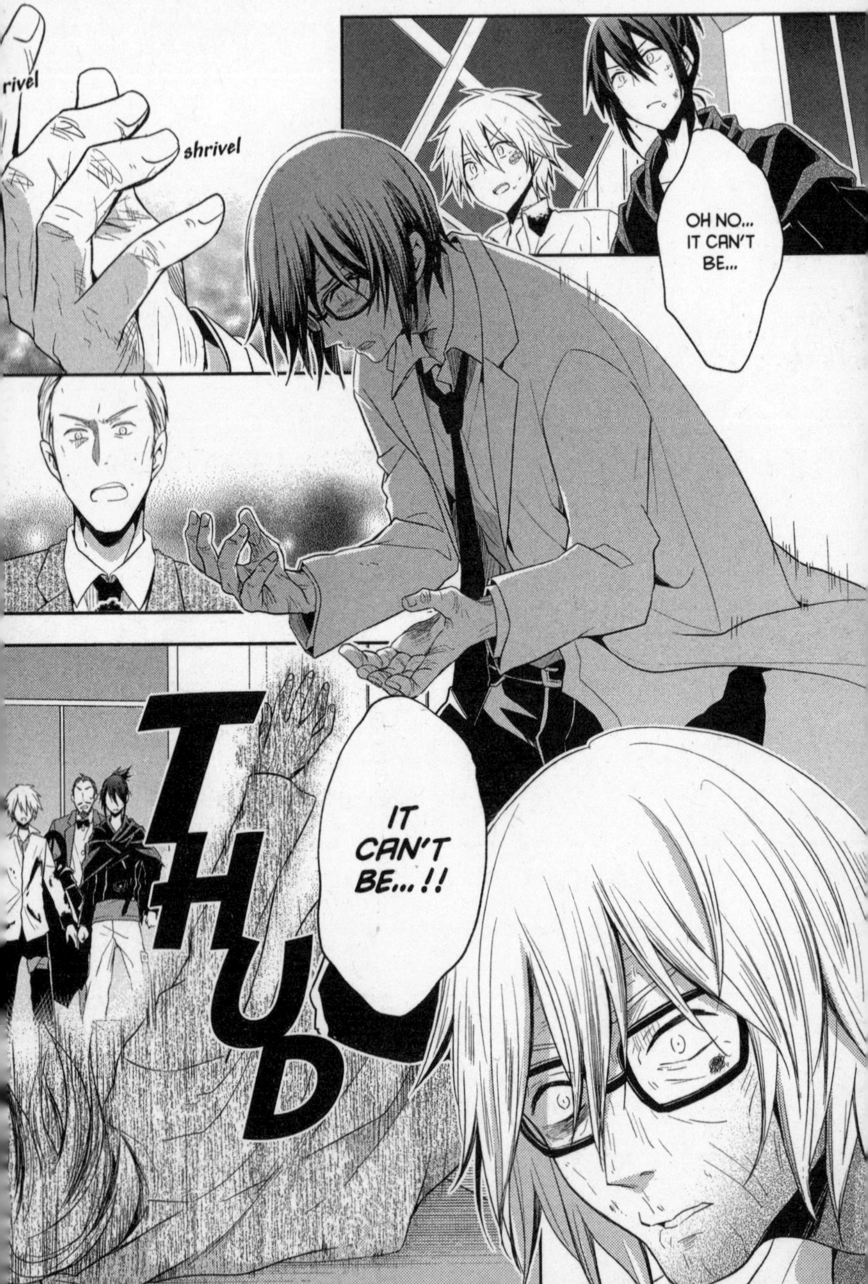
OH NO... IT CAN'T BE...
shrivel
rivel
IT CAN'T BE...!!
THUD

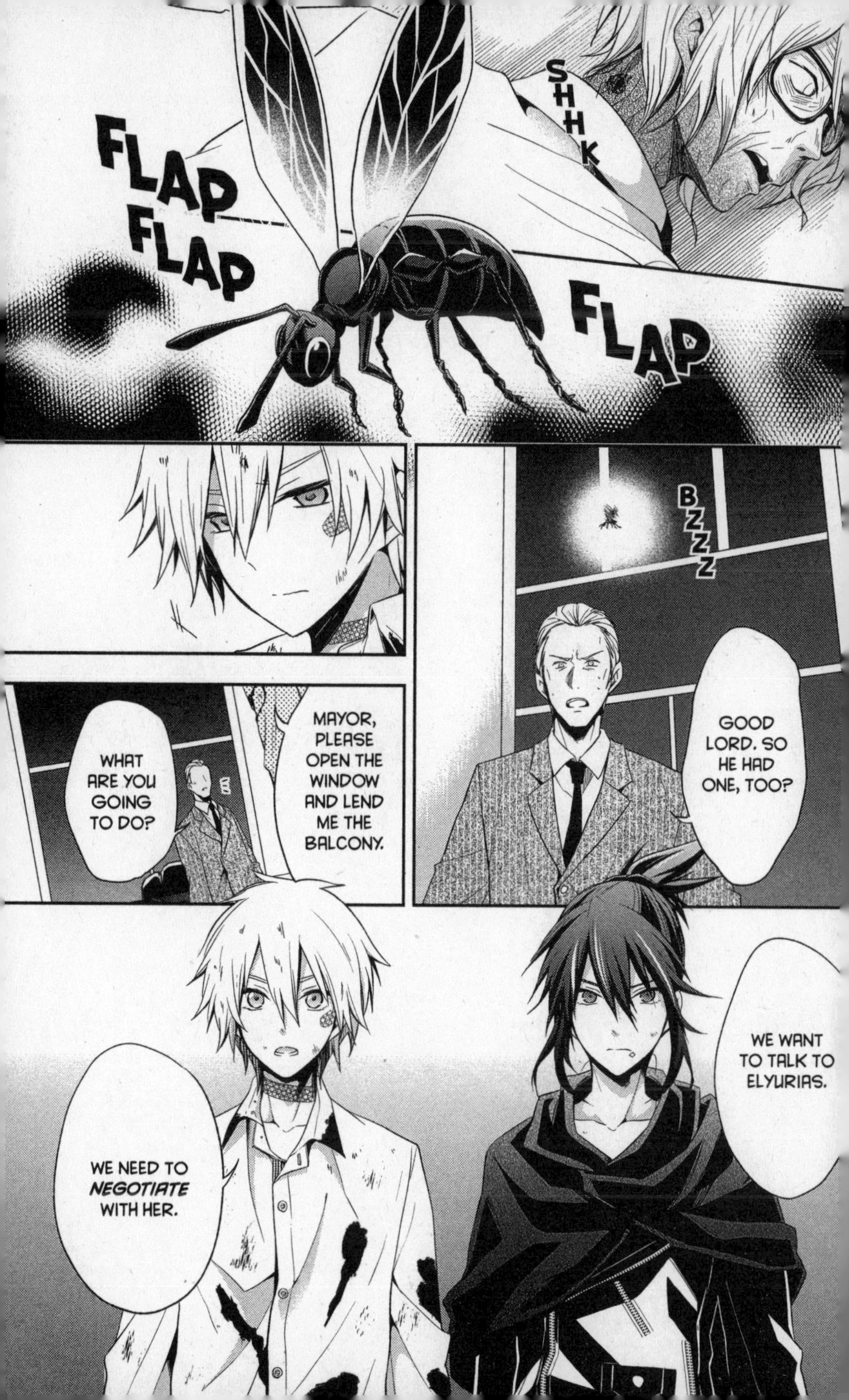
SHHK
FLAP FLAP
FLAP
BZZZ
GOOD LORD. SO HE HAD ONE, TOO?
MAYOR, PLEASE OPEN THE WINDOW AND LEND ME THE BALCONY.
WHAT ARE YOU GOING TO DO?
WE WANT TO TALK TO ELYURIAS.
WE NEED TO *NEGOTIATE* WITH HER.

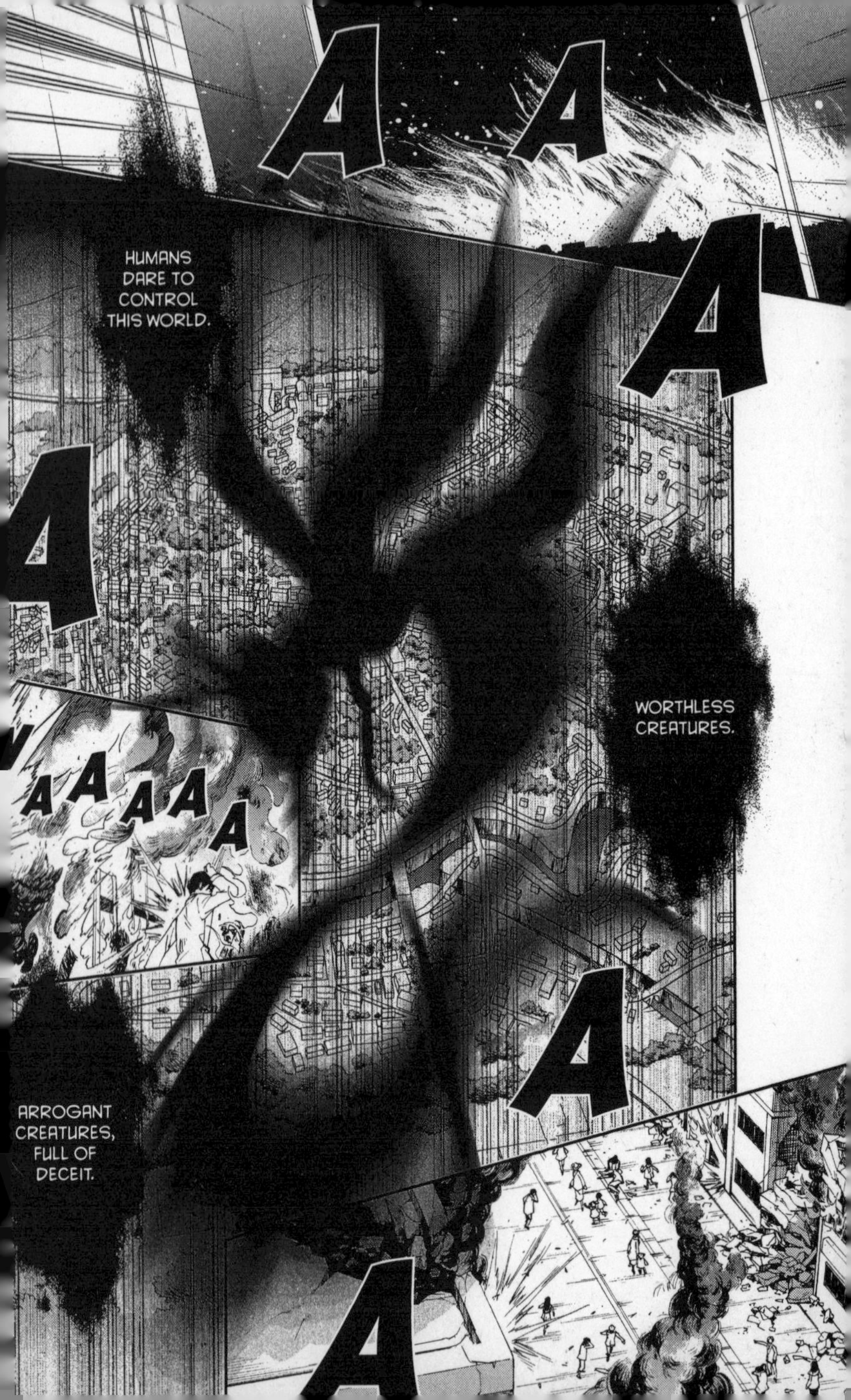
AAA
HUMANS DARE TO CONTROL THIS WORLD.
A
WORTHLESS CREATURES.
AAAAAA
A
ARROGANT CREATURES, FULL OF DECEIT.
A

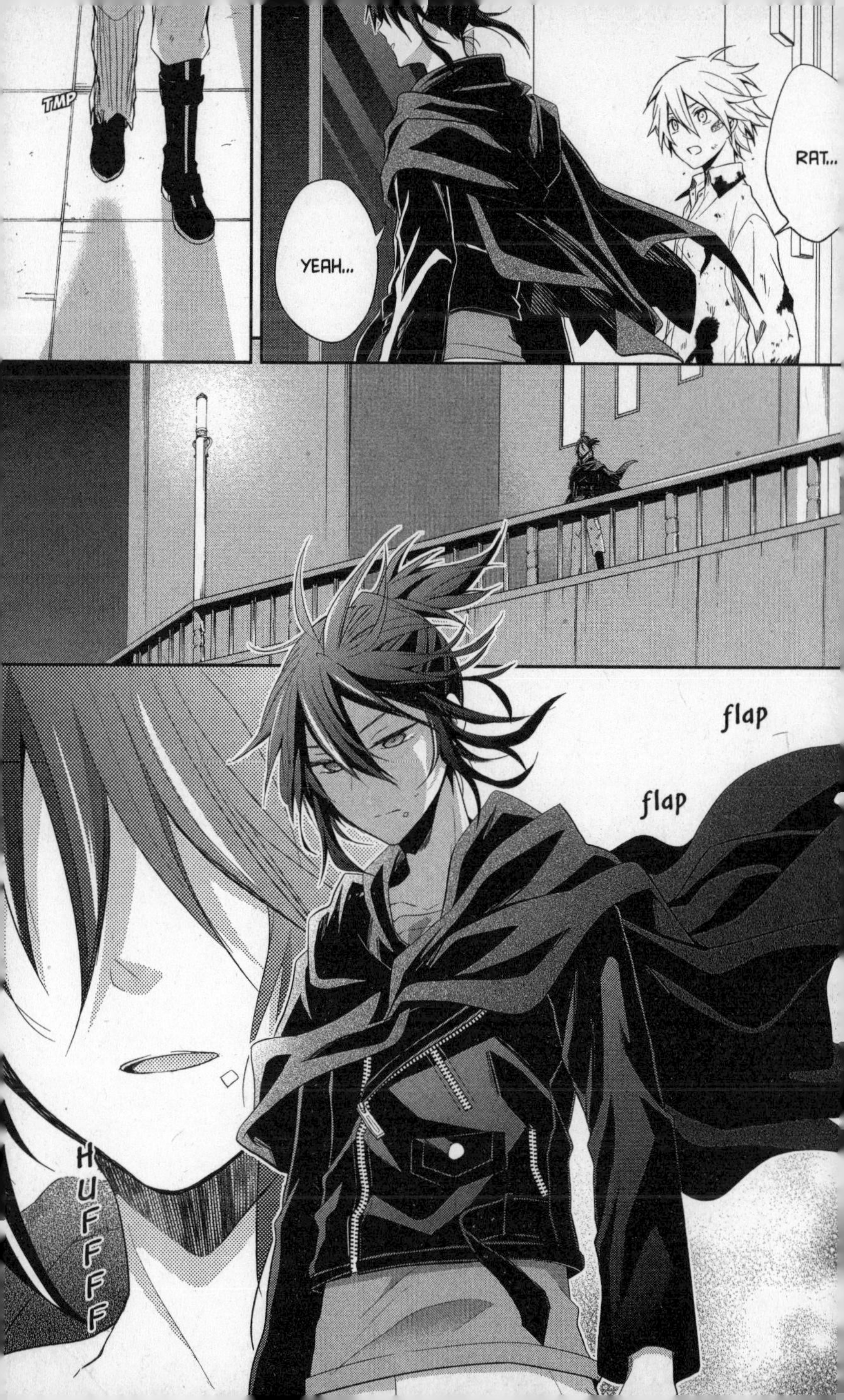
RAT...
YEAH...
TMP
flap
flap
HUFFFF

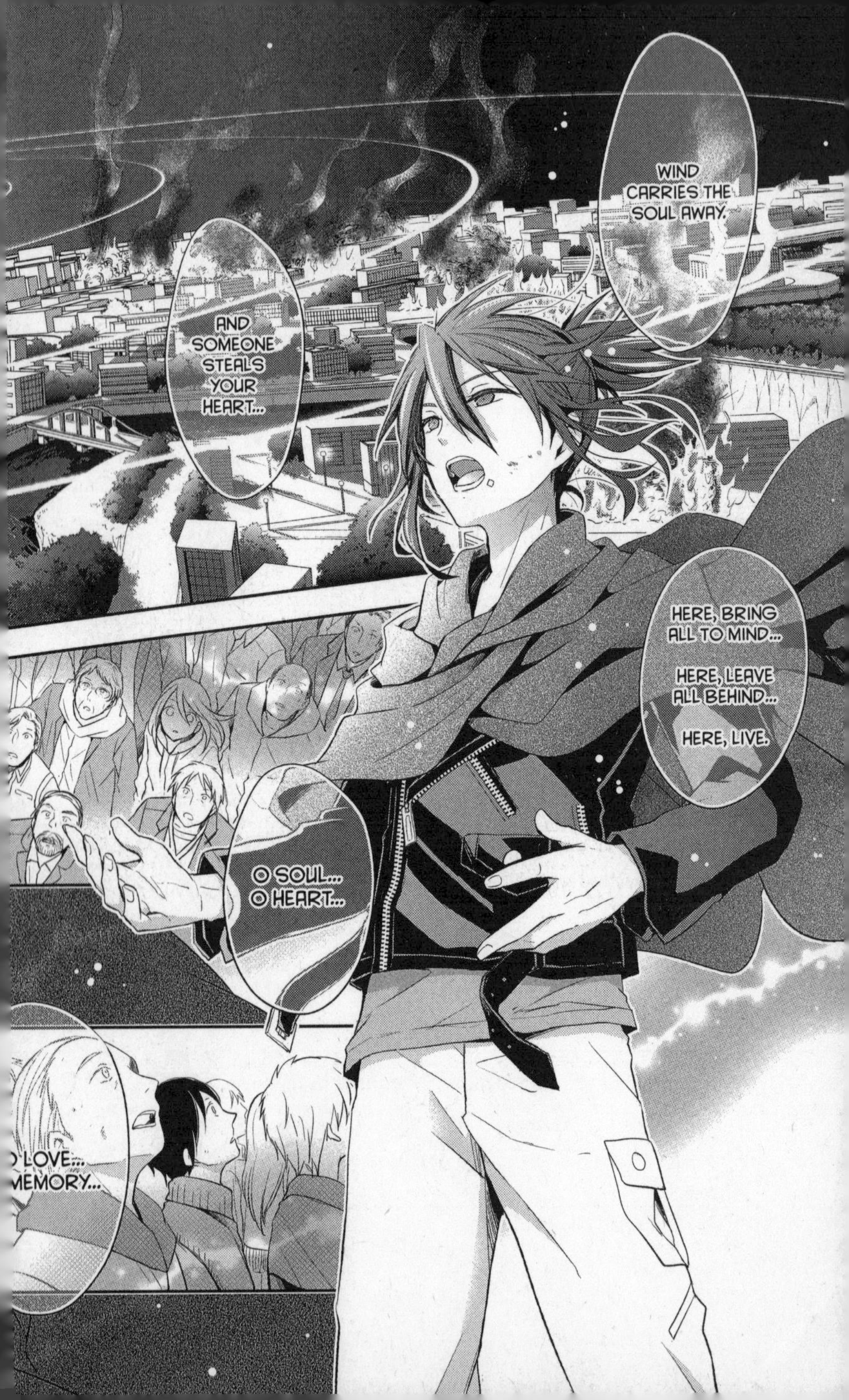
WIND CARRIES THE SOUL AWAY.
AND SOMEONE STEALS YOUR HEART...
HERE, BRING ALL TO MIND... HERE, LEAVE ALL BEHIND... HERE, LIVE.
O SOUL... O HEART...
O LOVE... MEMORY...

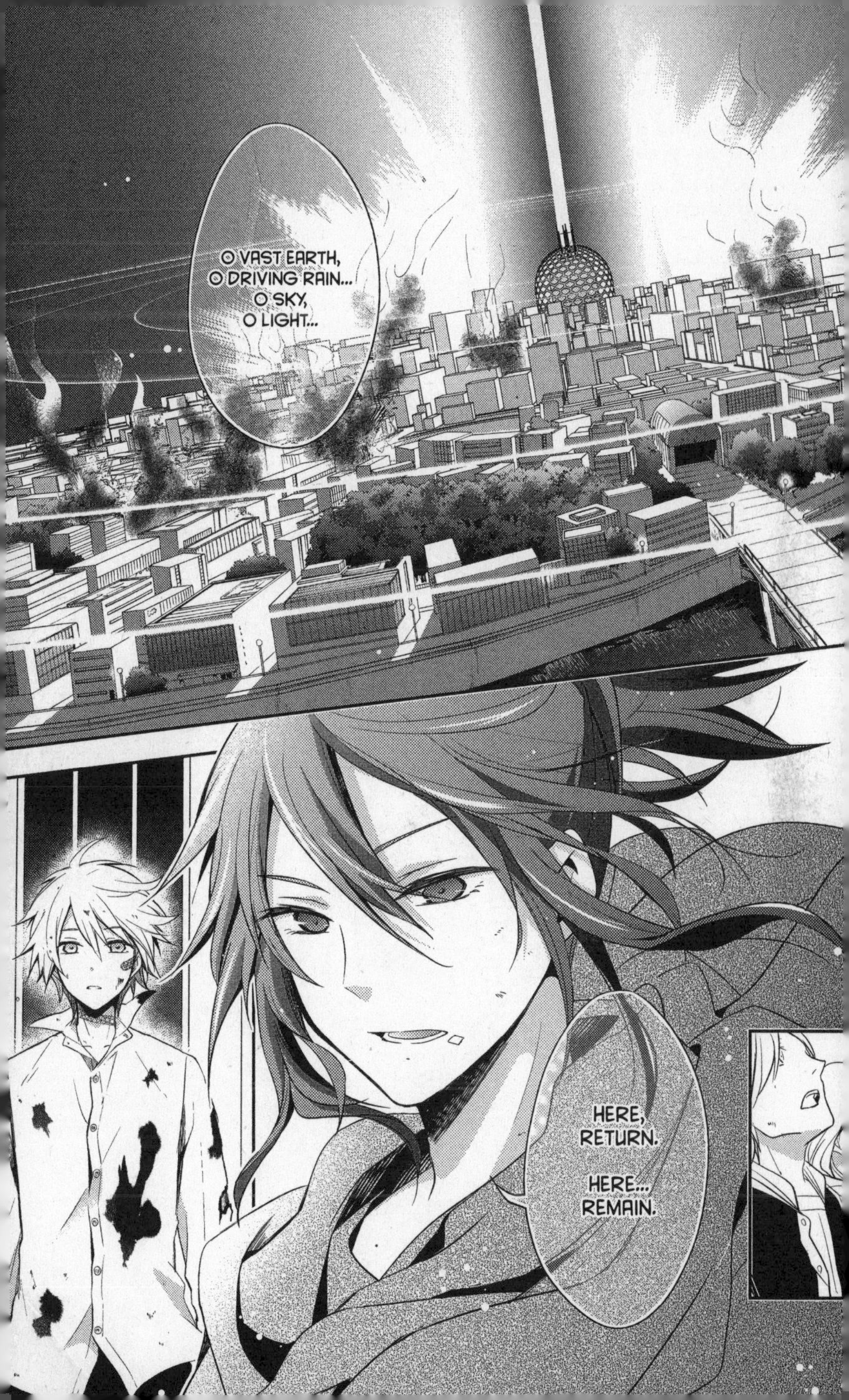
O VAST EARTH,
O DRIVING RAIN...
O SKY,
O LIGHT...
HERE, RETURN.
HERE... REMAIN.

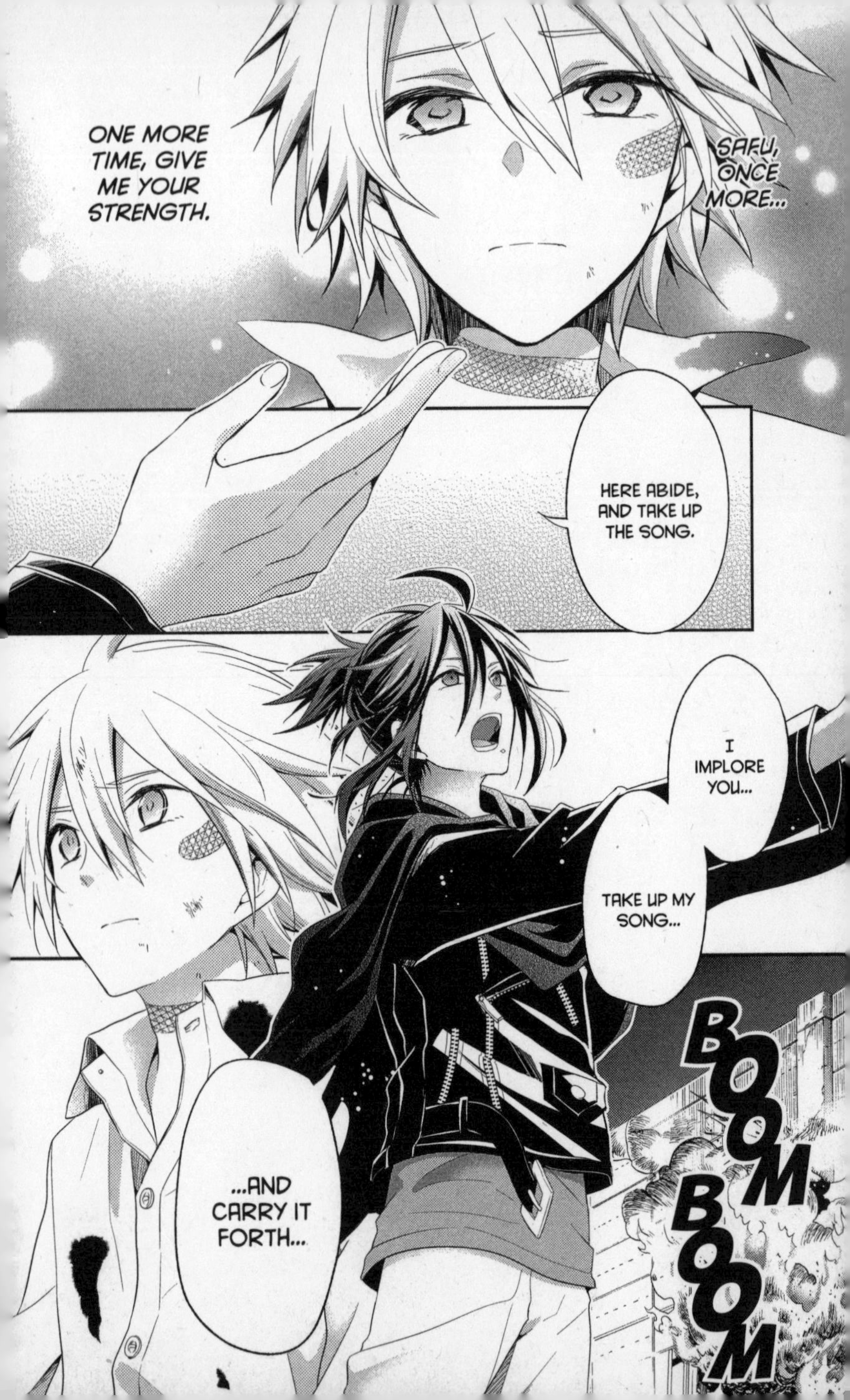
SAFU, ONCE MORE...
ONE MORE TIME, GIVE ME YOUR STRENGTH.
HERE ABIDE, AND TAKE UP THE SONG.
I IMPLORE YOU...
TAKE UP MY SONG...
BOOM BOOM
...AND CARRY IT FORTH...

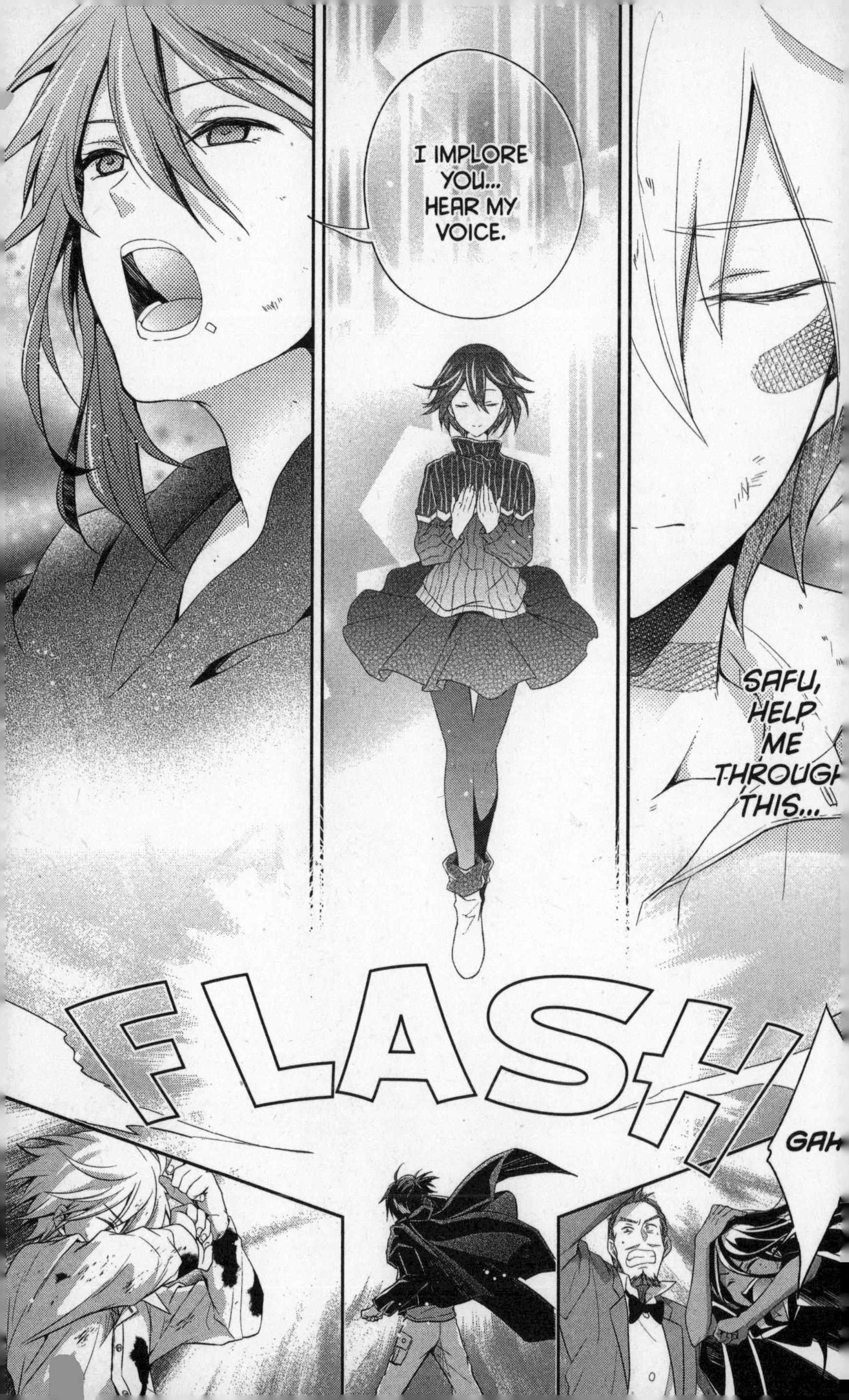
SAFU, HELP ME THROUGH THIS...
I IMPLORE YOU... HEAR MY VOICE.
FLASH
GAH

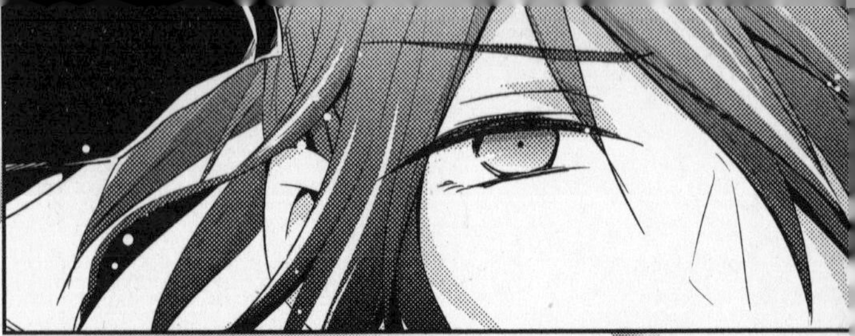
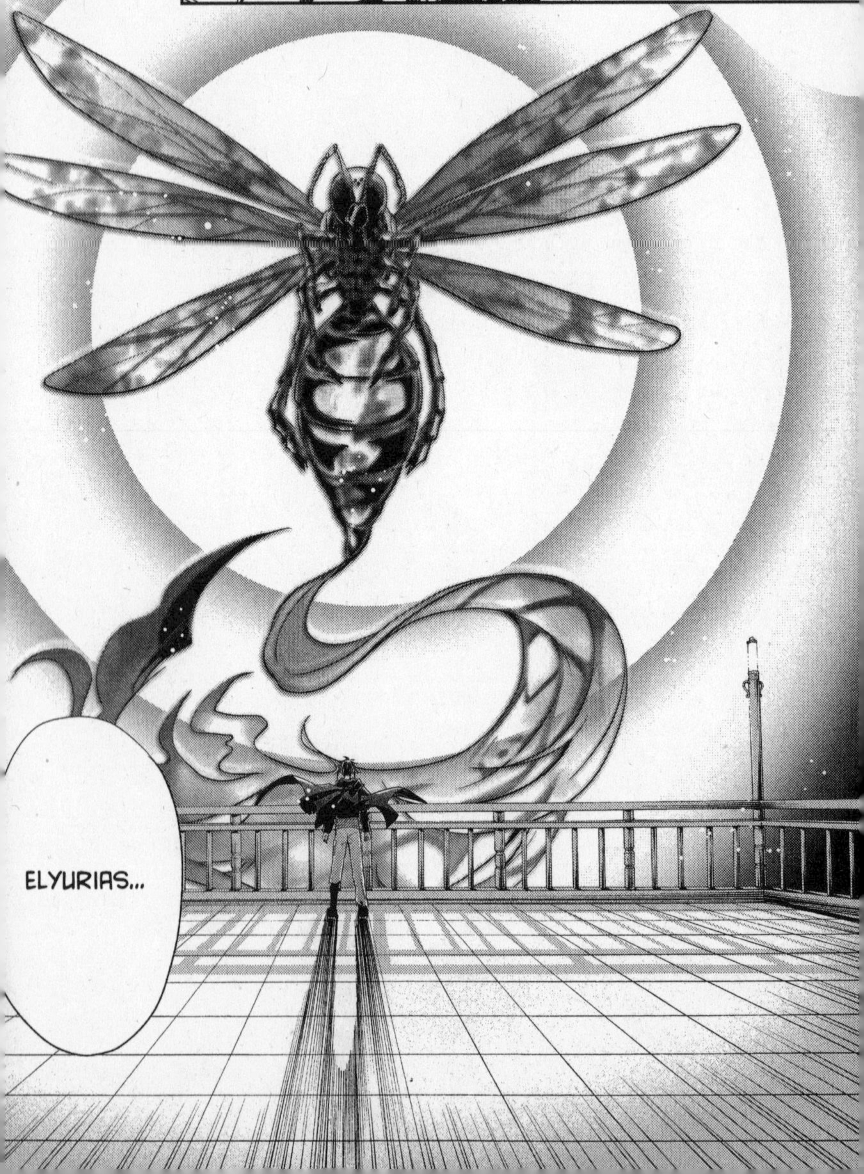
ELYURIAS...

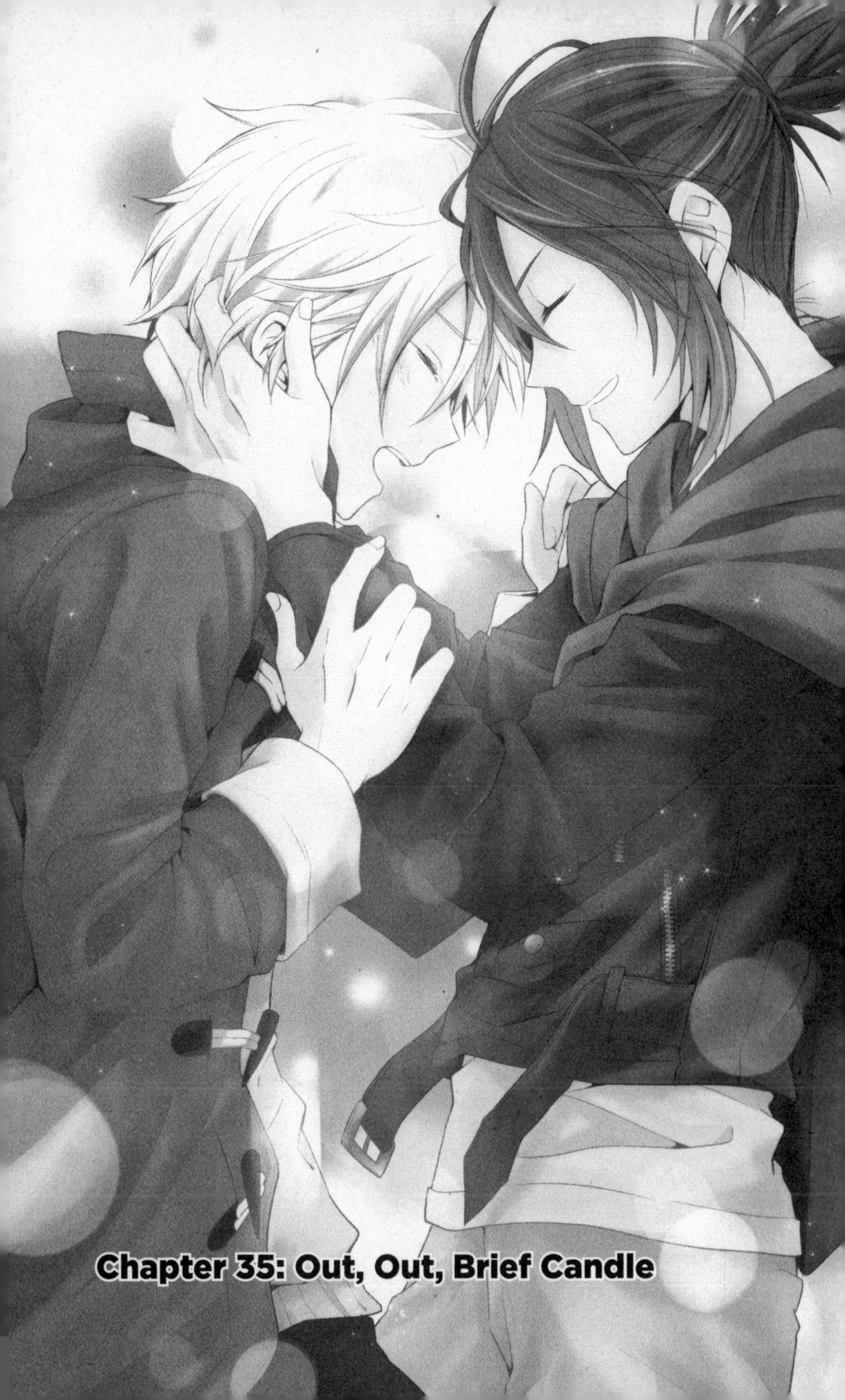
Chapter 35: Out, Out, Brief Candle

NO.6

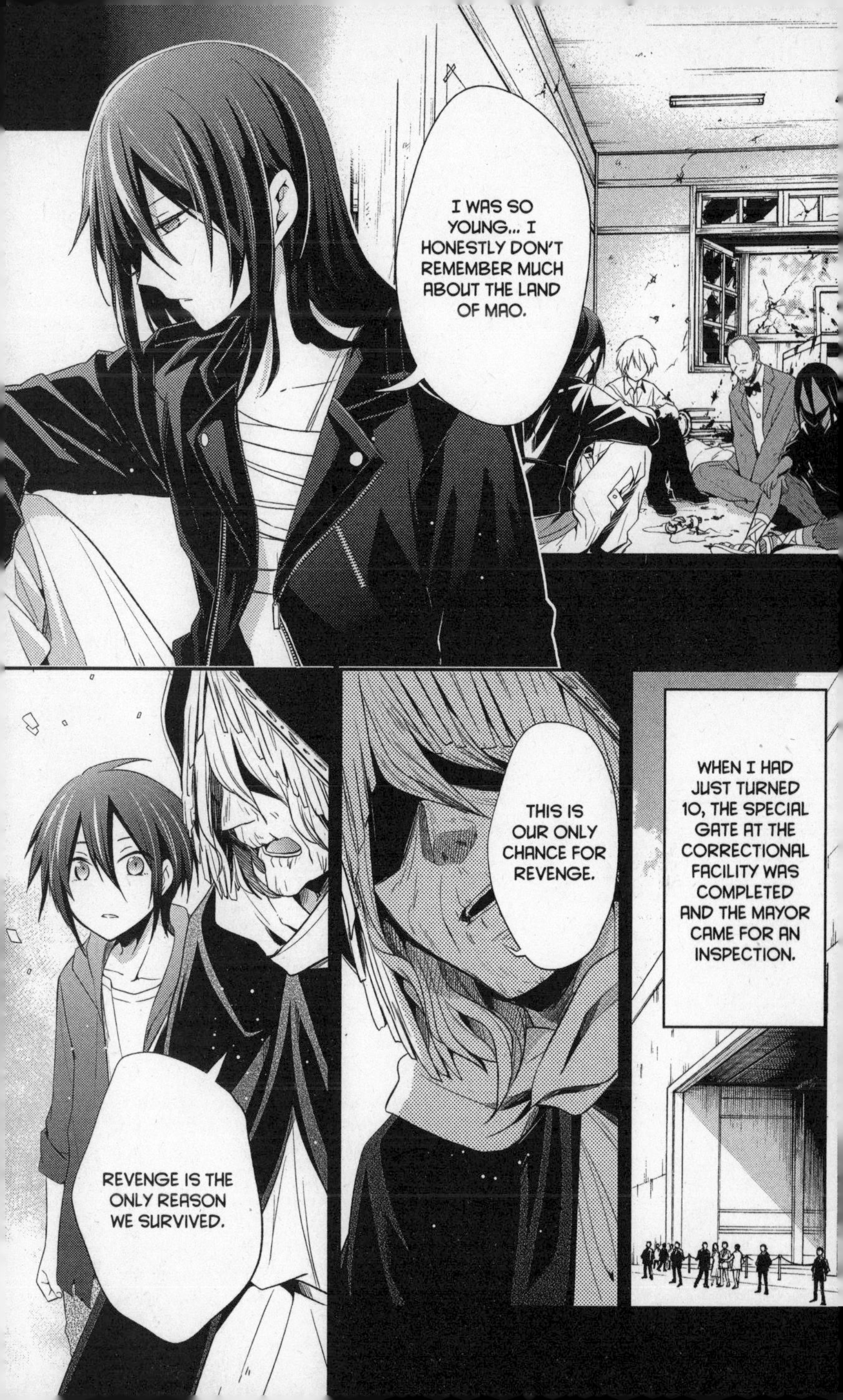
I WAS SO YOUNG... I HONESTLY DON'T REMEMBER MUCH ABOUT THE LAND OF MAO.
WHEN I HAD JUST TURNED 10, THE SPECIAL GATE AT THE CORRECTIONAL FACILITY WAS COMPLETED AND THE MAYOR CAME FOR AN INSPECTION.
THIS IS OUR ONLY CHANCE FOR REVENGE.
REVENGE IS THE ONLY REASON WE SURVIVED.

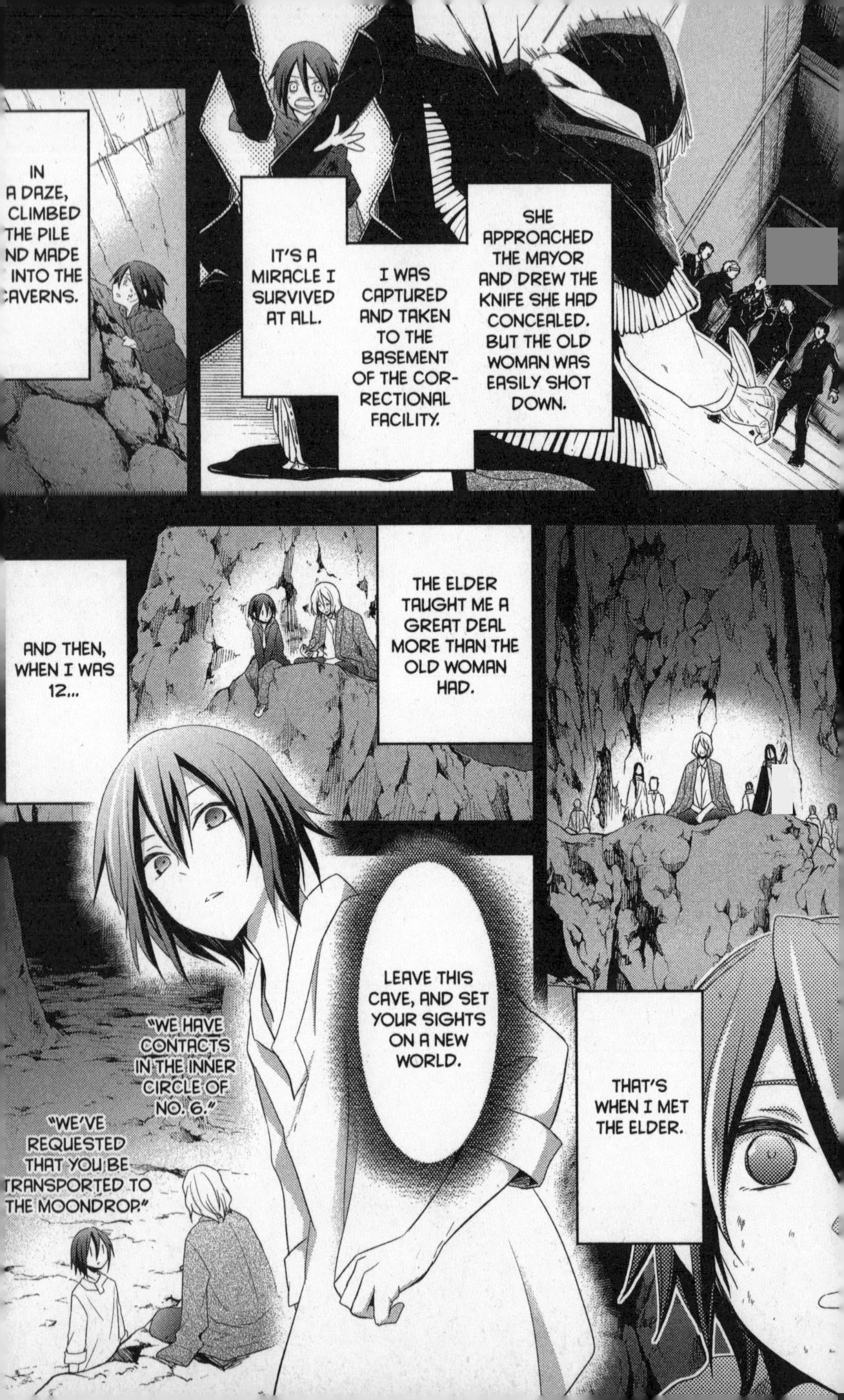
SHE APPROACHED THE MAYOR AND DREW THE KNIFE SHE HAD CONCEALED. BUT THE OLD WOMAN WAS EASILY SHOT DOWN.
I WAS CAPTURED AND TAKEN TO THE BASEMENT OF THE COR-RECTIONAL FACILITY.
IT'S A MIRACLE I SURVIVED AT ALL.
IN A DAZE, CLIMBED THE PILE ND MADE INTO THE AVERNS.
THE ELDER TAUGHT ME A GREAT DEAL MORE THAN THE OLD WOMAN HAD.
AND THEN, WHEN I WAS 12...
THAT'S WHEN I MET THE ELDER.
LEAVE THIS CAVE, AND SET YOUR SIGHTS ON A NEW WORLD.
"WE HAVE CONTACTS IN THE INNER CIRCLE OF NO. 6."
"WE'VE REQUESTED THAT YOU BE TRANSPORTED TO THE MOONDROP."

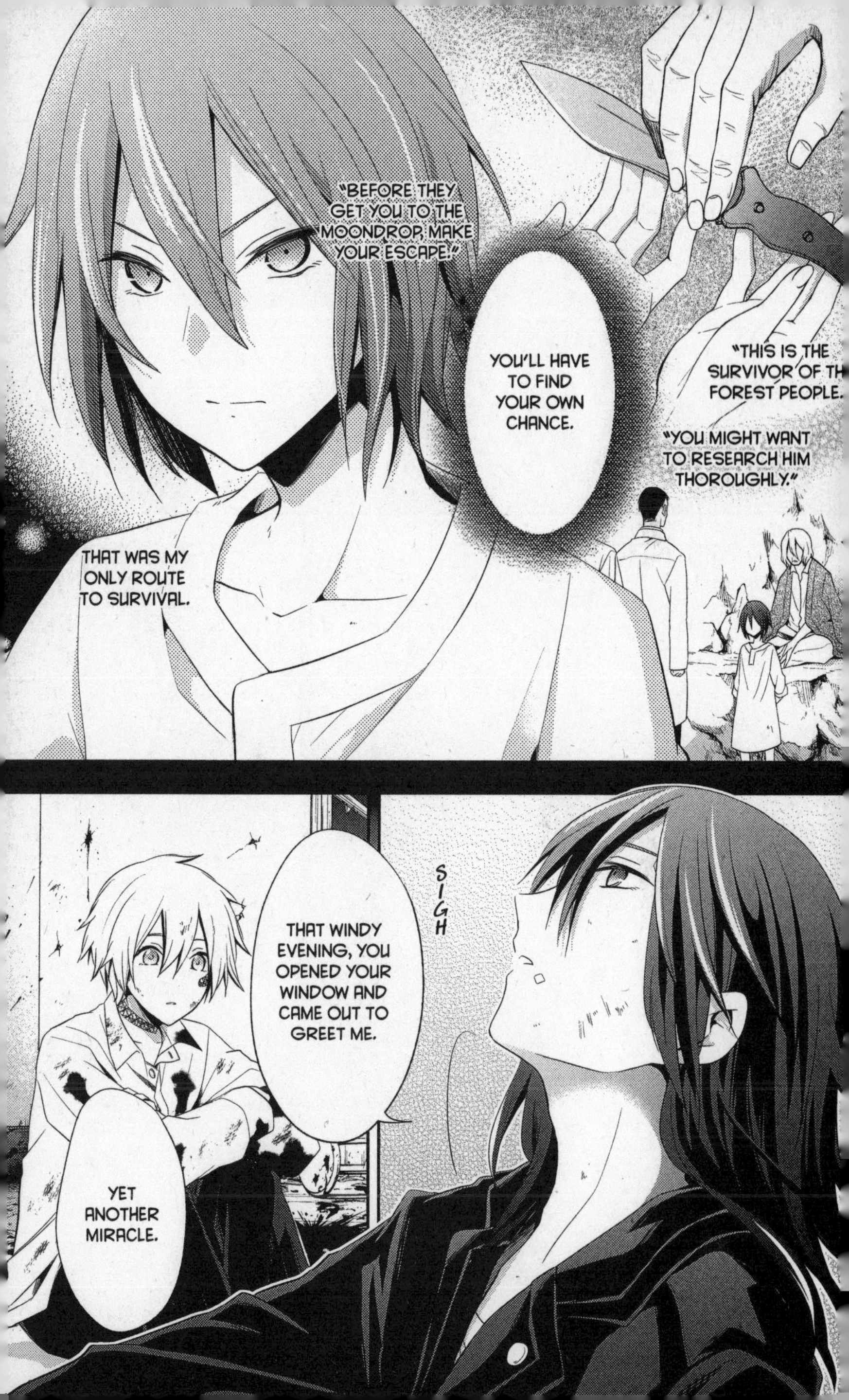
"THIS IS THE SURVIVOR OF TH FOREST PEOPLE.
"YOU MIGHT WANT TO RESEARCH HIM THOROUGHLY."
"BEFORE THEY GET YOU TO THE MOONDROP, MAKE YOUR ESCAPE."
YOU'LL HAVE TO FIND YOUR OWN CHANCE.
THAT WAS MY ONLY ROUTE TO SURVIVAL.
SIGH
THAT WINDY EVENING, YOU OPENED YOUR WINDOW AND CAME OUT TO GREET ME.
YET ANOTHER MIRACLE.

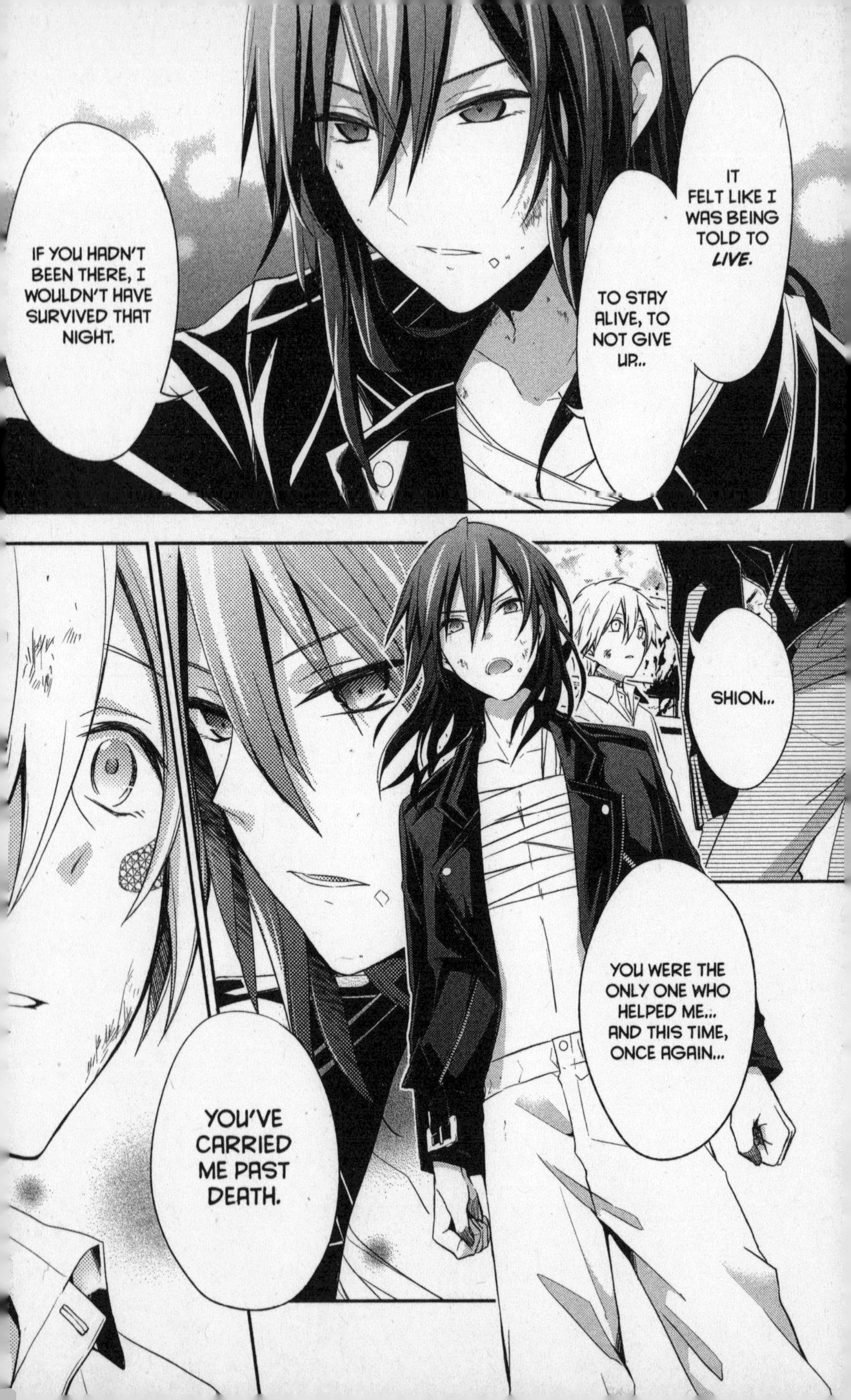
IT FELT LIKE I WAS BEING TOLD TO *LIVE.*
TO STAY ALIVE, TO NOT GIVE UP...
IF YOU HADN'T BEEN THERE, I WOULDN'T HAVE SURVIVED THAT NIGHT.
SHION...
YOU WERE THE ONLY ONE WHO HELPED ME... AND THIS TIME, ONCE AGAIN...
YOU'VE CARRIED ME PAST DEATH.

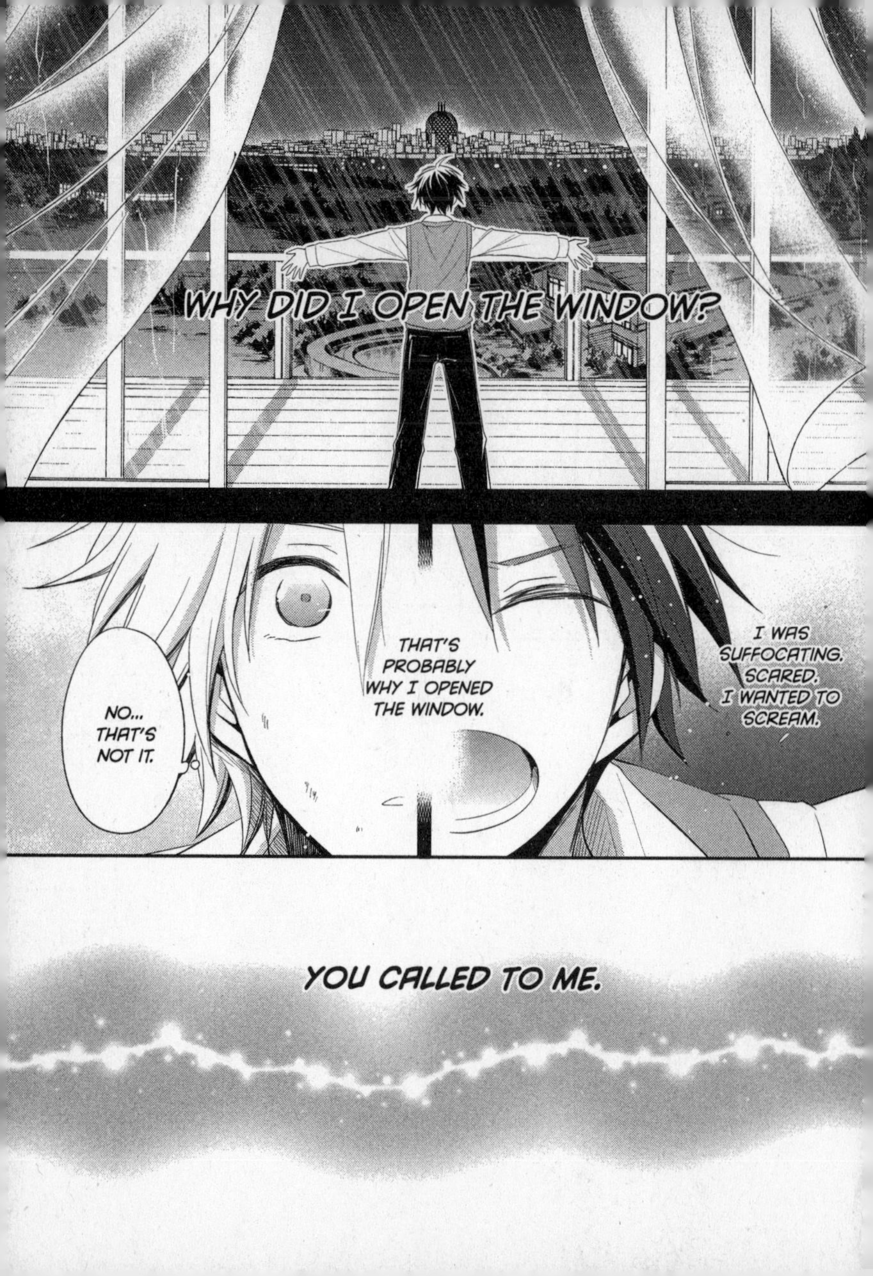
WHY DID I OPEN THE WINDOW?
I WAS SUFFOCATING. SCARED. I WANTED TO SCREAM.
THAT'S PROBABLY WHY I OPENED THE WINDOW.
NO... THAT'S NOT IT.
YOU CALLED TO ME.

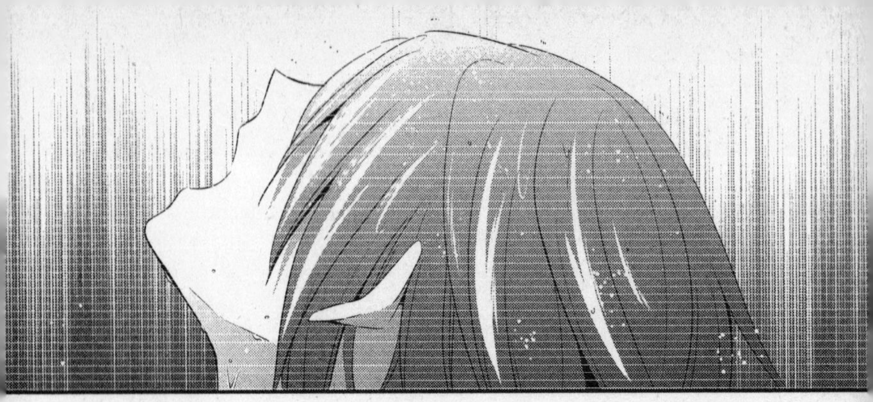

YOU CALLED OUT TO ME. I HEARD THAT VOICE.

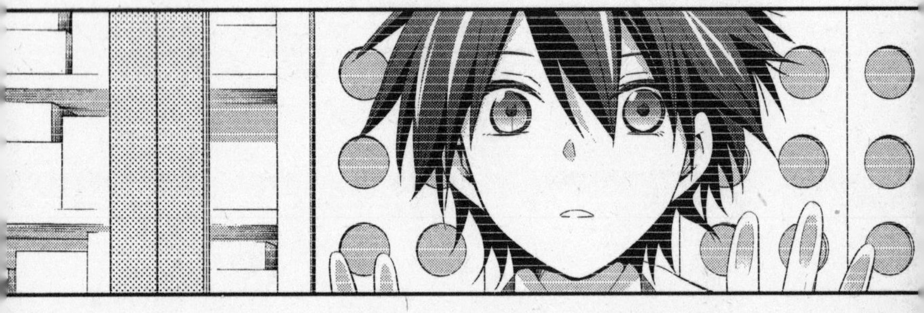

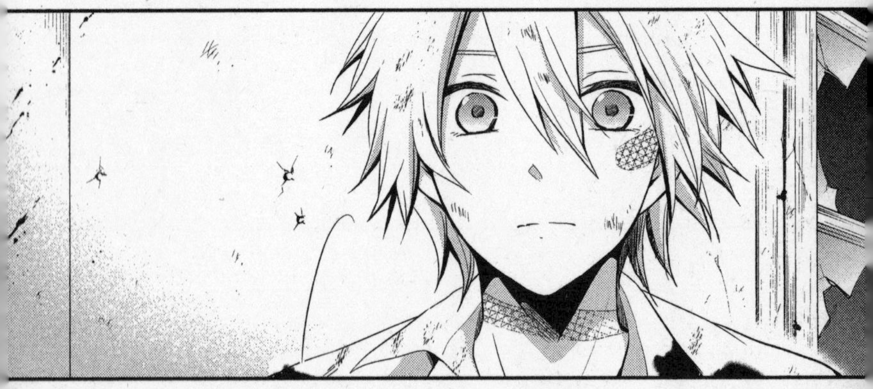

I...

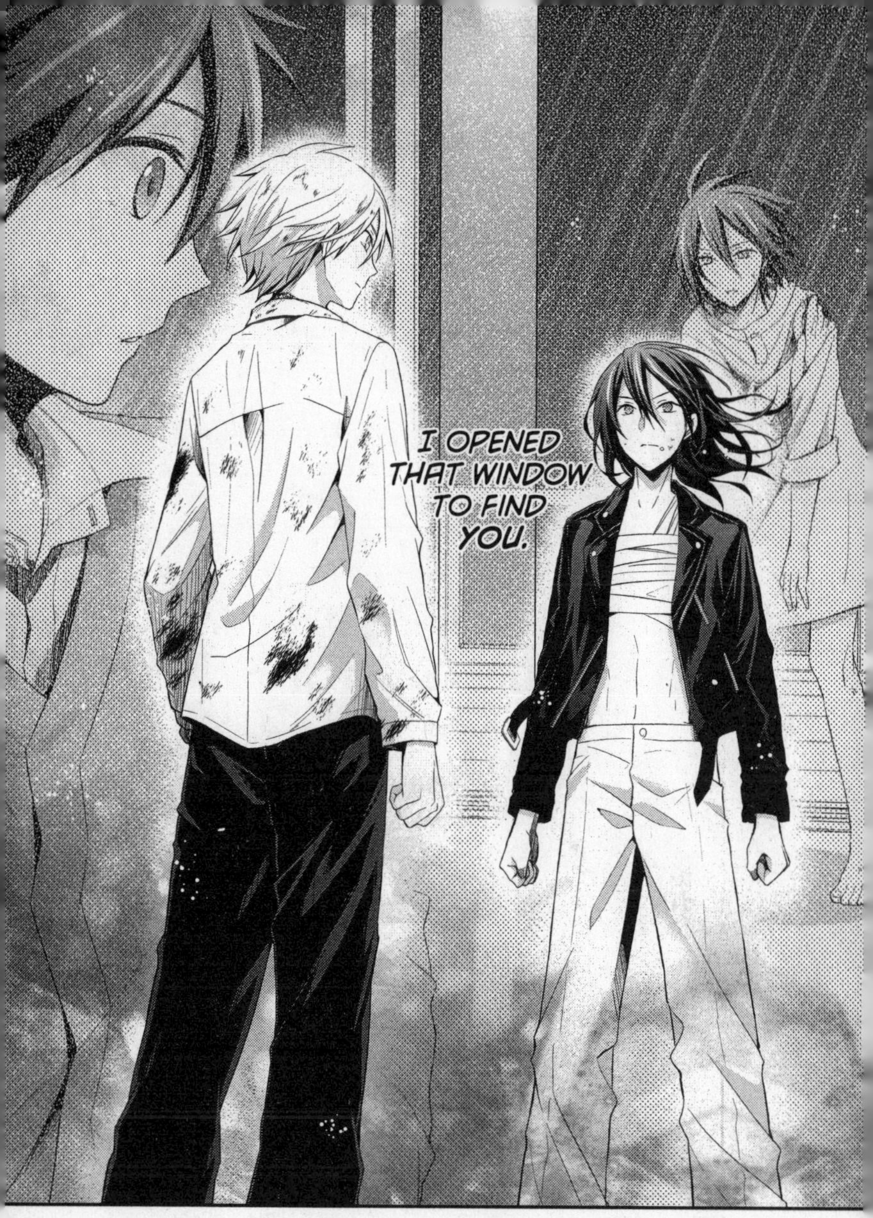
I OPENED THAT WINDOW TO FIND YOU.

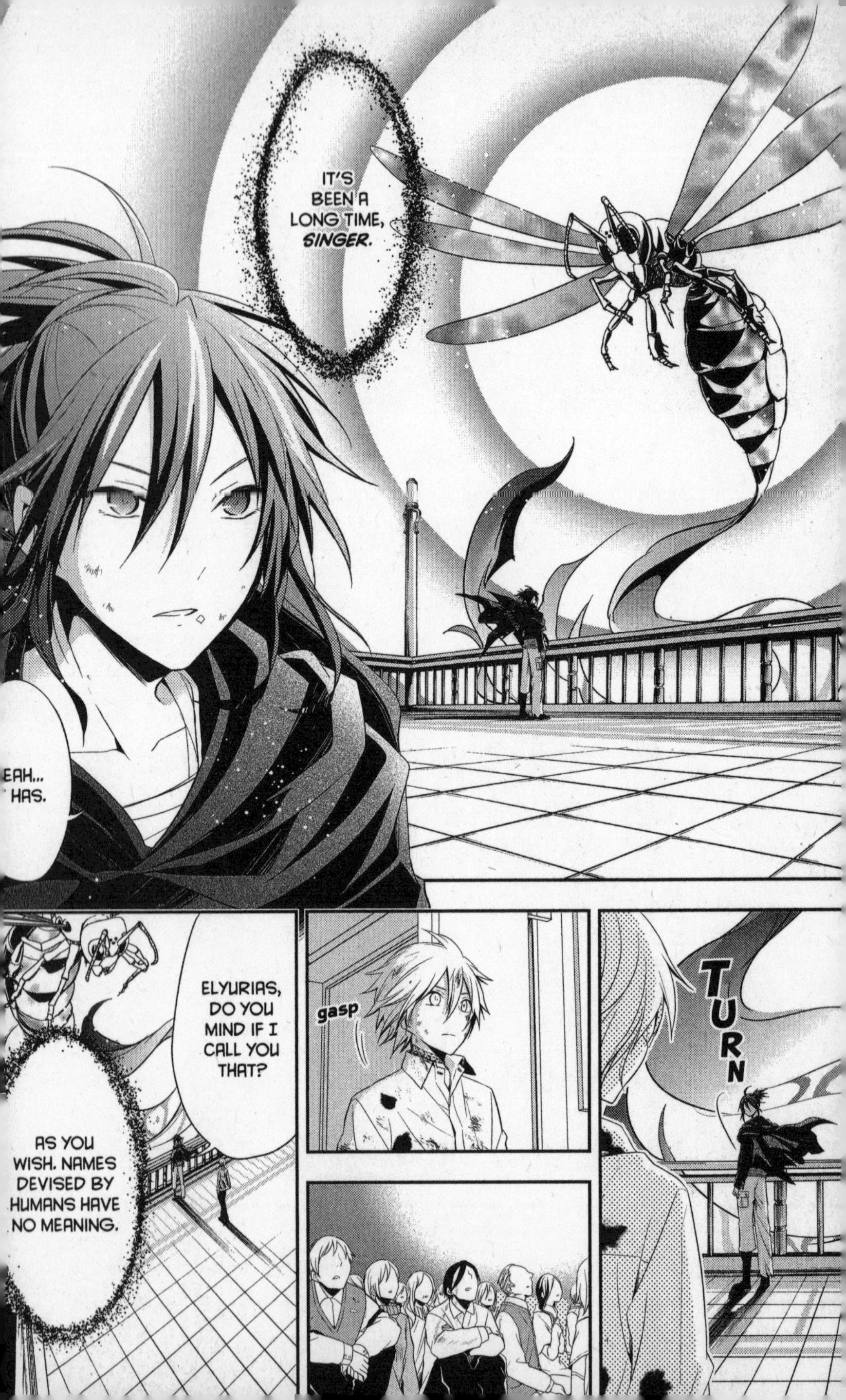
IT'S BEEN A LONG TIME, *SINGER*.
EAH... HAS.
TURN
gasp
ELYURIAS, DO YOU MIND IF I CALL YOU THAT?
AS YOU WISH. NAMES DEVISED BY HUMANS HAVE NO MEANING.

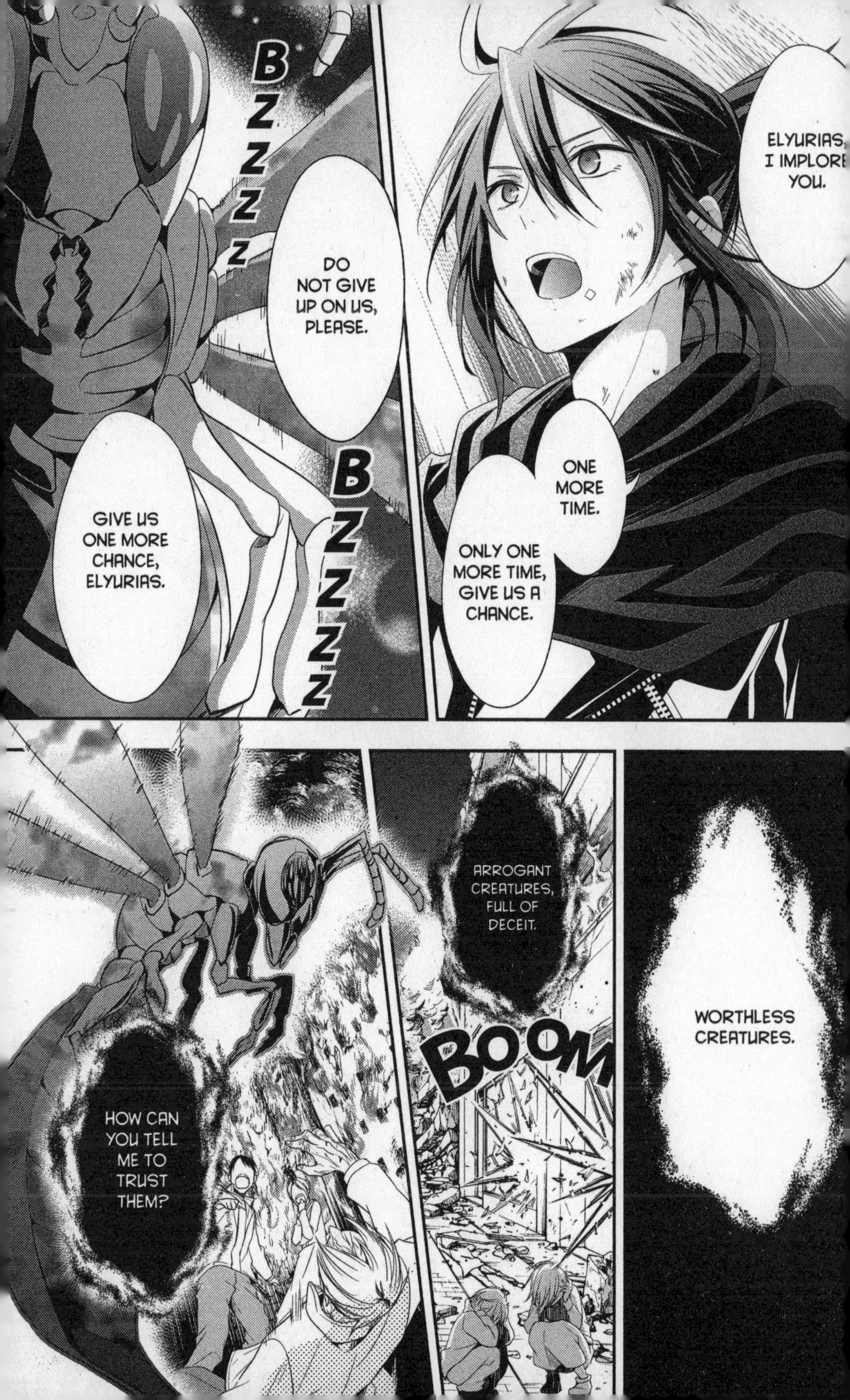
ELYURIAS, I IMPLORE YOU.
ONE MORE TIME.
ONLY ONE MORE TIME, GIVE US A CHANCE.
DO NOT GIVE UP ON US, PLEASE.
BZZZZ
GIVE US ONE MORE CHANCE, ELYURIAS.
BZZZZZ
WORTHLESS CREATURES.
ARROGANT CREATURES, FULL OF DECEIT.
BOOM
HOW CAN YOU TELL ME TO TRUST THEM?

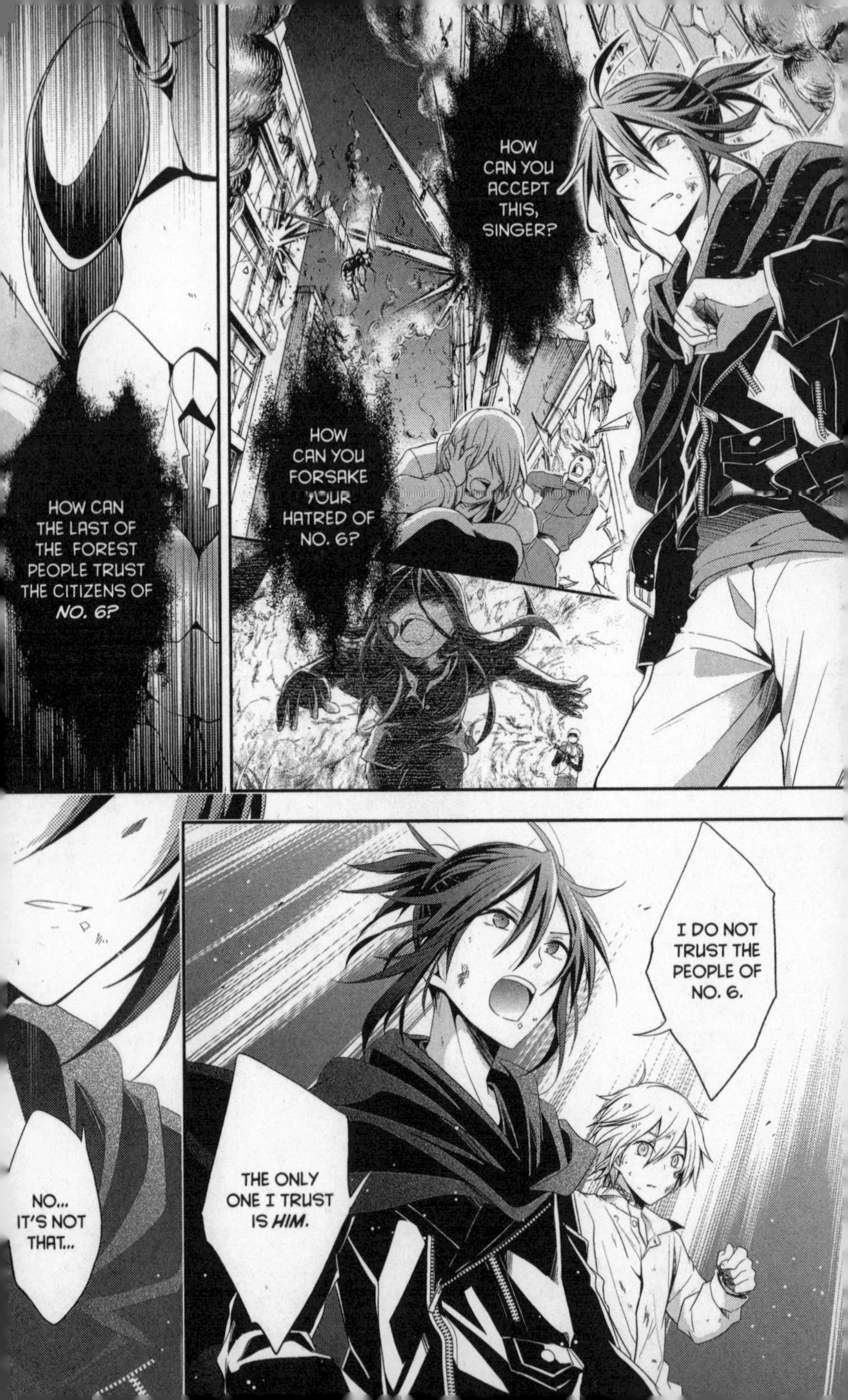
HOW CAN YOU ACCEPT THIS, SINGER?
HOW CAN YOU FORSAKE YOUR HATRED OF NO. 6?
HOW CAN THE LAST OF THE FOREST PEOPLE TRUST THE CITIZENS OF *NO. 6?*
I DO NOT TRUST THE PEOPLE OF NO. 6.
THE ONLY ONE I TRUST IS *HIM.*
NO... IT'S NOT THAT...

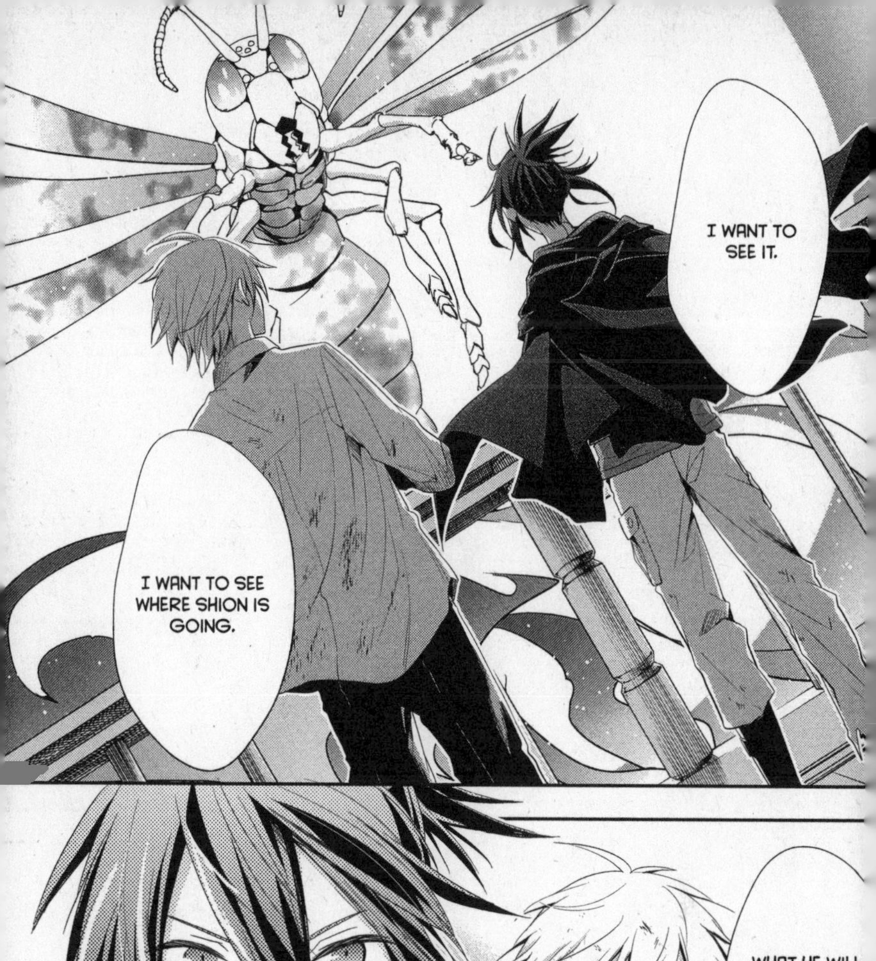
I WANT TO SEE IT.
I WANT TO SEE WHERE SHION IS GOING.
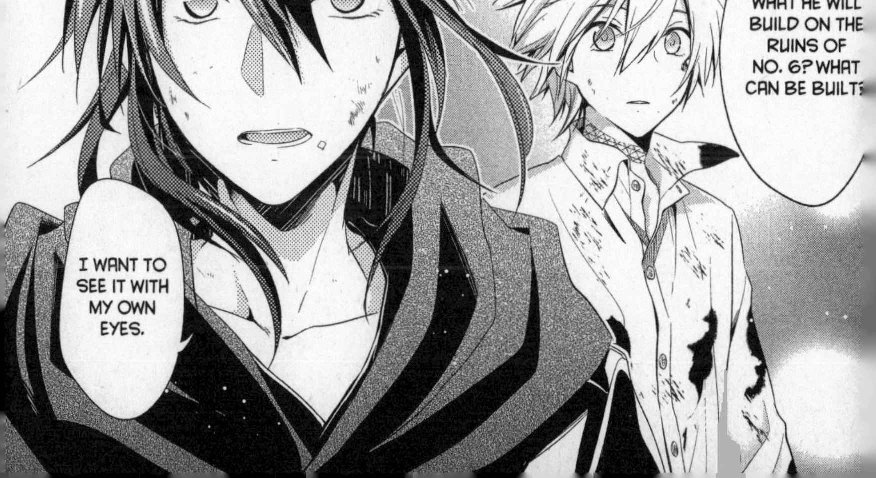
WHAT HE WILL BUILD ON THE RUINS OF NO. 6? WHAT CAN BE BUILT?
I WANT TO SEE IT WITH MY OWN EYES.

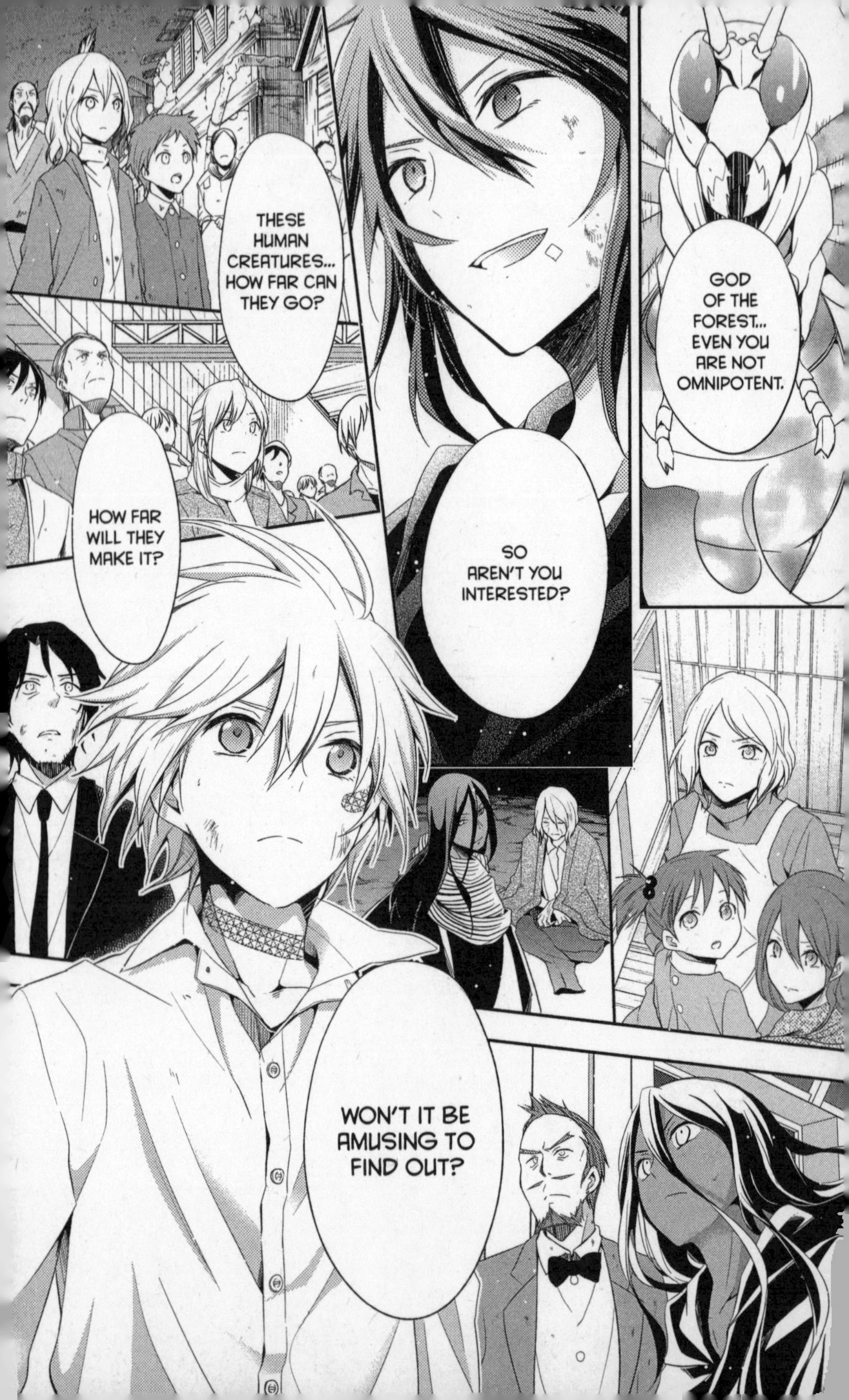
GOD OF THE FOREST... EVEN YOU ARE NOT OMNIPOTENT.
THESE HUMAN CREATURES... HOW FAR CAN THEY GO?
HOW FAR WILL THEY MAKE IT?
SO AREN'T YOU INTERESTED?
WON'T IT BE AMUSING TO FIND OUT?

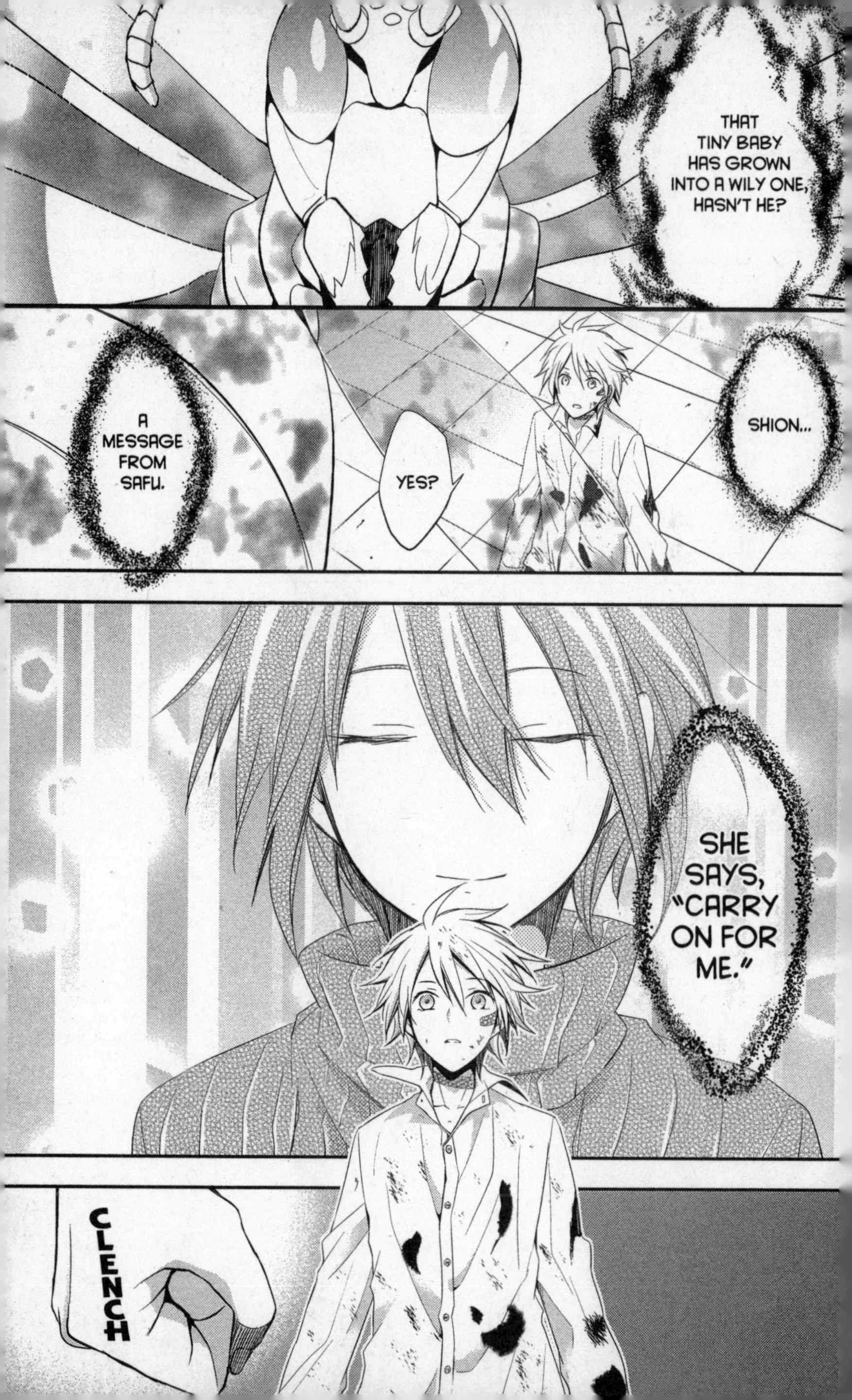
THAT TINY BABY HAS GROWN INTO A WILY ONE, HASN'T HE?
SHION...
YES?
A MESSAGE FROM SAFU.
SHE SAYS, "CARRY ON FOR ME."
CLENCH

TELL SAFU I RECEIVED THE MESSAGE.

AND THAT, AS LONG AS I LIVE, I WILL NEVER FORGET HER.

ELYURIAS, WAIT.

UNDER-STOOD.

B Z Z Z Z

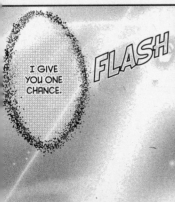

I GIVE YOU ONE CHANCE.

FLASH

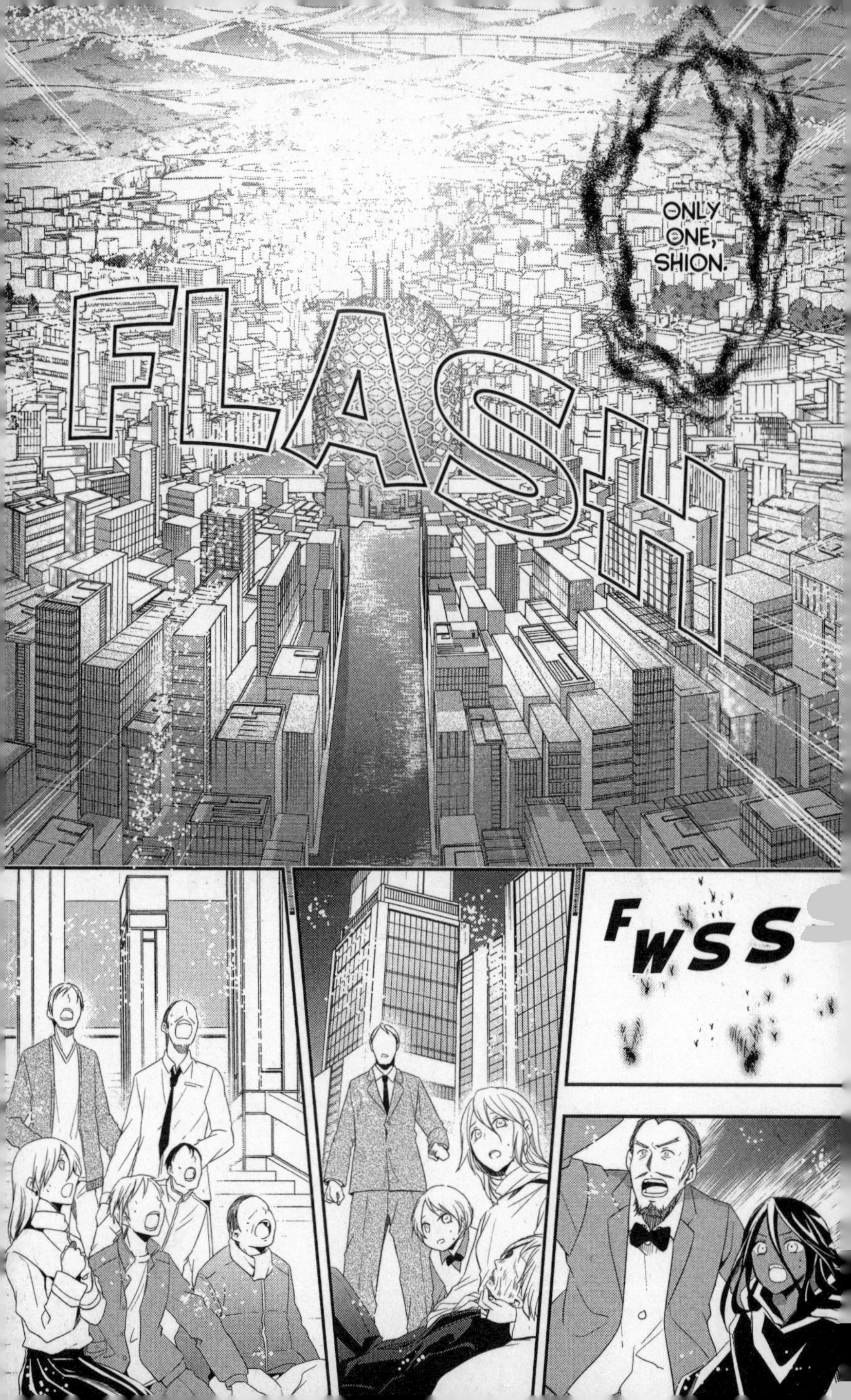
ONLY ONE, SHION.
FLASH
FWSS

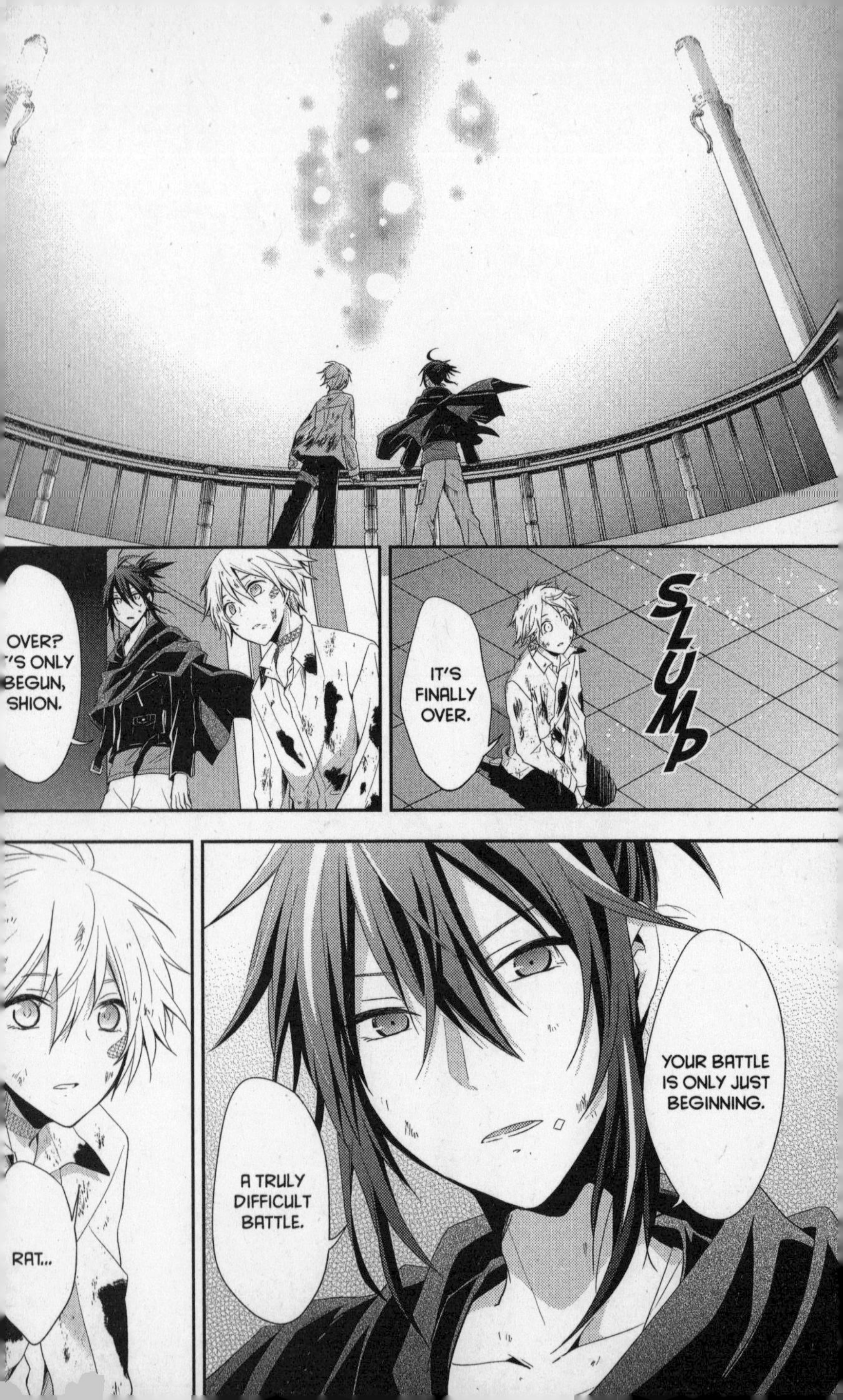
SLUMP
IT'S FINALLY OVER.
OVER? IT'S ONLY BEGUN, SHION.
YOUR BATTLE IS ONLY JUST BEGINNING.
A TRULY DIFFICULT BATTLE.
RAT...

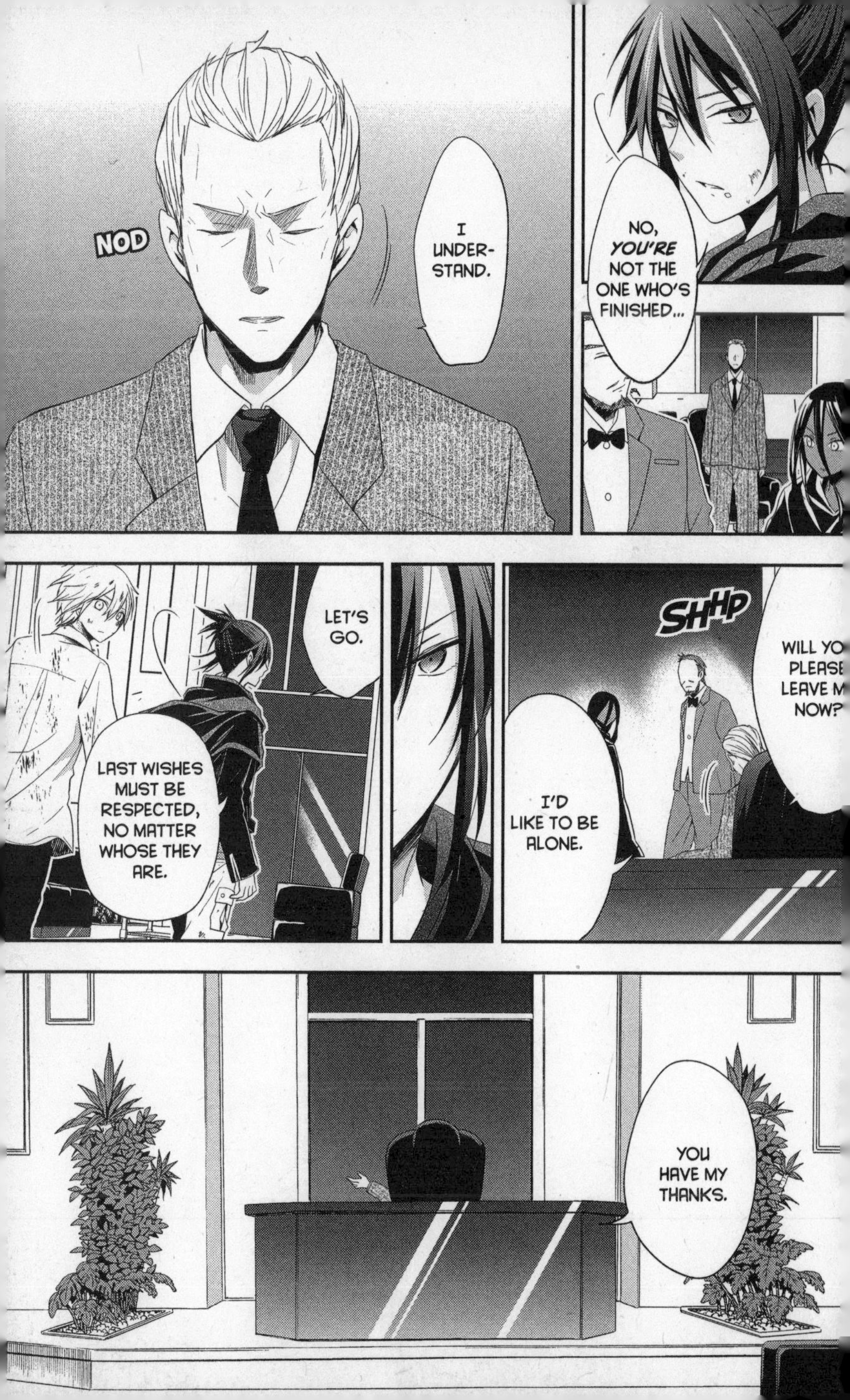
NO, *YOU'RE* NOT THE ONE WHO'S FINISHED...
I UNDER-STAND.
NOD
WILL YO
PLEASE
LEAVE M
NOW?
SHHP
I'D LIKE TO BE ALONE.
LET'S GO.
LAST WISHES MUST BE RESPECTED, NO MATTER WHOSE THEY ARE.
YOU HAVE MY THANKS.

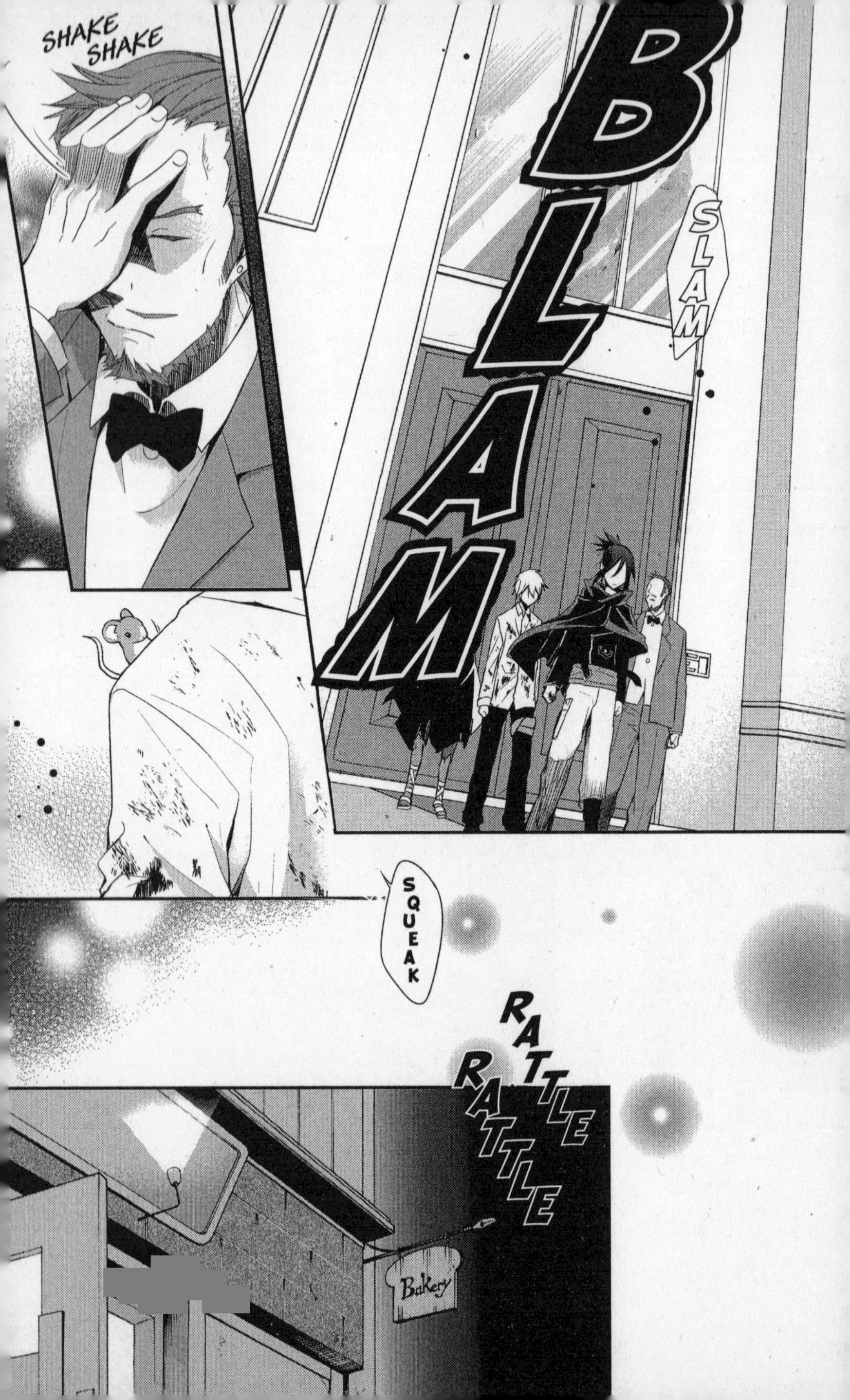
BLAM
SLAM
SHAKE SHAKE
SQUEAK
RATTLE RATTLE
Bakery

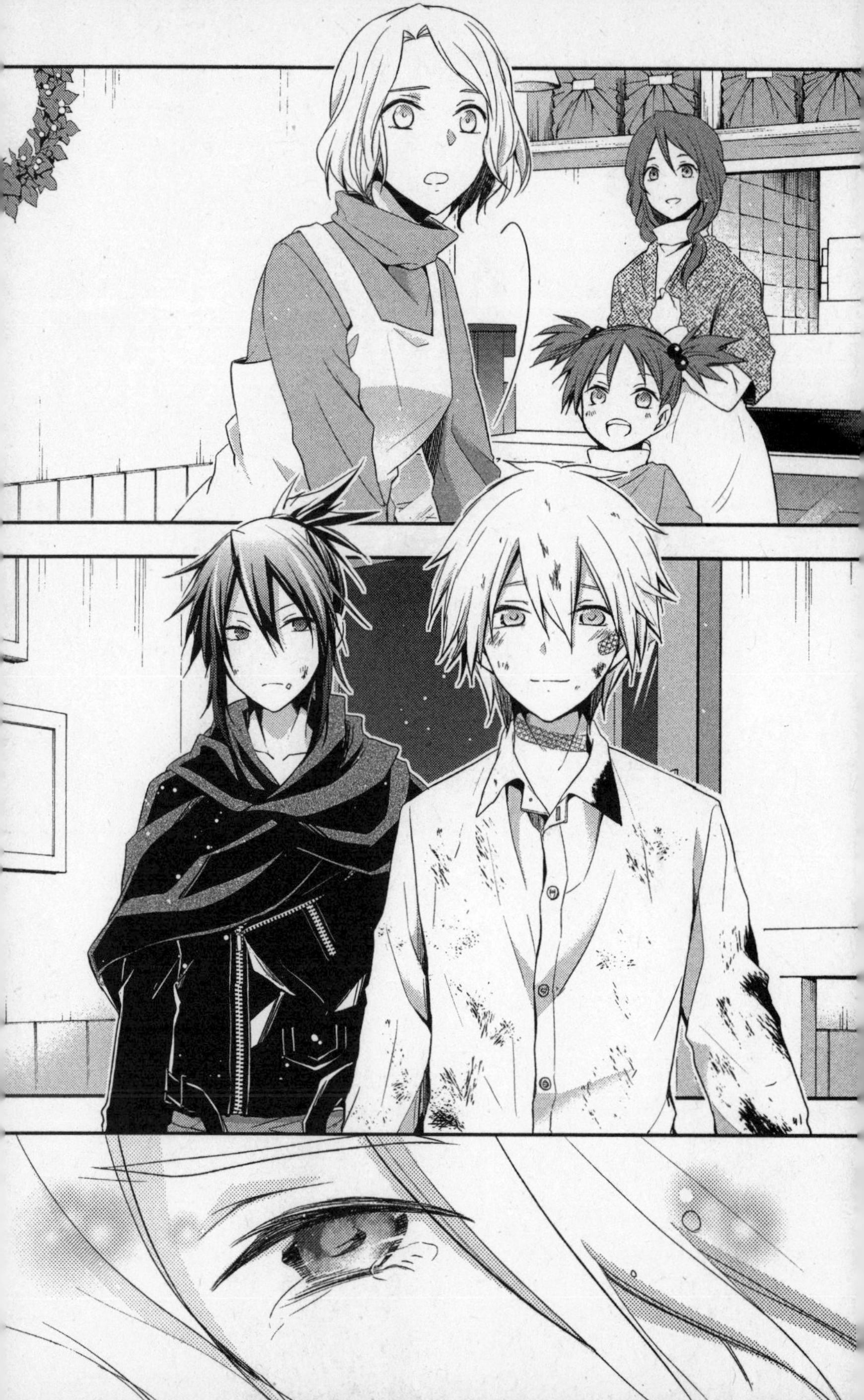

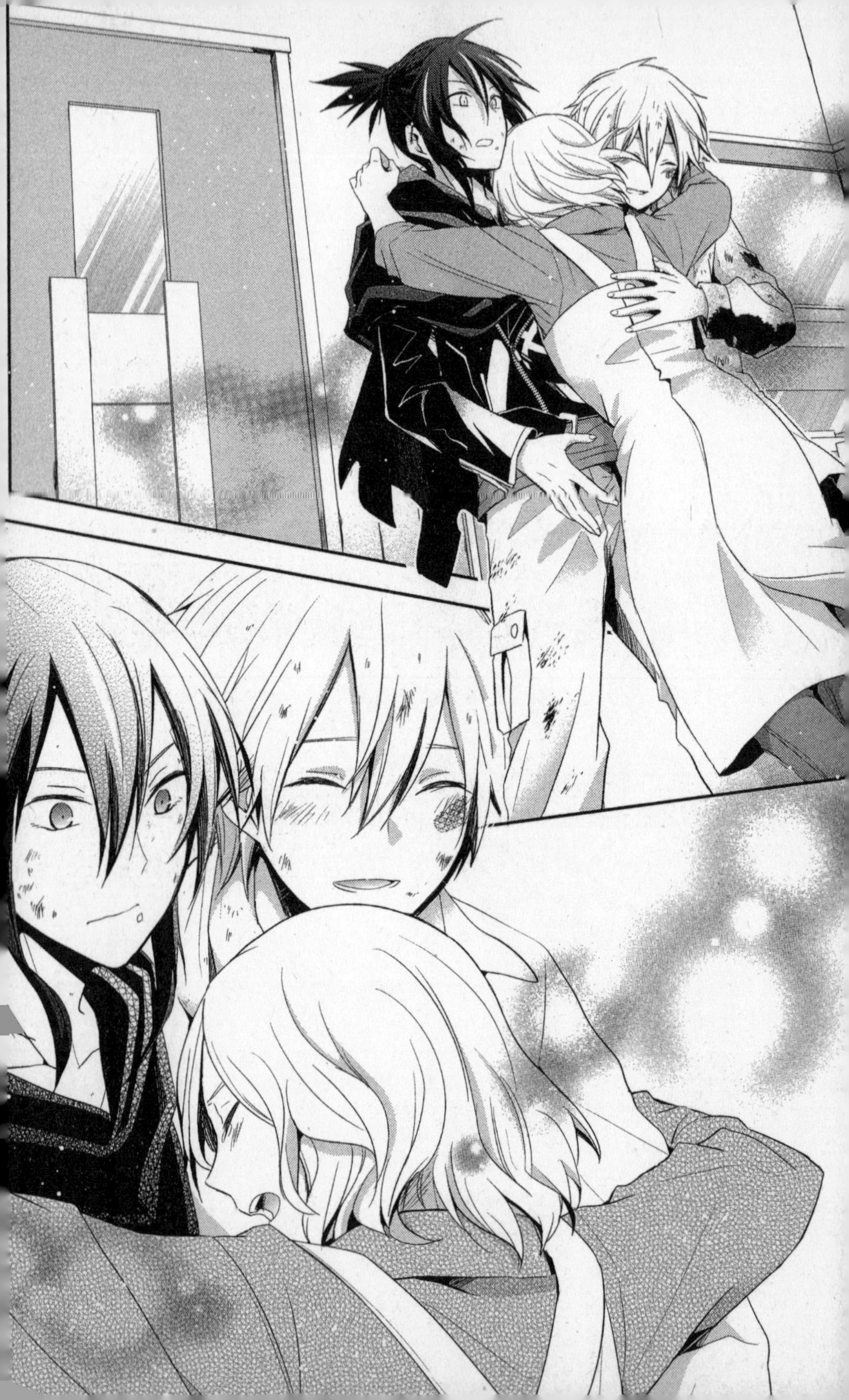

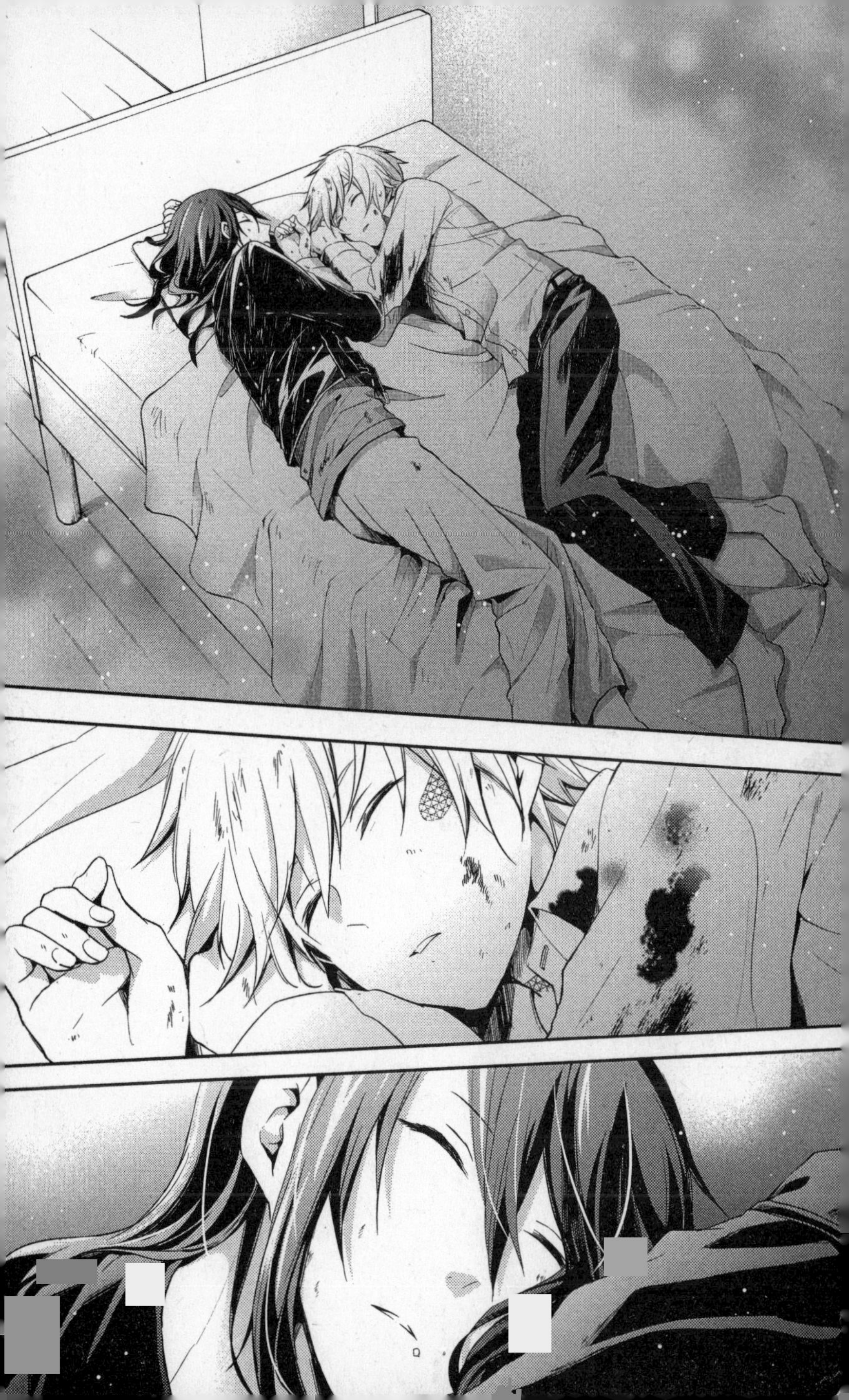

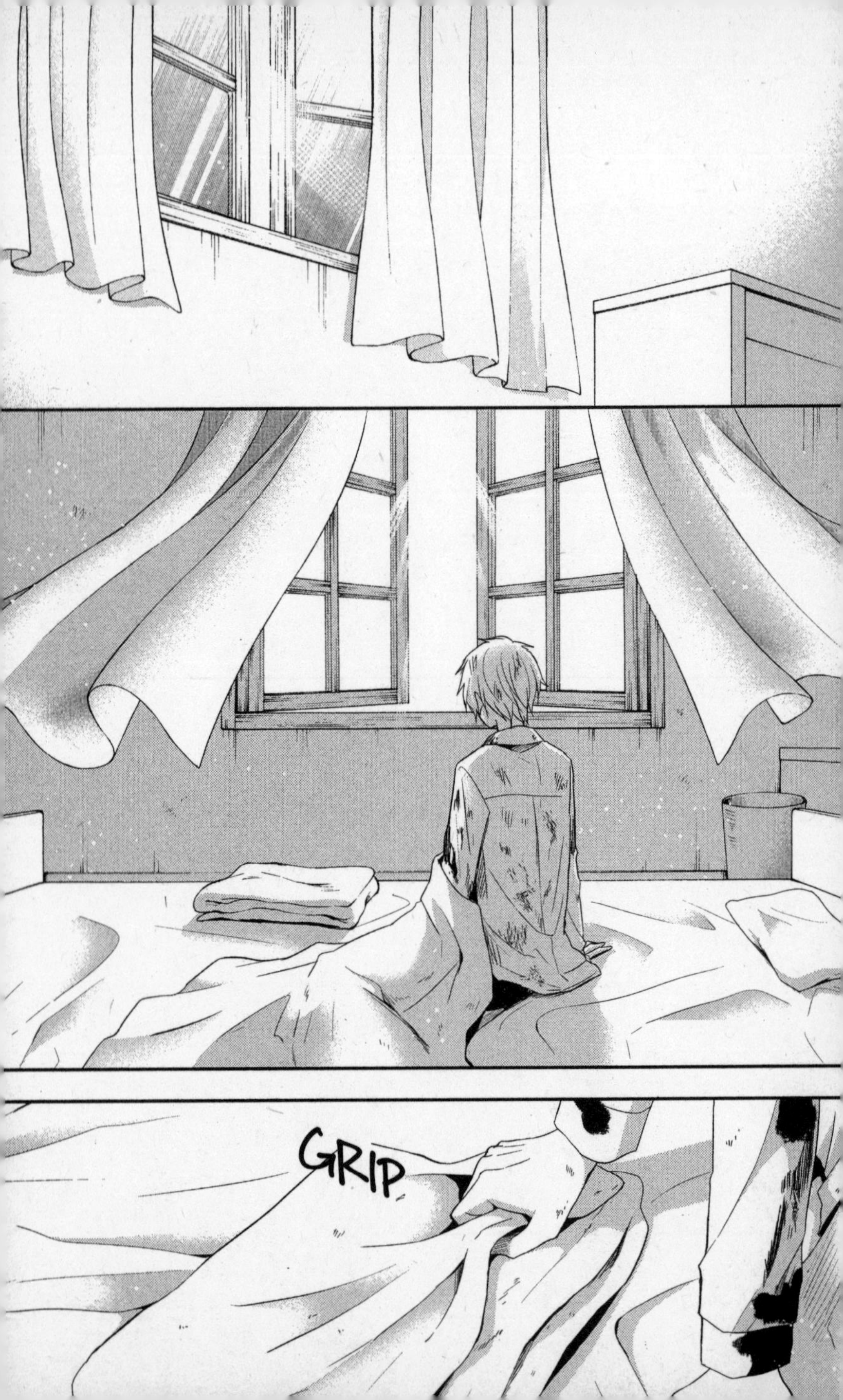
GRIP

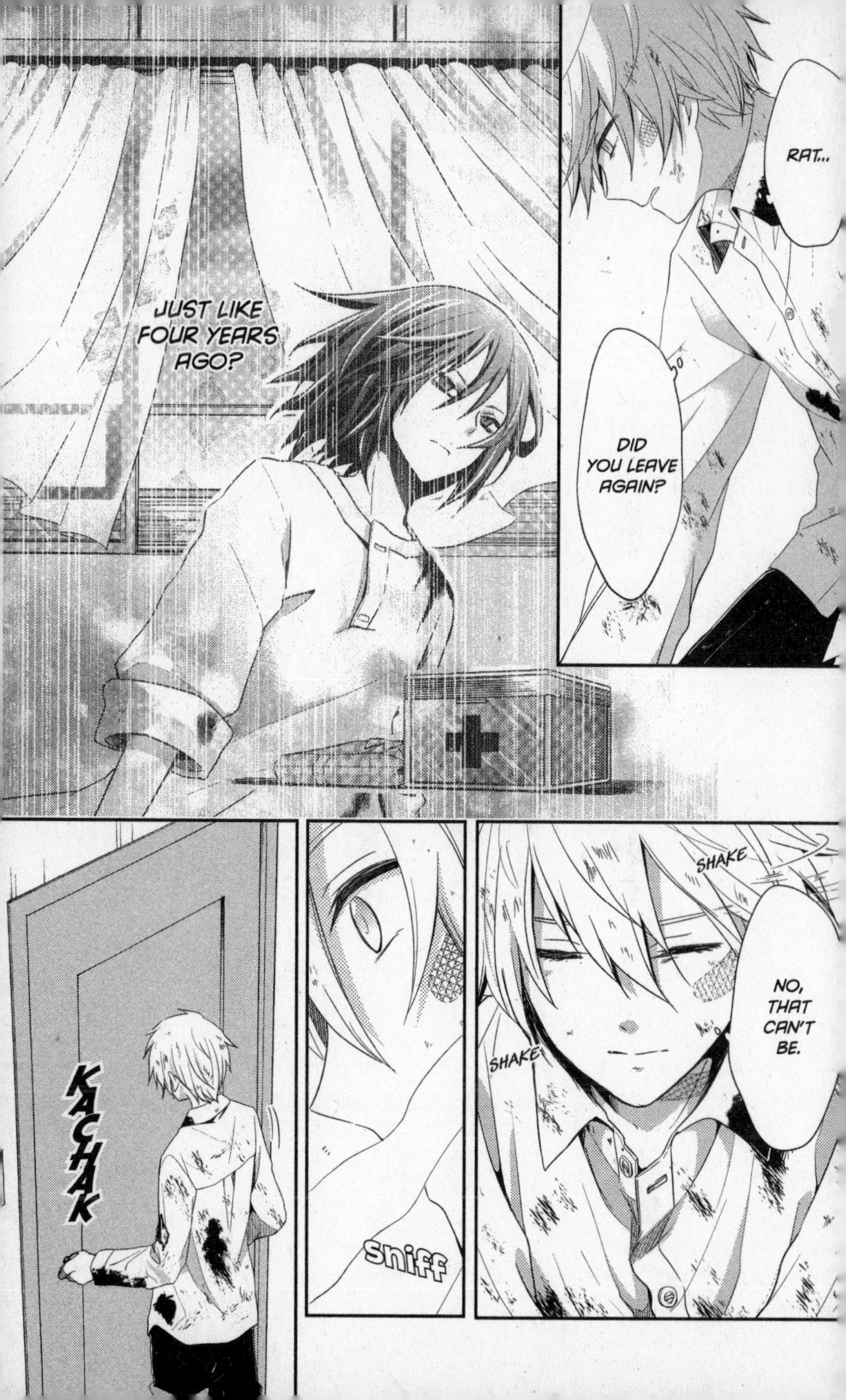
RAT...
DID YOU LEAVE AGAIN?
JUST LIKE FOUR YEARS AGO?
SHAKE
NO, THAT CAN'T BE.
SHAKE
sniff
KACHAK

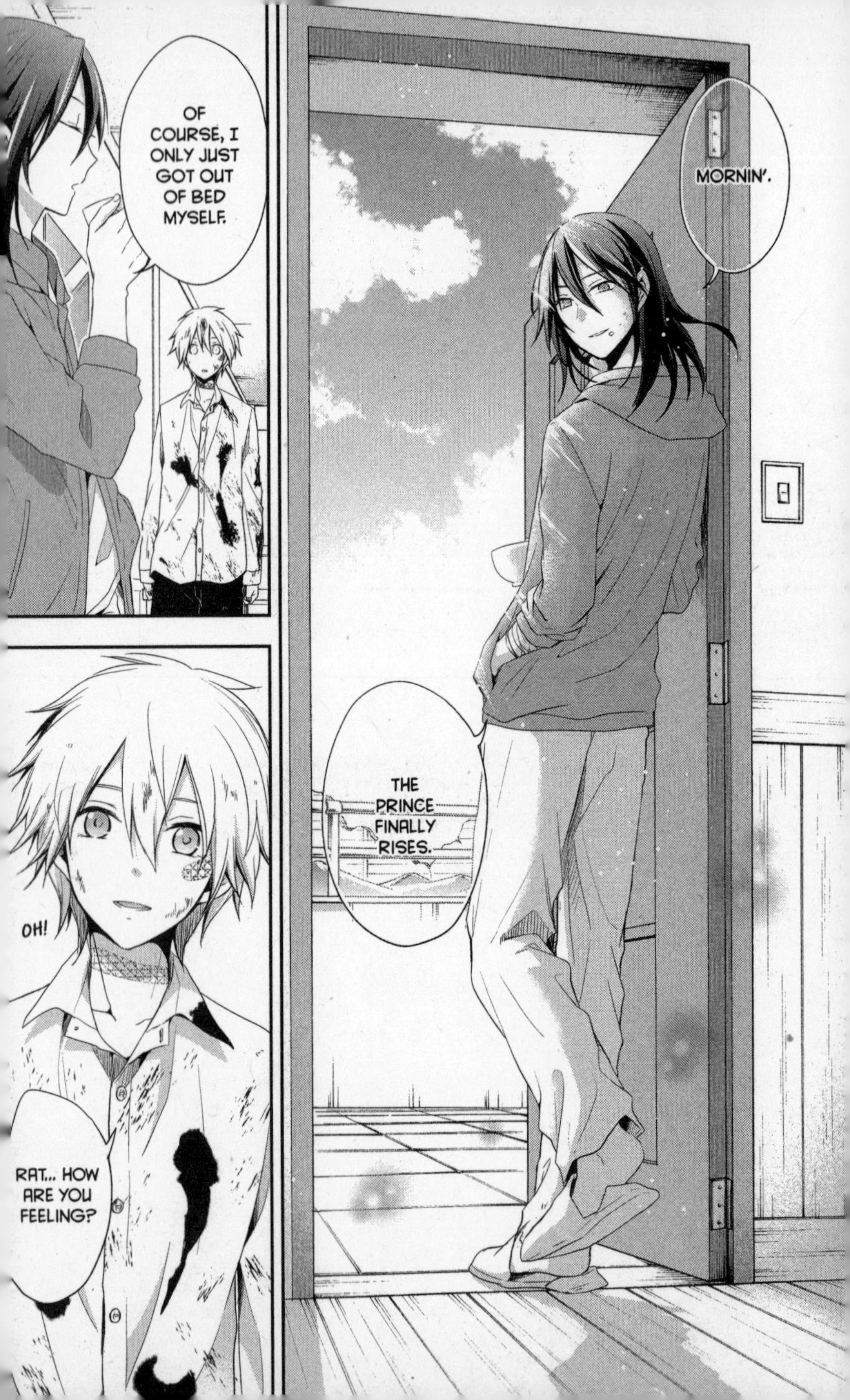
MORNIN'.
THE PRINCE FINALLY RISES.
OF COURSE, I ONLY JUST GOT OUT OF BED MYSELF.
OH!
RAT... HOW ARE YOU FEELING?

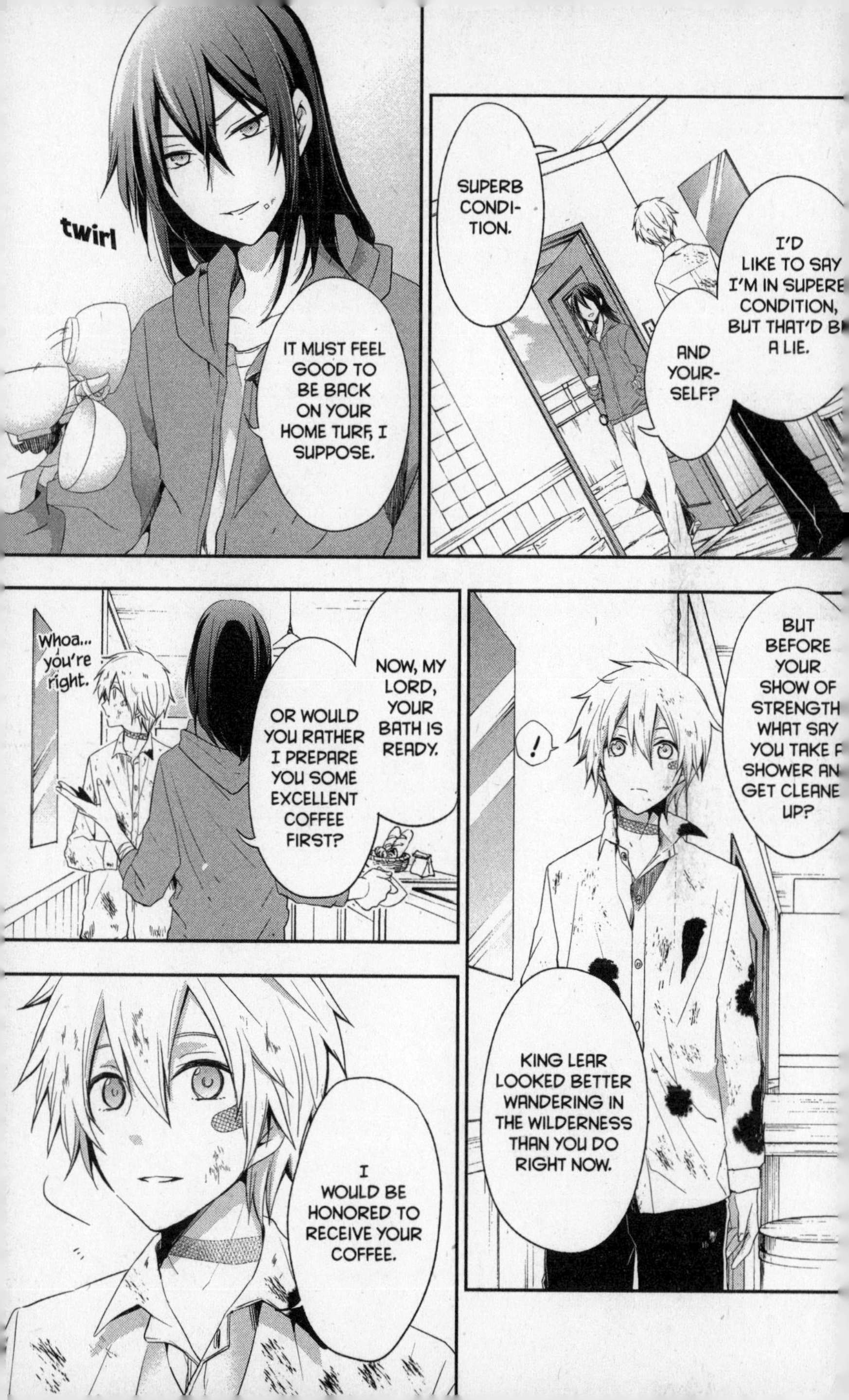
I'D LIKE TO SAY I'M IN SUPERB CONDITION, BUT THAT'D B A LIE.
AND YOURSELF?
SUPERB CONDITION.
twirl
IT MUST FEEL GOOD TO BE BACK ON YOUR HOME TURF, I SUPPOSE.
BUT BEFORE YOUR SHOW OF STRENGTH WHAT SAY YOU TAKE SHOWER AN GET CLEANE UP?
!
KING LEAR LOOKED BETTER WANDERING IN THE WILDERNESS THAN YOU DO RIGHT NOW.
NOW, MY LORD, YOUR BATH IS READY.
OR WOULD YOU RATHER I PREPARE YOU SOME EXCELLENT COFFEE FIRST?
Whoa... you're right.
I WOULD BE HONORED TO RECEIVE YOUR COFFEE.

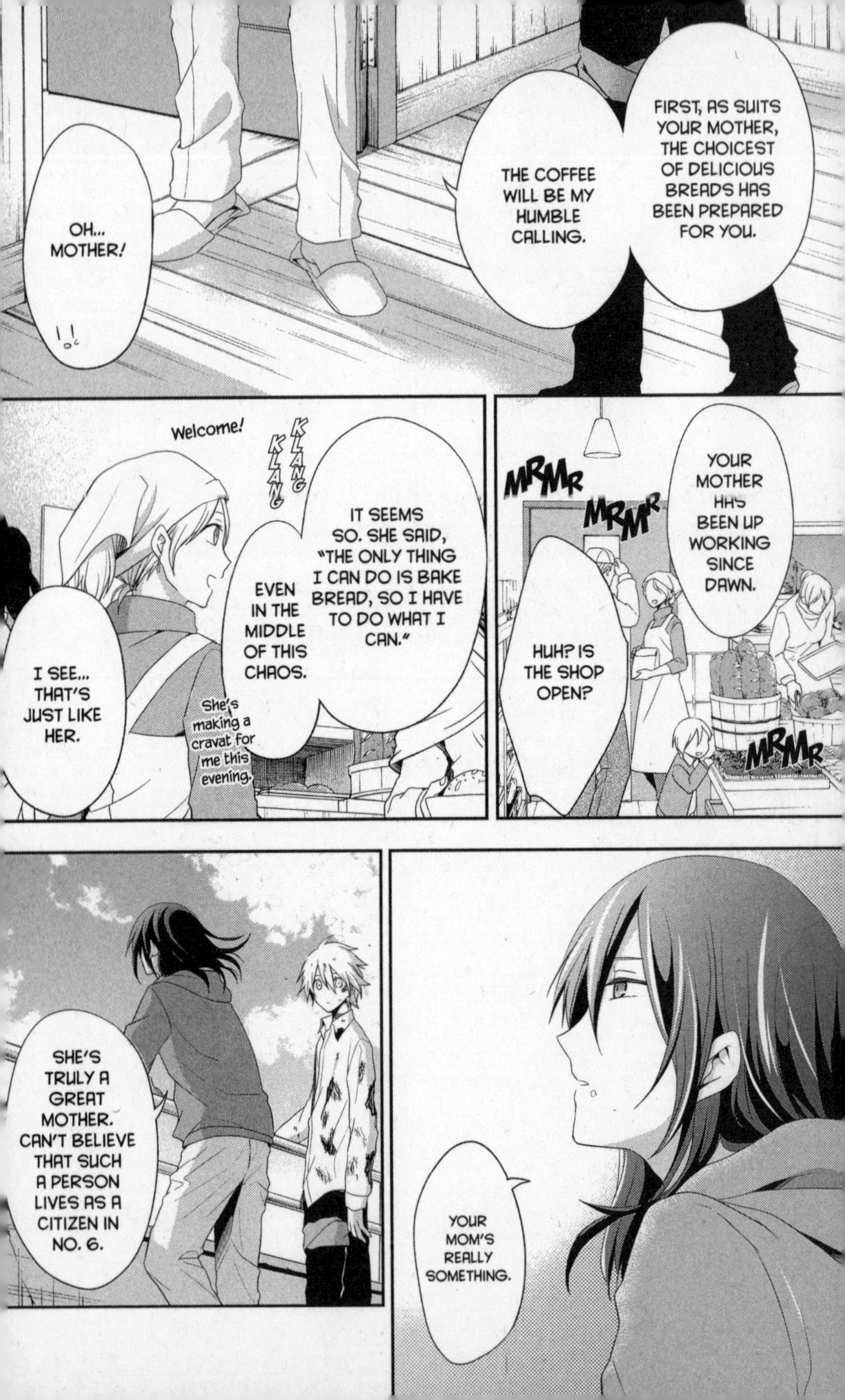
FIRST, AS SUITS YOUR MOTHER, THE CHOICEST OF DELICIOUS BREADS HAS BEEN PREPARED FOR YOU.
THE COFFEE WILL BE MY HUMBLE CALLING.
OH... MOTHER!
!!
MRMR
MRMR
YOUR MOTHER HAS BEEN UP WORKING SINCE DAWN.
HUH? IS THE SHOP OPEN?
MRMR
KLANG
KLANG
Welcome!
IT SEEMS SO. SHE SAID, "THE ONLY THING I CAN DO IS BAKE BREAD, SO I HAVE TO DO WHAT I CAN."
EVEN IN THE MIDDLE OF THIS CHAOS.
She's making a cravat for me this evening.
I SEE... THAT'S JUST LIKE HER.
YOUR MOM'S REALLY SOMETHING.
SHE'S TRULY A GREAT MOTHER. CAN'T BELIEVE THAT SUCH A PERSON LIVES AS A CITIZEN IN NO. 6.

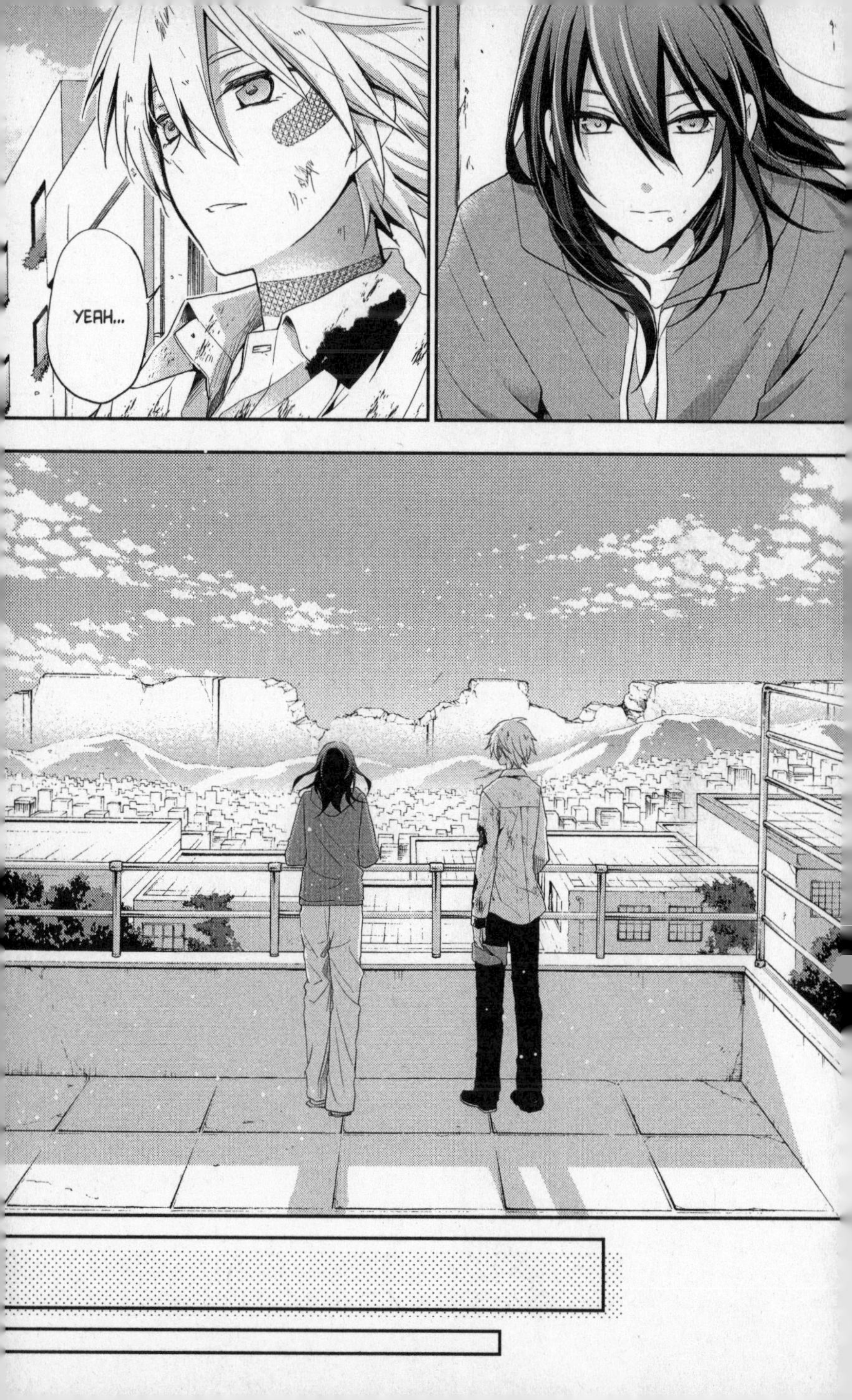
YEAH...

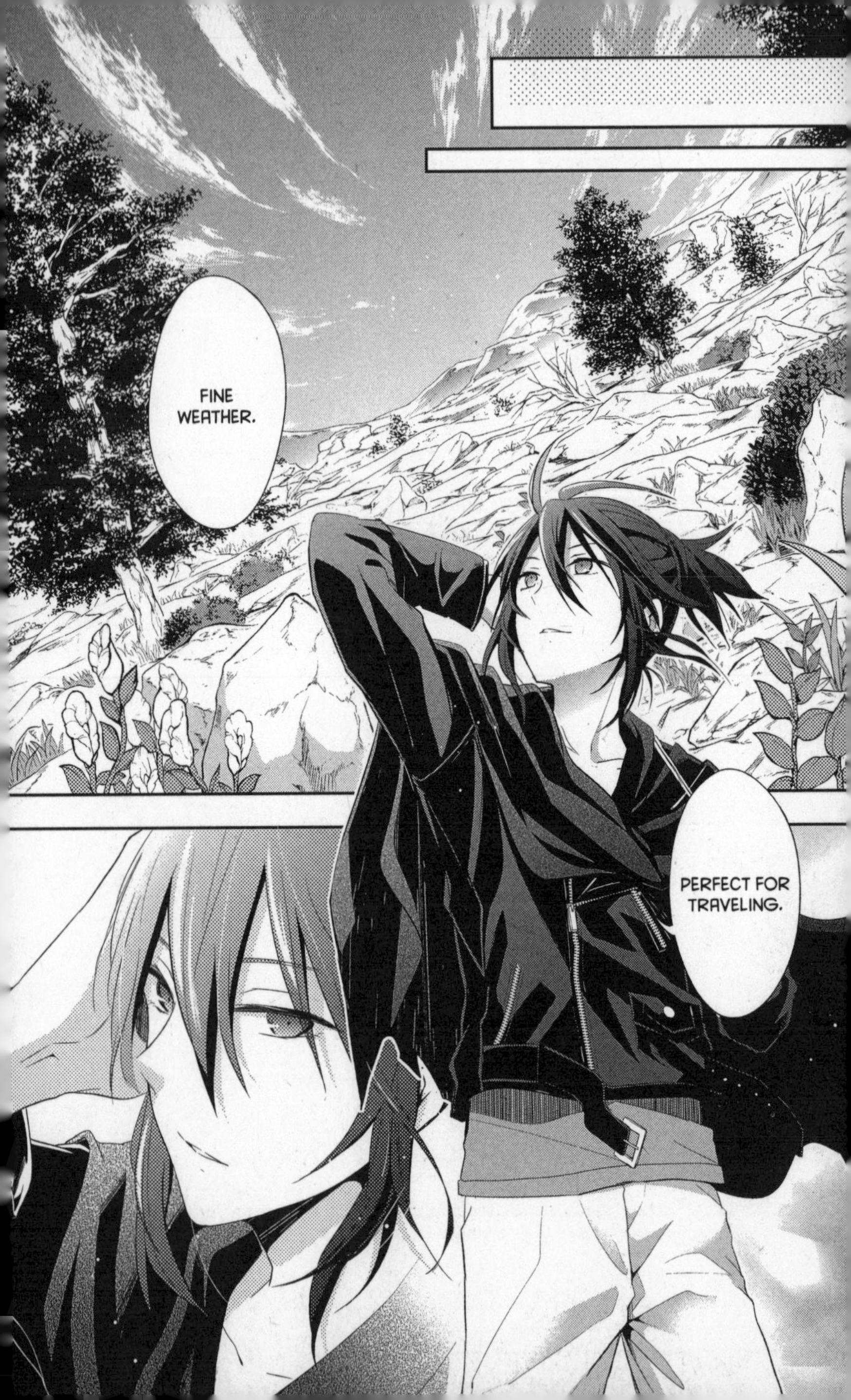
FINE WEATHER.
PERFECT FOR TRAVELING.

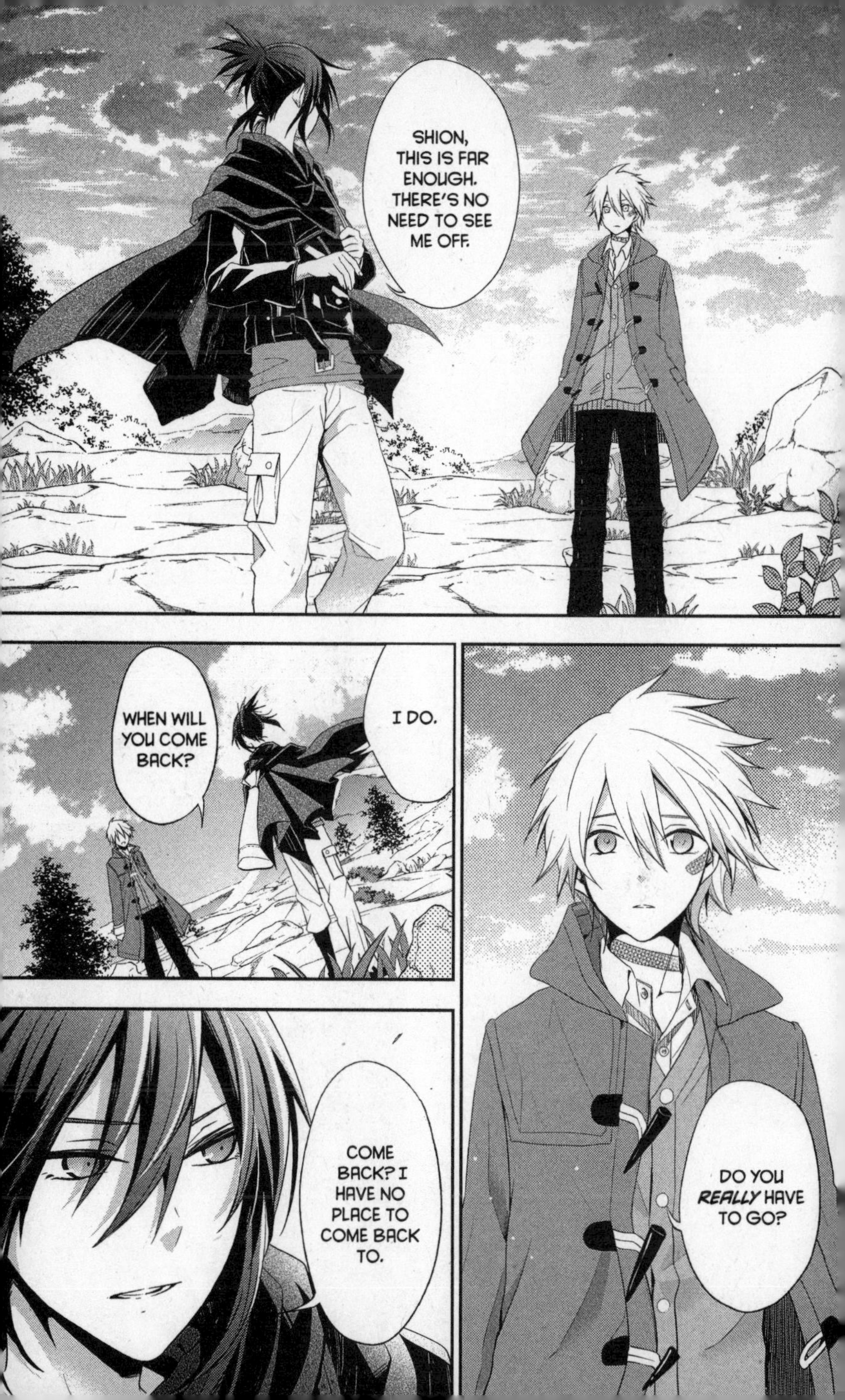
SHION, THIS IS FAR ENOUGH. THERE'S NO NEED TO SEE ME OFF.
DO YOU *REALLY* HAVE TO GO?
I DO.
WHEN WILL YOU COME BACK?
COME BACK? I HAVE NO PLACE TO COME BACK TO.

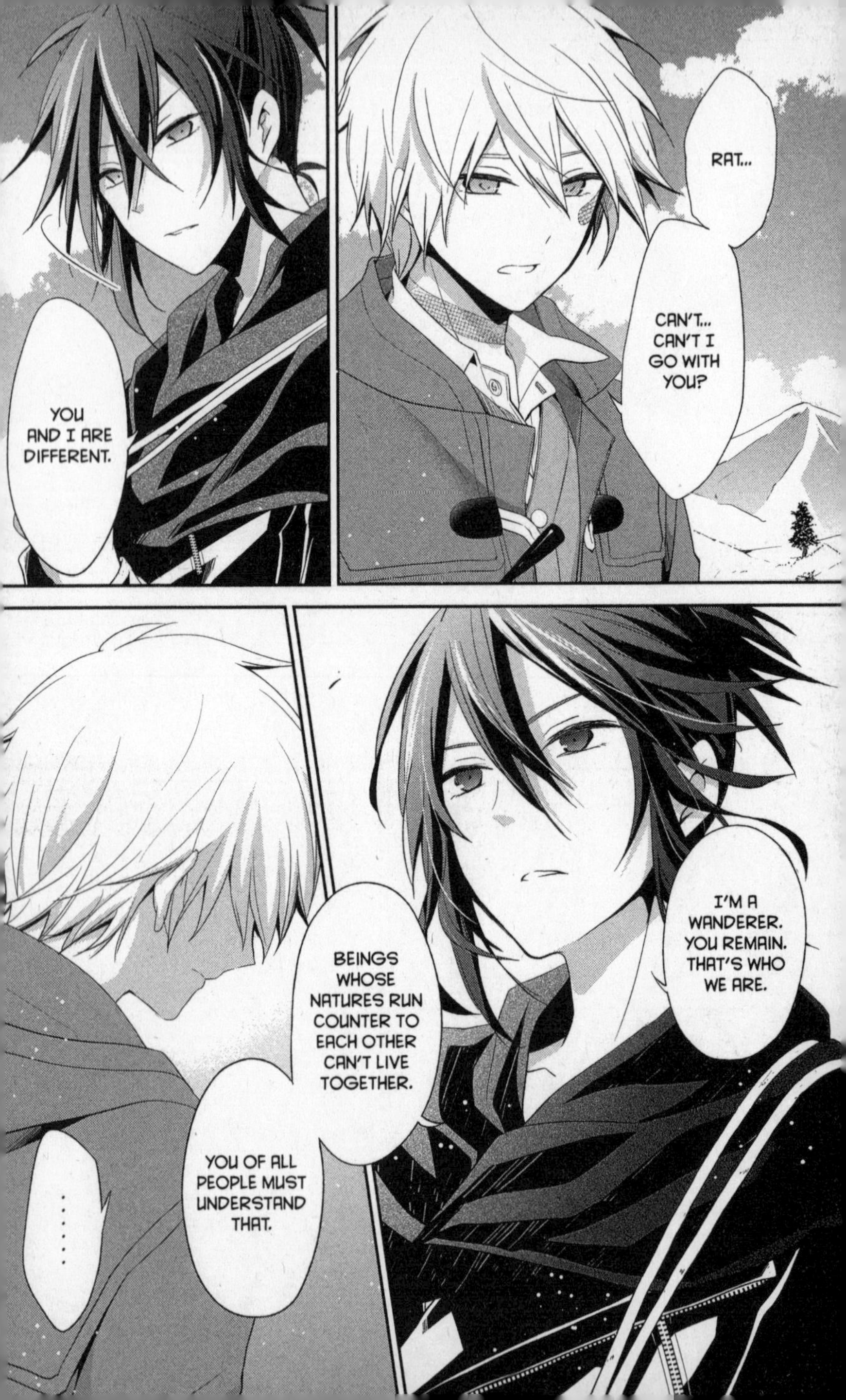
RAT...
CAN'T... CAN'T I GO WITH YOU?
YOU AND I ARE DIFFERENT.
I'M A WANDERER. YOU REMAIN. THAT'S WHO WE ARE.
BEINGS WHOSE NATURES RUN COUNTER TO EACH OTHER CAN'T LIVE TOGETHER.
YOU OF ALL PEOPLE MUST UNDERSTAND THAT.
......

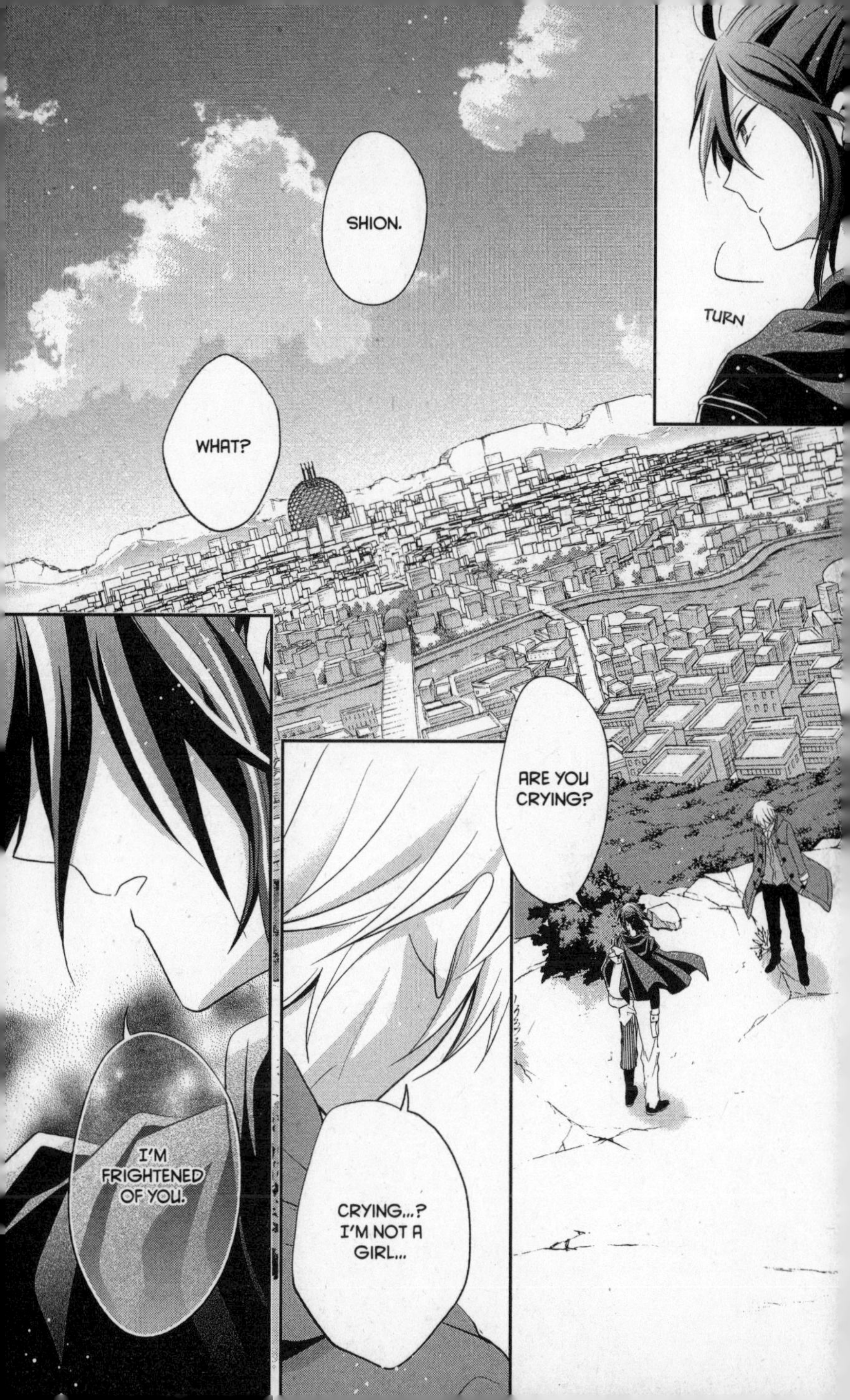
TURN
SHION.
WHAT?
ARE YOU CRYING?
CRYING...? I'M NOT A GIRL...
I'M FRIGHTENED OF YOU.

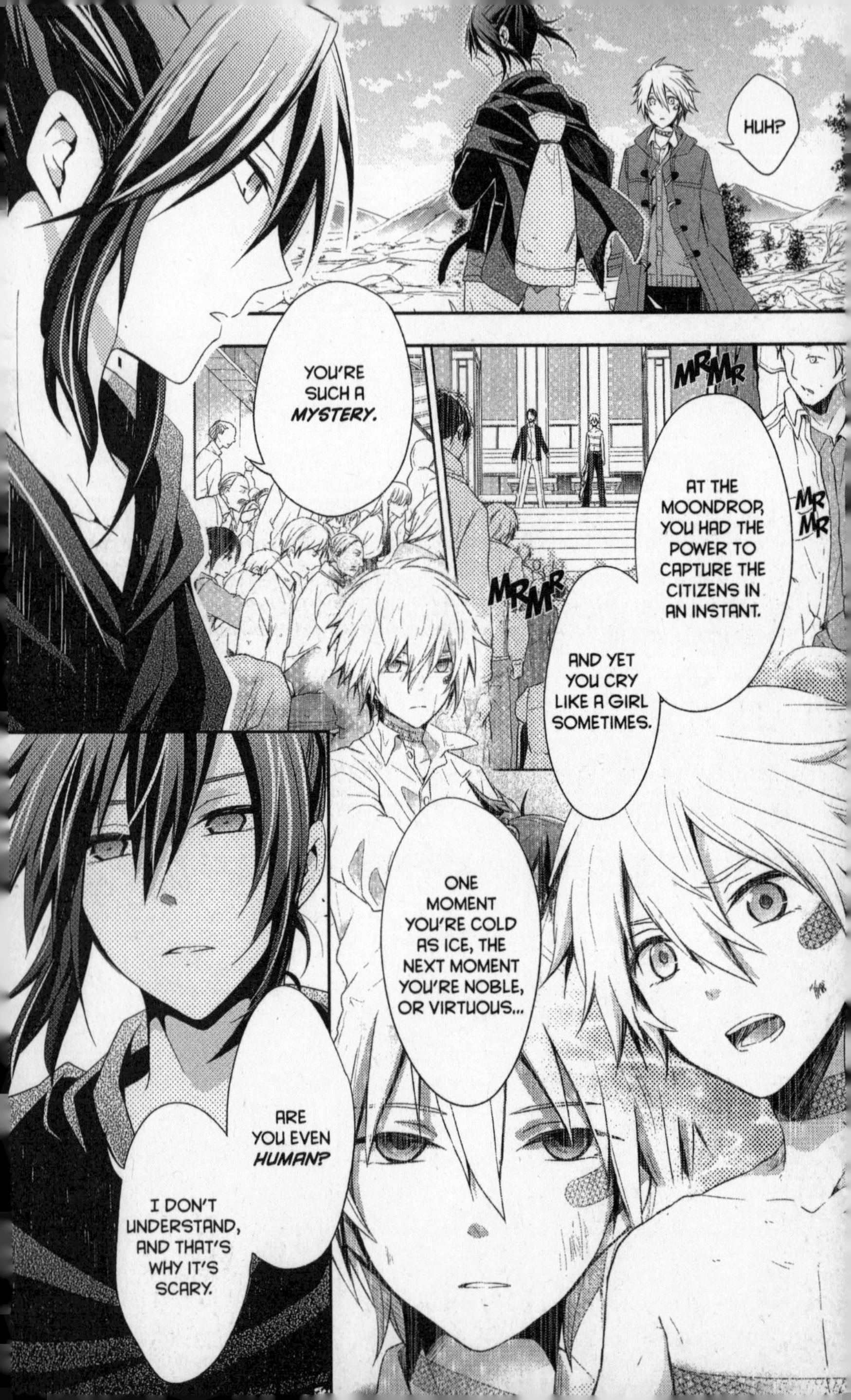
HUH?
YOU'RE SUCH A *MYSTERY.*
MRMR
MRMR
MRMR
AT THE MOONDROP, YOU HAD THE POWER TO CAPTURE THE CITIZENS IN AN INSTANT.
AND YET YOU CRY LIKE A GIRL SOMETIMES.
ONE MOMENT YOU'RE COLD AS ICE, THE NEXT MOMENT YOU'RE NOBLE, OR VIRTUOUS...
ARE YOU EVEN *HUMAN?*
I DON'T UNDERSTAND, AND THAT'S WHY IT'S SCARY.

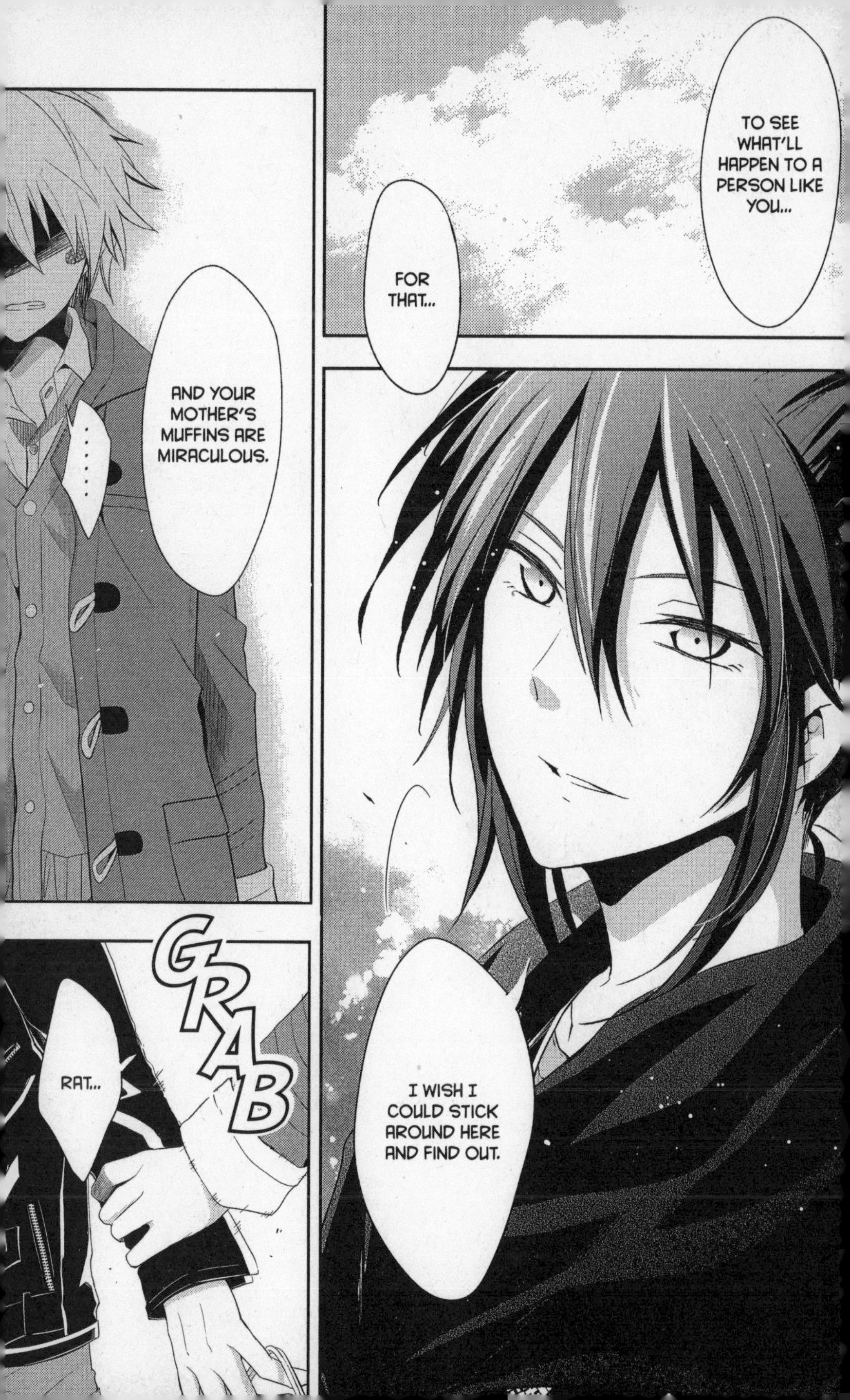
TO SEE WHAT'LL HAPPEN TO A PERSON LIKE YOU...
FOR THAT...
I WISH I COULD STICK AROUND HERE AND FIND OUT.
AND YOUR MOTHER'S MUFFINS ARE MIRACULOUS.
......
GRAB
RAT...

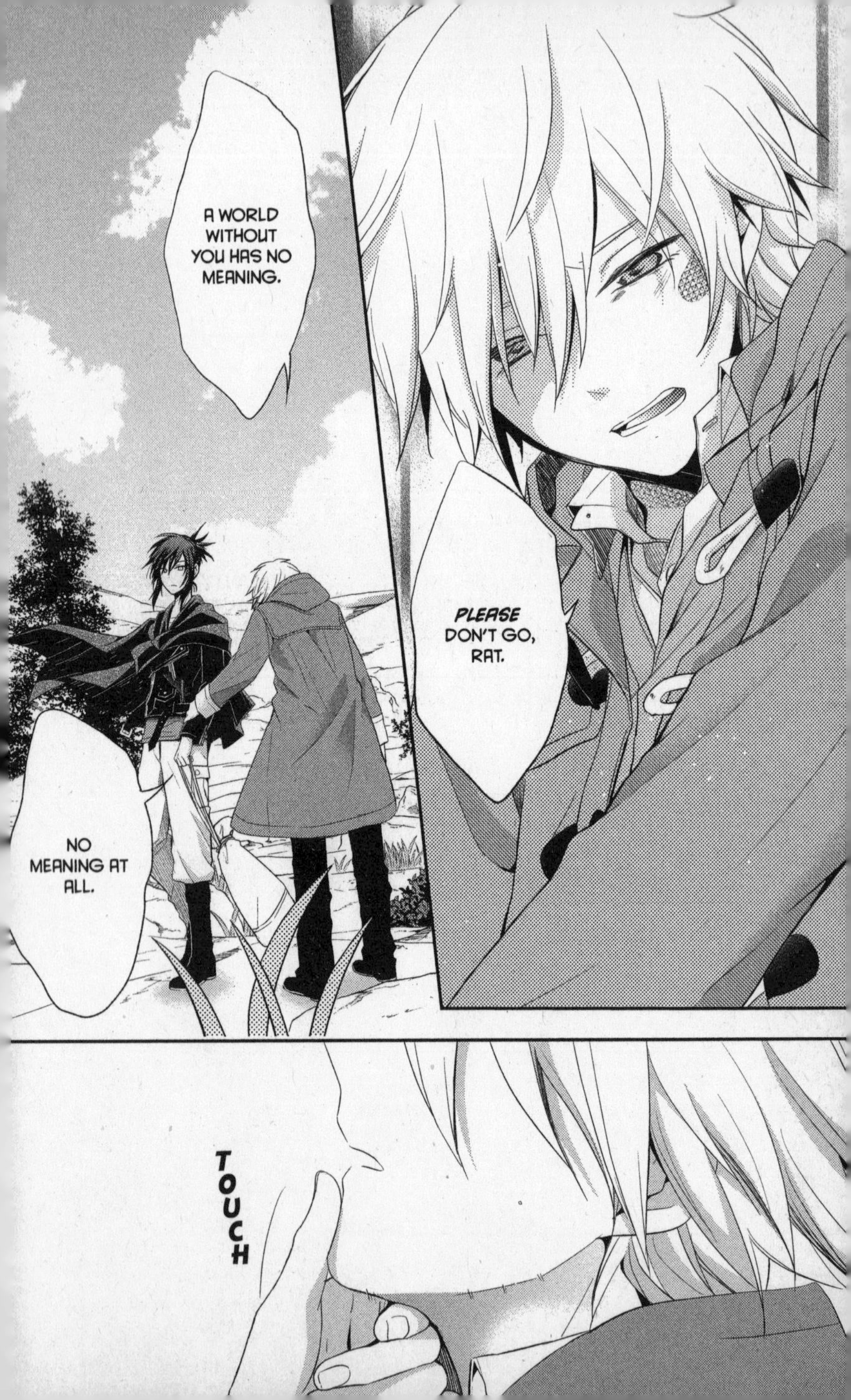
PLEASE DON'T GO, RAT.
A WORLD WITHOUT YOU HAS NO MEANING.
NO MEANING AT ALL.
TOUCH

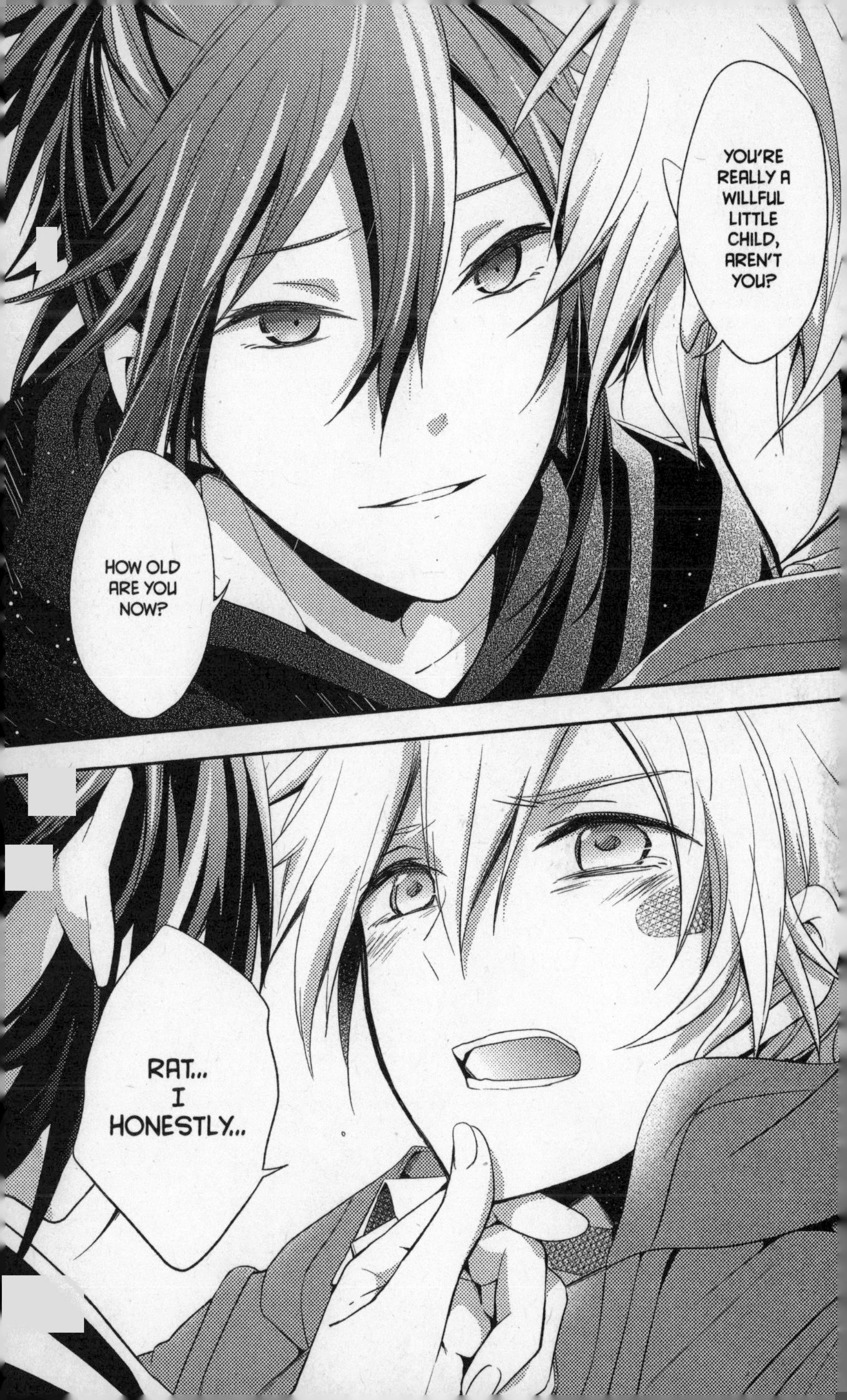
YOU'RE REALLY A WILLFUL LITTLE CHILD, AREN'T YOU?
HOW OLD ARE YOU NOW?
RAT... I HONESTLY...

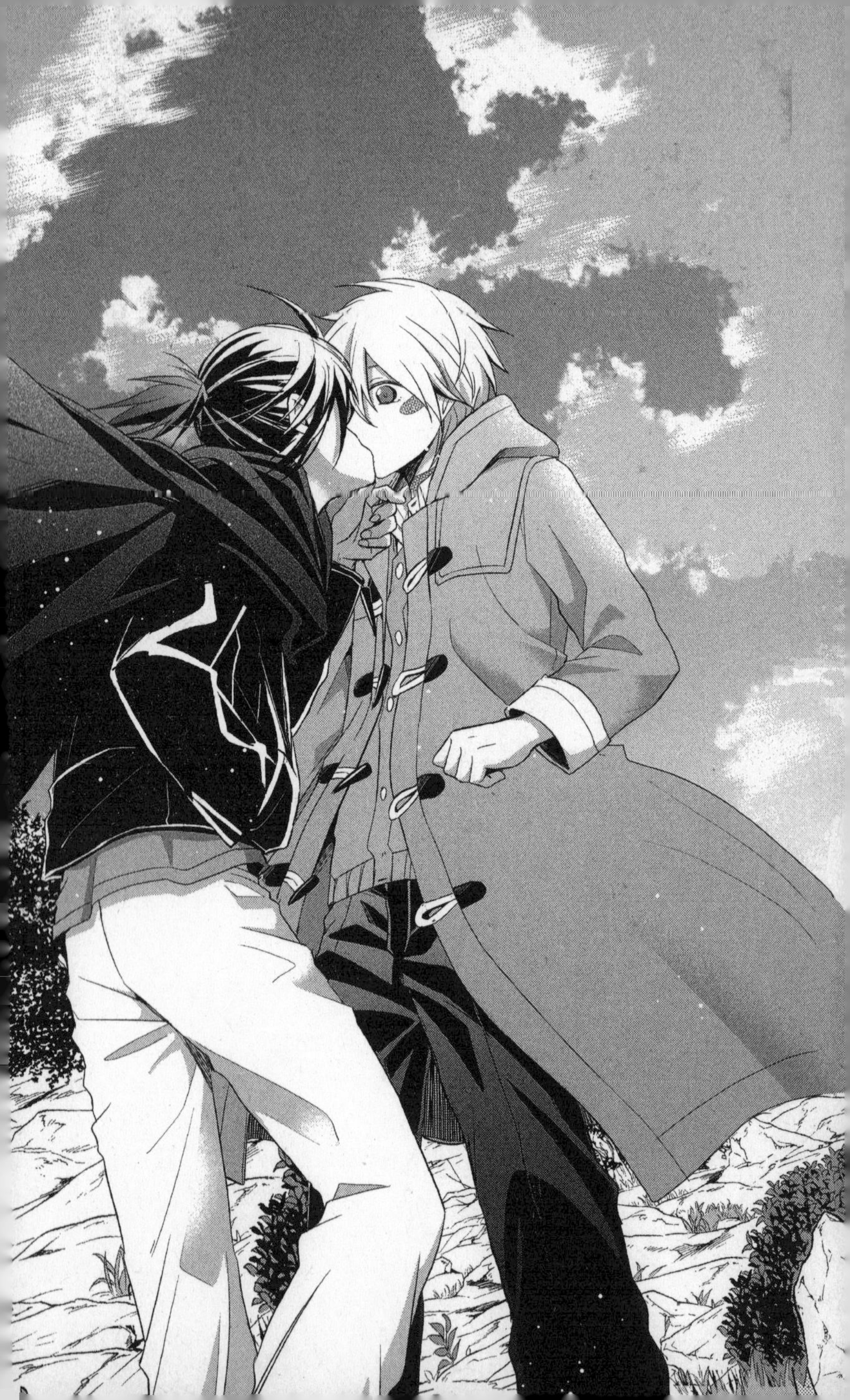

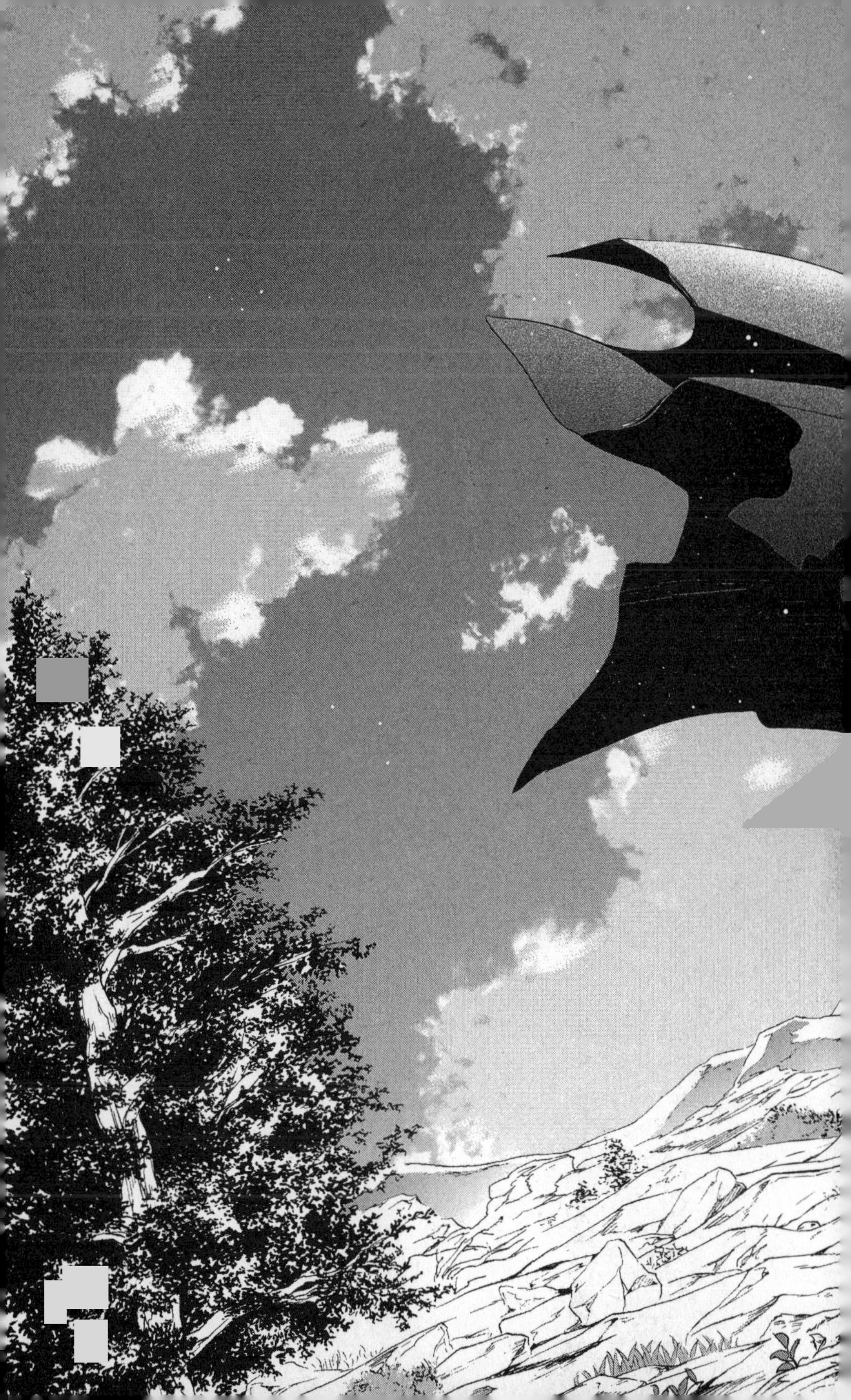

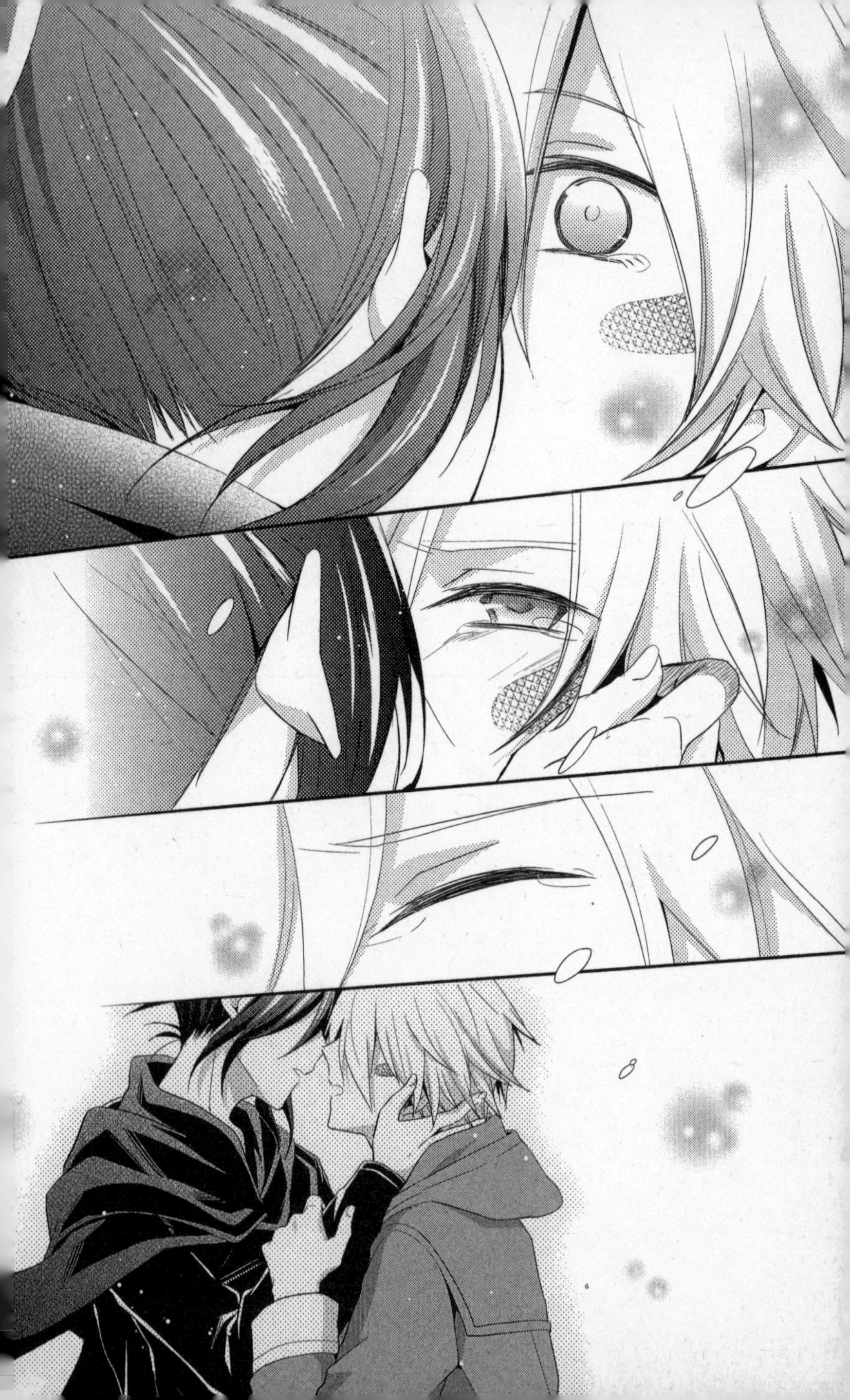

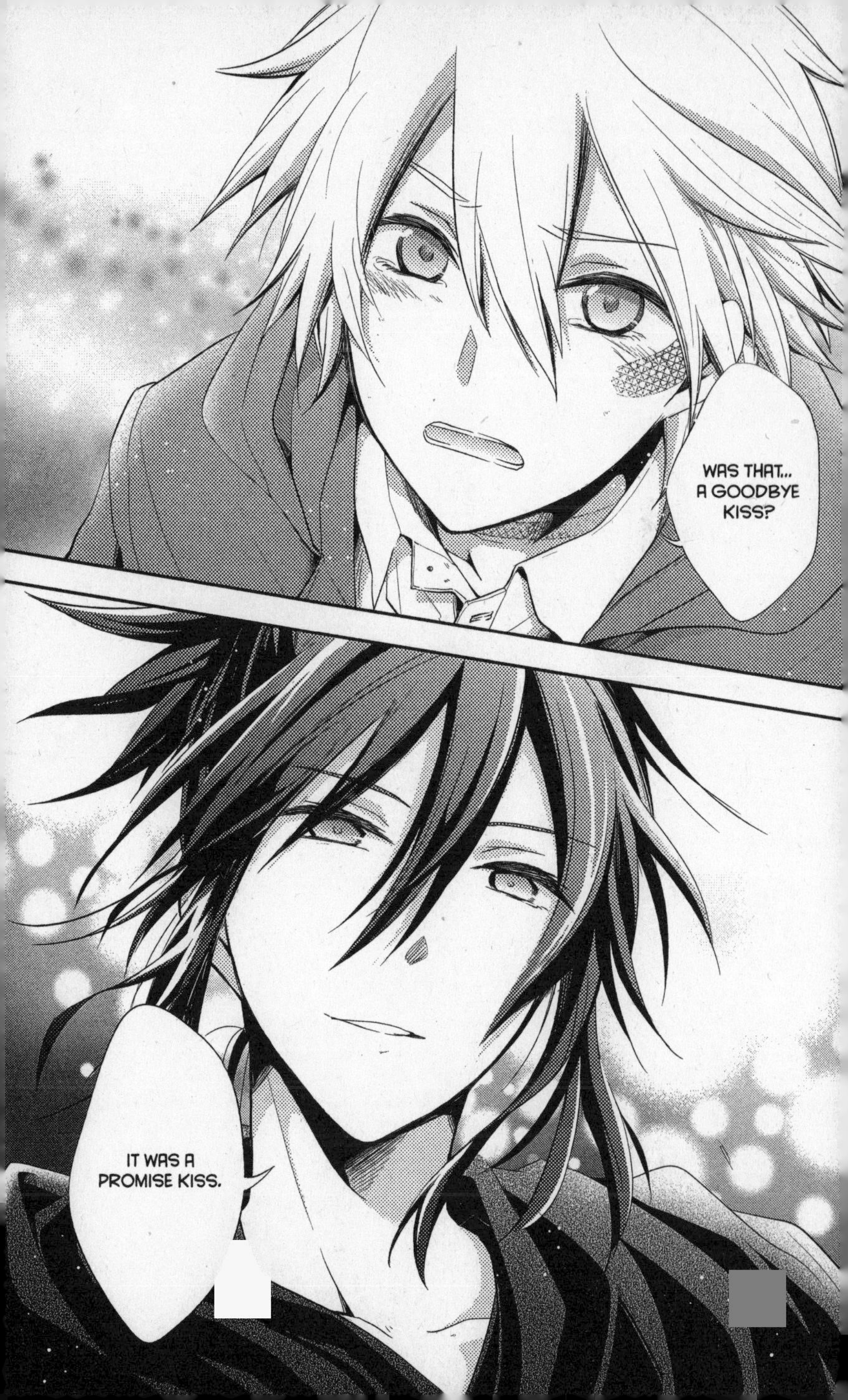
WAS THAT... A GOODBYE KISS?
IT WAS A PROMISE KISS.

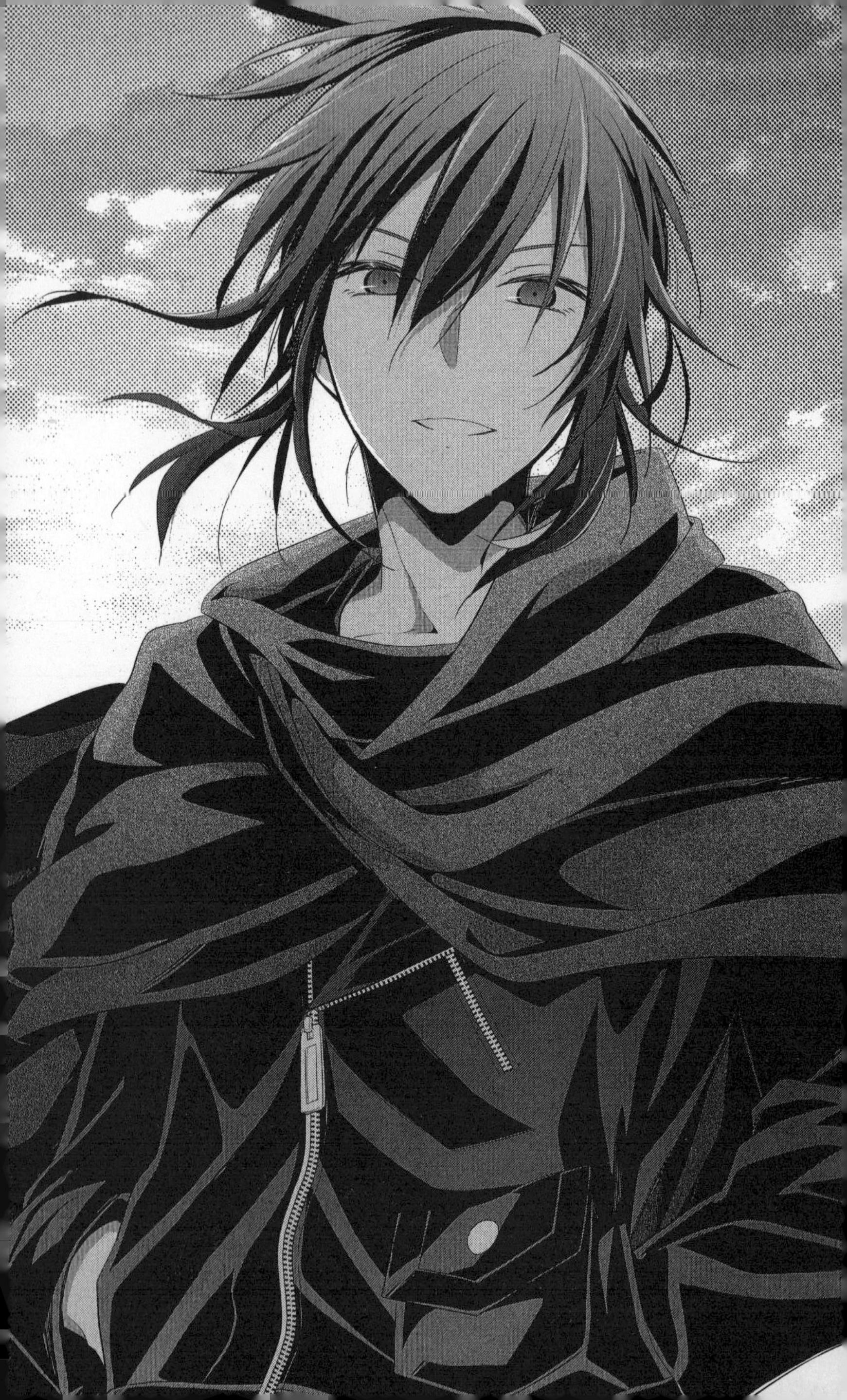

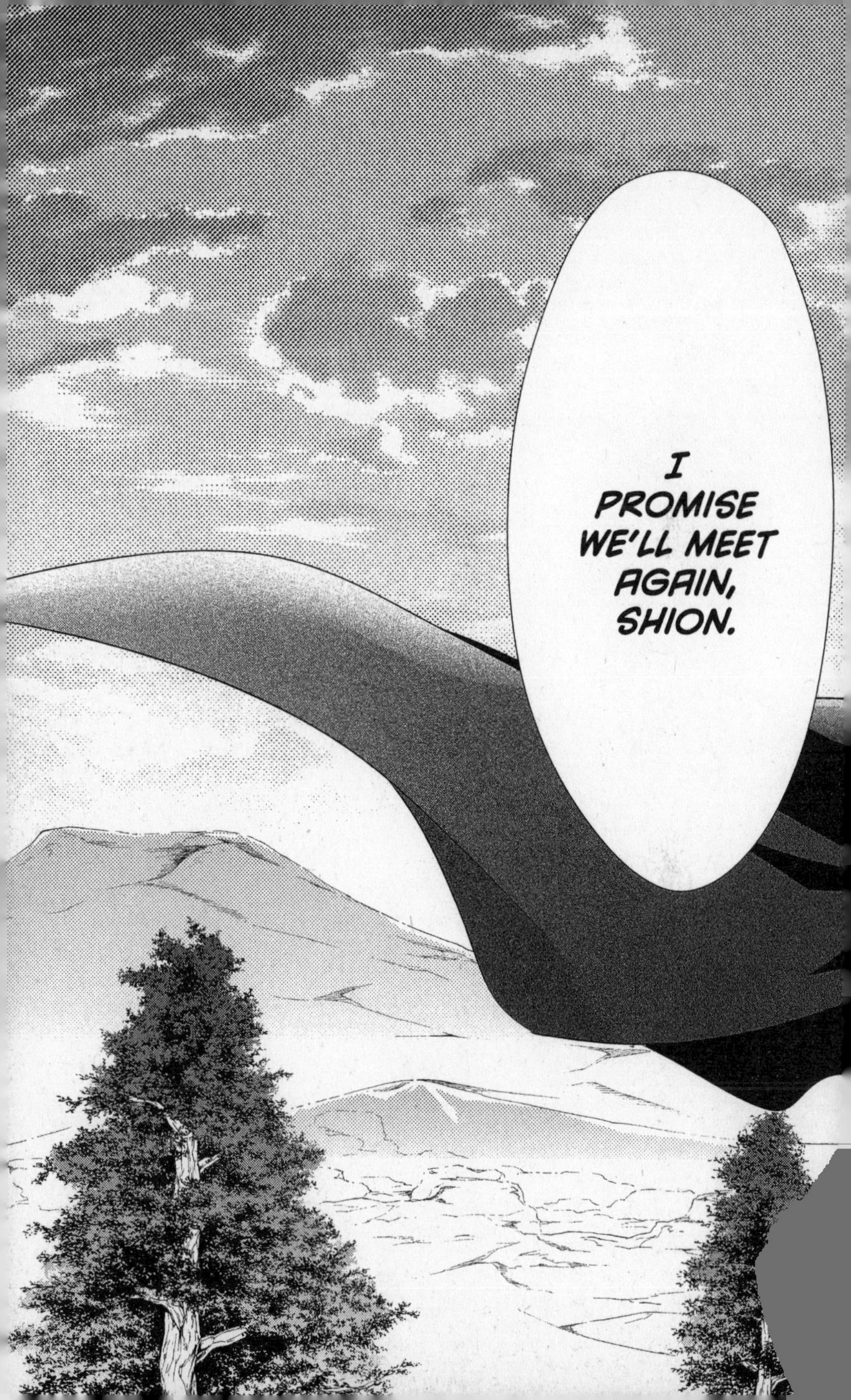
I PROMISE WE'LL MEET AGAIN, SHION.

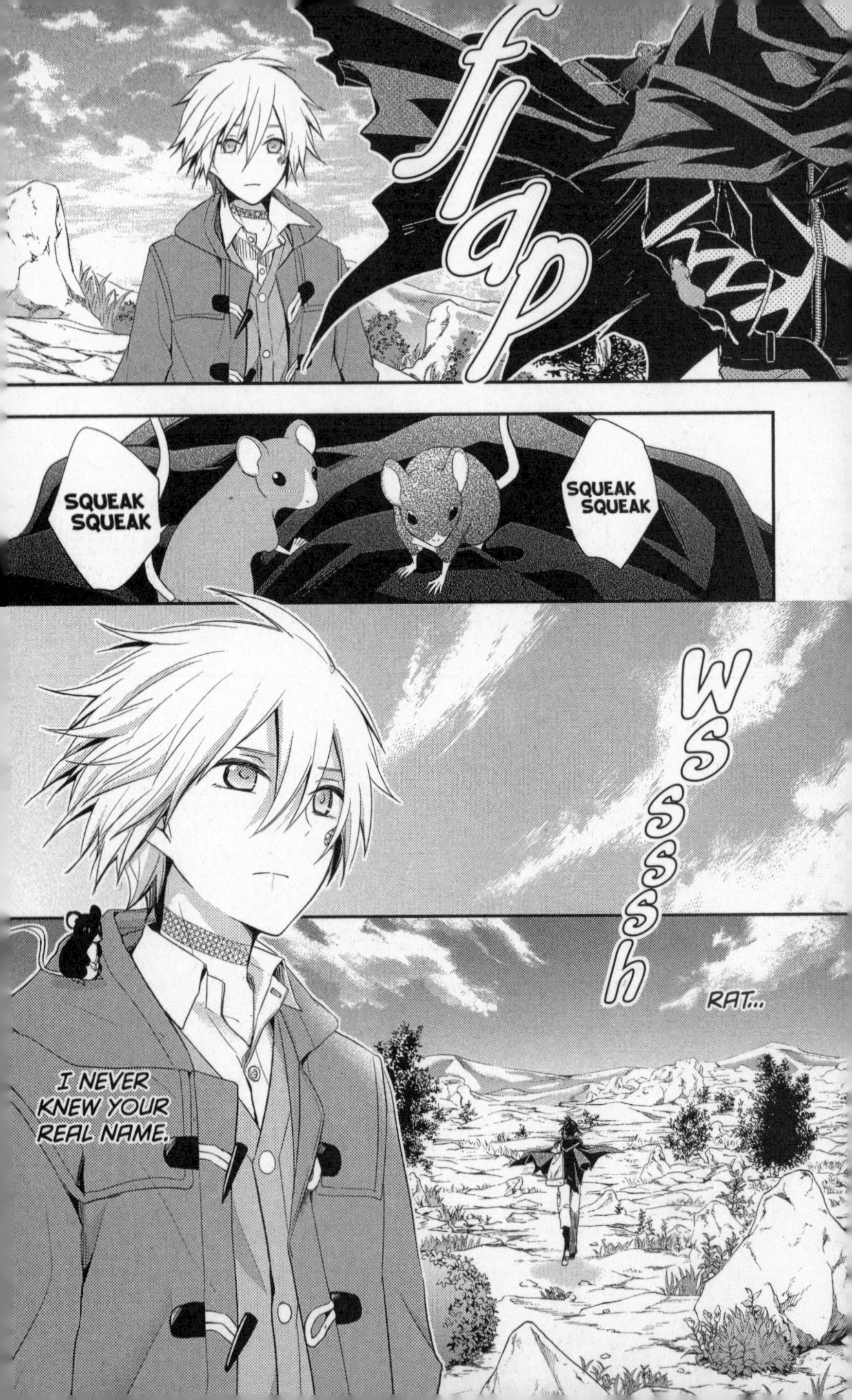
flap
SQUEAK SQUEAK
SQUEAK SQUEAK
wsssssh
RAT...
I NEVER KNEW YOUR REAL NAME.

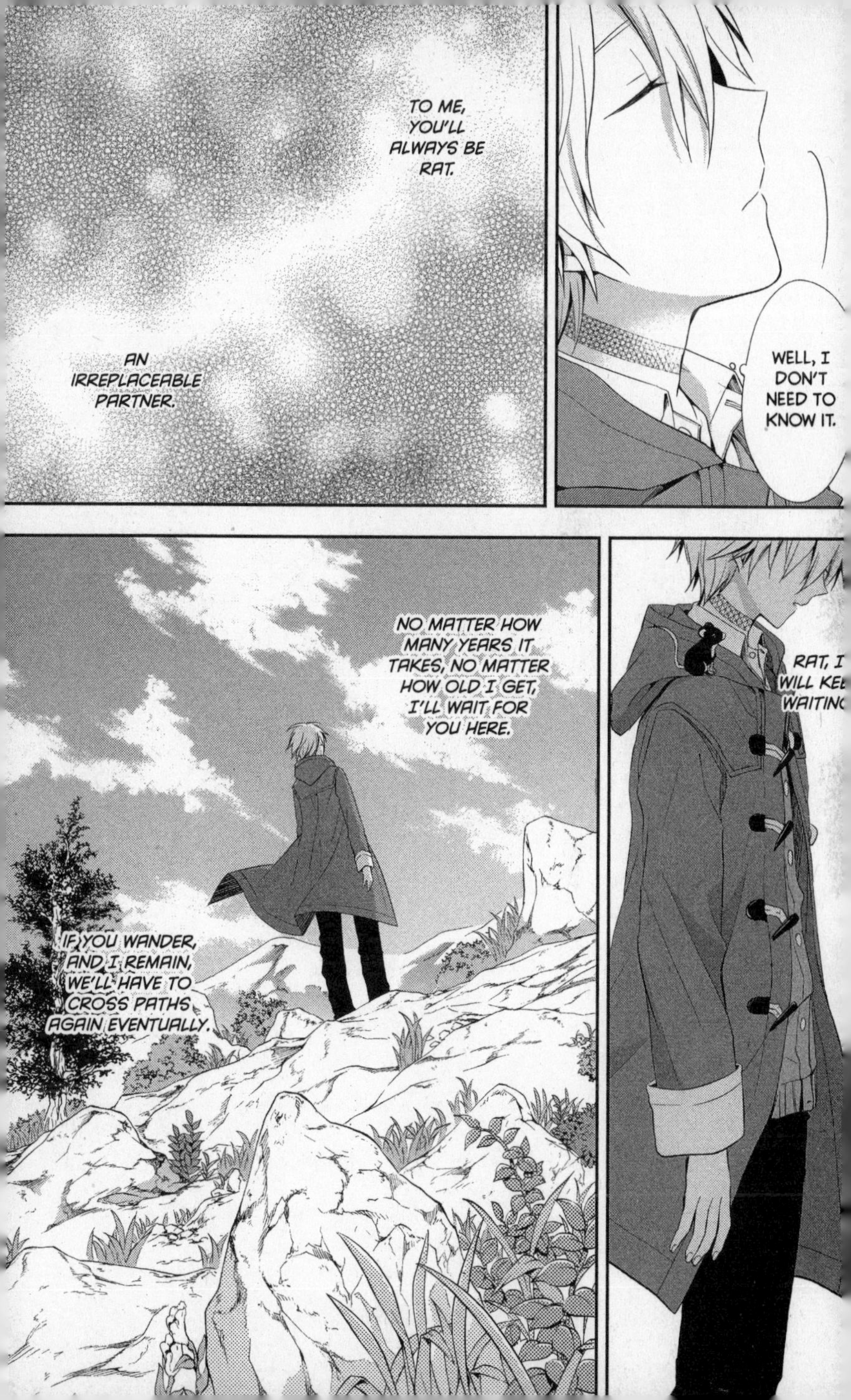
WELL, I DON'T NEED TO KNOW IT.
TO ME, YOU'LL ALWAYS BE RAT.
AN IRREPLACEABLE PARTNER.
RAT, I WILL
NO MATTER HOW MANY YEARS IT TAKES, NO MATTER HOW OLD I GET, I'LL WAIT FOR YOU HERE.
IF YOU WANDER, AND I REMAIN, WE'LL HAVE TO CROSS PATHS AGAIN EVENTUALLY.

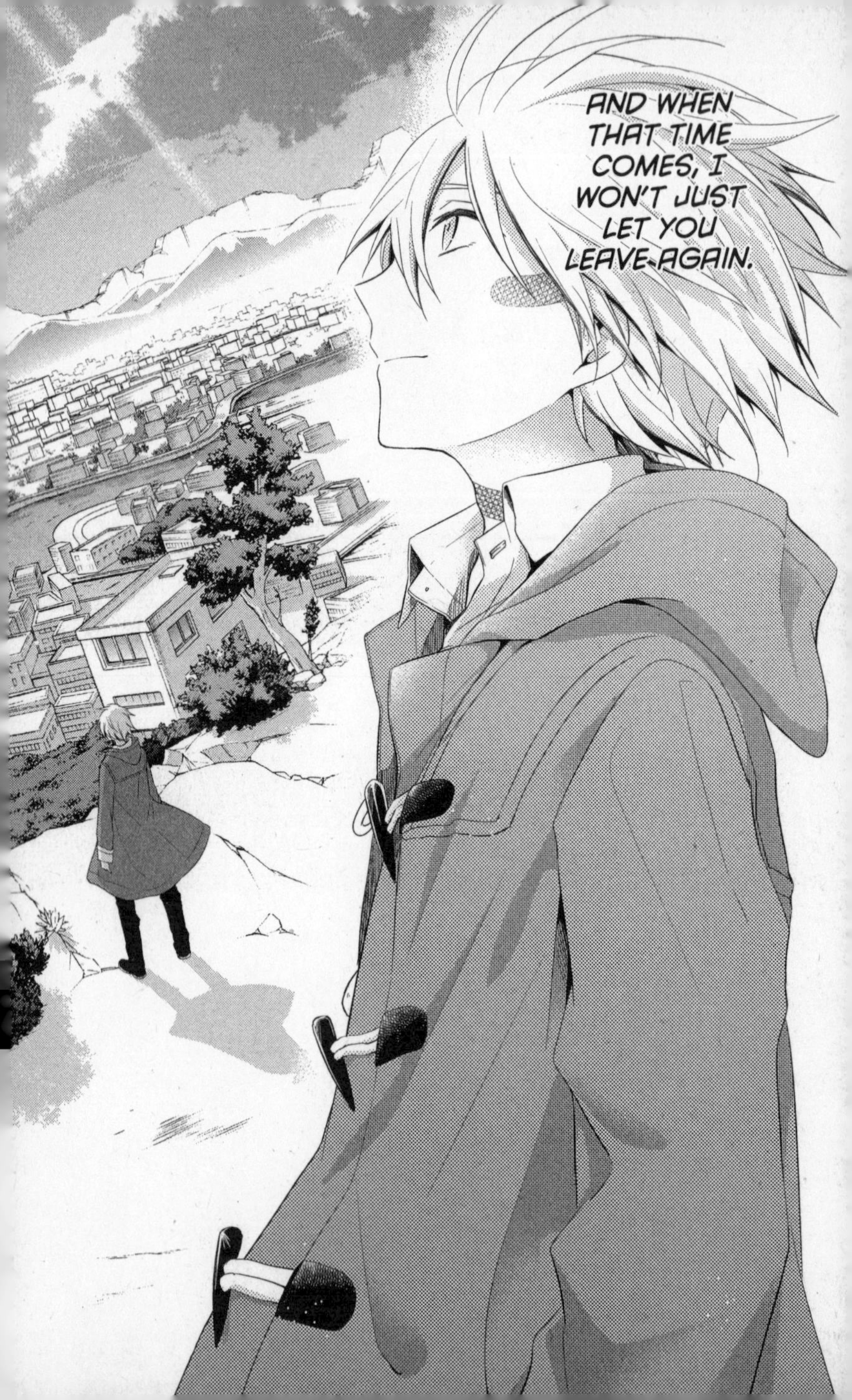
AND WHEN THAT TIME COMES, I WON'T JUST LET YOU LEAVE AGAIN.

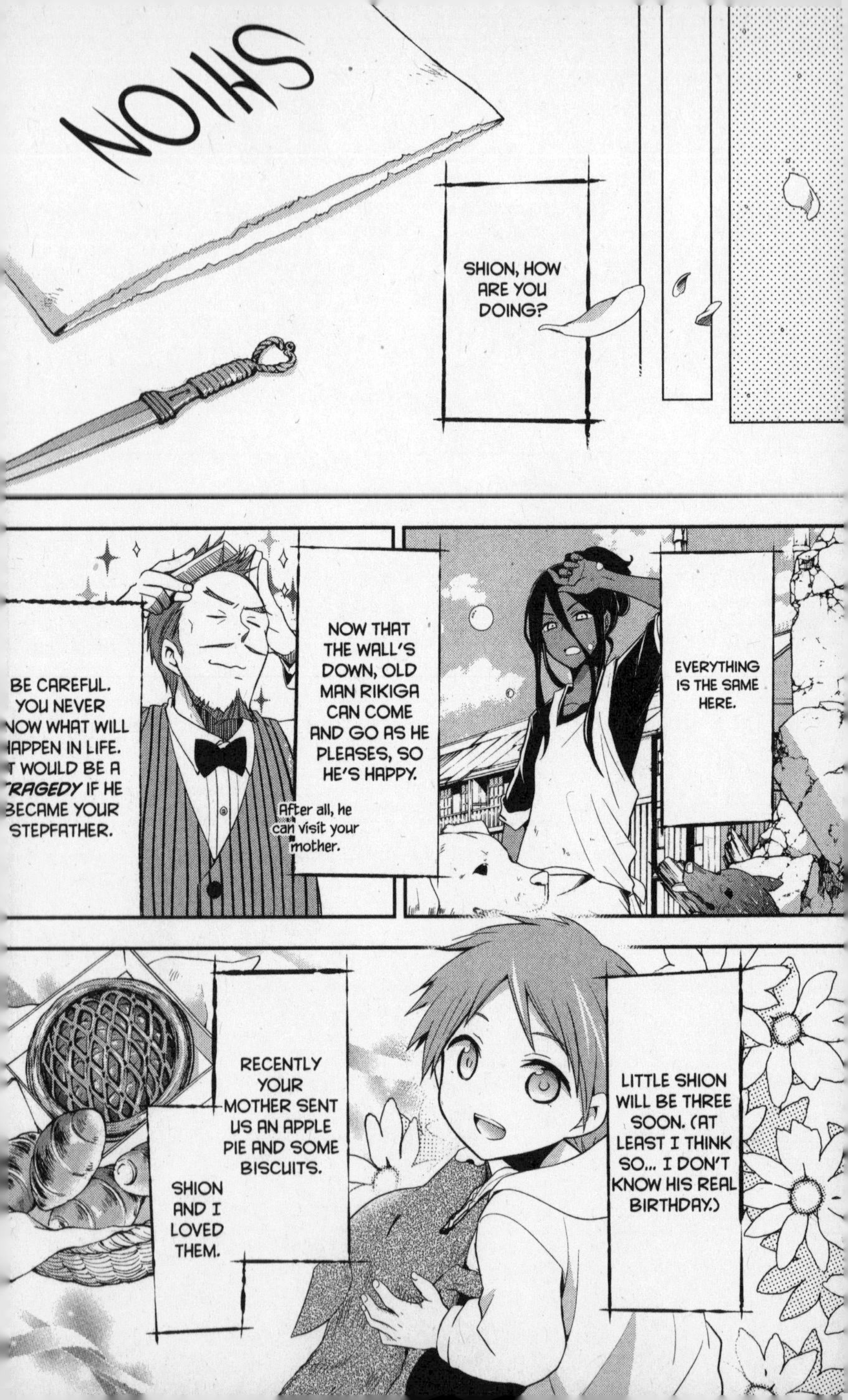
SHION
SHION, HOW ARE YOU DOING?
EVERYTHING IS THE SAME HERE.
NOW THAT THE WALL'S DOWN, OLD MAN RIKIGA CAN COME AND GO AS HE PLEASES, SO HE'S HAPPY.
After all, he can visit your mother.
BE CAREFUL. YOU NEVER NOW WHAT WILL APPEN IN LIFE. T WOULD BE A RAGEDY IF HE BECAME YOUR STEPFATHER.
LITTLE SHION WILL BE THREE SOON. (AT LEAST I THINK SO... I DON'T KNOW HIS REAL BIRTHDAY.)
RECENTLY YOUR MOTHER SENT US AN APPLE PIE AND SOME BISCUITS.
SHION AND I LOVED THEM.

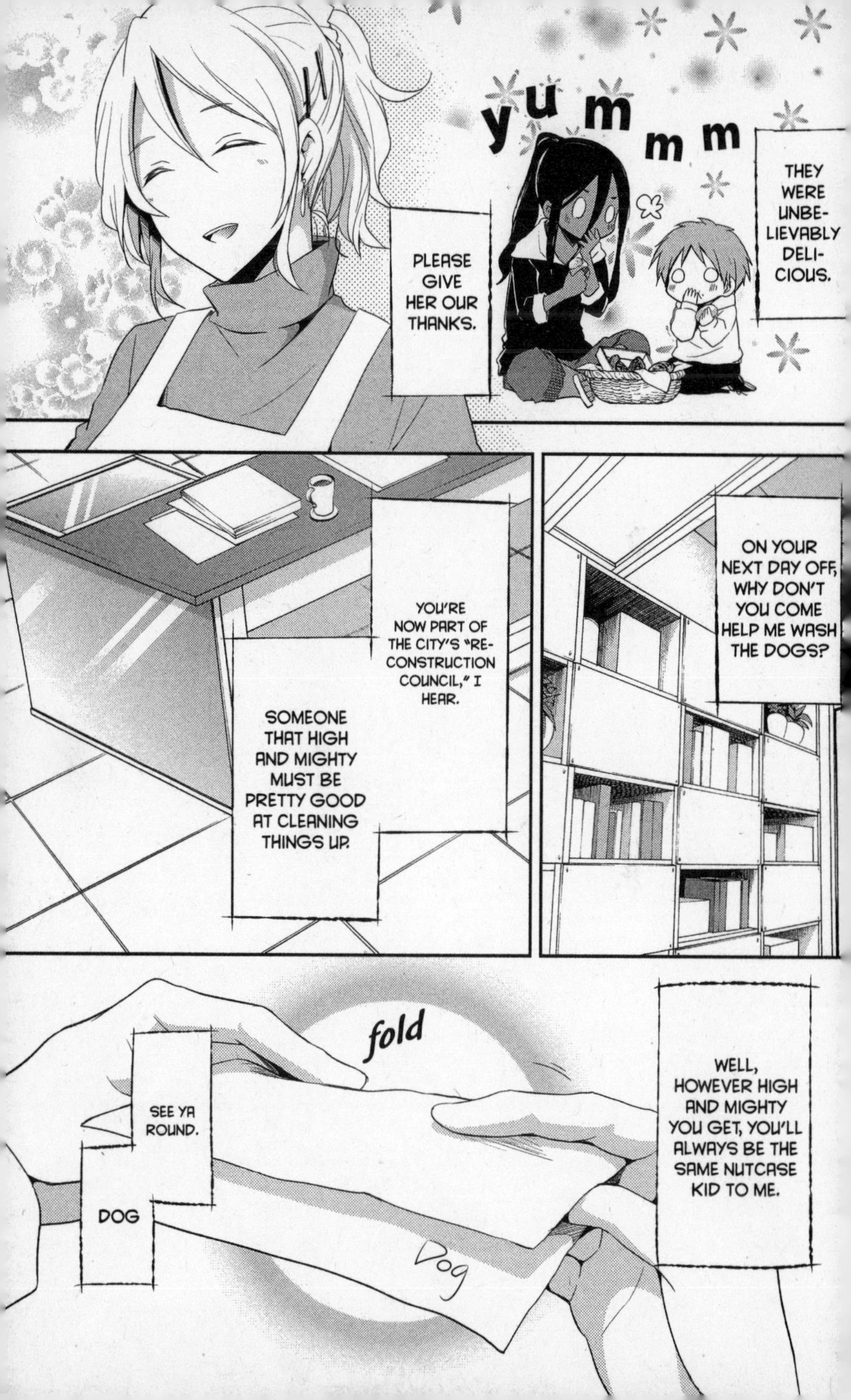
THEY WERE UNBE-LIEVABLY DELI-CIOUS.
yummm
PLEASE GIVE HER OUR THANKS.
ON YOUR NEXT DAY OFF, WHY DON'T YOU COME HELP ME WASH THE DOGS?
YOU'RE NOW PART OF THE CITY'S "RE-CONSTRUCTION COUNCIL," I HEAR.
SOMEONE THAT HIGH AND MIGHTY MUST BE PRETTY GOOD AT CLEANING THINGS UP.
WELL, HOWEVER HIGH AND MIGHTY YOU GET, YOU'LL ALWAYS BE THE SAME NUTCASE KID TO ME.
fold
SEE YA ROUND.
DOG
Dog

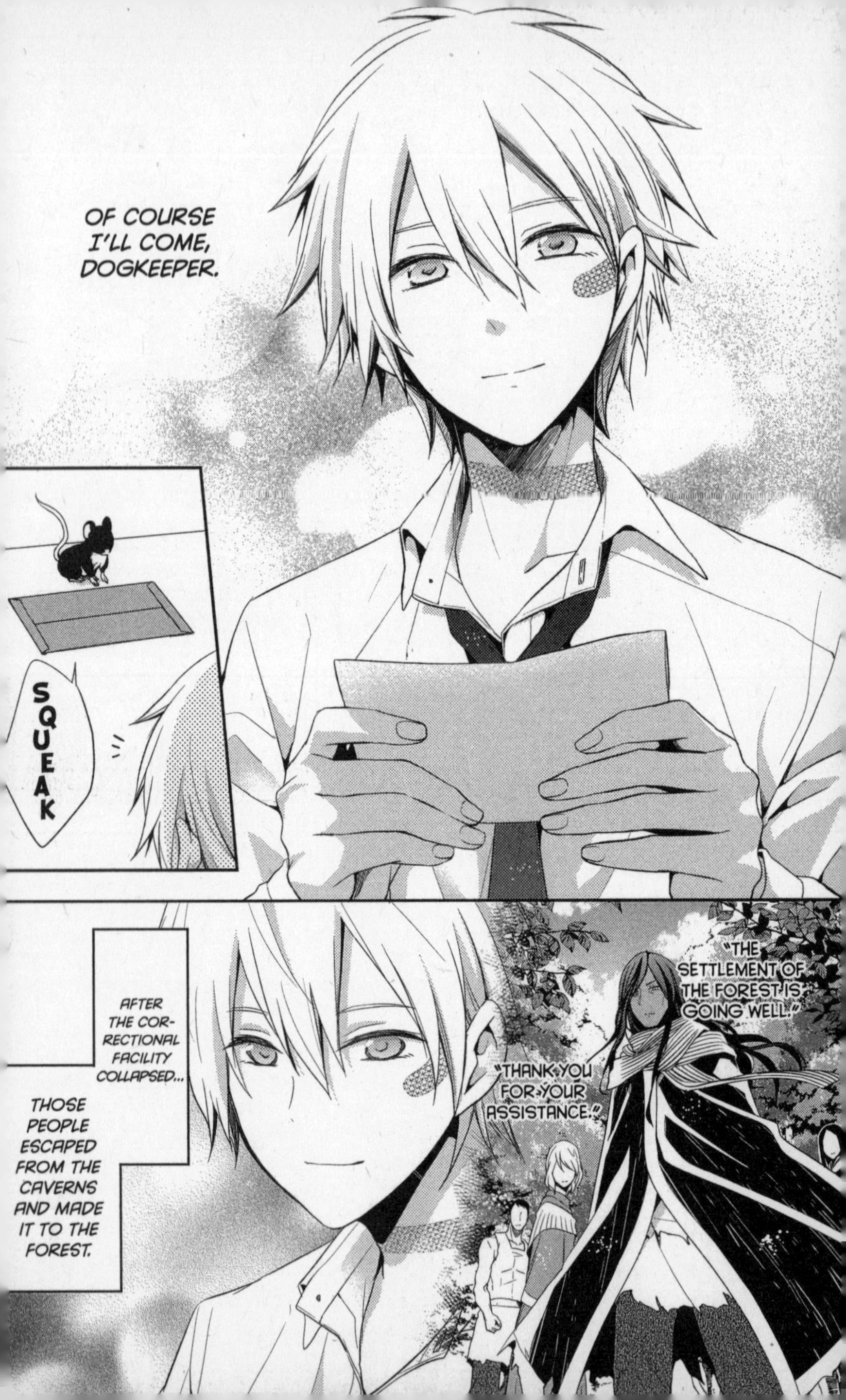
OF COURSE I'LL COME, DOGKEEPER.
SQUEAK
"THE SETTLEMENT OF THE FOREST IS GOING WELL."
"THANK YOU FOR YOUR ASSISTANCE."
AFTER THE COR-RECTIONAL FACILITY COLLAPSED...
THOSE PEOPLE ESCAPED FROM THE CAVERNS AND MADE IT TO THE FOREST.

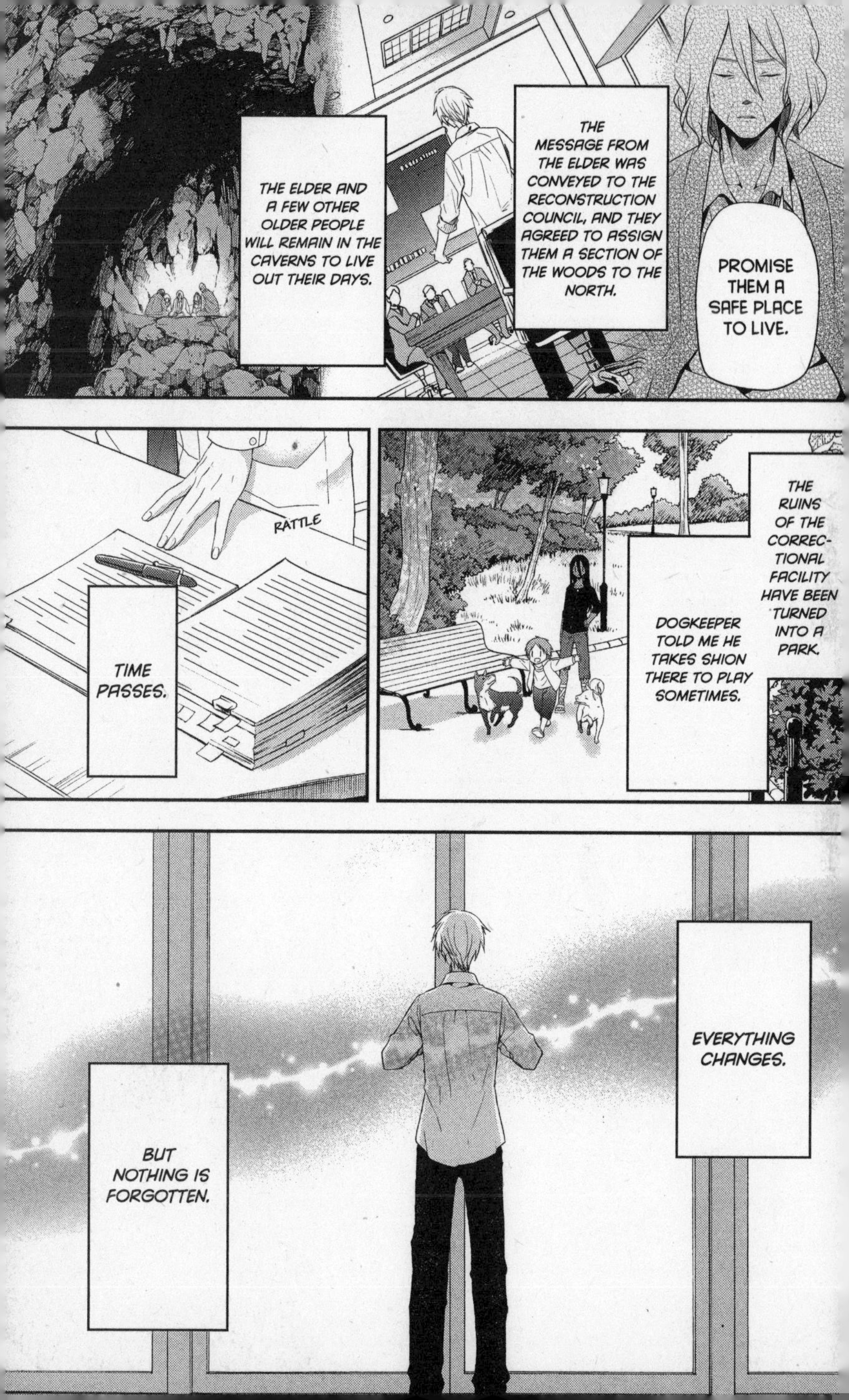
PROMISE THEM A SAFE PLACE TO LIVE.
THE MESSAGE FROM THE ELDER WAS CONVEYED TO THE RECONSTRUCTION COUNCIL, AND THEY AGREED TO ASSIGN THEM A SECTION OF THE WOODS TO THE NORTH.
THE ELDER AND A FEW OTHER OLDER PEOPLE WILL REMAIN IN THE CAVERNS TO LIVE OUT THEIR DAYS.
THE RUINS OF THE CORREC-TIONAL FACILITY HAVE BEEN TURNED INTO A PARK.
DOGKEEPER TOLD ME HE TAKES SHION THERE TO PLAY SOMETIMES.
RATTLE
TIME PASSES.
EVERYTHING CHANGES.
BUT NOTHING IS FORGOTTEN.

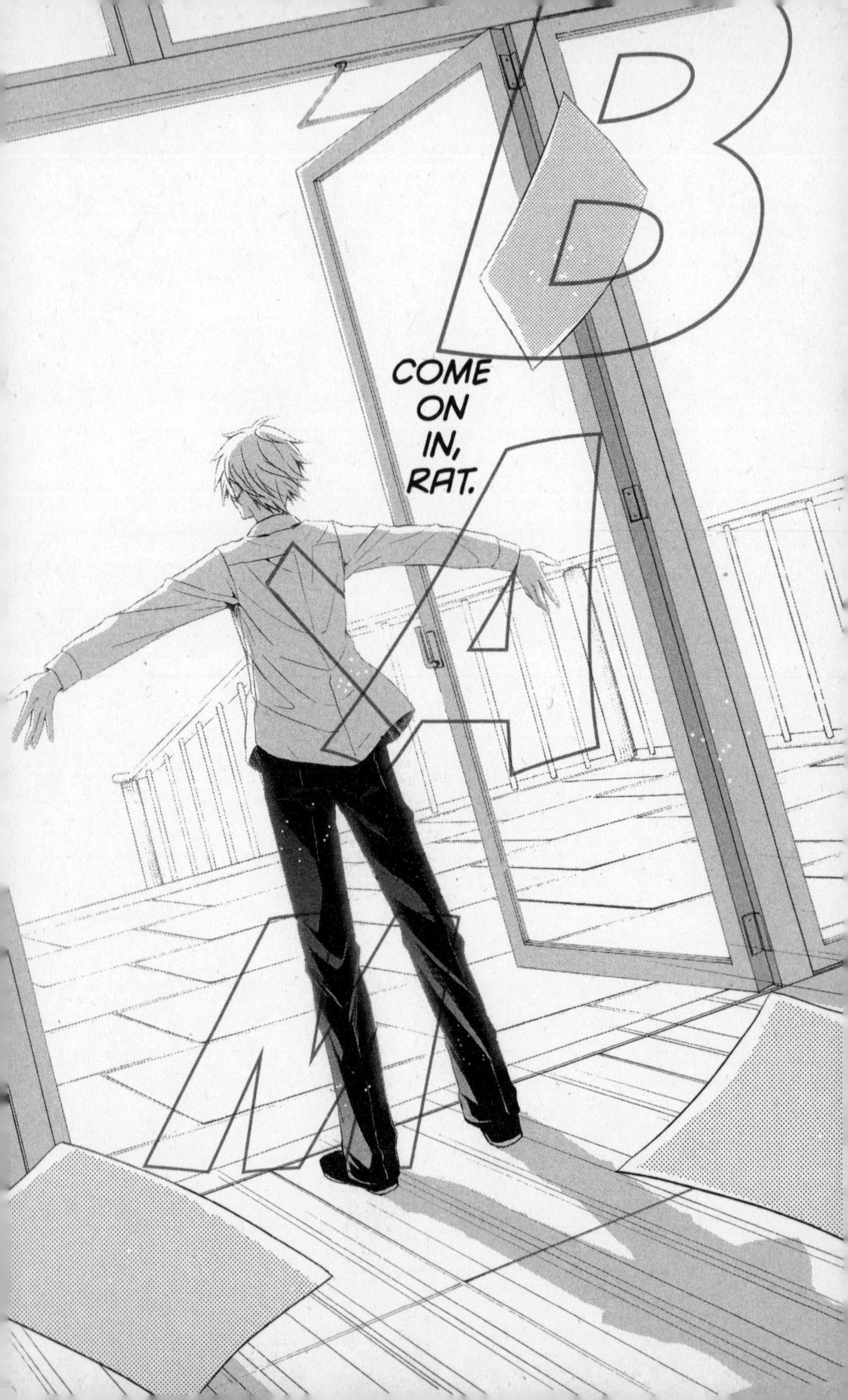
BAM
COME ON IN, RAT.

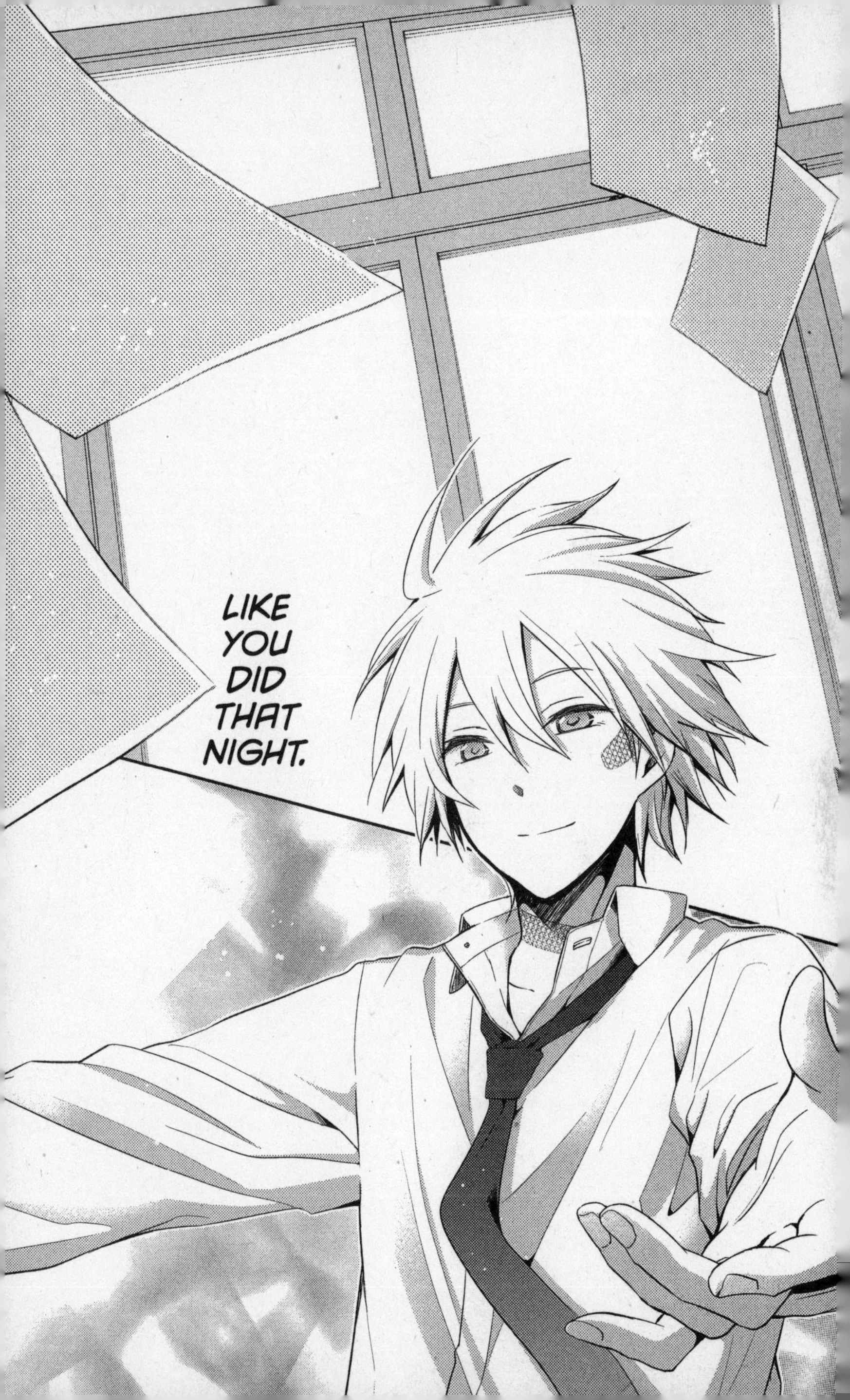
LIKE YOU DID THAT NIGHT.

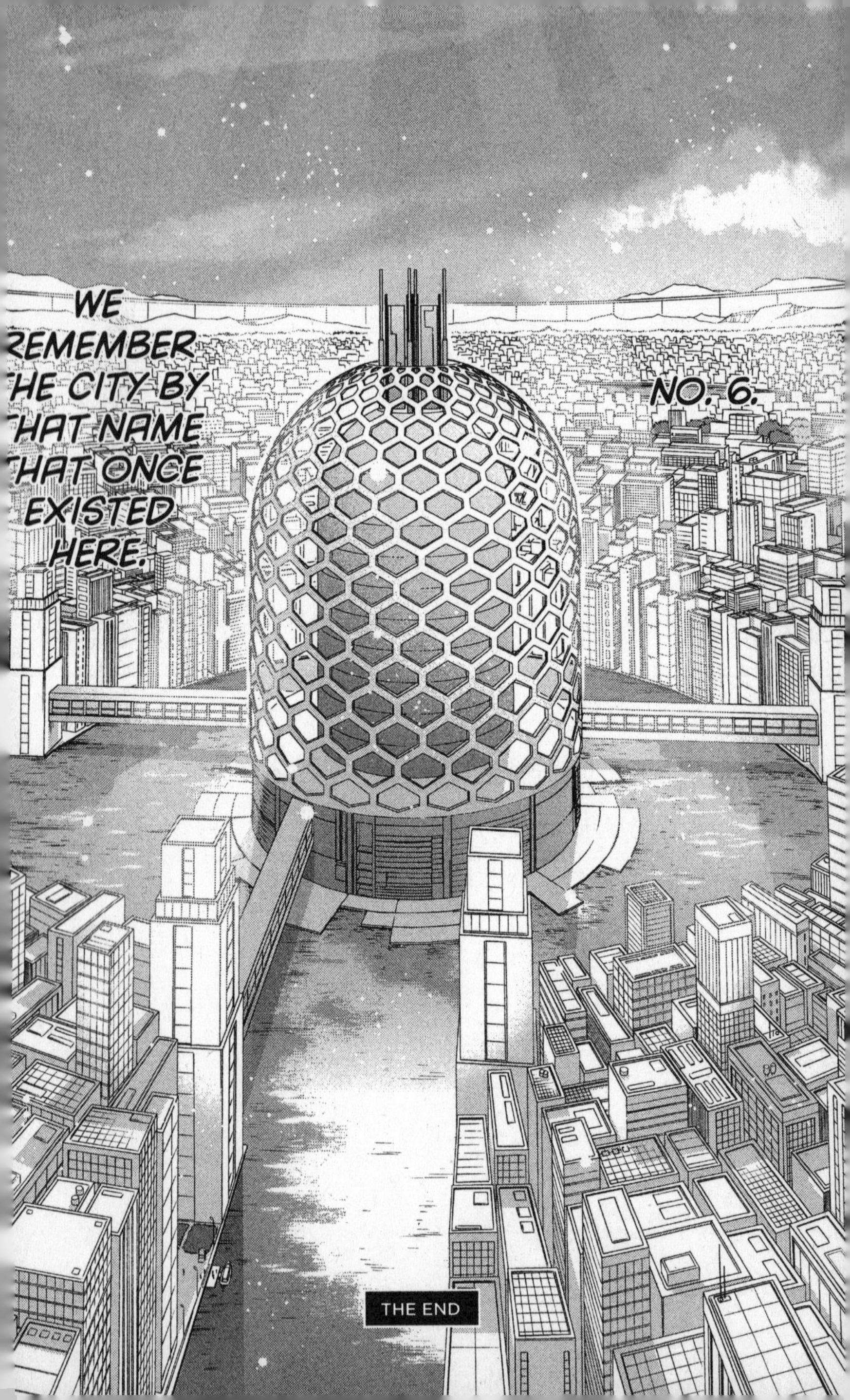
WE REMEMBER THE CITY BY THAT NAME THAT ONCE EXISTED HERE.
NO. 6.
THE END

NO.6

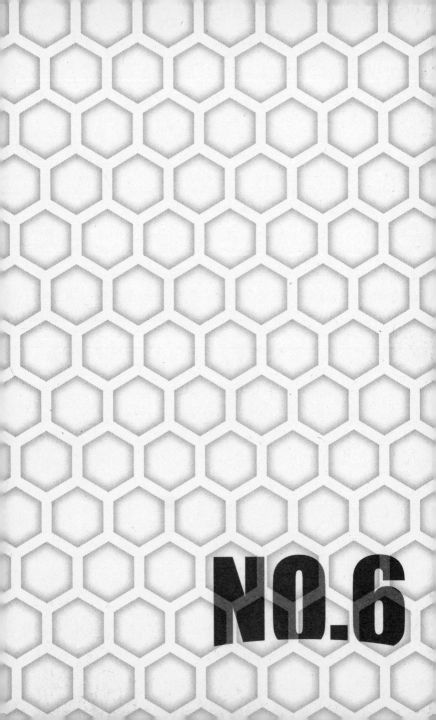

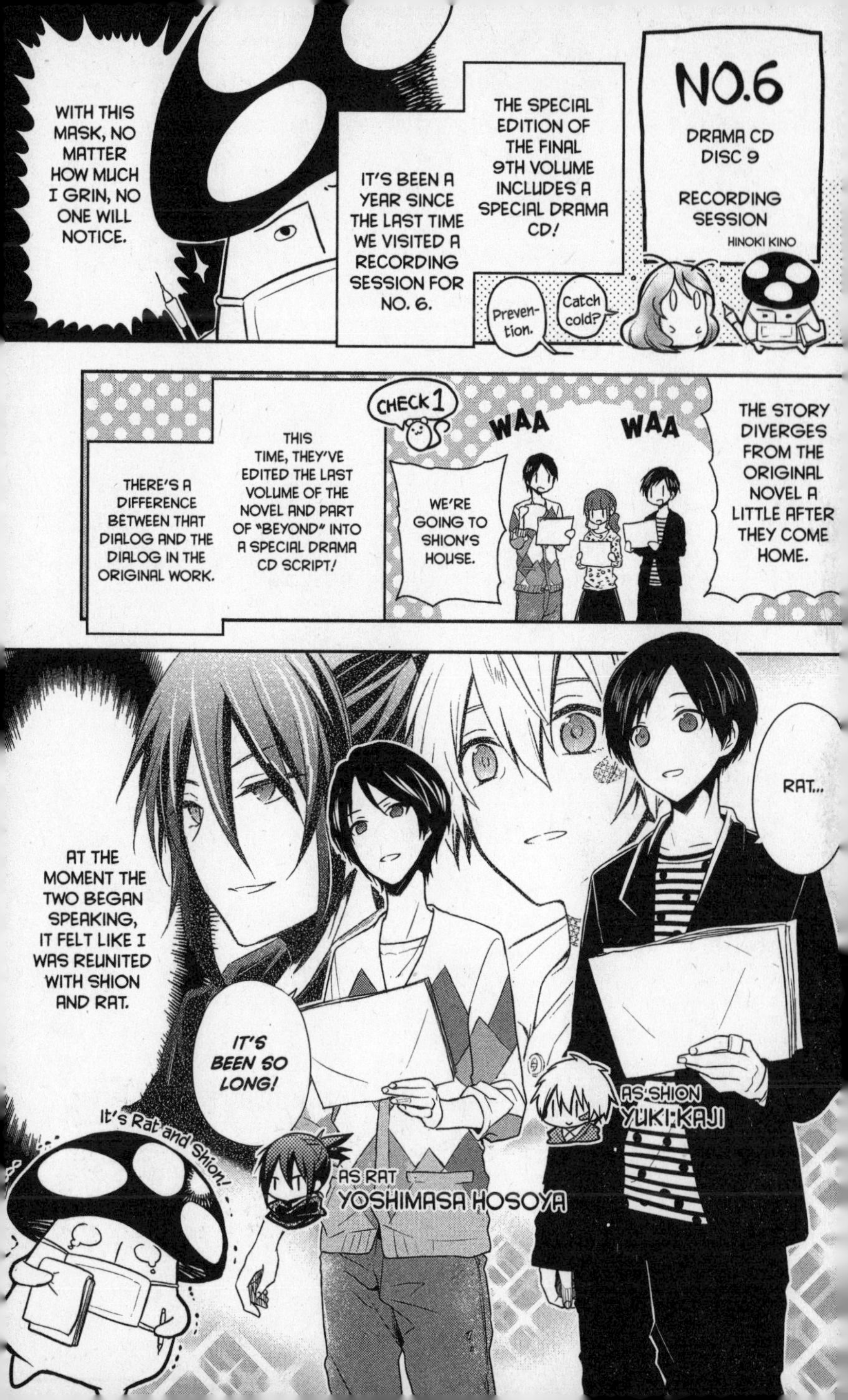
NO.6
DRAMA CD
DISC 9
RECORDING SESSION
HINOKI KINO
THE SPECIAL EDITION OF THE FINAL 9TH VOLUME INCLUDES A SPECIAL DRAMA CD!
IT'S BEEN A YEAR SINCE THE LAST TIME WE VISITED A RECORDING SESSION FOR NO. 6.
WITH THIS MASK, NO MATTER HOW MUCH I GRIN, NO ONE WILL NOTICE.
Catch cold?
Prevention.
CHECK 1
THE STORY DIVERGES FROM THE ORIGINAL NOVEL A LITTLE AFTER THEY COME HOME.
WAA
WAA
WE'RE GOING TO SHION'S HOUSE.
THIS TIME, THEY'VE EDITED THE LAST VOLUME OF THE NOVEL AND PART OF "BEYOND" INTO A SPECIAL DRAMA CD SCRIPT!
THERE'S A DIFFERENCE BETWEEN THAT DIALOG AND THE DIALOG IN THE ORIGINAL WORK.
RAT...
IT'S BEEN SO LONG!
AT THE MOMENT THE TWO BEGAN SPEAKING, IT FELT LIKE I WAS REUNITED WITH SHION AND RAT.
AS SHION
YUKI KAJI
AS RAT
YOSHIMASA HOSOYA
It's Rat and Shion!

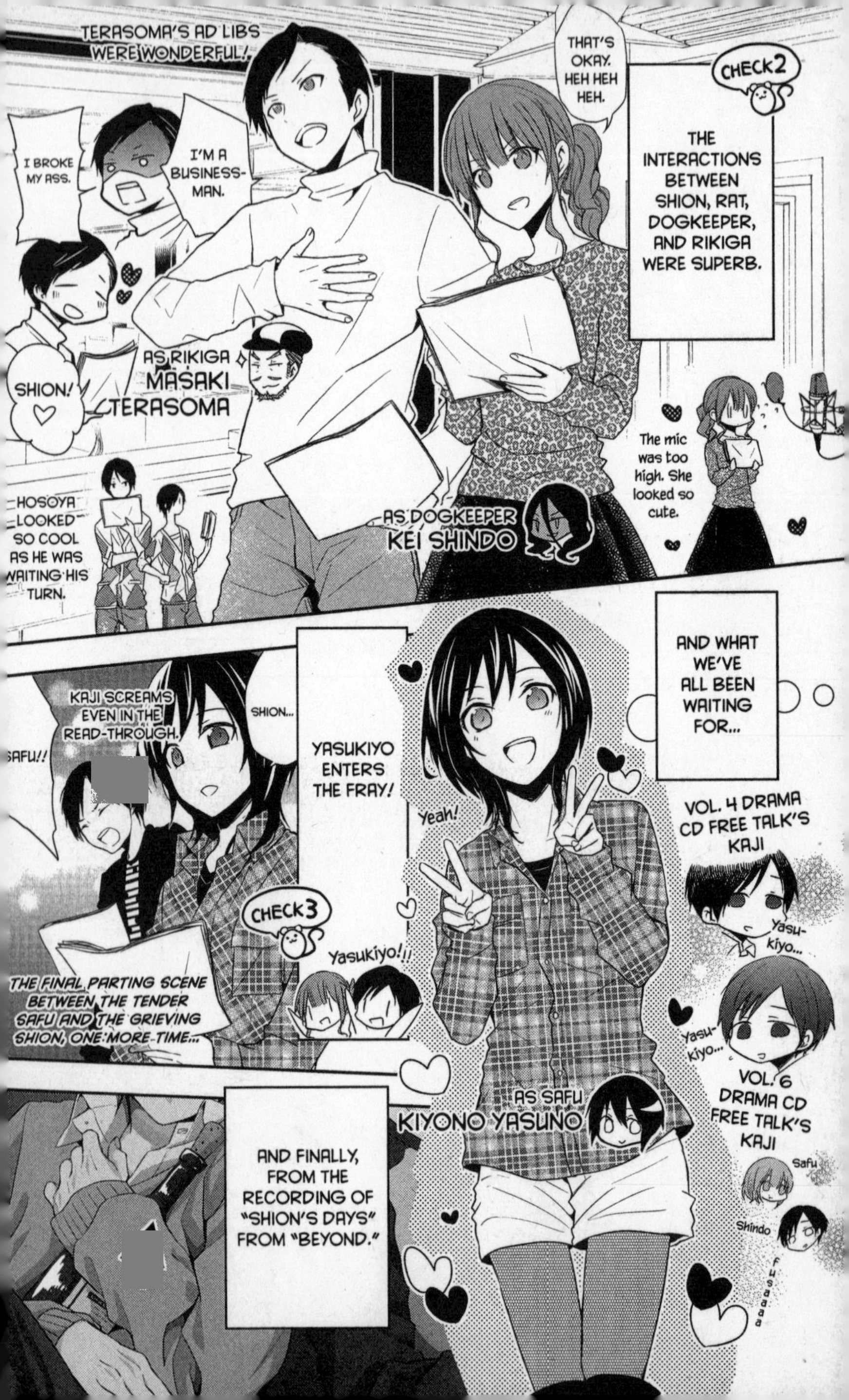
THAT'S OKAY. HEH HEH HEH.
CHECK 2
THE INTERACTIONS BETWEEN SHION, RAT, DOGKEEPER, AND RIKIGA WERE SUPERB.
The mic was too high. She looked so cute.
AS DOGKEEPER KEI SHINDO
TERASOMA'S AD LIBS WERE WONDERFUL!
I'M A BUSINESS-MAN.
I BROKE MY ASS.
SHION! ♡
AS RIKIGA MASAKI TERASOMA
HOSOYA LOOKED SO COOL AS HE WAS WAITING HIS TURN.
AND WHAT WE'VE ALL BEEN WAITING FOR...
VOL. 4 DRAMA CD FREE TALK'S KAJI
Yasu-kiyo...
Yasu-kiyo...
VOL. 6 DRAMA CD FREE TALK'S KAJI
Safu
Shindo
Fusaaaa
Yeah!
AS SAFU KIYONO YASUNO
YASUKIYO ENTERS THE FRAY!
Yasukiyo!!!
SHION...
KAJI SCREAMS EVEN IN THE READ-THROUGH.
SAFU!!
CHECK 3
THE FINAL PARTING SCENE BETWEEN THE TENDER SAFU AND THE GRIEVING SHION, ONE MORE TIME...
AND FINALLY, FROM THE RECORDING OF "SHION'S DAYS" FROM "BEYOND."

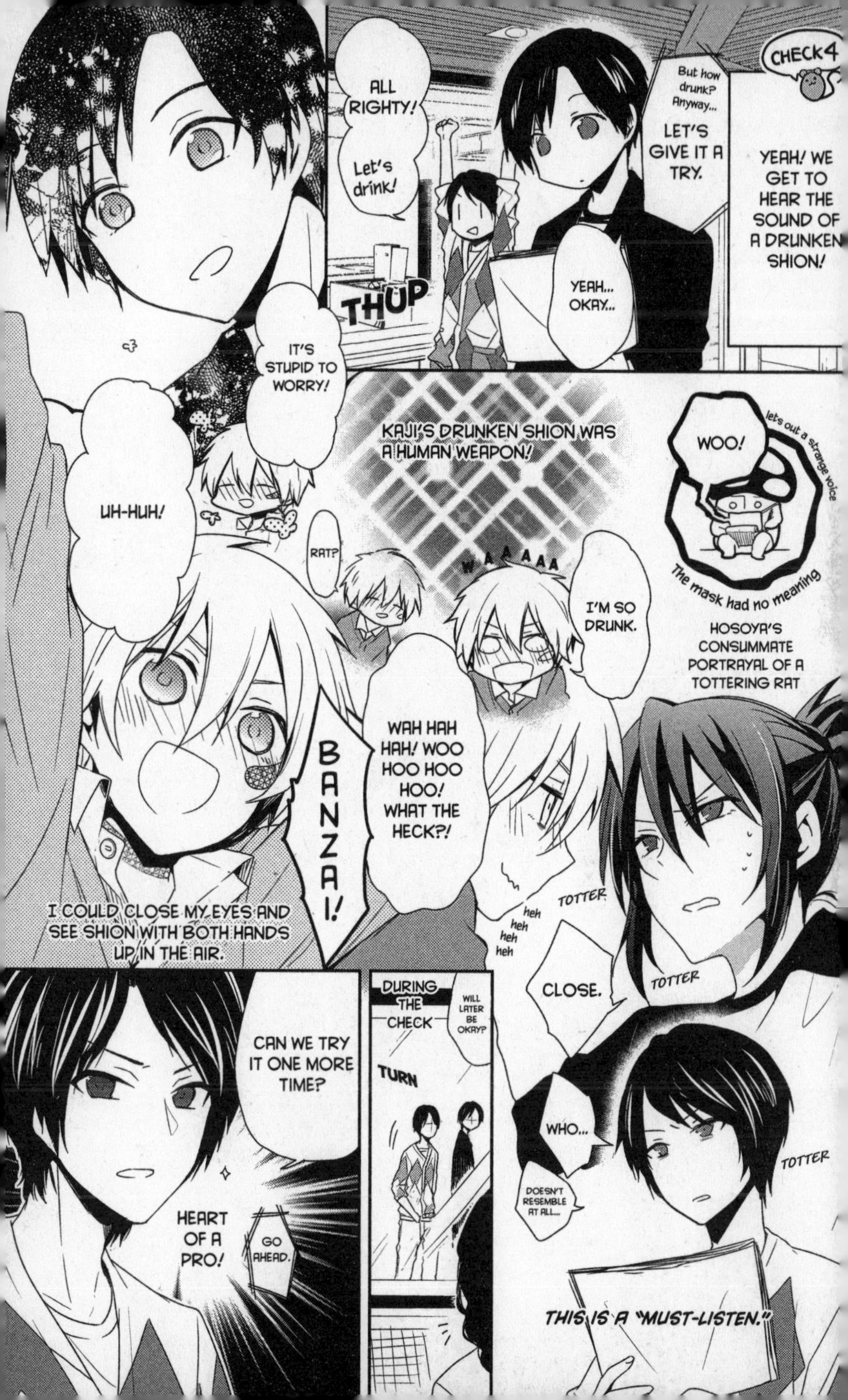
CHECK 4
YEAH! WE GET TO HEAR THE SOUND OF A DRUNKEN SHION!
But how drunk? Anyway...
LET'S GIVE IT A TRY.
YEAH... OKAY...
ALL RIGHTY!
Let's drink!
THUP
WOO!
lets out a strange voice
The mask had no meaning
HOSOYA'S CONSUMMATE PORTRAYAL OF A TOTTERING RAT
KAJI'S DRUNKEN SHION WAS A HUMAN WEAPON!
WAAAAAA
I'M SO DRUNK.
RAT?
WAH HAH HAH! WOO HOO HOO HOO! WHAT THE HECK?!
TOTTER
heh heh heh heh
TOTTER
CLOSE.
IT'S STUPID TO WORRY!
UH-HUH!
BANZAI!
I COULD CLOSE MY EYES AND SEE SHION WITH BOTH HANDS UP IN THE AIR.
WHO...
DOESN'T RESEMBLE AT ALL...
TOTTER
THIS IS A "MUST-LISTEN."
DURING THE CHECK
WILL LATER BE OKAY?
TURN
CAN WE TRY IT ONE MORE TIME?
HEART OF A PRO!
GO AHEAD.

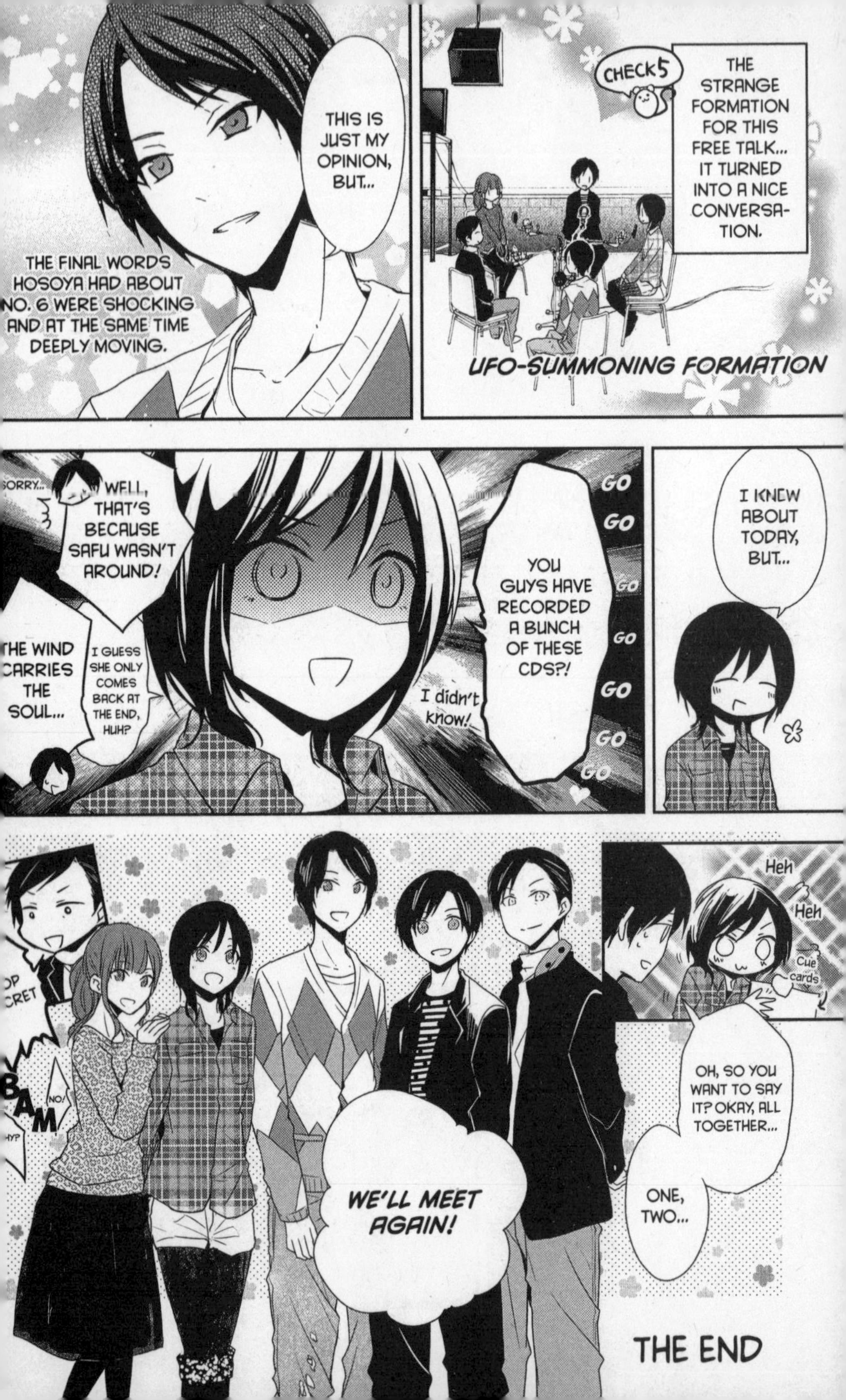

CHECK 5
THE STRANGE FORMATION FOR THIS FREE TALK... IT TURNED INTO A NICE CONVERSA-TION.
UFO-SUMMONING FORMATION
THIS IS JUST MY OPINION, BUT...
THE FINAL WORDS HOSOYA HAD ABOUT NO. 6 WERE SHOCKING AND AT THE SAME TIME DEEPLY MOVING.
I KNEW ABOUT TODAY, BUT...
GO GO GO GO GO GO GO
YOU GUYS HAVE RECORDED A BUNCH OF THESE CDS?!
I didn't know!
SORRY...
WELL, THAT'S BECAUSE SAFU WASN'T AROUND!
I GUESS SHE ONLY COMES BACK AT THE END, HUH?
THE WIND CARRIES THE SOUL...
Heh Heh
Cue cards
OH, SO YOU WANT TO SAY IT? OKAY, ALL TOGETHER...
ONE, TWO...
WE'LL MEET AGAIN!
BAM
NO!
THE END

NO.6

NO. 6, the story of Shion and Rat, has come to an end. Naturally, so many memories flash by, but first of all, I want to thank from the bottom of my heart all the readers who supported this series for so long. I feel there's no way to adequately express my appreciation.

Honestly, when I heard about the plan to make it into a manga, I was a little worried. Well, it was only a little, but I thought, "Is this going to be okay?"

I've poured a lot of my time, and feelings that have not faded despite all the time that's passed, into telling the story of these two young men, Shion and Rat. Set in the near future, this series poses questions on the nature of the individual and the state. I realize that this pondering can sometimes be idle, and as a narrative it also has many flaws.

However, I kept going to challenge myself as a writer, determined to pit myself against the reality of it. How could this be expressed in the medium of manga? I was worried that vital parts might be cut away.

However, my fears were groundless. With true sincerity and earnestness, employing masterful technique, Kino brought expression to the world of NO. 6. She deftly depicted not only Shion's frailty and strength, but also his ominousness; not only Rat's extreme beauty but also his fragility. As just another reader, I thought Kino succeeded magnificently.

To Kino, who loved this story, and also to the editor, Kamagata, thank you so much. This was a job well done.

Atsuko Asano

何でだ、イヴ
おまえは観客席で見物を決め込むんじゃなかったのか
そのつもりだったんだがな
役者根性ってのは因果なもので、
舞台に上がってスポットライトを浴びなくちゃ我慢できないようになっているらしい

Hello, Hinoki Kino here.

The manga version of NO. 6 is now complete. The serialization started only three years ago. Those three years passed in what seemed like a moment. It's said that happy times pass quickly, and it was certainly true. There were times when I suffered and hit a wall, but thanks to you kind readers watching over me, most of it was happy, and we were able to make it to the end. When I found out that the amazing author, Asano was probably going to let me draw the series, I danced around and a shouted a resounding "I'll do it!" But afterwards, thinking calmly, I worried if I'd be okay. Could I even do it? Would Ms. Asano and the fans be disappointed?

Repeatedly mulling over these doubts, I considered asking to leave the project before heading off to my first meeting with Kodansha. With a face white as a sheet, I apparently looked dreadfully unenthusiastic (according to my editor). But the chief editor and my assigned editor plowed along, fearlessly talking about the project, vigorously encouraging me. They continued to follow up with me (I'm so sorry for that occasion). I realized how much I really wanted to do it, how I wanted them to let me do it. Those feelings won out, and by the time I was going home, I was so full of desire to do it I was shaking on the train. There were times when I didn't have the power to draw it, and times when I was overwhelmed with frustration at not being able to execute the things I wanted to draw. Oh no, this is becoming an apology.

Just as I wrote at the end of Vol. 1, "I'm grateful to have all of you watching over me," you readers have watched over and encouraged this unseasoned amateur. To all my art and production assistants, whose high-quality backgrounds gave depth to the work; to everyone on the animation staff, whose technical expertise created a warm, vibrant atmosphere I could never have created myself; to the cast and director of the audio drama CDs, who breathed voice and life into the story with a clear, precise vision (especially during those times you took care of me during my visits to the recording sessions); to toi8, whose character designs created a beautiful Rat and a guileless Shion; to Ishino, who encouraged me so well on Twitter; to the NARTI:S Design staff, who created such incredibly riveting designs; to everyone at Ginnansha who strove to produce the paperbacks; to everyone at the ARIA Editorial Department who happily produced the magazine version; and to my editor K-gata who met with me everyday, discussed through sickness and health, who stuck with me like a partner in a three-legged race—thank you all.

Finally, to the great mother of NO. 6, Ms. Asano. I've learned so much from NO. 6. I was inspired by Rat's words so many times. I was so lucky to read this story, and being able to draw this work was such a delight! No matter how many years pass from now, to me it will be my best, most loved work.

Thank you all so very much! I LOVE – LOVE – LOVE NO. 6!

Kino Hinoki, March 2014

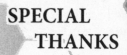

SPECIAL THANKS

Atsuko Asano

Everyone on the editorial
staff at Kodansha's ARIA

Everyone on the NO. 6 team
My editor K-gata
toi8
Everyone on the anime staff
Everyone at NARTI;S
Ginnansha

* Drawing Help
Honma
Megi
Matsugi

* Finishing
Tsunocchi

* 3D
Lim Wan-Gu

* Color Backgrounds
Mr. dominori

My family (Mom, Dad,
siblings, Granny, the dog)
Everyone else who helped

And all of the readers!

To all of you who stayed with
me to the end, thank you
very much! May we all meet
again.

けれど子どもを殺すのだけはいやだ

俺はマオの虐殺の生き残りだ

だからこそ虐殺の側にだけは回りたくない

おれはNO.6と同じにはなりたくないんだ

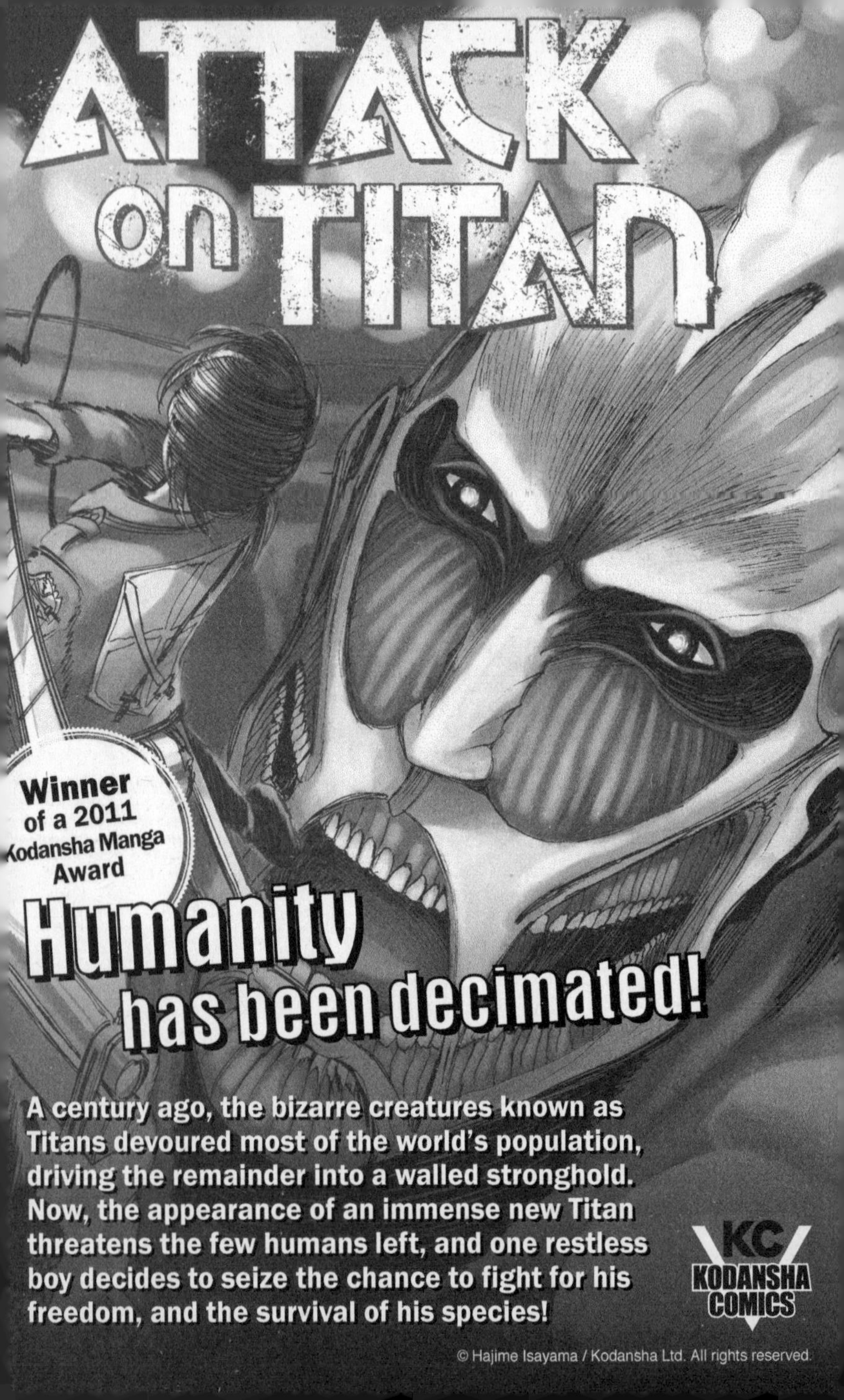

ATTACK ON TITAN

Humanity
has been decimated!

A century ago, the bizarre creatures known as Titans devoured most of the world's population, driving the remainder into a walled stronghold. Now, the appearance of an immense new Titan threatens the few humans left, and one restless boy decides to seize the chance to fight for his freedom, and the survival of his species!

KC/
KODANSHA
COMICS

KC KODANSHA COMICS

Mei Tachibana has no friends — and says she doesn't need them!
But everything changes when she accidentally roundhouse kicks the most popular boy in school! However, Yamato Kurosawa isn't angry in the slightest— in fact, he thinks his ordinary life could use an unusual girl like Mei. But winning Mei's trust will be a tough task. How long will she refuse to say, "I love you"?

My Little Monster

OPPOSITES ATTRACT...MAYBE?

Haru Yoshida is feared as an unstable and violent "monster." Mizutani Shizuku is a grade-obsessed student with no friends. Fate brings these two together to form the most unlikely pair. Haru firmly believes he's in love with Mizutani and she firmly believes he's insane.

KC KODANSHA COMICS

SANKAREA
undying love

"I ONLY LIKE ZOMBIE GIRLS."

Chihiro has an unusual connection to zombie movies. He doesn't feel bad for the survivors – he wants to comfort the undead girls they slaughter! When his pet passes away, he brews a resurrection potion. He's discovered by local heiress Sanka Rea, and she serves as his first test subject!

KC KODANSHA COMICS

Kodansha Comics Trade Paperback Original.

No. 6 volume 9 copyright © 2014 Atsuko Asano, Hinoki Kino
English translation copyright © 2014 Atsuko Asano, Hinoki Kino

Published in the United States by Kodansha Comics, an imprint of Kodansha USA Publishing, LLC, New York.

Publication rights for this English edition arranged through Kodansha Ltd., Tokyo.

First published in Japan in 2014 by Kodansha Ltd., Tokyo
ISBN 978-1-61262-794-6

Printed in the United States of America.

www.kodanshacomics.com

9 8 7 6 5 4 3 2 1

Translation: Jonathan Tarbox/Arashi Productions
Lettering: Christy Sawyer
Editing: Ben Applegate
Kodansha Comics edition cover design by Phil Balsman